THE RULES OF THE GAME IN PARIS

THE
RULES OF THE GAME
In Paris

NATHAN LEITES

TRANSLATED BY DEREK COLTMAN

WITH A FOREWORD BY RAYMOND ARON

THE UNIVERSITY OF CHICAGO PRESS

CHICAGO AND LONDON

Originally published in 1966 as *La règle du jeu à Paris*
© 1966 Mouton & Co.

Library of Congress Catalog Card Number 69-19276

The University of Chicago Press, Chicago 60637
The University of Chicago Press, Ltd., London W.C. 1

English translation © 1969 by The University of Chicago
ALL RIGHTS RESERVED
Published 1969
Printed in the United States of America

CONTENTS

Foreword by Raymond Aron   vii

Introduction   1

BOOK I: THE RUT AND THE SENSE OF ADVENTURE

  1   Don't Fence Me In   9
  2   My Watchdog Is Diversity   25
  3   Renewing the Lease or Moving On   54
  4   Distinctions and Mixtures   91

BOOK II: UNREASON AND WISDOM

  5   The Horror of Completion   123
  6   Good Luck and Near Misses   154
  7   Blunders and the Happy Knack   161
  8   Waste and Wiles   180
  9   Excess and Moderation   197
 10   Haste and Patience   212
 11   Swift Movements and Slow Progress   231
 12   Short Term and Long Run   249

BOOK III: VELVET GLOVE AND IRON HAND

 13   Brutal Tactics and Consideration   259
 14   Outbursts and Oil on the Waters   277

BOOK IV: LIGHT AND SHADE

15 The Facade and What Is Behind It   285
16 Lucidity and Blindness   290
17 Honesty and Lies   301
18 Words and Silence   312
19 Stark Language and Veiled Meaning   319
20 Precision and Ambiguity   342

Bibliography   351

FOREWORD

Does this book by Nathan Leites need a foreword? He himself claims that it does, and I must therefore accept his argument. But I should like first of all to say why I was tempted to reply in the negative.

Nathan Leites is no stranger to all those, in France, who take an interest in politics and political science. In collaboration with Constantin Melnik, he has already written a controversial and instructive book devoted to M. René Coty's election to the presidency (*The House without Windows*). In it, he provided a minutely observed, day-by-day, hour-by-hour account of that long battle, full of unexpected incidents and ricochets, whose outcome nevertheless seemed in retrospect to have been determined by the rules of the game. Being already vice-president of the Senate, was M. Coty not inevitably predestined to the highest office by the customs of the Third Republic, once the presidency had been vacated? And yet, when analyzed in detail, the second and final congress of the Fourth Republic produced an image, perhaps caricatured but certainly very striking, of the strange world in which our deputies were living a short while ago.

M. Leites's *Du malaise politique* had similar aims, but used a slightly different method to attain them. He was no longer concerned with a specific episode but with constant practices, which he undertook to make intelligible by means of a subtle concatenation of comparisons and quotations. French politics under

the Fourth Republic obeyed certain rules, and the French political science elucidated by Nathan Leites is also a game subject
to rules.

What is this game and what are its rules? The reason why I
thought a foreword would be superfluous is that the author's own
Introduction seems to me quite sufficiently explicit in this respect
for anyone who can read it. What Nathan Leites is looking for,
and finds, is a set of tendencies, of ways of feeling, of attitudes,
that appear to him to be more or less characteristic of a given
sector of the French people. He observes the French as they live
and speak, as they behave, and above all as they write. And he
does so with the utmost possible detachment. Then, making use
of his exceptional erudition, and of a familiarity with our country and its curious inhabitants acquired during long years of
residence in it, he selects an incident, a remark, or a written
quotation, and goes on to suggest innumerable overtones and
undertones. It was not mere coincidence that a previous work
of his on France employed the word *theme* in its title.

What criticism can be made of this method? Nathan Leites
tells us himself: "The inadequacy of my data, and their bizarre
nature, may possibly endow the pages you are about to read with
a character of oddity that the predominance of quotations is
likely to exaggerate still further. Take a few lines of Jules Renard
echoing a passage from Montaigne; follow it with a remark made
by Edgar Faure linked with a passage from *L 'école des parents*;
round the whole thing off with a paragraph or a witticism from
Le canard enchaîné, and there is your French characteristic; but
which will predominate, the fundamental or the oddity?"

Moreover, the author himself answers this objection better
than than I ever could. I therefore urge the reader to read section
19 of the Introduction to this book with the utmost attention. He
will then understand our friend's phrase: "To achieve an evocation of the nuances in a certain climate," which requires not only
that the observer should be present at every instant of his re-
searches, but that those being observed, the French, should themselves give expression, in their own fashion, to the mental
characteristic that the theoretically noncommitted spectator is
attributing to them.

What more can I add? A simple piece of advice to the reader:
that he should be patient, that he should accept the rules of the
game—Leites's game as well as that of the French themselves;
or, better still, that he should enter into the game himself. That
he should continue the enquiry for himself. Sometimes he will
discover further illustrations of the same theme; sometimes he
will seek to illustrate his own themes, even contradictory themes

perhaps. Sometimes he will recognize himself in the image of the French being presented to him; sometimes he will protest indignantly. And in addition to this participation, beyond it, in order to make his pleasure complete, I also hope that he will ponder the question of Nathan Leites himself, the question of what his relationship to the French people really is. Let the reader glance at chapter 19, for example: "Stark Language and Veiled Meaning." La Fontaine promises his readers: "Many expressions . . . that speak and yet do not speak." And our friend continues: "To say things clearly, what eccentricity!" (chap. 19, sec. 16). But does he himself speak quite clearly? Is he intending to tell us everything? The truth is, I do not believe there is an author alive who leaves so much for his readers to divine for themselves. And when, in section 53 of the same chapter, commenting on a passage from Racine, he writes: "I didn't ask you to say it; but I'm glad you recognized yourself," or again: "Heavens, no, my dear fellow, how could you possibly have thought I meant you?," is Nathan Leites talking *about* the French or *to* the French? Has he been won over to the French way of thinking? Or does he recognize himself in them? If we knew the answer, then the game would have lost its fascination, because its rules would then have become too immediately apparent.

RAYMOND ARON

INTRODUCTION

In order for the reader to give the assertions made in this book the sense that I should like them to have, it is essential that he should take several aspects of my procedure into account. These are as follows:

1. I am putting forward hypotheses only. Their verification would require a fund of data far in excess of what I have been able to assemble.

In order to avoid weighing my positive offerings with a recurring burden of precautions, I shall quite often take the liberty of formulating what I have to say as though I were dealing with well-established theories.

2. This being so, the few data I do offer in support of any assertion are intended to be valid as illustrations only, not as proof.

3. On the other hand, it seems to me more or less certain that almost every chapter in this book confronts an important dimension of the contemporary French sensibility. It so happens, however, that though a great many observers have called attention to the questions I raise, it is extremely unusual, in my experience, for anyone to dwell upon any of them at length. The pedantry of such a procedure on my part will, I hope, be redeemed by a consequent gain in knowledge.

4. I am calling attention to tendencies rather than to phenomena that will always occur in certain given conditions. It is

for the future to transform such approximations into propositions expressing constant relations.

5. The formula toward which the elements set out in this study tend is as follows: such and such a feeling (or belief, or type of behavior) has manifested itself with such and such a frequency within such and such a group of people at such and such a period. It is easy enough to be fairly precise in indicating the period concerned, to delimit the group being examined, and to express the reaction in question. But the frequency of its appearance will be indicated in a vague fashion only, by such words and phrases as "often," "frequently," or "on numerous occasions."

The reason for this is twofold. First, it is difficult in many cases to gain access to the secret feelings and private thought processes we are dealing with. And second, on the few occasions when the pertinent data are in fact generally accessible—for example anything that took place in a parliamentary session and therefore recorded in the *Journal Officiel*—I have not taken the time or care that a quantitative analysis would have required.

6. When passing from one statement to the next, I might very well often say with Paul Valéry: "Another idea occurs to me on this subject. An idea no less fragile than the preceding one" (Valéry, *Tel quel*, 2: 182). To me, there is nothing very shocking about this. In the particular field we are dealing with, I do not feel that there is any necessity to limit ourselves, at this point, to those propositions that can already be proved. Why should we not put forward what may well in fact be false, provided that it is not obviously false, and that we do not present it as a certainty? As long as a hypothesis is not wholly without interest, the effort that its future demolition may require seems to me outweighed by the chance that it may prove to be not wholly false, as well as by the ideas that it may, in turn, provoke.

7. In other places it would have been more appropriate for me to make my transitions by saying: another thought occurs to me on this subject; one no less familiar than the previous one. But to spell out something obvious in the right place—even taking several pages over it if it is of prime importance—sometimes seems to me a good way of avoiding the temptation to repeat it, albeit more briefly, far too often.

8. I shall put forward a great many hypotheses without stopping to establish their exact weight. This is because I feel that it often goes without saying that such and such a characteristic is more—or less—important than such and such another. It is also because the precise meaning of "importance" frequently seems to me obscure, and because, even if one succeeded in penetrating

that obscurity, the task of determining a characteristic's exact degree of importance would still very often be a rather tricky one.

9. Some readers will say that I merely set out numbers of characteristics one after the other without indicating how they combine to make a whole. But in what could that whole consist other than in the relationships that link those characteristics? And I do point out such relationships, except when they seem to me to go without saying.

10. It will also be said that my accounts of the causes of the phenomena I describe are something rather less than detailed. I agree, and regret having so far lacked penetration—like my predecessors. I console myself to some extent, however, with the argument that a more detailed description, such as I attempt, may facilitate the subsequent discovery of explanations. At present, those that resist a first logical or empirical examination are, in the field of study being investigated here, extremely rare. Although according to Montesquieu, "we know more about what gives a nation a certain character than about what gives an individual a certain cast of mind, about what modifies an entire sex than about what affects a man, about what forms the genius of whole societies that have embraced a particular way of life than about that of a single member of society" (Montesquieu, "Essai sur les causes qui peuvent affecter les esprits et les caractères," Œuvres complètes, 2: 39), in the present state of the human sciences it nevertheless seems to me that the contrary is true.

11. When I do in fact offer conjectures about the causes of the phenomena under examination, I am not professing to reveal the complete network of causation involved.

When I refer to "psychological" factors, for example, this does not mean that I am trying to deny the role of "institutions," or that of "history," or that of "economics," etc.

12. My interest is not directed solely to people's behavior but also, and often principally, to the beliefs related to that behavior and the feelings that accompany those beliefs. Myths, as we know only too well today, are as worthy of interest as the facts they distort.

13. In order to simplify the exposition of my material, and to render more likely the evocative process I am attempting spark off, I shall frequently express the feelings and beliefs I attribute to my subjects as though I subscribe to them myself.

14. A consideration of the broad tendencies of contemporary French sensibility in no way obliges us to deny (which would be absurd) the diversity of intellectual or other groups that exist within the country, or the changes that the country undergoes. However, analysis can sometimes reveal shared characteristics

in people or groups who believe themselves to be absolutely different; it can also demonstrate on occasion that they are simply reacting in different ways to a problem whose common basis has scarcely been perceived.

15. My aim is in no way to seek out only characteristics exclusive to France—an undertaking that would in any case be rendered impracticable by the absence of comparable studies on other Western nations. I am certainly not asking: does this characteristic differentiate France from the rest of the Western world? but rather: is this important in Paris (without its being evident that it is so everywhere)? Differences do not exclude resemblance, either between individuals or between groups of individuals. "Anything that resembles nothing else does not exist" (Valéry, *Mauvaises pensées et autres*, p. 169). The existence of these two factors is beyond doubt; their distribution is still for the most part unknown. If future studies were to establish perceptible resemblances between, say, Paris and Rome as regards the material of any given chapter or paragraph in this book, and notable divergences as regards some other aspect, then my expectations would be fulfilled.

Should any of the emotional configurations sketched in this book be revealed, in the light of subsequent comparative studies, as common to the entire Western world, I should be extremely surprised. Nevertheless, even in that case I should not think it nugatory to have written a chapter devoted exclusively to ambiguity, for example, since such a chapter is written very rarely.

16. I juxtapose data drawn from very different spheres of life —a leading method of the human sciences in our day. It is of little importance in any case; it is for the reader to judge whether or not any given trait is in fact to be found in places that appear to be far removed from one another.

17. I suggest various links between childhood and adulthood. At such points, it may be said that I ought to have made use of the formulations of psychoanalysis to buttress my hypotheses. It seemed to me better to reserve such elaborations for a future work.

18. Montaigne will be found associated with *France-Soir*. This use of the literature of the past is not a devious means of maintaining that France never changes. The works I quote all still continue to interest the living; and it is with them that we are dealing. "You can always find what you want," Gide asserts, "in a well-stocked library, if you look properly." It is of small concern to me whether the maxim of La Rochefoucauld I quote is true, provided a Parisian of today is prepared to hail it as the

perfect expression of a widespread attitude among the people he knows.

19. The inadequacy of my data, and their motley character, may possibly endow the pages you are about to read with a character of oddity that the predominance of quotations is likely to exaggerate still further. Take a few lines of Jules Renard echoing a passage from Montaigne; follow it with a remark by Edgar Faure linked with a passage from *L'école des parents*; round the whole thing off with a paragraph or a witticism from *Le canard enchaîné*, and there is your French characteristic. But which will predominate, the fundamental, or the oddity?

Why bother to present such doubtful data? In any successfully executed intellectual operation, must the raw materials not have been transmuted into the author's own utterance? Whatever the labors he has been obliged to undergo, do not propriety and intellectual taste require that their traces should have been concealed? We may be interested in the author's ideas, but certainly not in his index cards. If the latter intrude, and intrude persistently, does that not prove that we are in the presence of nothing more than a compilation—and a pitifully incomplete one at that?

I disagree, as far as the kind of study we are dealing with here is concerned.

My purpose: to achieve an evocation of the nuances in a certain climate.

This requires in the first place that I express every detail I believe I have observed, as well as its relation to the other aspects of the whole, in my own words. This I have tried to do.

But it also requires that I link with my own formulations some of the expressions that my subjects themselves might employ, or in which they are recognizable. To resort to paraphrase, merely in order that everything can be got through more rapidly and more conveniently, would seem to me to be showing a lack of fidelity to the object. It seems to me rather undesirable that I should interpose myself to such a degree between the reader and what I wish to show him.

20. There is no quotation anywhere in this book that is anything other than an illustration of what I as the author am trying to say. This allows—and even requires—me to reduce every passage quoted to what I judge to be essential, from that single point of view. I shall perhaps be taxed with having dared to separate certain passages from their proper context, or even with having savagely hacked great chunks out of them and left no trace of such gaps apart from a few dots. If the theme I am

attempting to illustrate does in fact occur in the text I quote from, and if my version preserves it, then it seems to me that I have achieved my aim. That said, a certain exchange occurs to me:

Siéyès: "I'll tell you my way of thinking on this."

Rivarol: "Spare me the way; just give me the thinking."

BOOK 1

**THE RUT AND THE SENSE
OF ADVENTURE**

1

DON'T FENCE ME IN

1. The child is always in danger of finding itself fenced in by grown-ups—literally shut up in a room, perhaps even in the "junk room," when it has managed to "get on their nerves" too much, or until it has "calmed down." These are measures in which the desire the adults feel to protect themselves from the child and the desire to inflict punishment upon it are mingled—or are thought to be active—in varying degrees. Grown-ups may also deprive the child of outings, thereby constraining it to remain in a proximity to them that cuts across the isolation with which the reprobate is being punished.

Since *enfermer* (to shut up) is also used, according to Paul Robert's dictionary, "to express limitation," the child would appear to be fenced in to some extent in every sense: it is not allowed to choose for itself, or, at least, the number of possibilities it is free to reject or retain is narrowly circumscribed.

2. Having attained adulthood, the child may experience a strong inner tendency to shut itself up inside situational frames that will restrict its possible paths of action. We often prefer—or behave as though we prefer—everything we do in a given sphere to be governed by rules that are not at all easy to obey. The fact that they may appear arbitrary or even absurd—thus resembling many of the laws imposed upon the child—produces scarcely any diminution in our attachment to them, an attachment whose deep hold on us is often masked by surface movements of lively

but feeble opposition. On the one hand, we insist that "where there is constraint there can be no pleasure"; on the other, we claim with Montesquieu that "restraint is good for us; it is like a wound up spring" (Montesquieu, *Mes pensées*, p. 1307).

Paul Valéry reminds us, for example, that "in eras of high civilization" (*Pièces sur l'art*, p. 8) "the poet was kept in chains. He was burdened with curious embargoes and shackled with inexplicable prohibitions" (*Variété*, p. 741).

This perpetuation of one aspect of childhood is not limited to the poetic use of language, for "our syntax . . . equals our classical prosody in the rigor of its conventions. It is remarkable that a people generally considered to be excessively free in its thought . . . should have restricted itself in its speech with constraints that are in many cases inexplicable" (Valéry, *Regards sur le monde actuel*, p. 183).

3. There are other pleasures that can be experienced only by shutting oneself up. The junk room may be succeeded by the dreamer's loft, by the cellar night club, or by the speleologist's unfathomable abyss.

4. My childhood once past, on the other hand, I enjoy refusing to allow myself to be circumscribed. Or rather it pleases me to believe that I do. (In fact, my very insistence upon this attitude may give rise to suspicions that I am only too willing to accept a quite converse reality.) This means that I have a horror of feeling myself ensnared in any way, of being like Ronsard's lover (quoted by Paul Robert under *empêtrer*, to ensnare): "The lover is an animal, an animal ensnared/In the toils of love. . . ." The idea that I may become *embourbé*, bogged down—"I am caught in a bog, there is no way out of it" (Robert under *embourbé*)—is an anxiety-producing prospect, whereas that of casting off bonds brings relief and sets me at peace with myself.

"I wanted to remain free for all the possibilities hovering over me," as Montherlant puts it (*Service inutile*, p. 23). "To retain one's liberty of action"—"to remain free to act, to have freedom of action,"—"to keep oneself unattached" (available), "to tie oneself up" (commit oneself) as little as possible: this is a strong aspiration, or at any rate a vigorous myth we entertain about both ourselves and others. Paul Valéry notes that "power and money have the glamor of the infinite; it is not such and such a thing, nor such and such a faculty of action that we desire to possess specifically. No man feels an insane yearning for a reasonable power; or for the exercise of government as a simple and everyday profession; or for money as the value of precisely determined objects.

No, it is the vagueness of power that is the source of the vast desire, because I never know what I may come to desire" (Valéry, *Tel quel*, 2: 39–40).

During the phony war, a certain writer (Lucien Rebatet) discovered that one of his colleagues (Thierry Maulnier) had succumbed to a passion for warlike matters, but that his fascination was exclusively with naval operations: " 'Maulnier,' I said to him, 'war is also fought on land.' 'This time that's not so certain,' he replied. 'And besides, I know nothing about that side of it. The fascinating thing about ships is that you can move them about so easily in any direction you like. You can plan everything, imagine everything, set no limits on yourself . . .' " (Lucien Rebatet, *Les décombres*, p. 214).

5. The best moment is therefore that which precedes the act. "I have already said," Valéry reminds his readers, referring to the works of man, "that the starting point of our works is various freedoms: freedom of material . . . of form . . . of duration." These are all "things apparently forbidden to the mollusc—a creature confined by its one simple lesson" (*Variété*, p. 900). But they are also things that are lost, in man, in the transition to the act. While the orchestra is tuning up before the concert we experience an "emotional stirring" that "has something more universal about it than any possible symphony," a "disturbance" that "contains all such symphonies mingled in it . . . that suggests them all." It is "a simultaneous presence of all futures" (ibid., p. 721). In such a context "the mind" is "pure expectation" in which "I am still distinct from all thought; equally aloof from all the words, from all the forms that are inside me. . . . O my presence without a face, what a gaze, that gaze of yours without person or object, what a power that undefinable power of yours . . ." (*Tel quel*, 2: 127–28).

6. When the number of possible paths before me is reduced, what may shock me most is not the loss of specific advantages from a particular act henceforth excluded—an act that I could be sure of not wishing to perform as long as there was nothing to prevent my doing so—but simply the fact itself of my liberty's having been curtailed. On his way to a post in the Sahara, a lieutenant of Montherlant's invention is obsessed by the fear that he will be unable to find a woman there to make love to. But having located one, this is what he feels: "The obsession had existed in his brain long before it had existed in his flesh, if it ever had existed in his flesh. What had been angering and disturbing him was not so much the idea of continence as the sensation of a material impossibility. And now that he was certain of possessing, his peace of mind was almost as great is if he had already possessed" (Henry de Montherlant, *L'histoire d'amour de la Rose de Sable*, p. 29).

7. Once obstacles have occurred in the path of any given action, an inclination to perform it is likely to arise. At the time when French political circles first began to pay some attention to the Euratom treaty, in the summer of 1956, the ambition for France to produce her own nuclear weapons was, in those circles, very weak. But the formal agreement proposed at that time seemed to be creating obstacles in this respect, so that the interest now being taken in the treaty suddenly strengthened many politicians' conviction that their country ought not to be without the new weapon.

8. Though we may perceive that there are several "solutions" to any given problem, in the sphere of politics or any other, we may also observe, regretfully, that "there are not *that* many. In order to combat this notion, we may say with Marshal Juin (speaking of what would happen if the C.E.D. were rejected), "There are substitute solutions available in plenty. . . . I have mine just as everyone else has his" (speech at Annebault, April 4, 1954; *Combat*, April 5, 1954).

There are those who openly say: "Let us not deceive ourselves for an instant: we are not free to choose from a large number of hypotheses" (on the subject of Algeria's future, Maurice Violette, A.N., October 11, 1955; *J.O.*, p. 5018*), and those who say, of a still pending solution to a major problem, that "it is tomorrow's secret, but that secret is nevertheless enclosed within certain limits. Juridical subtlety will certainly be able to think up many formulas within those limits. But it is impossible, all the same, to think of any that cannot be contained within one of the three following categories . . ." (on the extent to which West Germany should be rearmed, Antoine Pinay, A.N., August 31, 1954; *J.O.*, p. 4484). But such people, in political circles, are often held to be jackasses—or else cunning devils who are trying to promote their own formula by deceitfully obscuring the number of "substitute solutions."

Any attempt to "hedge me in with false alternatives," or to "spreadeagle me between false options" will excite a reaction of lively distrust mingled with indignation. Refusing to "allow myself to be hedged in by false dilemmas," I shall assert that "it is not impossible to find a solution," "on the sole condition that the full extent of my liberty shall be preserved (on the conflict between the Sultan and the Glaoui. Pierre-Albin Martel, *Le Monde*, April 13, 1953).

9. Since experience has shown that "everything can happen in France," that even the most unexpected combinations are

* A.N. denotes the National Assembly, and *J.O.*, the *Journal officiel* of the debates in question.

eventually realized with the passage of time, the future—when it is not dominated by a belief in the inevitable and/or desirable continuance of the *status quo* (see chap. 3, sec. 3)—is often impregnated with the belief that "everything is possible," that "no hypothesis can be excluded," that "you never can tell," that "the whole question may suddenly be reopened" (though even this belief, when strongly held, can also in fact help on occasion to perpetuate the established state of things).

Before and during an important debate or parliamentary crisis, for example, those who claim to know all about the particular question often do their utmost to predict as many possible outcomes to it as they can.

10. Though I may tend to take pleasure in limiting the possibilities open to others, or in considering them as being limited, when it comes to myself I am only too anxious to deny that the fact of my having ventured into a specific present has in any way reduced the future paths still open to me. What? People think that by doing this or that I have restricted my own freedom of movement? They will soon seen how wrong they are!

According to Bernard's angel in *Les faux-monnayeurs*, "we are the dependents of a past . . . that past puts us under an obligation. Our entire future has been blue-printed by it" (André Gide, *Les faux-monnayeurs*, p. 440).

But there is a likelihood that the man to whom such a remark is addressed will reply, again with André Gide, "I do not wish to be a slave . . . to my past, a slave to my future projects, a slave to my faith, to my doubt, to my hate or my love.

"Though I may agree to serve . . . I want the terms upon which I lease out my life to be both freely consented to and renewable at any given moment" (Gide, *Journal 1889–1939*, p. 670).

The idea that the stakes may all be down on the table from the very start often inspires a revulsion whose violence is proportionate to our secret conviction that such is in fact the case.

11. In opposition to the attraction of the rut there is my refusal to accept the continual "renewal" of my past as an inevitability. According to Montaigne, "the quality most objectionable to a proper man is . . . the obligation to a fixed, particular fashion" (*Essais*, bk. 3, chap. 13). In *Le Rouge et le Noir,* "the most *fin de siècle* of men" exclaims: "Why am I expected to be of the same opinion today as I was six weeks ago? That would mean I was the slave of my opinions" (Stendhal, *Le Rouge et le Noir*, pt. 2, chap. 4).

12. In other words, becoming aware of having predetermined my future—by having ventured into some present obligation— may arouse a wish to reestablish the liberty thus compromised.

This may be specifically observed in the case of resolutions taken by persons or assemblies with regard to their own future conduct. Grown-ups insist that children shall think consistently; but adults may see the fact that they themselves are acting against their own expressed intentions as a precious sign of their privileged status.

"If I knew what I must do tomorrow, I should immediately try to find something else," Jules Renard confesses (*Journal*, p. 110). Parliamentary assemblies under both the Third and Fourth Republics—according to a widespread belief in political circles that was doubtless also a reality—were very fond of jettisoning official schedules established either by themselves or their competent organs in order to follow, without warning, the unpredictable desire excited by unpredicted events. Similarly, to take one example, a parliamentary group faced with the task of resolving some internal problem may "decide not to apply its own ruling in this instance" (the Socialists in the A.N. dealing with a problem of discipline, Raymond Barrillon, *Le Monde*, January 14, 1955). And in the case of a law already formally passed it often appears desirable to be able to apply it "without . . . allowing ourselves to be trapped by its dispositions as though in a prison" (on the subject of the 1947 Algerian statute, Roger de Saivre, A.N., October 13, 1955; *J. O.*, p. 5089).

In order to make myself capable of obeying a particular resolution, I sometimes do my utmost to close my eyes to the fact that I have made that resolution, as with the soldier at the front who never stops protesting: "heroism, what crap!"—until the day he dies a hero.

13. People may claim that some particular and precipitate act on my part must perforce entail the performance of such and such another, upon which I have not yet decided; but is this a truth or a trap? Might I not maintain, ultimately, that nothing obliges us to anything? Thus, under the Fourth Republic, to be a minister in a government could still be viewed as compatible with all sorts of actions expressing a really rather imperfect solidarity with one's colleagues. To approve, as a member of the National Assembly, of a general policy statement by the government did not apparently oblige me to support the specific measure with which the group in power eventually executed the declared policy (if the wording used in the particular case was sufficiently precise to permit such a formulation); in fact, under the Fourth Republic, the "contract of investiture," so punctiliously drawn up and analyzed at the time of a government's formation, had always long fallen into oblivion by the time of its demise.

14. If, at the moment of envisaging a given path of action, we see ourselves threatened by some trammeling obligation, is it not possible for us to avoid it by altering the course of that path slightly, so that we are still able to perform the desired action while also reducing its dangers? As, for example, when the members of a political group (the Socialist Republicans), at a time when Félix Gaillard was forming a government, "authorized M. Chaban-Delmas to accept the Ministry of Defence . . . [he] will nevertheless hand in his resignation as chairman of the Socialist Republican party. Thus the latter will not be committed by his presence in the government" (Jacques Fauvet, *Le Monde*, November 6, 1957). When the transition from one government to another (from Guy Mollet's to that led by Maurice Bourgès-Manoury) eliminated a party (the Socialists) from the Hôtel Matignon while allowing it to retain certain key posts, the advantage that the party in question expected to reap from the "operation" was explained as follows: "a government that includes Socialists will enable the [Socialist party] and its secretary to keep a tight hand upon French politics . . . without taking any direct responsibility for them, thus retaining its freedom of critical opposition" (Jacques Fauvet, *Le Monde*, June 9 and 10, 1957).

15. Why should I not commit myself to a course of action I intend later to abandon? It is often seen as both legitimate and profitable to advance far in the direction of an apparent goal only to do an about-face at the last moment; one is always free to "go into reverse"; it's the other fellow who gets "his fingers burned"! Changing one's mind about what one is apparently in the very process of performing—that's freedom!

For example, when a parliament is required to pronounce upon the principle or even the details of a projected law or treaty while it is still being drawn up, many members are tempted to take up specific positions with the feeling that they will nevertheless still be free, when the moment of final decision arrives, to adopt the opposite point of view; even though there is likely to be some difficulty in justifying such a reversal of opinion by claiming that the case has altered in the meantime.

When the French parliament came to make its decision on the extent to which West Germany should be rearmed, this tendency played a major role. In the autumn of 1954, the government presented the Assembly with the *Acte de Londres*, which was a detailed prefiguration of the U.E.O. treaty shortly to be drawn up. This act was put through by the Assembly "as though it were mailing a letter"; but this was because "once more, while giving their approval in principle, many will make mental reservations as to the future and see to it that they are still able to reverse this initial approval" (Adolphe Aumeran, A.N., October 7, 1954; J.O., p. 4581). And, indeed, when the moment of decision arrived (several months later), the treaty in question did experience the greatest difficulties. This is why, on a comparable occasion (before a vote on a motion in favor of the then embryonic Euratom treaty), a prime minister (Guy Mollet) insisted: "A vote in favor of this motion will also signify that we are committed in advance to approving, in several months' time, the treaty that will by then have been drawn up, if it is in conformity with the decisions we make at this point" (A.N., July 11, 1956; J. O., p. 3385). But this is how a deputy (Valéry Giscard d'Estaing) described the attitude of certain of his colleagues as they prepared to vote in favor of the treaty instituting the Common Market, despite their belief that it could well cause havoc in the economy: " 'That doesn't matter. Let's ratify the treaty for the moment, there's always a chance we may leave the Market.' " The speaker then judged it expedient to refute this line of thought: "If we leave the Common Market, we shall leave it humiliated, diminished, discredited. We cannot entertain such a hypothesis" (A.N., July 24, 1957; J.O., p. 3252).

On the other hand, those obsessed with a concern to collect sufficient votes to get them over the next bridge are tempted to encourage rather than to destroy this belief that one can always "take back one's vote." I may take the same attitude toward myself—for example, when attempting to reconcile myself to some line of action that I consider repugnant but also inevitable. By persuading myself that such and such a first step is easily reversible, I end up by getting myself irretrievably enmeshed in a mechanism of which I refuse to let myself become aware until it is too late.

16. A member of the opposition (Camille Titeux) once said to a party leader (Edgar Faure) in the Assembly: "there is no member of this Assembly more adept than yourself . . . at entering into commitments that do not commit you" (A.N., February 23, 1955; J.O., p. 885). But is this not precisely the principle of a branch of wisdom whose practitioners are often extremely respectable men? "His philosophy," one writer (Valéry) said of his predecessor in the Académie (Anatole France) "safeguarded him against excessively rigid resolutions. . . . He did not pledge (*engager*) his future" (Valéry, *Variété*, p. 726). Under "pledge the future" (*engager l'avenir*) Paul Robert refers us to the figurative sense of "mortgage," for which he quotes "mortgage one's present chances," and also Chateabriand's lament when selling his memoirs: "No one can ever know what I have suffered from

being obliged to mortgage my own tomb." In order to explicate "to bind someone" (*engager quelqu'un*), Robert first of all gives "this signature or contract binds you," but follows it with: "Words bind no one. That doesn't bind me in any way. He avoids anything that might bind him." For *engager* also signifies, in a literal sense, "to cause to enter or penetrate into something that fastens onto, that does not leave free," and, in the corresponding figurative sense, "to cause someone to enter into an opinion, a feeling, an affair, an undertaking, etc. that will hold him fast, that will not leave him free"; which is to say, in colloquial and vulgar terms, "to drag into, to draw into, to con into." That the first illustration Robert gives of this meaning of *engager*—"he succeeded in drawing him into this business"—may already be assumed to conjure up an undesirable situation is perhaps indicated by those that follow: "He has drawn him into a nasty business, into hot water. A dictator who commits his country to a military venture." Similarly, for the reflexive form *s'engager*, "to engage oneself in an enterprise," is followed by: "To engage oneself in a tricky affair. . . . He went into it head down, without thinking. . . . He committed himself too far." Then come all the other verbs immediately brought to mind by this sense of *engager*: "venture, commit, expose, risk, compromise." And in the case of *s'engager*; "venture oneself, embark upon, undertake, throw oneself into, hurl oneself into, place oneself in the van. . . ." Here again, words evoking danger seem to predominate.

As an illustration of *engagement*, Robert gives: "He is bound, hampered, prevented from acting, by a previous engagement." How frightful! What a good deed it must be then "to free, to set loose, to disentangle someone from an engagement." And corresponding to this meaning we also find an example of the figurative use of *dépêtrer*, to extricate: " to extracate someone . . . from a thoughtless engagement."

That I may engage or commit myself with pleasure, that my happiness may depend upon it does, it is true, seem possible; but it would also appear to be the act of a most extraordinary man: "This work, this choice, this decision . . . engages his whole being." This exalting and exalted sense of *s'engager* is, as we know, a neologism created by "intellectuals": "To participate actively, in accordance with one's deepest convictions, in the life of the human community, while willingly engaging (committing) one's conscience, one's reputation, one's goods . . . to such a project." But before presenting us with the cliché: "A committed writer," the dictionary takes just one more backward glance at the more ordinary human emotions: "To be afraid of committing oneself."

Corresponding to the perils incurred by those who commit themselves, or allow themselves to be committed, we find—as I have already remarked—the relief experienced by the person who is freed, or who frees himself, from an engagement or commitment. (The former risks desertion; the latter inflicts it). *Dégager* (to disengage) is "to withdraw what has been given in pledge (*gage*). It is also "to free, to deliver, to extricate from a critical or embarrassing position." Or again, "to free from that which is enveloping . . ., to rid of that which impedes, from that which restrains . . . from that which conceals . . ., to free a mixture of its impurities . . ., to untie bonds, to loose shackles." Applied to clothing, *dégager* means "to make looser, freer, to restore ease of movement," to medicine: "to free an organ from that which is incommoding it." To be *dégagé* means to possess freedom and ease of manner. There is "work *dégagé* from all ambition, from all material considerations," and also the "soul *dégagée* from all terrestrial bonds." It is against this background of good things that we should consider the meaning of particular interest to use here. *Dégager* is: "To free from an obligation. . . . See enfranchize, liberate. To release someone from his word, his promise; to give him back his word, his promise. To release someone from a sin he has committed. See absolve. To release someone from a burden, a debt. . . . See unload, disencumber, dispense, exonerate. . . ." And similarly with the reflexive form *se dégager*, which Paul Robert illustrates as follows: "To free oneself from all responsibility. . . . To free oneself from a promise, an undertaking. . . . To free oneself from one's bonds. To detach oneself from a crowd. . . . To rid oneself of a habit, a routine, a prejudice."

17. We sometimes hear of politicians unwise enough to have spoken in rather too precise a way about their own future actions —announcing some specific goal, letting fly with a "never" or an "always" on some specific subject—only to find themselves constrained, shortly afterward either to give themselves the lie, which is embarrassing or to abstain from some useful line of action. Although the politician is unlikely to neglect the advantages to be gained from a nicely calculated false promise, he also experiences the feeling described by Montaigne with regard to "undertakings wholly mine own and free": ". . . if I tell the goal, I feel that I am obliging myself to it, and that committing it to another's knowledge is to bind oneself to it in advance; I feel that I am promising it when I tell it. So I air my intentions very little" (*Essais*, bk. 3, chap. 9).

"Let us not hedge in the future with excessively strict formulas!" the veteran politician cries to those of his colleagues who are in danger of letting themselves be carried away by the present situation (Paul Ramadier referring to the omission of a particular status for Algeria from the 1958 Constitution, Socialist Party Congress, September 12, 1958; *Paris-Presse*, September 13, 1958).

18. One should never go into anything, or any place, without making sure that one has some convenient means of egress. Which is to say, both easily accessible and inconspicuous—after the model of Costals entering marriage: "I am going into this business as I went into the war, and perhaps as I go into everything: concerning myself at my moment of entry with the means I may need to get out of it again" (Montherlant, *Le démon du bien*, p. 56). Or after that of M. d'Auligny drawing up a contract: "Whenever M. d'Auligny had successfully inserted some phrase into a contract that constituted, in his mind, an open door that would enable him to evade his commitments, then he was in his seventh heaven" (Montherlant, *Les Auligny*, p. 29). "The artist," Montherlant says finally, this time referring to himself, "ought never to commit himself to a state that is either irreparable or too difficult to modify" (*Carnets*, 1930–1944, p. 390), a maxim that appears to be equally valid for the politician; indeed, for any man. "Everything you do that takes the form of an irremediable, unrecapturable act—is another step toward old age. Oh cling to the reversible! (Valéry, letter to Pierre Louys, May 21, 1917; *Lettres à quelques-uns*, p. 120).

19. Thus, ambiguity, so often decried, here appears an indispensable tool in the hands of the man struggling to retain his freedom. By using vague words we keep the future open and inconclusive—as a mother may when negotiating her daughter's marriage: "Two years earlier, Solange had refused a young civil service engineer. But Madame Dandillot, succumbing to the attractions of inconclusiveness . . . had made it quite clear when passing Solange's refusal on to him that 'the future was not closed' . . . Once a year, for two years, the tenacious engineer continued to call upon Madame Dandillot; the same inconclusiveness still reigned, and the door was still left ajar" (Montherlant, *Le démon du bien*, p. 181).

20. Cardinal de Retz, when recommending a certain "decision" to Monsieur, notes that "he is not decisive, he leaves or always appears to leave his Royal Highness with a freedom of choice, and consequently with the power to select whatever may suit him from the 'chapter of accidents'" (Retz, *Mémoires*, p. 622). It is in this same spirit that we find Camille Chautemps, in Bordeaux during June of 1940, suggesting that the government should continue its flight as far as Perpignan. Once there, it would have greater freedom to choose: "either to remain in

France, or to board a cruiser at Port-Vendres" (Jacques Benoist-Méchin, *Soixante jours qui ébranlèrent l'Occident*, 2: 378). When faced with opposing arguments that we are unable to decide between, we like to adopt a course of action that does not apparently exclude the subsequent application of either.

21. But the surest method of safeguarding my freedom of action is still that of abstaining from action altogether (see sec. 5 above). During the Algerian war, a general officer (Paris de la Bollardière) refused a decoration as a token of protest against certain methods employed in the prosecution of that war. But an individual who subscribed to the point of view being discussed here, if pressed by his friends to imitate this gesture, would have exclaimed: "You can't be serious! If I sent my ribbon back, I should no longer be in a position to send it back!" Or, in abstract language, "The accomplishment of the exterior action does not radically deprive us of the ability to think that it is still to be performed. . . . How often one catches oneself reliving the state of oscillation and equipoised possibilities in which one existed before having acted, as though it were some Other who had subscribed to the act, and as though it were impossible for the Self, under pain of no longer being the Self, to accept that *the deed counted*? It is as though our Self felt a repugnance at becoming that Other who has committed himself to the irreversible. . . . We recognize ourselves solely in the provisional and the pure possiblility: that is what is really us" (Valéry, *Regards sur le monde actuel*, p. 55).

22. The passage of time—if I am to give credit to a feeling closely associated with that just described—gradually curtails the number of possibilities open to me, until that moment when the last of all disappears with my death: "I was born *several* . . . and I die *only one*. The child on the way is a numberless host that life quickly narrows down to a single individual; the one that actually manifests itself then dies. A quantity of Socrates was born with me, from which, little by little, the Socrates due to appear before the judge and drink the hemlock emerged" (Valéry, *Eupalinos*, pp. 71–72). Similarly: "We are made (*faits*) of something that happens (*se fait*); something that happens at the expense of the possible" (Valéry, *Variété*, p. 772), since "life's sequence eats up our initial reserves . . . of possibilities" (Valéry, *Mélange*, 1: 326). "I do not know what to think of M. Paul Valéry considered as a determined object," the same author wrote in his old age; "even though at my age one is of course bound to end up as one" (letter to R. P. Rideau, 1943; *Lettres à quelques-uns*, p. 246). The young André Gide expressed the same feeling: "I sense a thousand possible beings within me; but I cannot resign

myself to wishing to be only one of them. And I am terrified, at at every instant, at every word I write, at every gesture I make, to think that each of those things is one more ineradicable stroke added to the image of me that is gradually becoming fixed" (Gide, *Journal 1889–1939*, p. 28).

Is this death in life unavoidable? Perhaps not, Valéry suggest: "We believe that if we start again from our childhood we could become another person, have a different history. . . . This possibility of grouping the same elements in various ways persists. . . .

"There is no time *lost*, no time really past, as long as those other personae are still possible" (Valéry, *Tel quel*, 2: 263). Is refusing to let oneself be trapped not the same as escaping old age—escaping death? "Life is the preservation of the possible" (Valéry, *Mélange*, p. 288).

23. By dint of impositions of all sorts, grown-ups try to make that disturbing creature, the child, into a predictable being. Once an adult himself, this creature imagines himself capable of caprices, if not actually capricious. The use that grown-ups make of their time must not appear too predictable, especially when such predictability is, less consciously, very much desired, and when the grown-up is in reality rather rarely given to leaving his rut. "To do no more than is required," Montherlant asserts, "is one of the great secrets in the service, in art, in love—in life" (*Le solstice de juin*, p. 245).

24. If the child lies, we tend to classify it "a liar"; if it gets itself dirty, a label saying "dirty" may even be attached to it physically; if it steals, it may have to copy out "I am a thief" a hundred times. A single act conjures up the idea of a permanent essence. In school, a child psychiatrist (M. H. Revault-d'Allonnes) tells us, "when setbacks occur . . . the resulting failure situation immediately appears almost impossible to break out of. . . . The child is held to be a poor student" (*L'école des parents*, December 1953, p. 27). There is a strong tendency to "establish rigid student types: the good student, the student with an academic bent, the dunce, the trouble-maker. Once the label has been applied it often becomes definitive, and the child has to drag it around like a ball and chain" (Didier Anzieu, *L'école des parents*, May 1954, p. 35).

This is yet another aspect of childhood that the adult is attempting to slough off by preferring to be considered unpredictable. Since grown-ups often are in fact unpredictable in their dealings with children, thereby causing them suffering, the children will later transmute the distress inflicted upon them into delight in inflicting it. To the degree in which their parents sometimes spoil them, sometimes yell at them, sometimes take no interest in them at all, passing from kisses to slaps, from praise to insult, children are likely to be impatient for the moment when the privilege of being unpredictable devolves upon them in their turn.

25. "This man was so crammed with inner riches that his replies were difficult to predict, and he himself did not know what he would come up with . . . what feelings would prevail in him, what desires would spring up, what ripostes, what illuminations!" (Valéry, *Monsieur Teste,* pp. 69–70)—a precious quality indeed in that Monsieur Teste! According to "a friend," Colette "proclaims that the true charm of life consists in not knowing exactly, at any given moment, what one will be doing an hour later" (Sylvain Bonmariage, *Willy, Colette et moi,* p. 144). "I don't know what I shall do . . . but *I shall give myself a surprise*; if I doubted that, I should be nothing," Paul Valéry declares: (*Variété,* p. 483).

To claim that I am unpredictable, and to require that others should not destroy that belief, may be all the more important to me if the converse is in fact true: "When dining out, Maurice always eats boiled beef followed by cheese, and the glum waiter asks him before every meal: 'What would Monsieur like today?' " (Jules Renard, *Journal,* p. 273).

26. What may prove particularly attractive is a mixture of the expected and the unforeseen, such as that provided by knowing an end result without knowing how it will be achieved. Montherlant, observing the beginning of a love affair, writes: "It is exquisite to watch her coming and going, knowing now that she will be mine, whereas an hour ago nothing was certain. . . . This moment, when one has the certainty that the thing will take place, without knowing exactly how it will take place, is perhaps the most exquisite in the whole of any affair. . . . To say to oneself: 'She is mine,' without her being so, and yet her being so, all the same" (Montherlant, *Carnets,* 1930–1944, p. 262). Or the mixture may be provided by a mutable interplay of elements within a fixed framework, as in the case of Pierre Herbart's brothel: "At the Big Ape, Madame Jeanne controlled the frolics of her inmates with the severity of a ballet mistress. . . . Whatever random chance presided over the composition of the clientele, the same play was played out every night, full of the unexpected, yet subject to rigorous rules" (Herbart, *L'Age d'Or,* p. 52). Under the Third and Fourth Republics, those who moved in political circles often employed the same image when referring to "the play being performed"—and enjoying such a long run—in the Assembly.

27. Reminding us that we "sometimes do things that 'are not at all like us,' " Paul Valéry adds: "It is good to do such things

with deliberate intent, in order . . . to render ourselves . . . less easily predictable both to ourselves and to others" (*Tel quel*, 2: 186). "Sleep must be caught," Proust advises us, "at the very moment when we thought we were doing anything but going to sleep" (Marcel Proust, *Sodome et Gomorrhe*, p. 982). "I like not being where people think I am" André Gide tells us (*Si le grain ne meurt*, p. 250).

28. We can make ourselves less predictable by means of frequent and abrupt changes in behavior, such as those that characterized the life of the French parliament under the Third and Fourth Republics. Those who took part in it sensed, with a feeling of unease that marked their pleasure, that "the unpredictable is king" (André Stibio, *Carrefour*, November 7, 1951), the "volteface, normal."

Whenever a difficult problem presented itself, a cascade of contradictory votes—particularly in committee—was by no means unusual. For instance, in a committee of the *"chambre de réflexion"*: "An amendment of major importance proposed by M. Maroger, accepted at 4 p.m. by 14 votes to 8, then rejected at 11 p.m. by 13 votes to 12, was finally adopted at 4 in the morning" (*Année politique, 1948*, p. 227).

According to one great parliamentary journalist (Jacques Fauvet), "the Assembly . . . totally disrupts its work schedule every three days" (*Le Monde*, November 28, 1952). A few years later, a deputy generally considered by his colleagues to be a very serious politician (Jean Minjoz), when commenting upon the improvement that had taken place in this respect, recalled a quite recent period when "our labors were paralyzed almost daily by continual disruptions of the agenda" (A.N., July 21, 1955; J.O., p. 4001). But several month later, one of the most respected members of that parliament (Charles Barangé) was still able "to invite" the National Assembly "to undertake discussions that shall at least be inspired by a purposeful order" (A.N., November 23, 1955; J. O., p. 5954). It was in order to restrain this tendency that the Fifth Republic introduced so many "safeguards," in a spirit that led the chairman of its first Assembly (Jacques Chaban-Delmas) to say: "After the division, I shall give the Assembly precise indications as to its daily agenda for this week and the week following, so that each of you, my dear colleagues, will know what to expect (applause)" (A.N., January 21, 1959; J.O., p. 151).

29. Although someone else's unpredictability may appear distressing or dangerous, it can also appear fascinating, or even, and quite often, as the necessary condition of a strong attraction. Costals says of his mistress: "I am incapable of predicting what

her reaction will be in any specific case. When dealing with her, I have the impression of being engaged in subtle diplomatic maneuvers; I do everything by groping in the dark and the grace of God" (Montherlant, *Les jeunes filles,* p. 221). A journalist (Jean Ferniot) once said of a great politician: "The secret of fascination is surprise. George Bidault can be excellent or execrable. We flock in crowds to find out 'what he'll be like today' " (*La Nef,* January 1958, p. 31).

The other ceases to appear unpredictable as soon as he or she is no longer the object of an intense attachment. Having observed at Balbec that "every time we see them, young girls are so little like what they were the time before," Proust adds: "I am not saying that a day will not come when, even to these . . . young girls, we shall assign extremely rigid characters, but that is because they will have ceased to interest us, because their every appearance will no longer be an apparition for the heart quite different from what it was expecting, leaving it overwhelmed each time by a fresh incarnation. Their rigidity will be the product of our indifference" (Proust, *La prisonnière,* p. 66)

2

MY WATCHWORD IS DIVERSITY

1. Though the child is often firmly thought of as all of a piece, grown-ups rather like to be spoken of in terms resembling those used by the Abbé describing M. Teste to the latter's wife: "Your husband's faces are without number" (Valéry, *Monsieur Teste,* p. 50). Since "diversity is a great source of pleasure" (La Motte-Houdar), to say of someone that he has "a very diverse intelligence" (a phrase quoted by Paul Robert under divers) is strong praise; even stronger is that which attributes "a great, an infinite diversity" to some object. According to Pascal (again quoted by Robert under *diversité*), "God *diversifies* . . . [the] unique precept of charity, in order to satisfy our curiosity, which leads us in quest of diversity." According to Gide's Lafcadio: "A shrewd man, in the jargon that both Protos and he used . . . , was a man who, for whatever reason, did not present the same face to all people and in all places . . . opposed to which was . . . [the] great family of the *crustaceans*, the representatives of which . . . always stood foursquare" (Gide, *Les Caves du Vatican,* p. 274). Let some great politician express the attitude he sets store by not only in the House but in the lobbies, let him say the same things to too many people, and he risks their disregard; what can one be expected to make of a fellow who's all of a piece!

To be all of one piece is to be less or more than human. "The whole of a dog," Paul Valéry notes, "is in his eyes. He hurls himself upon me with a look expressing the very same impulse of

affection as his movement. He is undivided" (*Mélange*, p. 400).
The mollusc, as we have seen, is a "creature that knows only what
it has been taught," whose work is "beyond repentance, beyond
reservations, beyond retouching" (Valéry, *Variété*, p. 900). Moreover, "if a being can do one thing only, and in one way only . . .
that action is not . . . human" (ibid., p. 895). The same author
has his Faust say to Mephistopheles: "You are only a spirit. . . .
You are infinitely simple. As simple as a tiger that is all predatory
power. . . . There is nothing more in you. . . . You cannot even
suspect that there is a great deal more in the world than Good and
Evil" (Valéry, *Mon Faust*, pp. 45–46).

The powerful attraction of what Valéry rejects does not lack
for direct expression either: "When you invent the idea of a new
character/ Let him appear in all respects to be in harmony
with himself/ And let him remain to the very end just as we see
him first," Boileau insists in *l'art poétique*, while a man of Colette's
invention has the following feeling toward the woman he loves:
"He sighed with relief upon seeing her so very like herself"
(Colette, *Duo*, p. 28).

Whatever the power of the rut in our lives, our aversion to it
is glaringly apparent in the tastes we wish to experience and
like to credit ourselves with. "Our principal sufficiency," in
Montaigne's estimation, "is to be able to apply ourselves to various
ways of behavior. It is being, but it is not living to attach ourselves . . . solely to one way of doing things. The noblest souls
are those with . . . the greatest variety" (Montaigne, *Essais*, bk
3, chap. 3). And here is how a young man of Gide's invention
feels about his friend: "Bernard . . . felt an ever increasing astonishment, an ever increasing admiration . . . at the diversity of
which that friend showed himself capable" (Gide, *Les faux-monnayeurs*, p. 148) "The important thing," Montherlant declares,
"is not being different from others, but being different from
oneself" (Montherlant, *Carnets*, 1930–1944, p. 302).

2. This much prized diversity often appears to have been
achieved by human beings. "Man is a diverse being," Paul Robert
writes when illustrating that adjective. "And there is as much
between us and ourselves as between us and others," Montaigne
is led to believe by his observations, (*Essais*, bk. 2, chap. 1), a
belief in which he is joined by La Rochefoucauld: "We are sometimes as different from ourselves as we are from others"
(*Maximes*), and by Gide: "From myself to myself, what a distance!" (*Journal 1889–1939*, p. 365), and again: "Nothing could
be more different from me than I myself." When such is not the
case, then "it seems to me that my life slows down, stops, and
that I am literally about to cease being" (Gide, *Les faux-mon-*

nayeurs, p. 93). It is therefore "an absurd folly always to behave like oneself" (Gide, *La tentative amoureuse*, p. 39). One must, on the contrary, "remain faithful to oneself by never resembling anything less than oneself" (Gide, *Journal 1889–1939*, p. 628).

"When we remember the vigor of a glance, or some boldness of demeanor," Marcel Proust reminds us, "it is inevitably by an almost languid profile, by a . . . dreamy gentleness . . . that we shall be astonished at the next encounter. . . . So great is every individual's multiplicity. . . . The human face is truly like that of God, of the god of some oriental theogony, a whole bunch of faces juxtaposed on different planes and impossible to view all at the same time" (Proust, *A l'ombre des jeunes filles en fleurs*, pp. 916–17). (Were it not, then it would appear "flat with nothing beneath it, made up of a single piece without any thickness" (ibid., p. 818).

3. The same holds true of the country as a whole. "A diverse country or people" Paul Robert gives us under the adjective in question. Paul Valéry, itemizing the "essential variety of France," observes that its territory is "one of the most varied in existence," that "there is almost no geographical definition of which we cannot find an example here," and that "the recipe for the constitution of the French people is one of the most complex in the world" (*Regards sur le monde actuel*, pp. 179–81). "What strikes one immediately," Montherlant writes after looking through a book of photographs depicting many different aspects of France, "is the extreme variety of the landscapes. France appears at every moment different from herself" (*Carnets*, 1930–1944, pp. 353–54).

4. How can we love someone who is not diverse? "Do you wish to merit the public's affection?/ Then vary your language without cease as you write," Boileau instructs us in *L'art poétique*. If "women with a degree of resistance . . . are the only interesting ones" to Marcel Proust, that is because "to conquer them is to vary the form, the magnitude, the relief of the human image," whereas "women one first meets at a brothel are not interesting because they remain unchangeable" (Proust, *Du côté de Guermantes*, 2: 362–63). Lying beside Albertine, it seemed to the narrator that "every time she moved her head she created a new woman, often unsuspected by me. It seemed to me that I was in possession, not of one, but of innumerable young women" (*La prisonnière*, p. 72). Costals feels of Solange "that she had revealed herself to him as a twofold being, both tart and socialite, and he was never interested in anyone who was not twofold (twofold being a minimum)" (Montherlant, *Le démon du bien*, p. 42). Attempting to explain the pleasure he finds in a painting

of Venus reclining, Paul Valéry observes: "This painting presents us with a white and rounded person. It is also a happy distribution of lights and darks. It is also a collection of noble parts and regions of delight. . . . It is also a system of values, of colors, of curves, of domains. . . ." If this object were not "so many things at the same time," it would "lack all poetry," as "totally abstract thought" lacks it, because "it follows its thread and . . . is nothing but what it follows" (*Tel quel*, 1: 12).

5. And how, with even stronger reason, are we to remain faithful to someone who is not multiple? "Constancy in love," La Rochefoucauld explains, "is a perpetual inconstancy that causes our heart to attach itself successively to all the qualities of the person we love . . . so that this constancy is nothing other than an inconstancy arrested and imprisoned inside one and the same subject" (*Maximes*). "Fidelity," one of Montherlant's characters declares, "is the power to embody a hundred different beings in one single being" (*Celles qu'on prend dans ses bras*, act 2, sc. 1). A contemporary writer (Hervé Bazin), writing of fashion, has expressed the opinion that "the only, the great excuse" for this "institution" is "to render woman different, thus enabling us to remain faithful to her by deceiving her with herself" (*Paris-Presse*, March 26, 1958). A paragraph in one of the weeklies expresses the same cliché: "To possess three women in one, as any husband will tell you, is the most common thing in the world! After all, if the wife didn't change, how could the poor husband be faithful to her?" (*Artaban*, November 29, 1957).

6. Just as a child is in its seventh heaven when given a selection of "dressing-up" outfits (an observation made by Constantin Melnik), so the adult likes to feel himself *several*. "A man of changeable humor is not one man," La Bruyère notes, "he is several: he multiplies himself as often as he acquires new tastes and different manners; he is at every moment what he is not, and he is about to be what he has never been: he is his own successor" (La Bruyères, *Les Caractères*, "De l'homme," 6). "I am not some one, but several," asserts one of Gide's characters (*Les faux-monnayeurs*, p. 75); "every one of us is not one, but contains a number of persons" Proust declares (*La fugitive*, p. 529); exalting "the faculty of not being one" (*Histoires brisées*, p. 160), Paul Valéry proudly claims: "I believe more than ever that I am several!" (letter to Pierre Louys, August 30, 1890; *Lettres à quelques-uns*, p. 17). In a weekly that does not go in for unusual ideas (*Demain*), a novelist (Roger Rabiniaux) who is also a civil servant and a propagandist for the main industry (cutlery) in his subprefecture (Thiers), has published an article entitled: "I have the right to be several" (*Demain*, April 11–17, 1957).

7. The man in love with plurality sets out to look for means of *self-multiplication*. Baudelaire discusses "wine and hashish . . . as means of multiplying the individuality," while Proust speaks of "that possible multiplication of the self we call happiness" (*A l'ombre des jeunes filles en fleurs*, p. 794).

8. What a windfall then, when an error on someone else's part endows me with a diversity that has cost no effort on my part to achieve! "For those who are not actors," Marcel Proust observes, "the boredom of living constantly inside the same character is dissipated for an instant, as though we were suddenly on a stage, when some other person conceives an erroneous idea of us, believing that we have a close relationship with some lady we are not acquainted with and whom we are known to have met during the course of a charming journey that we have never made. A multiplicatory and delightful error . . ." (*Du côté de Guermantes*, 2: 499). "It is better than the kiss of life," Montherlant points out, "when a newspaper prints your name in error beneath a picture that is not of you. A dam-burst of possibilities!" (*Carnets*, 1930–1944, p. 252).

9. How are we to create multiple lives for ourselves? First of all, by increasing the number of our names. "He gave himself a hundred or so pseudonyms," Valéry says of Stendhal, "less for purposes of concealment than in order to feel that he was extant in several versions" (Valéry, *Variété*, p. 571). According to François Mauriac, Alexis Léger, alias Saint-Léger-Léger, alias Saint John Perse, is "so complex and various a character that it took three names . . . to designate him" (Mauriac, Préface à Jacques Dumaine: *Quai d'Orsay 1949–1951*, p. 8). "To have three or four households, and a dozen 'words of honor,'" Valéry muses wishfully (*L'idée fixe*, p. 124), while in Montherlant we find the following description of a character who "collected alternative residences": "In Algiers, he had three residences; in Paris, four. Here a bungalow; there an apartment; elsewhere a studio, and each of them under a false name or that of a third party, needless to say" (Montherlant, *L'histoire d'amour de la Rose de Sable*, pp. 81–82). The contemporary theater and cinema abound in characters leading multiple lives until the moment when a breaching of the compartments brings about either a tragic resolution or comic euphoria. And akin to such figures are the doubles, whether twins or not, who create the illusion of a double life around themselves.

10. To the multiple existence being led at any given moment may be added the metamorphosis in time. "To start from the beginning again," I am "starting life afresh," I am "casting off my old skin," I am "growing a new skin"—these are some of the

phrases the French use to convey this idea. "The 'schoolmaster of La Baule' died four times . . . not just twice as was generally believed until now," began an article in one newspaper covering a story of multiple and successive personalities (*Paris-Presse,* June 28, 1958). For Paul Valéry, the possibility of such a metamorphosis presented itself, fortunately, every morning: "Why, this particular morning, should I choose myself? What is there compelling me to resume my particular goods and ills? What if I were to say good-bye to my name, to my truths, to my habits and my chains . . . as the man who wants to disappear and start life afresh carefully abandons his clothes and his papers at the edge of the sea?

". . . Is not the morning the moment and the imperious counsel not to resemble oneself?" (*Tel quel,* 2: 121). To André Gide, self-metamorphosis sometimes appears as an involuntary and angst-creating thing rather than a purposeful and exalting one (thus revealing itself as one of the multiple phenomena denoted by double signs that will be encountered during the course of this book): "Not being able to count on oneself. Will the person who keeps the engagement be the same as the person who made it?. . . Not to be able to recognize oneself, how trying it is" (Gide, *Ainsi soit-il,* p. 1203).

11. One of the motives urging us toward diversity, or toward laying claim to it, is the desire to escape from ourselves. According to one of Valéry's close friends, the latter "claimed to be always wavering . . . between delight at being himself and disgust at being nothing but that" (Henri Mondor, *Propos familiers de Paul Valéry,* p. 71). In fact, as Vauvenargues points out, those who "are all of a piece" are also those "who never step outside themselves" (quoted by Gide, *Journal des faux-monnayeurs,* p. 97). "The only true journey," Marcel Proust wrote, in disparagement of those aspiring to Mars or Venus, "would be . . . to have other eyes, to see the universe through someone else's eyes, through a hundred other people's eyes" *La Prisonnière,* p. 258). By making myself diverse, or by imagining others so, I may attempt to approach that state from which I am excluded by the human condition.

12. At the same time, I shall be achieving a certain freedom with regard to what I am now living.

Proust dreams of Albertine, partly as a woman he will shortly take in his arms, and partly as a being belonging to Elstir's paintings, to Bergotte's books, to Vinteuil's music: "Albertine . . . gained . . . from being transported in this way back and forth . . . between two worlds . . . thereby escaping the crushing pressure of matter" (ibid., p. 56). Paul Valéry asks himself whether: "a mind that . . . does not swiftly attempt to escape from its own judgments when they are still scarcely formed . . . merits the name of mind at all?" (*Variété*, p. 727). So that any supreme example of mind (Leonardo) "has the fascination of always thinking about something else" (ibid., p. 1159), just as the complicated man will think about a different partner from the one with whom he is actually making love. "Man's great characteristic" may appear in fact to be that "of not being what he does," of "being able to act in total absence . . . sometimes better than if he were participating in what he is doing" (Valéry, *Tel quel*, 2: 317). A character in a Camus novel is able to say of the Dutch people: "I like them because . . . they are here and they are elsewhere" (Albert Camus, *La chute*, p. 18).

The inclination to be fought against is therefore that of the soul "to employ itself only at full stretch and in its entirety. However slight a subject the soul is offered, it tends to enlarge the matter and draw it out to the point where it needs to labor at it with all its force" (Montaigne, *Essais*, bk. 2, chap. 3).

This is where diversity becomes useful as a tool in the cause of liberty: "If your affection in love is too strong . . . break it into diverse desires so that they may accept a regent and master. . . . For fear that it should take you over and tyrannize you, weaken it . . . by dividing it" (ibid., bk. 3, chap. 4). And also: "The mayor and Montaigne have always been two, with a very clear distinction between them" (ibid., bk. 3, chap. 10), which recalls a remark of Tristan Bernard's: "He doesn't like giving himself; the most he will do is distribute himself" (Michel Chrestien, *Esprit es-tu là?*, p. 161). After his victory over the Présidente de Tourvel, the Vicomte de Valmont writes to the Marquise de Merteuil: "So you think me a subjugated lover? . . . I am already on may way, before many days are out, to weakening—by dividing it—the perhaps too lively impression made upon me; and if a single division does not suffice, then I shall multiply it" (Choderlos de Laclos, *Les liaisons dangereuses*, letter 133). Paul Valéry confided to a close friend (Henri Mondor): "I am preparing . . . an exhibition of etchings and engravings. A second profession: to be at last something larger than oneself!" (Mondor, *Propos familiers de Paul Valéry*, p. 175). When "the mind flits from folly to folly like a bird from twig to twig," "the essential" is that it should always "be ready for flight, that highest final proposition" (Valéry, *Mélanges*, p. 307), that victory over seriousness, "The seriousness of animals, the seriousness of children eating, of dogs in love. . . . It is as though such an exact life leaves no room . . . for the hiatus of mockery" (Valéry, *Tel quel*, 1: 30). "We should say of a surgeon that he is nothing but a surgeon," another writer reminds us, "if he never thinks of anything but his surgery" (Félicien Marceau in *Arts*, April 20–27, 1955). But Charles de Gaulle is able to say of Edward Spears that "he belonged . . . to many categories without being classifiable in any single one of them" (de Gaulle, *L'appel*, p. 85), thus escaping the fate of the colonel of police at whose funeral a fellow officer was able to say: "Until his dying breath . . . Colonel Vohl lived only for the police. It contained everything for him; it circumscribed everything. Born in one of our barracks, his eyes opened for the first time upon a police uniform. As a child, then as an adolescent, he spent his time within the walls of those 'monasteries in which we are taught and practice the religion of Duty.' . . . He was possessed of a vibrant faith that brought a shining light into his eyes when he spoke of the Police, like that in the eyes of a believer when he speaks of his God" (*Bulletin du Cercle Républicain*, November 14, 1955, quoted in *Le canard enchaîné*, November 30, 1955). Degradation or perfection? Speaking of God, of things, of the angels and the animals in "the age of purity," Paul Valéry says:

> . . . All were pure
> Each being what he was
> Each doing without error and miraculously
> What he was formed to do."
> [*Mélange*, p. 198]

13. While making man freer, diversity also makes him less vulnerable.

Here is the precautionary motto adopted by a friend of Jules Renard: "Never to become attached to anyone . . . to have a great many acquaintances, to leave them as soon as they become, or one becomes, unbearable" (Renard, *Journal*, p. 313). And here is an occurrence that Proust's narrator seems to observe taking place in himself after the loss of his beloved: "The character I had still been such a short while ago and who lived solely in perpetual expectation of the moment when Albertine would come to say goodnight to him and kiss him, that character now appeared to me, by a kind of multiplication within myself, as being no longer anything more than a slight part . . . of me, and like a flower beginning to open I was experiencing the refreshment of an exfoliation" (Proust, *La fugitive*, p. 534).

For the diverse being, no loss can ever be total, whereas "any convenience upon which I was obliged to depend wholly would have me by the throat" (Montaigne, *Essais*, bk. 3, chap. 9). Having affirmed France's great diversity and also her particular capacity for recovery from misfortunes, Montesquieu adds: "Perhaps she owes this to that very diversity, which has prevented any ill from ever striking deep enough root . . ." (Montesquieu, *Mes pensées*, p. 1099).

The diverse man will be able to make better use of whatever happens to him. "One must work on several things at once. The returns are higher," Valéry tells us. "Because as the ideas come one can dispatch each to the most suitable site for it, there being several sites waiting to be filled" (*Tel quel*, 2: 60). "Each Greco-Roman divinity had . . . a number of very different roles and attributes," Montherlant notes, "so that if he or she was not honored and entreated in one particular line, there was still the possibility of being so in another. The Greco-Roman divinities were most resourceful characters" Montherlant, *Carnets*, 1930–1944, p. 361). And of himself, the same writer tells us: "Possessing all natures as I do, even the most contrary ones, whatever happens there will always be at least one of them experiencing satisfaction, and I shall always be able to say without ceasing: 'Oh world, your wish is my wish also' " (*Aux fontaines du désir*, p. 29). If I chase several pairs of lips at the same time, then I am assured of keeping at least some of them within reach of my own.

14. Diversity makes me impossible to imprison: it enables me to thwart any attempt on the part of others to pin me down by creating a fixed image of me. It means I can prevent anyone from saying of me, "in the end, there's not really much to him" —which was what those grown-ups thought when they were constantly sticking such elementary (and often unfavorable) labels on me as a child. "Not content with ceasing to allow people to see through me," Madame de Merteuil says of herself as a child, "I amused myself by deliberately appearing in different guises" (Choderlos de Laclos, *Les liaisons dangereuses*, letter 81). Just as one of Montherlant's characters moved from one of his residences to another "in order to throw people who were after him (women especially) off the scent, or simply because that was his way of 'escaping' without actually leaving town" (*L'histoire d'amour de la Rose de Sable*, p. 82), so the ex-child employs diversity as a means of "losing" those who thought they could catch him red-handed in the indubitable possession of a given attribute: "Grace or nature? The wing or the thigh? . . . Both. . . . Since I always belong to both worlds at the same time I can always say, fairly sincerely: 'whom do you take me for?' " Montherlant, *Carnets*, 1930–1944, p. 333). Since "I disturb and trouble myself by the instability of my attitude," Montaigne explains, "those who take heed of it . . . scarcely ever find me twice in the same state. . . . All opposites are to be found in it at some moment and in some fashion. Bashful and insolent; chaste and

lustful; talkative and taciturn; plodding and sprightly; quick-witted and stupid; sorrowful and gay; lying and truthful; learned and ignorant; liberal, miserly, and prodigal, I see all of this in me to some extent, as I turn myself about," so that "there is nothing I can say about myself wholly, simply, and solidly" (Montaigne, *Essais*, bk. 2, chap. 1). It is by virtue of an "essential property," Valéry suggests, that "the Self" "rejects . . . all attributes" (letter to Heidsieck, November 23, 1943, *Lettres à quelques-uns*, pp. 242–43). And here, again according to Montaigne, is the secret of how Augustus succeeded in "escaping" the "best writers": "There is in this man a variety of actions so conspicuous, sudden and continual . . . that he has evaded the grasp, whole and without precise outlines, of even the boldest judges" (*Essais*, bk. 2, chap. 1). Even if I do not succeed in taking out an injunction in advance against anyone who tries to give me an outline, I can render his efforts sufficiently arduous to ensure that I can easily reject any result he may achieve. So we find a specialist in the human sciences, taking up a much worn theme, remarking upon "the extreme difficulty of analysis presented by the French temperament" (Charles Morazé, *Les Français et la République*, p. 46).

15. Diversity is a means of combating attrition, of staving off those disillusioned mornings-after toward which all power and pleasures persistently drift.

We are often apprehensive lest a weapon should quickly become blunted, lest a "taste" should be "followed by a prompt distaste," in the words of Voltaire that Paul Robert quotes under "distaste" (*dégoût*), as he gives La Harpe's remark under "criticism" (*critique*): "In France, the first day is for infatuation, the second for criticism, the third for indifference." "Progressive disenchantment with the entire universe on the one hand, satiety on the other": according to André Gide, there is no state "that is more easily and more commonly attained" (*Journal 1889–1939*, p. 792). "The difficult part of life," one of his characters declares, "is to take the same thing seriously for any length of time" (Gide, *Les faux-monnayeurs*, p. 76). "The fable does not inform us," Montherlant points out, "how long the spell that Orpheus cast on the wild beasts continued to work; I am of the opinion that after ten minutes of it they must have gone back to their usual occupations" (Montherlant, *Mors et Vita*, p. 103).

Whether swift or not, the destructive effect of an absence of diversity seems certain. According to Pascal, "persistent attachment to one and the same thought tires and ruins man's mind" (*Discours sur les passions de l'amour*). "Men grow bored in the end," La Bruyère notes, "with the very things that charmed them when they were new" (La Bruyère, *Les caractères,* De l'homme," 145). "One does not please for long when one has but one sort of wit," La Rochefoucauld observes (*Maximes*). Speaking of Xerxes, Condillac reminds us "that it was he who issued an edict promising a reward to any man who invented a new pleasure" (quoted by Littré under *plaisir*), "The soul sickens of everything that is uniform, even of perfect happiness," Stendhal declares (a remark quoted by Paul Robert under *bonheur*). "Nothing more blindly wears out the ancient joy/Than a noise flowing evenly with never a change" Paul Valéry says (Le rameur). (But elsewhere, Chamfort tells us that "La Fontaine, hearing someone pitying the lot of the damned surrounded by hellfire, said: 'I flatter myself that they grow accustomed to it, and eventually take to it like fish to water'" [Chamfort, *Maximes et anecdotes,* p. 139].)

During the Third and Fourth Republics, one of the recurrent themes in expressions of unfavorable public reaction to the "performances" of politicians was that of monotony. "Is it surprising," Robert de Jouvenel was asking in 1914, "that the public should have acquired a distaste for politics? The program is never changed, and the play has overstayed its welcome" (Jouvenel, *La république des camarades,* p. 67) And similarly, it was thought that any government under those regimes had only to continue for a few months in order to provoke a standard reaction in political circles toward its premier: irritated exclamations of "He never changes! It's time we had a new face!"

The absence of fatigue or wear often seems to be a thing too wonderful to be probable (happiness consists in continuing to desire what we possess). And this is even truer in the case of fatigue's opposite, the appetite that never flags despite our continually satisfying it: "Enjoyment adds force to the desire,/ An aging tree, its roots enriched by pleasure" according to Baudelaire (*Le voyage*) "The more I kiss you, the more I want to kiss you/ The more I hold you, the more I want to hold you" in the words of the song—a theme whose purpose is probably to a large extent that of fighting back our apprehension that desire is in fact doomed to exhaustion (see chap. 13, sec. 22).

It is in the context of this apprehension that we ought to consider the use of "that variety which refreshes the mind" (Montesquieu, *Discours sur les motifs qui doivent nous encourager aux sciences*) as an antidote to "monotony, that half of nonexistence" (Baudelaire, *Le spleen de Paris,* 48). The maneuver is rather like that of replacing a child's gruel, or some other invariable form of food, with less uniform menus when its lack of appetite is thought to be caused by monotony. One might also make a comparison with the investigation of "little (or big) love-games" by older couples who are experiencing the eventual dulling of physical pleasure by time; sense-lulling time that transforms predilections into habits and habits into routines, which must then be renewed, rejuvenated. For

> Beauty itself, however sharply felt
> Sickens and sates in the end,

and La Fontaine also admits that

> I need a little this, a little that:
> My watchword is diversity.
> This lady, something dun
> Is bright to me: and why is that?
> She's new, you see; whereas that other,
> Who has been mine for some long time,
> White as she is, leaves me now,
> In every way, untouched
> [La Fontaine, *Pâté d'anguilles*],

which becomes, on the joke level: "What is polygamy?" the schoolteacher asks one of his prep school students.—"The opposite of monotony" (Carmen Tessier: *Bibliothèque rosse*, p. 288). Monsieur Fenouillard, tied to a strut, still tries to achieve variety in his positions, being secretly convinced that uniformity is always bound to lead eventually to boredom. For, Montaigne reminds us, even when "nothing profits me . . . variety alone still profits me, and the possession of diversity" (*Essais*, bk. 3, chap. 9).

What delight when we discover that we can vary our positions in the performance of acts that seemed at first acquaintance to exclude such variety! Here is a novelist (José Cabanis) on an adolescent's first encounter with a woman skilled in the art of love: "The discoveries she led me into . . . stupefied me. What variety and what nuances where I had imagined nothing till then but a monotonous recurrence!" (Cabanis, *Le fils*, p. 95).

But what is our horror, on the other hand, when we sense that the possibilities offered by the human condition are limited! "Sensuous pleasure . . . always runs the risk of some monotony," Valéry tells us (*Variété*, p. 485), and even: "Living is an essentially monotonous practice" (*Variété*, p. 1027). Appalled, Montherlant realizes that he has exhausted his own diversity: "And the person complaining here is all mobility! But all immobile mobility. The horses on the merry-go-round: they go past one by one, but there are only seven of them and no eighth will ever go by. So what horror must those who are all of a piece feel?" (Montherlant, *Aux fontaines du désir*, p. 102). And here is his hero with a new mistress: "After dinner, in the evening dark, they made their way along the Avenue des Acacias. There was scarcely a bench not providing a couch for some heavily embracing couple. . . . 'Will they at least teach me some new gestures?' Costals wondered. But no, their every gesture merely reduced him to mirth: 'Oh come on, dimwit, we know that one!' How dismally limited is the catalogue of physical caresses" (Montherlant, *Les jeunes filles*, p. 252).

16. The greedy and unreasonable child forever wanting to be in two places at the same time is curbed by adults imposing a choice upon it—as Odette still does upon Swann when he asks her to play Vinteuil's "little phrase" for him: "He made Odette play it over and over, ten times, twenty times, while at the same time insisting that she go on kissing him. . . . Whereupon she made a show of stopping, saying to him: 'How do you expect me to play like this with you holding me? I can't do everything at once, at least make up your mind what you want. Am I to play the phrase or play at kissing?" (Proust, *Du côté de chez Swann*, p. 238).

The child is taught that if it insists on being interested in everything, on wanting to do everything, it will never get anywhere; it has the dangers of dispersion, of fragmentation constantly waved in front of it. And adults continue to attribute this dangerous inclination to others. Even though "as they say, to be everywhere is to be nowhere" (Montaigne, *Essais*, bk. 1, chap. 8), Montaigne still feels able to say himself: "A little of everything, and nothing at all, in the French manner" (*Essais*, bk. 1, chap. 14). Under the Fourth Republic, one of the stock insults in political circles was to accuse one's colleagues in power of pursuing too many overambitious goals with invariably insufficient means, thereby guaranteeing failure in every field.

It is almost always expeditious, when in the wings oneself, to insist upon such truisms as "choice is a restriction" or "a door must be either open or closed"—precisely because the ex-child, now exploring the prerogatives of the adult world, has difficulty in renouncing the attempt not to renounce anything. "During the course of this debate," one deputy declared when the National Assembly had decided to discuss "Europe" in 1953, "I have frequently been reminded of Alain's remark that 'any choice is a limitation.' We cannot at the same time preserve all the advantages of the national framework in which we now live, and reap all the benefits . . . of an enlarged European framework" (Pierre de Félice, A.N., November 20, 1953; *J.O.*, p. 5337)—a theme whose frequent appearance indicates the strength of the refusal to choose.

As I prepare to obtain such and such an advantage or pleasure for myself, I may be seized by a misgiving: why precisely that one rather than some other, since my desires are so numerous?

Especially since each such realization must exclude so many others that are equally, if not more, desirable. Here we are confronted with the poignant idea that every life is "an existence that could be QUITE OTHER" (Valéry, *Variété*, p. 1158), that "of the thousand ond one forms of life, each one of us can know only one" (Gide, *L'immoraliste*, p. 169). "Your decision, once effected," Paul Léautaud notes, "makes you regret what you rejected and what might have been" (Léautaud, *Journal littéraire*, 1:104). Marcel Proust writes of "the regret at having fixed happiness in this particular form at the expense of all the others thus excluded" (*La fugitive*, p. 461). The narrator of *Paludes* elaborates the point even further: "As soon as we are in the street, I began. 'What an intolerable existence! Can you bear it, dear fellow?' 'Well enough,' he said. 'But why intolerable?' 'Simply because it could be different and isn't' " (Gide, *Paludes*, p. 65). "The necessity of choice was always intolerable to me," the young Gide says again elsewhere (quoted by Paul Robert under *choisir* "to choose): "to choose seemed to me not so much to elect as to reject what I was not electing." Bringing God into the matter, one of Jean Anouilh's characters talks of "the anguish with which He has endowed certain people at not being able to have everything" (Anouilh, *Ornifle*, act 3). Gide tells us of "the cause of my anxiety during the first fine days: I should like to be able to contemplate the spring everywhere at once, which means that I cannot be perfectly content anywhere. . . . Oh, only ever being able to be somewhere! Only ever being able to be someone!" (Gide, *Feuillets d'automne*, p. 1084). Paul Valéry says of himself that when faced with "the whiteness of his paper" he is seized by "regret for all the signs that will not be chosen" (*Variété*, p. 1181). "Have you never wanted to yell out loud in the street," one of Anouilh's characters asks another, "because a girl walks past you and lifts up her arms? A girl who will never be yours— because you already love another" (*Ornifle*, act 3). And Montherlant's Don Juan drives the same point home even more firmly: "The only boring thing about the creatures is that while you are doing it with them, you can't be doing it with others, or even be on the hunt for others" (act 1, sc. 1).

Choice may appear difficult, not only because we find ourselves confronted with an abundance of riches, but also because we experience a more or less equal detachment with regard to all the numerous possibilities offered. "Why these things and not others?" Figaro asks. "It is a little foolish to imagine that we have any reason to be there rather than elsewhere," Jules Renard muses as he thinks of his native village in the Nivernais. Better "to be anywhere at all, better never to accept being fixed in any place" (Renard, *Journal*, p. 737). "To be," the narrator confesses to Monsieur Teste, "remains, you will admit, strange. And to be in a particular way is even stranger. It is uncomfortable even" (Valéry, *Monsieur Teste*, p. 108). "Our observable life" being no more than "one of the innumerable lives" that my "SELF . . . could have assumed" (Valéry, *Variété*, p. 1093), there results a certain "ridiculousness in any particular form and existence" (ibid., p. 514). "We ought to say to ourselves," Montherlant exhorts us, "of any truth we are used to living with, what every married man has said to himself at least once of his wife: 'Why this one?'" (Montherlant, Postscript to *Le maître de Santiago*, *Théâtre*, p. 659). A character in the novel remembers "the growing irritation aroused in me by Laurence's voice, by her words, by her gestures. This feeling of absurdity that was shattering my head like a migraine and making me constantly repeat under my breath (which is not a figure of speech, because I really was speaking aloud, albeit quietly): 'Why this one rather than another? Venice rather than some other city?'" (François Nourissier, *Les orphelins d'Auteuil*, p. 144).

For the various painful aspects of the human condition just described, diversity offers a certain relief. Grown-ups forbid the child to be a jack-of-all-trades; the ex-child can then become, or believe itself to have become, the Jupiter of Molière's play, of whom Night says: "I don't understand all these disguises he gets into his head," to which Mercury replies: "It's his way of trying to experience all sorts of conditions" (Molière, *Amphitryon*, Prologue). "A man who lived obstinately enough," Valéry calculates, "could experience in succession all the attractions, all the repulsions, could become acquainted with all the virtues perhaps; certainly with all the vices; would eventually exhaust, in relation to every thing that is, the total of the affects . . . that it is able to excite" (*Variété*, p. 535). "Let us translate that into the language of my own age," Montherlant suggests: "I want to have a finger in every pie. . . . I want to have everything, because I can use everything" (*Les olympiques*, p. 128). In opposition to the appalling idea of a non-coincidence between the possibilities for pleasure and the capacity of a given life, he maintains that "There is room for everything, all together or successively" (Henry de Montherlant: *Maletestiana*, p. 562). And he imagines this dialogue: " 'How can you sleep with such an awful-looking woman when you have another who's so beautiful?' 'It's precisely the fact of having a woman who's so beautiful that enables me to have one who's so awful-looking' " (Montherlant, *Carnets* 19–21, p. 68).

The aspiration to diversity thus entails the acceptance, at a given moment or for a long period, of acts that the average man would take to be incompatible—as with the good La Fontaine, who spent many long years composing salacious tales on the one hand and edifying, Jansenist-inspired works on the other. "I can understand how it is possible to desert a cause in order to know what one will experience by serving another" Baudelaire says in *Mon cœur mis à nu*; while the prospect of imminent social upheaval suggests this possibility to him: "Not only shall I be happy to be a victim, I shall also not hate being an executioner—in order to experience the Revolution in two different ways!" (Baudelaire, *Argument du livre sur la Belgique*, 33). "It is always from my most recent offspring that I am most different," André Gide says of his works (*Journal*, p. 276); so that "each of my books turns against all those who admired the one before it" (ibid., p. 787). Quoting the criticism: "Montherlant's tragedy is that he was never able to choose among his tendencies," Montherlant himself reacts as follows: "And what if that were my good fortune—and my pride?" (*Carnets*, 1930–1944, p. 116). Because for man "the secret pleasure he experiences in 'disowning himself," is that of "bringing to light those parts of himself that were previously choking him" (Montherlant, *Le solstice de juin*, pp. 308–9).

More particularly, the "Cartesian" discipline that grown-ups attempt to impose on children, and upon each other, provokes a fundamental tendency to revolt against it, a spirit of contradiction. Leaving Joseph Prudhomme to his "That's my opinion and I share it," André Gide says of himself: "I cannot affirm anything that does not arouse within me a desire to champion the contrary" (*Si le grain ne meurt*, p. 256). "A good mind," Valéry tells us in confirmation, "contains, retains, and maintains in good condition everything that it needs to destroy its own opinions and systems. It holds itself in readiness to attack its own 'feelings' and to refute its own 'reasons' " (letter to R. P. Rideau, 1943; *Lettres à quelques-uns*, p. 243).

17. The aspiration to diversity also finds itself in the service of our desire to believe ourselves powerful. The more strings one has to one's bow, the more tricks up one's sleeve, the more of a "one-man-band" one is, the more one can delight in an awareness of one's own capability. Quoting Barrès—"My dream was always to make my soul like a mechanical organ, so that it would play me the most varied tunes every time I chose to press a given button"—Montherlant tells us: "That defines me exactly" (*Carnets* 19–21, p. 35) since "the real gamble is to have a stake on

every number" (Montherlant, *Service inutile*, p. 258). "I like the same man to be able . . . to present himself with difficulties of more than one sort," says Valéry (*Degas, danse, dessin*, p. 15). "The power of the mind," Charles de Gaulle asserts, "implies a diversity that is not to be found in the exclusive practice of a profession, for the same reason that home life is rarely very entertaining" (*Vers l'armée de métier*, p. 200).

My feeling of power will similarly be increased if I can feel myself to be in possession of a tool that will lend itself to a great many uses. The great politician is skilled in dealing with the most diverse affairs, even though he has not had time to study them; top quality arms or armies are suitable for doing battle in the most varied conditions and against the most diverse adversaries.

In rendering myself diverse, I am also proving my power—as an "acrobat"—by organizing the coexistence within my life of acts that might, at first glance, be seen as incompatible. Here is a dream of Valéry's: "I am cut in two. . . . I perceive myself in two incompatible persons. An oscillation is set up between these two presences. . . . I have interests in two worlds that have no communications between them. I dream *or* I am awake. I see *or* I formulate. . . .

"Little by little this double-entry life achieves an organization. The oscillation of the pendulum *Self* slows down. I consent *to be* and *to construct*, more or less simultaneously. Something has changed. I pass from the state of alternating perturbation, from the state of 'one or the other,' to the state of 'the one and the other' (Valéry, *Tel quel*, 2: 107–8). And here is how he describes one day in his life to a friend. "You wouldn't believe how hard I struggle to control my three or four different existences crushed together inside that single day. Paris, as hard and packed as an egg, is a torturer's rack" (*Correspondance entre Paul Valéry et Gustave Fourment*, p. 141). But that could well be a satisfying and honorable exhaustion, since Valéry seems to share the feeling expressed by Montherlant: "What I admire in a life is the patterning" (Montherlant, *Les olympiques*, p. 127), an example of "patterning" being provided by Costals' behavior at a certain evening party: "By leaning slightly backwards, he could see behind Solange's back the young woman sitting beside her. . . . She was not pretty, but Costals desired her, first, because he felt it appropriate that, at the very moment he was caressing one young lady for the first time, he should be desiring another. . . . Costals therefore stretched out his arm behind Solange's chair and laid his hand on the back of the chair beyond, so that the unknown young lady's shoulder would press against it" (Montherlant, *Les jeunes filles*, pp. 227–28). And here, twenty years later, is another young man: "The most difficult part was to make sure that the compartments of his love life were kept perfectly watertight. . . . It was a matter of infinite detail, of various precautions to do with the telephone, with confidences, with meeting places; but the strain of it often gave Bernard a migraine, conscious as he was that the slightest false step, the least blunder could have fatal consequences, such as three revolver bullets for him or a tube of veronal for some innocent girl" (Jean-Louis Curtis, *Les justes causes*, p. 165). Or, in the words of another novelist describing the same milieu: "I had no feeling of being one person to Cécile and another to Laurence. Nor was I suffering from the anguish of an appetite so great, of a tenderness so rich that they could only be satisfied by two bodies and two hearts. No; my feeling was rather that of preferring money to what it buys, complication to simplicity. I liked each meeting to be made possible only by calculation, each evening spent with the one to necessitate a difficult and apparently affectionate rearrangement of the other's plans. . . . I liked to lie. I could not wait for an accumulation of circumstances to bring me to the point where it would no longer be possible for me to work at furthering one of my affairs without deception. Before long, pleasure and lying would no longer be distinguishable" (François Nourrissier, *Les orphelins d'Auteuil*, pp. 66–67).

More particularly, what gives us a feeling of power is the facility with which we manage to "pass through separations and partitions" (Valéry, *Variété*, p. 1180), "the feeling of being that which passes *immediately* from one thing to another, of cutting across . . . the most diverse orders" (Valéry, *Monsieur Teste*, p. 71). Having postulated a multitude of clearly compartmentalized sectors in the desirable life, Montherlant goes on to emphasize the necessity for a "perpetual and easy passage from one to the other" (*Carnets* 19–21, p. 27).

Thus the wretchedness of the child subjected by grown-ups to excessive discipline—aggravated by interruptions stemming from those adults' own needs—is eventually transformed into a triumph. But this victory for the adult is not stable; the man adored by countless women may grow tired of the glorious struggle to accommodate them all in a single life, the man burdened with many tasks may experience as a torment the multiplicity of acts he is required to perform. Paul Valéry, though so frequent a eulogist of diversity, confessed to a friend: "What I find so backbreaking is the infinite fragmentation of my occupations. I start, I leave off . . . my day is completely shattered"

(*Correspondance entre Paul Valéry et Gustave Fourment*, p. 172).

18. Since a simple life is alarming in so many respects, the introduction of diversity into it may be intended to prove to ourselves that we have evaded the forces dragging us toward a life wholly without diversity. "Monsieur X, who had become engaged," Montherlant tells us, "decided to go, on his own, to a boxing match, with the sole purpose of proving to himself that one world did not exclude the other" (*Carnets*, 1930–1944, p. 180). And he is even more emphatic on this point in the case of one of his fictional characters: "Even in that confusion of love that possesses a man between the moment when a woman accepts and the moment when she yields . . . even then his reason still upheld so strongly the *principle* of the multiplicity of women that, his mind still full of the woman now promised, he nevertheless rushed out into the street, as though to fulfill a sort of obligation, in order to snap up another—*any* other" (Montherlant, *L'histoire d'amour de la Rose de Sable*, p. 72). According to a widespread belief, the very fact of having married, or having had a child, may spur a man on to take a mistress in order to prove to himself that he is not prepared to let himself be inescapably trapped by a second instalment of family life; some psychiatrists believe it true to say that there is a certain type of man who can only be fully potent with his wife if he is being unfaithful to her.

19. One of the aspects of the aspiration toward diversity is an infatuation with the complexity of the object, whether it be myself or someone else.

Those in charge of children and those who attempt to control the darker areas of adult life—the police and the courts, sometimes hospitals and the armed forces— often tend, it is believed, to entertain simple and unfavorable views of those with whom they have to deal; according to the victims, summary and unjust views. "One may steal," Montherlant reminds us, "and *also* retain one's honor." But "it is still not a living idea . . . that men are not all of a piece. We fail to understand the importance of the word *also*" (*Service inutile*, p. 150).

20. Our childhood over, the uneasiness conjured up in us by school reports is succeeded by the desire for citations; the adult's witticisms avenge and annul the unpleasant remarks of which he has himself been a victim.

But this is also the time when free rein may be given to that particular reply which children find so difficult to throw back at the terrible simplifiers with whom they are forced to struggle:

it's not as simple as that; I'm not as simple as that. "What shocks us in the judgments made about us," Paul Valéry notes, "is the simplification . . . imposed upon us. . . . What is more mortifying than to be simplified?" (*Mauvaises pensées et autres,* p. 87). To those grown-ups who used to dismiss me with their "You're nothing but a . . .," I can now at last reply with the dogma; he who sees life simply is nothing but a simpleton. "That which is simple is always false" Valéry proclaims (ibid., p. 143).

21. The world, people tend to think, is extremely complex. "Everything," Montaigne points out, "can be seen from several angles and in several lights" (*Essais,* bk. 1, chap. 38).

22. That which excels is particularly complex. As in the case of man. "There is no character so simple," André Gide claims, "as not to offer complications and meanders (*Un esprit non-prévenu,* p. 36). According to Montherlant, "anything human . . . is made up of difficult and subtly gradated things" (*Le démon du bien,* p. 72).

23. When faced with the complexity of the world, it is as well to have subtle reactions. "Although there are several epithets qualifying wit that appear to come to the same thing," La Rochefoucauld notes, "the moment and the manner of uttering them introduces differences." For example, "when we say that a man *has* wit, that he *certainly has* wit, that he has a *ready* wit, and that he has an *excellent* wit, it is only in the tone and manner of our speech that we are able to differentiate between these expressions . . . which express . . . very different sorts of wit" (La Rochefoucauld, *Réflexions diverses*).

24. We sometimes affirm the existence of subtleties of attitude that it would perhaps be difficult to establish if those in relation to whom we allege them were to break the tacit agreement that confers upon everyone the right to pass for subtle and complicated. Toward the end of the Fourth Republic, an unpleasant debate flared up (February 4, 1958) in the National Assembly: what political factors had possibly entered into the advancement of certain high-ranking officers? The discussion was reduced to a series of allusions to alleged irregularities, countered by summary denials. Yet the speaker still referred to the debate as one dealing with "matters . . . allowing of many subtle gradations" (A.N., February 4, 1958; *J.O.,* p. 506).

25. On the other hand, at that same time a journalist (Jacques Fauvet) was able to write, with reference to certain proposed reforms of the Constitution: "Everything complicated is disturbing" (*Le Monde,* January 16, 1958). Life is quite complicated enough as it is, we often hear it said among friends. How you manage to complicate even the simplest things! "Oh God, every-

thing could be so simple! Why do we complicate our lives?"—a classic remark that Jean Anouilh gives to one of the characters in his *Valse des toréadors* (act 3).

26. Among the good kinds of simplicity is that displayed, admirably, by the classic in art: it conceals an extreme complexity that has the added advantage of knowing how not to appear so. There is also the reassuring simplicity of rustic sturdiness; of the simple tool and the simple happiness that do not go wrong so easily, that are less subject to "complications" than complex machines or arrangements that also entail a risk of being "complicated." "It is the same with happiness as it is with watches. The least complicated are those that go wrong least often" (Chamfort, *Maximes et anecdotes*, p. 69) "To complicate a mechanism," "to complicate the gears of a machine excessively" —phrases given by Paul Robert under the verb in question—is therefore a risky procedure. Analyzing a military measure, a high-ranking officer was able to say, in characteristic terms, that "the perfecting of the system was in danger of leading to a gigantism whose complications would have constituted a grave risk; there were some who even wondered whether we should not eventually have at our disposal a machine which though it might be perfect, would 'resemble a watch in which the tiniest wheels are as important as the large ones. Only one has to give way and the system is brought to a halt' " (Paul Gérardot, *Revue de défense nationale*, March 1956, p. 291).

Although the power of the mind is made evident in the first place by its capacity to grasp every detail, it is revealed in the end by a return toward simplicity. "The French," Valéry reminds us, "judge . . . it to be in conformity with the essence of things that even a prodigiously varied set of even the most complex phenomena can and must . . . be reducible in the end to a few clearcut formulas" (*Regards sur le monde actuel*, p. 277). When writing a composition, it is preferable for a student to avoid accumulating both data and hypotheses, and to concentrate instead on expounding an extremely limited number of key ideas. A new prime minister, while formally seeking investiture, was able to say to the National Assembly: "During the past few days I have come up against a great many complications. I do not believe there is any virtue in what is complicated. Great ideas . . . are expressed simply. The most highly developed technique can often be reduced to a few . . . basic outlines. Democracy itself requires simplicity" (Maurice Bourgès-Manoury, A.N., June 12, 1957; *J.O.*, p. 2697).

27. Linked to the taste for complexity we also find that of the nuance that will distinguish an object—whether it be myself or

not—from all others. One must be "distinct," which means "not confused with something else . . . nearby" (Paul Robert).

Georges Mauco, a psychologist, tells parents that they "should be glad of . . . the differences that exist between children and not try to destroy them" (*L'école des parents*, June-July, 1955, p. 14). And indeed, just as the centralizing state is thought of as savagely determined to annihilate all regional and local particularities, so many parents are thought of as wishing to render the unique soul of a given child as similar as is humanly possible to a particular model dear to their hearts. Similarly, according to Montherlant: "For a hundred years and more our public educational system has been a hothouse for . . . the cultivation . . . of the platitude. . . . I can remember those schoolboy compositions, mine and those of a more recent past, in which every view or expression with the slightest hint of freshness or originality was condemned, ironically, by the teacher" (*Le solstice de juin*, pp. 155–56).

28. Later on, the ex-child may well exclaim with Monsieur Teste: "Let's thump all those who want to make us just like them" (Valéry, *Monsieur Teste*, p. 109); let us insist that they respect an "originality" for which our parents and teachers don't give a damn.

29. By making myself unique I am also creating the necessary conditions for achieving the highest rank; or else I am discovering an honorable means of escape from a race in which I feel I am not well placed. If "the sufferer from the disease of not being unique consumes himself in inventing things that separate him from others . . . perhaps," Valéry suggests, "this is not so much in order to place himself above everything that is preying on him and tormenting him as to place himself entirely to one side, as it were beyond all comparison." So that " 'great men' become a source of smiles for certain 'incommensurable' men" (Valéry, *Variété*, p. 563).

30. In any case, this is that "frenzied will to dissimilarity" (Henri Mondor, *Propos familiers de Paul Valéry*, p. 229) that we observe in ourselves; by which we imagine ourselves possessed; that we attribute to men generally and the French in particular; naturally, since "to be in existence is to be different" (Rémy de Gourmont, quoted by Paul Robert under *dissemblance* "dissimilarity." I am not like anyone else: a precious affirmation, even though it may be necessary, in order to buttress it, to insist upon the fact that I too, like everyone else, have my little tics, my little drawbacks, my little vices. In an attempt to explain the occasional grinding noises produced by the Frenche political machine, it is often eagerly explained that "in France there are . . . ten parties . . . criss-crossed by many different currents, and forty

million opinions" (Jacques Fauvet, *La France déchirée*, p. 22). What could be more evident than the unfortunate effects produced by the fact—admirable in itself—of this "infinite diversity" (ibid.), of this "to every man his own opinion"?

31. It is often thought that there exists a widespread horror of recognizing oneself to be like someone else. " 'If he thinks like me,' he used to say"—Paul Valéry being reported by his friend Henri Mondor—"meaning anyone at all, 'then he renders my position intolerable. To think like others is to have ceased thinking' " (Mondor, *Propos familiers de Paul Valéry*, p. 183). According to one political leader (Guy Mollet)—who was merely reworking a long familiar observation—there is a tendency "that leads us to emphasize subtle differences when we are in agreement over the essential" (A.N., March 27, 1957; *J.O.*, p. 1909). "No Frenchman," affirms an editorial writer in a review, a man with ready access to political circles, "would dream of thinking, talking, living like another. . . . Every Frenchman thinks of himself as . . . having earned his fame through his originality" (*La Nef*, September 1958, p. 4).

32. Even if it were admitted that such feelings are so widespread, this would not apparently exclude their capacity to coexist with massive spiritual and behavioral uniformities (apart from that of rejecting and denying all uniformity). In Rousseau's words, quoted by Montherlant, "one must do as others do: that is the first maxim of the country's wisdom. It isn't done: that is the supreme decision" (Montherlant, *Carnets*, 1930–1944, p. 138). And Paul Léautaud said of the literary world he was part of in 1900: "All of them are afraid of showing any desire to singularize themselves" (Paul Léautaud, *Journal littéraire*, 1:328).

33. Corresponding to the self supposedly different from all other selves there is a world perceived as being full of subtle gradations.

34. Whatever the system of categories within which we attempt to "imprison" that system, it always proves possible to perceive differentiations within each of the categories that cannot be dismissed. As Bibendum reminds us in the *Guide Michelin*: "There are stars and stars" (see sec. 36 below).

35. The more valued a composite object is, the more its elements are often supposed to be different from one another. As with France itself. "French vowels are numerous and subtly differentiated," Paul Valéry observes (*Regards sur le monde actuel*, pp. 126–27). And having remarked that "one can still see hundreds of little wrought iron balconies in the old neighborhoods of Paris, none of which resembles any of the others," he adds:

"Nothing more clearly sums up what is most French in France" (ibid., p. 186).

36. "Always distinguish!" is one of the stock exhortations made by the teacher to the promising student. The number and intricacy of the nuances one is able to observe: that constitutes a good measure of intelligence and acuteness. To perceive slight, tenuous, almost imperceptible differences clearly is the property of a first-class mind. "As intelligence increases," Pascal notes, "so does the capacity to perceive men's individuality; ordinary people do not perceive the differences between men" (quoted by Paul Robert under *différence*). "Common sense," Montesquieu affirms, "consists largely in apprehending the gradations in things" (*Défense de L'Esprit des lois*, part 2, *Idée générale*); he also talks of "slight and delicate differences that are imperceptible to persons unfortunate in their birth or upbringing" (Montesquieu, *Essai sur les causes qui peuvent affecter les esprits et les caractères*). By studying the properties of animals and plants, Zadig "discovered a thousand differences where other men see nothing but uniformity." Writing about the Tunisian orange season from December to February, Colette notes that "one Tunisian orange is never exactly identical in taste with another Tunisian orange." So that "the slight difference encourages one to peel yet another orange and yet another" (Colette, *Flore et Pomone*, pp. 222–23). While thinking about his mistresses' mouths, one Montherlant character remembers "the smells of all those he had desired or known, all different . . . and each one different from the smell of the back of the neck, which was itself different from that of the throat, in its turn different from that of the backs of the hands, which was again different from that of the palms, which was again different from that of the brow" (Montherlant, *Le Songe*, p. 123). In *La reine morte*, a man says to the woman he loves: "Did you know that every time you move your head, you waft the smell of your hair toward me? And that smell is never quite the same" (Montherlant, *La reine morte*, act 1, tableau 2, sc. 4).

37. An appearance of identity between objects could thus very easily be a booby trap; a denial of identity or even of resemblance always gives an impression of acuteness. "But come now," you say, "it's not quite like that"—an affirmation sometimes devoid of risk, since I do not go on to back it up, and may not be required to. The important thing is to have implied that between two objects apparently similar at first glance there in fact exists the abyss of a nuance.

38. To remark upon "similarities"—to make comparisons— is thus an operation of the mind that can easily appear somewhat

lacking in refinement. Reminding a "lay" congress (of the Ligue française de l'enseignement, in 1957) that for Malherbe "will was possibly more precious than inspiration," the honorary dean of the Toulouse *Faculté des lettres* added: "In that sense—if you will forgive me the comparison—he makes one think of Valéry" (*L'Action laïque*, October 1957, p. 20).

39. The same attitude exists toward the world men create or champion. We often believe ourselves to be searching for something "different from the rest." In France, there is a generally accepted belief that "the particularism of the French home market has limited mass production" (*Le Monde*, January 30, 1954), thought the case is quite different for "the Americans with their bulldozers" (Jean Silvandre, A.N., August 27, 1954; *J.O.*, p. 4347).

40. Another aspect of the taste for diversity is that of the variation in time.

Childhood frequently seems marked by a distressing absence of such variations. "The principle characteristic of my family," the female narrator of a novel tells us, "was its power to distill boredom . . . . always the same gestures, the same amusements, the same endlessly repeated remarks" (Colette Priou, *Le miroir aux alouettes*, p. 15).

One of the childish "answers" that irritates parents most is: "You're always saying the same thing!"—the counterpart of a phrase frequently to be heard in parents' accounts of their dealings with their children: "I never stop telling him . . . ." "I've even stood in front of him for three-quarters of an hour," one mother has said, discussing her little boy. In an interview with Charlotte Roland "holding a candy in my hand, not letting him have it, and telling him again and again that he must say thank you." Extremely often, the naughtiness or lack of "intelligence" attributed to the child render a repetition of the acts supposedly bringing pressure to bear on it apparently indispensable. "She's like all children," another mother said of her little girl, "you have to tell her to do things again and again before she will obey." On other occasions, the parents repeat themselves not so much because of any pedagogic belief as because they are driven to it by their own feelings. "I get angry and say the same thing ten times over," another mother says when discussing her relationship with her child (*L'école des parents*, May 1956, p. 44). For parents powerless to make themselves obeyed there is always the refuge of repetition. Referring to this situation, a child psychologist, advising specifically on the chores expected of children, feels called upon to say: "Once it has been agreed that he is to perform a particular task, he must be trusted to do it . . . instead of saying the same thing over and over twenty times ('And above all don't forget that . . .')" (André Berge, *L'école des parents,* March 1950, p. 35).

In any case, however, the child's apprenticeship in the many and various forms of good manners is bound to require repetition. ("I'm always telling you the same thing because the thing is always the same," Molière's Don Juan says (*Don Juan,* act 2, sc. 1). When asked, "How do you set about teaching your children good manners?" another mother interviewed by Charlotte Roland replied, "You simply go on saying the same thing over and over again. Don't play with your fork, hold your knife straight, don't put your feet up on the table, sit up straight, keep your elbows to your sides, etc. You just have to go on saying it all through the meal, and then start again the next day."

At school too, exercises and, on occasion, punishments also entail repetition.

Parents and teachers have a tendency to demand a great deal of regularity in the child's use of its time, both at school and at home.

Yet at the same time as they are imposing such repetitions on the child, these authorities also deplore much of their charges' behavior precisely on the score of its repetitiveness: "Oh no, you're not going to start that again . . . !"

41. The result of this is that a contrast is created between the repetitions that made one's childhood so dismal and the variations that bring gaiety to the real or imagined life of the adult. After the monotony of a childhood diet, "change of dishes makes man rejoice" (La Fontaine, *Les troqueurs*). Having remarked that "the child's happiness resides in the fact of growth," a child psychologist (André Berge) adds more specifically that this happiness contains "the hope of becoming adult, the joy . . . of achieving the right to increasingly diverse activities" (*L'école des parents,* March 1955, p. 31). Here is Montherlant observing a young athlete running: "Everything that disappears and appears is transformed second by second! At every second there is a new world on his chest and on his back. And only there, for his legs are still just a shade too thick, like a young dog's. Scarcely free yet of theoir childhood padding . . ." (Montherlant, *Les olympiques,* pp. 155–56).

42. The exercise of this right to variation, a privilege of adulthood, is apparently made all the more urgent by the fact that even grown-ups can still feel themselves threatened by pressures tending to force them back into the repetition that marked their childhood. "If you usually write your capital M's with three legs," a certain civil servant and man of letters (Roger Rabiniaux)

explains with some indignation, "then by what right can you ever poach, even by chance, upon the territory of the men who write them with only two legs? . . . If you ordinarily eat only very rare meat, then make sure you don't happen to ask one day for your steak well done, because that would make you an eccentric, and what confidence could anyone ever have in you?" (*Demain*, April 11–17, 1957).

43. Such phantasms are a cover, at least in part, for a dominant tendency to preserve the rut.

"My timetable is immutable" a character in a novel can say in ecstatic tones when describing his vacations (José Cabanis, *Les mariages de raison*, p. 152).

44. As a means of opposing such tendencies—though often not very consciously—we employ the belief that we prefer things to follow one another and not to resemble one another; we lament the fact that being shackled to our individual selves renders the realization of this objective far from easy. As a weapon against the unpleasant feeling produced by inconstancy (in politics, the act of "dissociating oneself," or even of being a "weathercock"), there is the affirmation that "the absurd man is the man who never changes," that "only fools never change." According to La Bruyère, "the man with the best mind is irregular"; it is the "fool" who is "uniform," who "never takes back his words," who "is fixed and determined by his nature"; "When you have seen him once, you have seen him at every moment and at every period of his life" (La Bruyère, *Les caractères*, "De l'homme," 142).

"I am rather like a weathervane; for they never stay still until they are rusty," Voltaire proclaims, while Montesquieu made himself pleasant to the academicans who had just accepted him among their number by assuring them: "You are never like yourselves" (Montesquieu, *Discours de réception à l'Académie française*). The narrator of *Paludes* expresses his horror of those who "do exactly the same thing every day," and suggests to his mistress: "We should try to vary our existence a little!" (Gide, *Paludes*, pp. 51–55). When someone asks a character in *Les faux-monnayeurs* who is supposed to be following a course of lectures, "Which ones?" he replies "nonchalantly, 'I vary them' " (Gide, *Les faux-monnayeurs*, p. 132). "You are changing shades even now!" Paul Valéry exclaims in *Charmes*. And:

> What would you be without surprise?
> The mind cannot shine unless it break
> The resemblance mirrored in the past,

one of his fairies says (Valéry, "Le solitaire," in *Mon Faust*, p. 240). When Jaurès reproached Briand for his desertion of socialism, Briand is supposed to have replied: "The only things I know that always stay stuck on the same rock are mussels" (Charles Daniélou, *Dans l'intimité de Marianne*, p. 344).

The man who changes easily gives proof of levity—a quality both suspect and precious. Each one of his acts has the good fortune to be unique, as Paul Valéry sensed when walking among rocks being battered by the sea: ". . . each step is a special invention. . . . Not one of them resembles another. . . . No habit here. . . . All the muscles . . . working by improvisation; the center constantly has to invent the form of its man" (Valéry, *Tel quel*, 2: 136–37).

45. This being so, one can be horrified at not feeling a desire to change. Here is a character in a novel discussing with his friend the reasons that may have caused the latter to remain faithful to his wife: " 'It might also have been because you didn't want to be unfaithful to her, because the game wasn't worth the candle.'

"Roland started with outrage as though at the lash of a whip:

" 'Not want to be unfaithful to her? What do you take me for? By what right do you dare insinuate that I didn't want to be unfaithful to her?'

. . ." 'I restrained myself from being unfaithful to her,' Roland announced energetically, 'because my religious convictions forbade it' " (Jean-Louis Curtis, *Les justes causes*, p. 52). It was perhaps when moved by a similar emotion that La Fontaine was led to envisage the reactions to a "dispensation to barter a hymen, not just as often as one feels like it, but at least once in one's life":

> Such a thing as an indult in France
> Would be welcomed, I'll guarantee; for people here
> Are great on barter: God made us changeable.
> [La Fontaine, *Les troqueurs*]

46. Though "the French language slips more evenly off the tongue than any other" (Gide, Journal 1889–1939, p. 1202), though "French when well spoken scarcely sings at all" being "a discourse of rather narrow register, a more level language than others" (Valéry, *Regards sur le monde actuel*, p. 126), it would nevertheless be audacious to claim with Pascal that it is better to use the same word several times than to render one's discourse obscure under pretext of avoiding repetitions. It is quite normal that a journalist, reporting the beginning of the long governmental crisis in the spring of 1933, should write: "M. Paul Reynaud began his consultations yesterday in a favorable atmosphere," only to add "more specifically" later on: "The president of the finance committee did in fact receive a warm wel-

come from . . ." (*Le Monde*, May 25, 1953). Having given us the headline: "At the Tarbes regional congress," *Le Monde* (October 13, 1953) then gave as its first subheading "The radicals in the southwest put their hope in M. Mendès-France" with a second that read: "Speech by the Deputy for the Eure." Reporting the events leading up to the Suez expedition, a member of the French parliament claimed that after 1948 "Israel was never able to free itself from a feeling of being strangled," while "the Arab leaders, on the excessively vulnerable frontiers of M. Ben Gurion's country . . ." (Arthur Conte, A.N., March 26, 1957; *J.O.*, p. 1863). And though the liturgical tends to get the upper hand in Péguy and Claudel, according to Valéry "there exists in the mind an indefinable horror of repetition" (Valéry, *Variété*, p. 1026)—the all-important process of "finding the law of a succession" thus being another means of "dominating . . . surmounting . . . as it were exhausting the expected repetition" (ibid.)—a horror that makes us find something soothing in the idea of "a subject incapable of thinking the same thing twice" (Valéry, *L'idée fixe*, p. 130).

3

RENEWING THE LEASE OR MOVING ON

1. Nothing, fundamentally, ever changes; the multiple variations that may impress the superficial observer are no barrier to the astute eye that can see through this frequently disquieting facade to the immutable and reassuring background beyond: such is one great theme that recurs in various Parisian worlds. "In the long run," Paul Valéry declares, "nothing has ever happened" (*Mauvaises pensées et autres*, p. 109).

Toward the end of the Fourth Republic, one observer (Jacques Fauvet) decided to compare the percentages of the electorate that voted against MacMahon in 1877, against Flandin-Laval in 1936, and against Edgar Faure in 1956: 45 percent in every case. (Fauvet, *La France déchirée*, p. 28).

2. Often, the permanence of the background is clearly manifested by the absence of changes in particular aspects of the facade, even when the latter does not actually provide an illustration for the tendency to "live in the past" that provoked one observer into saying: "The Théâtre de France is like that these days; it doesn't create, it 'makes over'" (Morvan Lebesque in *Le canard enchaînéx*, June 20, 1956).

This is how Charles de Gaulle remembers his return to the rue Saint-Dominique after the liberation of Paris: "Immediately, I am gripped by the impression that nothing has changed inside these rooms. . . . Gigantic events have toppled the universe, our army has been annihilated . . . but at the War Ministry the way things look remains immutable. Out in the courtyard, a squad of the Garde Républicaine is presenting arms as usual. The vestibule, the staircase, the armor decorating the walls are all exactly as they used to be. There, in person, are the doormen who stood outside before. I go into the minister's office that M. Paul Raynaud and I left together during the night of June 10, 1940. Not a single piece of furniture, not a single tapestry, not a single curtain has been moved. On the table, the telephone is still in the same place, and the names visible on the call buttons are all exactly the same as before. In a moment someone will be telling me that the same is true of all the other buildings in which the Republic was embodied" (de Gaulle, *L'unité*, p. 306).

3. It is often supposed that the future will simply continue some particular and prominent feature of the present. "When the people are once stirred," La Bruyère notes, "one cannot understand how calm can ever return; and when they are peaceful, one cannot see how their calm can ever leave them" (La Bruyère, *Les caractères*, "Du souverain," 6). "When there are disturbances and confusion in some place," says Montesquieu in his turn, "one cannot imagine how peace can ever return to it," just as "when complete peace and obedience reign there one cannot imagine how they can ever cease" (Montesquieu, *Mes pensées*, pp. 1424–25). "The distinguishing feature of powerful emotions," says a contemporary writer taking up the same theme, "is that they can convince us of their immutability. . . . The present moment, what one is living, what one is doing, what one is feeling, is so indisputably evident that one cannot conceive of the past as ever having been otherwise, or of the future as ever being different" (Jean Dutourd, *Doucin*, p. 48).

Though regimes change, each of them, until the very moment of its collapse, may give the impression of being eternal to those who are governed by it, even if they are critical of it. "When one is accustomed to a settled system of abuses," notes one of the Third Republic's great politicians (André Tardieu), "one is inclined to think of it as eternal; and such is the case with the majority of Frenchmen. In 1789, the duc d'Orléans, who was for all that an intelligent man, wagered a hundred *louis* that the States General would disperse again without having done anything at all, and without even abolishing the *lettres de cachet*. And Frenchmen in the twentieth century are similarly convinced that what is will be" (André Tardieu, *La profession parlementaire*, p. 361)—a conviction that certainly accompanied the criticisms, most of them far from moderate, that political circles during the last period of the Fourth Republic were almost unanimous in hurling at the regime. It appeared to them, and in equal parts, both impossible to live under and impossible to shake.

When it is a matter of explaining a military reverse—such as Dienbienphu—there is a tendency to adopt the hypothesis that the command responsible must have fixed its assessment of the enemy's forces or methods once and for all at some arbitrary point in time, expecting to find them more or less the same at the time of the next engagement as experience had shown them to be in the past.

Although a national assembly may be experienced by its members as an extremely fluctuating entity, those within it are often carried away by an inclination to imagine the future as a continuation of the present. Having noted, with reference to Roger Duchot, that "the general secretary of the independents has found himself betrayed by half his forces" at the time of an important division, a weekly then concluded in characteristic terms: "He will now have to content himself with secondary roles" (Demain, October 3–9, 1957). When "a tone of great hostility to the Popular Republicans dominated the exchanges of opinion" within the Moderate group in the National Assembly, one observer (J. R. Tournoux) felt justified in adding: "Added to the S.F.I.O.-Moderate split, from now on we have the Moderate-M.R.P. split" (Combat, October 17, 1957). During a governmental crisis (in spring 1957), a possible prime minister (Pierre Pflimlin) found himself blocked one night by the incompatible demands of various groups, an episode that prompted one journalist (Georges Rotvand) to write: "Whether M. Pflimlin contrives to round this nocturnal cape or not, the same questions will persist. Should he persist in his attempt, then he will find things very difficult when it comes to fixing the proportions of his cabinet and distributing portfolios. Should he yield his place to another, however, the latter will only find himself faced with the same demands, if not the same prejudices" (Bulletin du Centre d'études politiques, June 5, 1957). And yet, once M. Pflimlin had given up his attempts, the next candidate to enter the lists (Maurice Bourgès-Manoury) succeeded instantly.

4. That which has succeeded in achieving existence will tend, it is frequently believed, "to maintain itself in being," to continue on the same track, the same trajectory. There are many things apparently "among the number of those that continue by a kind of impetus given in the beginning" (Montesquieu, Considérations sur les causes de la grandeur des Romains et de leur décadence, chap. 5); many groups that seem to recall those "companies" observed by the cardinal de Retz (such as the Paris parlement)

of which he wrote: "I have not seen one of them in which three or four days of familiarity have not caused them to accept as natural what they never even have begun without constraint" (Retz, *Mémoires*, p. 626). One of the great habits of things is that of forming habits. And a habit is caught so easily! There is a perpetual danger of a "transition from the level of caprice to that of habit" (J. Dublineau, *L'école des parents*, March 1955, p. 11). Just once doesn't make a habit? But oh Lord, what if it were to become one? "The only reason why it should endure," Baudelaire says of the world, "is that it exists" (*Fusées*). At a party given in his new apartment by *Dosithée*, the teacher of thinking, he was congratulated on the charming sparrows that did such honor to his balcony. "I have never given them any bread," he announced; "I am too much afraid of its becoming a habit." In the drawing-room of *Daphné*, wife of a high-ranking civil servant, there was talk of a couple said to have had fourteen children. "But certainly," put in a young woman whose opinions were valued, "once you've begun having them, why stop?" "One does something again," a Gide character says, "because one has done it before; each of our yesterday's acts seems to be crying out for us again today . . . every action becomes the hollow in a mattress one is constantly rolling back into" (Gide, *Paludes*, p. 99). Proust talks of "the tendency everything that exists has to prolong itself" (*A l'ombre des jeunes filles en fleurs*, p. 622). "Once launched," he remembers, "it seemed to me that I could have continued on my dismal course as far as the moon" (ibid., p. 821), and also, referring to a long sleep: "It is no easier to . . . emerge from such a sleep than it is to enter sleep after staying up too late, so strongly do all things tend to last" (ibid.).

Either I abstain from doing such and such a thing, or I run the risk of doing it all the time. Toward the end of the Fourth Republic, discussing a project for reforms of the Constitution that would tend to facilitate dissolution of the National Assembly, a Keeper of the Seals (Robert Lecourt) predicted that should this project be passed "there might be a temptation to look for every possible means of evading its terms. It could happen . . . that a government might be disbanded with the sole object of avoiding dissolution within the terms provided for in the act." While on the other hand, "the procedure for dissolution having been successfully employed once, there would be a risk of having recourse to it often, either because it had become an acquired taste or because the parties had all made it an integral part of their calculations" (A.N., February 14, 1958; *J.O.*, pp. 791–92).

5. Thus one or two manifestations of any new phenomenon can easily produce a prognostic of indefinite recurrence, or even

the illusion of an already protracted series; a reaction that lends itself easily to polemical or humorous ends.

When, during the death throes of a government (Joseph Laniel's) and those of a war (that in Indochina), the Assembly had debated the two predictable deaths on several occasions, one of the deputies (Guillain de Benouville) repeated in the house what had become a constant refrain in the lobbies: "It has become a habit in this Assembly to adjourn the problem of the war in Indochina regularly once a week" (A.N., June 12, 1954; J.O., p. 2973). Similarly, in a comedy by Henri Verneuil (*Pour avoir Adrienne*), the husband knows that the lover has had a previous affair with Rose Pompon. Consequently, when another man presents himself claiming to be a former lover of Rose Pompon, the husband asks: And now you are making advances to my wife? When the other denies this, the husband explains: Rose's former lovers usually do.

6. More particularly, there is often a readiness to believe that "the first fault invites us to other faults," that "one fall always brings on another fall." According to La Rochefoucauld: "One can find women who have never had a love affair, but it is rare to find one who has had no more than one" (*Maximes*). "Though a first theft may require some resolution," says Edouard in *Les faux-monnayeurs*, a character the author intended as subtle of mind and close to himself, "those that follow necessitate no more than yielding to temptation. Everything that comes afterward is merely a matter of letting oneself go. . . . Often, an initial action, one performed almost without thinking about it, irremediably traces out our form and begins to inscribe a characteristic that all our efforts, in the sequel, will never be able to erase" (Gide, *Les faux-monnayeurs*, p. 461).

As long as it doesn't continue! worried parents seem to think to themselves when confronted with some naughtiness on the part of their child. "One fit of temper," a child psychologist feels he ought to warn them, "does not mean that the future adult will necessarily be quarrelsome" (C. Koupernik, *La colère*, p. 10). According to another psychologist: "A certain number of parents are disturbed when they realize that their children tell stories that have no basis in truth. . . . They wonder whether their children are perhaps destined to become terrible liars" (Guy Durandin, *L'école des parents*, June-July, 1955, p. 16).

7. It is therefore indispensable to avoid a bad beginning, since that might lead to a bad habit which could very soon prove irresistible. "If you begin to rock a child, then you're obliged to rock it all the time," one of the mothers interviewed by Charlotte Roland said. Rock a child? "But if the child gets too used to it,

then your life is poisoned for years," was another mother's reply. A third, having described one of her child's "bad habits" as a tendency "to hang on to you and other people in order to get you to fondle her more and more," was then forced to face the objection that it is in fact normal for a small child to want to be fondled. "A small child perhaps," was her reply, "but a small child is going to become a grown-up eventually, and the habits you get into as a child stay with you."

8. Worse still, there is the fear that bad behavior, instead of simply continuing, may snowball. If you steal a sheep you'll steal a flock. "I have seen a great many parents . . . behaving in the most unfortunate manner to their children," a child psychologist notes, "simply because the slightest departure from perfect behavior on the part of their offspring immediately conjured up a vision of the magistrate's court" (André Berge, *L'école des parents*, October 1955, p. 18). "A child only has to take a sugar cube out of the sugar-bowl," he also observes, "and its parents immediately see a picture in their minds of a burglar being dragged into the dock" (André Berge, *Les défauts de l'enfant*, p. 109). A little girl accused of having brought so-called Algerian bombs into the school was informed by her teacher that "even a tiny pebble rolling down from the Himalayas could kill us!" "It is farther," Montaigne confirms, 'from nothing to the smallest thing in the world than from the smallest to the greatest thing in the world" (*Essais*, bk. 3, chap. 11). "You never know what it will lead to; there's no reason to stop" (*La famille Fenouillard*, p. 178).

9. Here, then, is a supplementary reason for calling a quick halt to bad beginnings, if you once catch a finger in the cogs you'll end up with your whole hand in the machine; if I give him that much (showing one finger), he'll take all that (moving my hand up to my shoulder). "Of all things," Montaigne observes, "births are the weakest and most tender. Yet we must keep our eyes wide open at the beginnings of things, for when things are still small we do not perceive the danger, but when it the danger increased we can no longer perceive the remedy" (*Essais*, bk. 3, chap. 10). As for what goes on inside me: "With very little effort I can halt that first stirring of my emotions and abandon the object of concern that begins to weigh on me, and before it carries me away with it. He who does not check the outset has no time to halt the course. He who cannot slam the door upon his feelings will not drive them out once inside. He who cannot control the beginning will never control the end. And he who could not withstand the first tremor will not withstand the fall" (ibid.).

10. The forces of change often appear inferior to those that

tend to maintain the established state of things. "How many times I must have wanted to write a book that took no account of my past," André Gide remembered towards the end of his life, but "There was nothing to be done: I simply slipped back into the same worn out themes" (Gide, *Ainsi soit-il*, p. 1173). And a politician who was often in the cabinet during the last decade of the Third Republic recalls that "it had become impossible to institute the slightest reform . . . other than by . . . producing exceptionally energetic efforts that left you exhausted, incapable of attempting anything fresh for a very long time" (Jean Zay, *Souvenirs et solitude*, pp. 41–42). "When those in power make timid attempts to improve governmental structures," a leader during the Fourth Republic (Pierre Mendès-France) commented with reference to what was then called the Union française, "they run up against resistances of such strength that they have never been overcome to this day" (*Le Monde*, April 10, 1953).

11. This being so, a retreat by the forces of conservation may be merely a prelude to the reconquest of the territory temporarily abandoned. Summing up the development of the attempts at change undertaken during the latter part of the Fourth Republic, one journalist (Jacques Fauvet) observed: "During its passage from 'round table' to 'round table' this constitutional reform has . . . been partly emptied of its content. It has met the same fate as the outline-law for Algeria. Passing from Council to Council, from Assembly to Assembly, this latter document has lost a great deal of its import. . . . Constitutional revision or outline-law . . . all reforms . . . gradually lose their substance in transit" (*Le Monde*, January 10, 1958).

12. As for certain reforms, the general conviction as to their utility is accompanied by an evaluation of the forces opposing them such that any announcement of a resolution to undertake them is seen as no more than a pious and somewhat ridiculous wish. Here is a passage from the investiture speech of the last prime minister but one under the Fourth Republic on "the concern preoccupying the government with regard to the food supplies of the Paris region": "The government will request the reorganization of the present system of municipal food markets in agreement with the Paris Municipal Council (laughter from various parts of the house). I do not think, ladies and gentlemen, that the Paris Municipal Council will be able to refuse, if it is invited in sufficiently pressing terms—which is what the government intends to do—to cooperate in the reorganization of a system of distribution which would permit great economies and quite certainly a lowering of prices. . . . Though certain of our colleagues have greeted this idea with scepticism or irony, I for

my part am justified in thinking that the Paris Municipal Council will not be able to refuse this necessary reorganization" (A.N., November 5, 1957; *J.O.*, p. 4651)—which, needless to say, was not immediately forthcoming.

13. There is also a risk that a continuance of the *status quo* will result from a multiplicity of efforts directed at a variety of changes. "Concentration," said a leader under the Third Republic (Waldeck Rousseau) referring to one of his broad formulas for government, "consists . . . in forming a cabinet in which the ministers come from every area, not in order to agree upon some specific point, but in order to achieve agreement upon that particular kind of immobility that results from many people's pulling in various directions" (quoted by André Tardieu, *La profession parlementaire*, p. 229). (In such a ministry, the major objective of each member is, in effect, to "block" what they take to be the others' plans.) When the fall of a government (Edgar Faure's) was foreseen just before an election (in the autumn of 1955), the following prognostication became current in political circles: "The formation of a new government now would entail extraordinary difficulties, because every deputy would like to be given, or given back, a ministry before having to seek reelection, while at the same time each one of them would like to stand in the way of the others elected from his own *département*.

"The solution: a change of prime minister and a continuation of the same government with an 'additive' " (chosen in that event from the ex-R.P.F. party, since they had left the government only two months before) (J. R. Tournoux, *Combat*, November 29, 1955). During the same period, a journalist (Bertrand Poirot-Delpech) wrote with reference to the entrance examination for certain important schools: "Even though there is unanimous agreement upon the obsolete character of certain educational subjects, often because there is no agreement upon the subjects that should replace them, and also from fear of offending such and such a professor or such and such a university group, all change has until now been rejected" (*Le Monde*, January 5, 1955).

Things could be worse still, however, while one at least has an existing state of things to fall back on, since it can be used to avoid any quarrel between the upholders of various reforms "leading to chaos," as in the case of the famous debate in the Assembly (June 20, 1952) on an important problem (that of Tunisia) during which a great number of tabled motions were rejected one after the other.

14. The most difficult of all appears to be the abolition of something that is hallowed by the very fact of its existence. If one suc-

ceeds in adding to it the measure one would like to have substituted for it, even though it is itself left intact, then one can think of oneself as highly efficient indeed.

This means, however, that the passage of time may cause the rules and arrangements in any given sphere to grow progressively more and more cumbersome. Here is how an inspector-general of public education (Maurice David) feels about the development of school programs: "As long as the specialists continue to rise in arms every time there is any question of their particular specialties being touched, as long as . . . we go on believing ourselves obliged to drag behind us the enormous weight of a past as cumbersome as those old cupboards . . . that people insist on keeping in their tiny apartments out of respect for some great-grandmother . . ." (*L'école des parents*, February 1955, p. 11).

But when it reaches a certain point, retention—"immobilism" —produces a movement of brutal and massive expulsion—"revolution."

15. For everything that has just been said applies solely to the feelings that are current during the long periods when institutions are functioning "normally." Whereas these periods are in fact interrupted at intervals by episodes during which "the facade crumbles," during which "the rigid framework explodes": 1936, 1944, 1958. At these times many things become possible, and are even realized, with the proviso that they themselves then form a new constellation which will itself quite soon appear just as difficult to modify.

This sequence of phases in the life of the nation calls to mind certain developments in the individual's transition to adult life; certain forms of discipline imposed in earliest childhood are often maintained, it appears, until a period quite late on in adolescence, at which point they suddenly give way to a status approaching that of the adult.

16. There is a widespread and powerful feeling, though it is one often decried by those in whom it is strongest, that immobility is preferable to agitation, rest to bustle, the tried to the new, the customary to the unknown, the habit to the innovation. Although it is not always easy to agree with it, we are often attracted by the very restful advice that the only thing to do is stay as we are. Shifting ground, whether inside or outside oneself, is a worrisome thing!

"The life of a sleeping cat," Jules Renard calls it. "From time to time, I hear a leap, a claw scratching, a yawning that has the air of being action, then everything draws into its fur and sleeps again" (Renard, *Journal*, p. 716). "You're waiting for someone to get up," the same author explains to certain well-intentioned men; "no one will get up. It is so pleasant sitting down and even more so lying down!" (ibid., p. 226).

"The first day, she asked: 'What am I gonna cook for your supper?' 'Some potato soup.' The next day, she asked: 'So what am I gonna cook you for your supper?' 'Some potato soup, I already told you.' The third day, she asked the same question and received the same reply. At which point she understood, and from then on, every day, without prompting, she cooked him his potato soup" (ibid., p. 106).

"Things that move disturb me," admits Maurice Barrès (quoted by André Gide, *Journal 1889–1939*, p. 1064), while Abel Ferry writes of Delcassé: "I admire his powers of immobility; it is not laziness of mind; it is almost a system of life" (*Les carnets secrets*, p. 42). In *Le visiteur*, Henri de Régnier describes the wonderful life of "those who have never desired anything else" and who live a life made up of "days resembling all their other days hour by hour." A contemporary novelist (François Nourissier) has used the following quotation from Benjamin Constant as an exergue to his *Les orphelins d'Auteuil*: "A deadly and doomed mobility."

17. This passion for the immutable, which is thought to be universal in its influence, is always being underlined. "In France," says a high-ranking and celebrated civil servant (Louis Armand), we like to teach subjects *ne varietur*, such as Latin grammar or mathematical theorems" (*Le Monde*, February 18, 1958). Early on during the economic expansion of the fifties, a specialist correspondent (Pierre Drouin) wrote in the country's number one newpaper of "the horror of changing one's horizon or one's trade that is to be observed from top to bottom of the social scale" (*Le Monde*, September 11, 1953). Three years later, at the very height of the expansion, the report of state organization (the Board of Productivity) asked the nation to "give up obsolete but traditional spending habits in favor of new and, for that very reason, suspect forms of investment" (*Le Monde* June 15, 1956).

18. Often, a situation achieved tends to take on the appearance of a precious and precarious "equilibrium": there are so many tiny accidents, so many minute moments of carelessness that might destroy it, replace it with a state much inferior to it, or even provoke a catastrophe. "Heavens, Monsieur d'Aurevilly," Jules Lemaître is said to have exclaimed when meeting that writer in the Champs-Elysées, "how marvelously well you are strapped into your topcoat today!" And the reply was: "If I were to communicate I'd burst!" (Gide, *Journal 1889–1939*, p. 948). During the Fourth Republic, the government appeared for most of the time to be in the situation of the man in *Wages of Fear*

at the wheel of his truck of nitroglycerine in Latin America: the slightest false move meant annihilation. It was said that ministers could be seen walking on tiptoe in order not to disturb anything; in the house, one *enfant terrible* (Georges Loustaunau-Lacau) compared the cabinet to a lot of "fakirs lying on beds of nails that prick them whenever they move, which is doubtless why they've never moved much" (A.N., December 3, 1954; *J.O.,* p. 5755). "I'm up to my neck in the shit; so don't make waves!"

So many states of equilibrium in an individual soul or within a group consist of a "skillful distribution" of advantages between a great many "payees," each of which is likely to be no more than moderately satisfied with the share allotted to him and to have resigned himself to the situation with some regret. Only one of those parties need seek to gain a supplementary advantage, or to be granted one, and all the others will very swiftly denounce the pact. Under the Fourth Republic, for example, specialists pointed out that there was a crisis in army recruitment for the officer ranks, and that this crisis was at least partly due to the drop in material benefits that had been affecting them. But the military correspondent of *Le Monde* (Jean Planchais), commenting on a certain project for a "revalorization" of army pay, was able to observe that "this project does not seem in theory to be excessively ambitious. Yet it does present one grave disadvantage: any substantial change in the wage index [fixing officer salaries] would certainly result in a complete revision of the entire system of laboriously worked out scales of civil service salaries. It is understandable that the government should hesitate before provoking the collapse of a pyramid it has been at such pains to construct" (*Le Monde,* December 13 and 14, 1953).

Frenchmen also frequently feel that they are involved in situations reminiscent of worm-eaten wooden buildings that will crumble at the slightest shock (whether their fragility is apparent on the surface or not). In 1936, we find Montherlant noting, for example, "the decrepitude of the first story of the Eiffel Tower. It's like some strange no-man's-land. Old amusement machines doubtless dating back to the inauguration (1889). Paintwork gone, wood worm-eaten. The keepers, centenarians keeping themselves warm with minute sticks of wood, like down-and-outs. The feeling (which I get on French liners, and which would prevent me from flying in French planes) that the whole thing is unsafe. What with the intellectual incapacity, the physical incapacity (when the Opéra caught fire the other day the only watchman on the premises was yet another centenarian) and the moral incapacity (the lack of conscience), one

feels that the whole thing is only kept together by a miracle"
(Montherlant, *Carnets*, 1930–1944, p. 240).

19. Though it is easy to destroy a state of equilibrium in an
instant (nothing is easier to commit than the irreparable), what
a long and arduous task it is to evolve one! And similarly, in order
to maintain it, one is obliged to engage in incessant, painful, and
painstaking labors. Describing the "balance" of the relationship
between two of his characters, Montherlant speaks of the "thousand and one little pains that Léon had gone to in order to maintain that balance" (*Les célibataires*, p. 276); every major aspect
of any life may well require as much. "Our life," a diplomat and
man of letters observes, "is a constant disruption of an equilibrium that we must then perilously restore at the very next step"
(Jacques Dumaine, *Quai d'Orsay, 1945–51*, p. 75).

20. In practice, the difficulties can become an enjoyable sport:
let the equilibrium be as precious as possible, fragile beyond
words—and then let it be preserved by feats of skill concealing
all the hard work!

Having learned to walk, children celebrate their new skill and
their victory over the fear of falling by performing prodigies of
balance. They will fill a beach bucket to the very brim with
water, then see if they can run at top speed without spilling any.
Montherlant recounts having once been in a park and having
seen a small boy walking on one of the wire fences round a
lawn like a tightrope walker and saying "balance . . . balance . . ."
to himself over and over again. He said it fifty times, visibly under
a spell (perhaps he was a future cabinet minister) before he
finally lost that all-important balance and ended up with his
hands and knees on the grass" (Montherlant, *Le solstice de juin*,
p. 172). He never slips off the pedals; his story stands up: good
points where grown-ups are concerned. Having referred to a
couple who made love standing up in a hammock, a comedian
added: "The manager of the club asked me to leave that bit out,
because next day there are always people who've got themselves
hurt; obviously, it's a question of balance." But Paul Valéry imagines "a state of balance . . . that is at the mercy of a mere breath
yet is maintained for almost half a century" (*Variété*, p. 1109).

21. To cultivate a state or states of balance means in the first
place to avoid destroying them by touching them unnecessarily.
There is no advantage to be gained by waking sleeping dogs; or,
to quote the subtitle of Armand Salacrou's play *L'archipel Lenoir*,
"Don't disturb anything not already in motion." "What madness
to risk disturbing a state of equilibrium!" one of Montherlant's
characters exclaims. "If you knew how precious it is, a moment

of equilibrium!" (Montherlant, *Demain il fera jour*, act I, sc. I).
How many times one must have said to oneself when it was too
late: I should probably have done much better to keep quiet!
Why was I so thoughtless as to start that hare running?

22. Similarly, in politics, there is a constant fear of the forces
that would be *unleashed* by incautious meddling with such and
such a delicate balance obtained at the expense of so much effort
and heartsearching (see sec. 18 above). "We now have to face
the problem of educational reform," a prime minister (Félix
Gaillard) once informed the Assembly. "The government," he
then added, "begs you not to evade it, as we are very frequently
tempted to do with difficult problems" (A.N., November 15, 1957;
J.O., p. 4633). But to those acquainted with the depths of the
"emotion," of the "undercurrents," of the resistance that every
attempt at change is said to provoke in that field, such a "temptation" does not appear wholly unreasonable. If radical innova-
tions are being proposed to some particular situation, then at
least let there be an acute crisis afflicting it that will provide the
impetus to overcome all the obstacles. Otherwise, it is the same
with every sector of the national life as with a certain day's
agenda upon which a parliamentary group finally decided to
agree even though it was divided upon the question. At the time
of the Assembly's debate on the *Acte de Londres,* on October 8,
1954, a journalist (Raymond Barrillon) wrote that "the text of
the Socialist agenda finally agreed upon had been worked out
with such difficulty, calculated with such care, that it became,
in view of this, an extremely delicate, if not impossible matter to
abandon or truncate it. The suppression of any one of its para-
graphs would have shattered the balance of the concessions and
risked reopening the quarrel" (*Le Monde,* October 10, 1954).
Another journalist (Georges Hourdin) wrote along the same lines
that the status of Roman Catholic Church "constitutes a complex
structure, slowly built up over fifty years of often agitated religious history, and now at last seems to have found a point of
equilibrium. It would be impossible to modify one of its elements
without the risk of shaking the entire structure and reviving past
conflicts" (*Le Monde,* April 30, 1957). When, toward the end of
any sizable governmental crisis under the Fourth Republic, the
political and personal composition of a new cabinet was apparently fixed, one could speak equally well of a complex structure,
slowly built up over several weeks of frequently agitated parliamentary history that now seemed at last to have reached a point
of equilibrium. And in this case too, it would be impossible to
modify one of the elements without a risk of undermining the
whole structure and reviving past conflicts.

23. Once "the established state of things has been called into question," there is a widespread feeling that one is at the mercy of "adventure." "Adventure," a journalist (Jean Ferniot) notes, "that word which is such a source of dreams for children, poets, and explorers, plunges the elected representatives of the nation into stark panic" (*La Nef*, April 1958, p. 19). To open the door to adventure, to embark upon an adventure: how horrible! In a speech requesting the application of the 1947 Algerian statute, a deputy (Jacques Chevallier) could say: "Deciding to depart from the statute and trust to blind chance (*se lancer dans l'aventure*) . . ." (A.N., October 13, 1955; *J.O.*, p. 5110). Referring to the case of a child (Elisabeth Irr) abandoned by its mother, another deputy (André Mutter) told the house that "the mother . . . simply left on adventure (*à l'aventure*)" (A.N., January 29, 1958; *J.O.*, p. 347).

When we depart from what is, we know what we are leaving behind, but not what awaits us; or at least, we have not yet experienced it. "One can never know," Montesquieu tells us, "what will be the result of any change one makes" (*Mes pensées*, p. 1461).

And there are a great many who might well say, with Madame de Sévigné, "Any kind of suspense kills me" (Madame de Sévigné, *Lettre à M. de Pomponne*, November 27, 1664).

"There is nothing unknown in it, there is no trap," a leader (René Mayer) assured the Assembly when attempting to calm its uneasiness at being faced with an innovation (A.N., January 1, 1952; *L'Année politique*, 1952, p. 415), being well aware that "of the unknown a wise man is ever wary." Explaining why he had proposed that an eventual C.E.D.—Community for European Defense—should be more closely controlled by N.A.T.O. than had originally been intended, a prime minister (Pierre Mendès-France) reminded the house: "Our idea was as follows: N.A.T.O. is an organization we know . . . within which we have contracted obligations of which we know the exact scope" (A.N., August 29, 1954; *J.O.*, p. 4425). "Objections have been made to the conception of the common market treaty fixed upon by the government," admitted another prime minister (Guy Mollet) a little later, only to refute them as follows: "In our estimation, the purpose of this treaty is primarily to set out principles and general directions. As for the methods of applying it . . . to attempt to fix all of these in advance and in all their details would be an illusory and somewhat unwise course. Is it proper, for example, to determine in a treaty, for decades to come and in its details, the whole of Europe's agricultural policy?" (A.N., January 22, 1957; *J.O.*, p. 214).

24. If we allow an idefinitely prolonged *instability,* an un-checked whirlwind of agitation, to maintain an endless disorder and restlessness in all our movements, shall we not be punished for it? "And he who changes once may change every day," Corneille says (quoted by Paul Robert under *changer*). The at-traction of such behavior, and the horror it inspires, are not limited to the political field. Discussing the nosology of child psychiatry in France, a specialist was able to say that "instability" is "a syndrome . . . comprising two-thirds" of the field in question, whereas in the "structural constructions" of the same science in Germany "there . . . is never any mention of instability" (André Beley, *L'enfant instable,* pp. 6–7).

25. Not knowing where one is going to end up produces a fear of ending up nowhere, of "being led into chaos": the punishment for having so lightly abandoned "that which at least has the merit of existing."

This apprehension often serves as a check to those sudden urges to political "massacre" that the very existence of any government tends to stir up. It is frequently said that the prime minister in office counts mainly upon the difficulty of finding a replacement for him to keep him in office; "What other policy and with what other majority?" he may throw in the faces of those who are meditating his fall (implying also: What other cabinet with what other leader?—even though—and this is the misfor-tune—the latter is a question for which it is much easier to pro-vide a reply). Thus a government may conceive (or a journalist impute to it) the plan of increasing its chances of survival by augmenting the conflicts between the groups represented within it (provided there is no alternative majority involved, as with the last Assembly of the Fourth Republic). According to one weekly, "M. Félix Gaillard, by his use of parliamentary "round tables," has created a new system which enables the parties concerned [in the government] to discuss . . . any projected plans quite publicly, and outside the government. . . . The parties achieve a clear awareness of their many disagreements, and, when they oppose one another openly in this way, it becomes more and more difficult for them to think of forming a new government together; a fact that strengthens the one now in existence" (*L'Express,* January 30, 1958).

26. Even if the events following the destruction of a state of balance do not lead to chaos, are we not bound before long to lose control over the forces we have unleashed? "We guide affairs in their beginnings," Montaigne reminds us, "and hold them in our power; but then later, when they are under way, it is they

that guide us and carry us along with them, and we must follow them" (*Essais*, bk. 3, chap. 10).

27. These "affairs" that carry us along with them" are in fact, inside us, the passions hitherto shackled by the habits we have shaken off. "If habit is a second nature," Proust says, "it prevents us from knowing the first, of which it lacks both the cruelties and the enchantments" (*Sodome et Gomorrhe*, p. 754).

28. Whatever the final effect of disrupting our equilibrium, anyone who does so is in danger of ending up with "his face in the mud." Though "a worm spends its whole life crawling on the ground" (and "it is well known that those who crawl never fall over"—editorial in *La Nef*, February 1958, p. 6), "the higher a monkey climbs the more you see of its behind (as *Clitiphon*, a great politician under the Fourth Republic, was fond of saying), and the easier it is to "bring him down." "If Bonaparte had remained an artillery lieutenant," as Joseph Prudhomme so sagely remarked, "he would still be on the throne."

During the Fourth Republic, the association between acting and falling (exploding or being toppled over) seemed quite evident to those in power. As one of them (François Mitterand) remarked, recognition of the fact that things that move about too much die much sooner was something in common between that regime and Louis XVIII (*La Nef*, February 1958, p. 8). Toward the end of the Fourth Republic, however, if the conflict over any question became sufficiently intense, even the "round table" method of sharing out governmental responsibility could prove inadequate. In which case, if it was to survive, the government would be obliged to consider abstaining from any action whatsoever in the matter. "M. Antoine Pinay has made a speech in the provinces in order to explain the unacceptable dangers of the Socialist plan for socialized medicine. The Socialists have replied. The disagreement is so strikingly apparent that no one would have the imprudence to expect the prime minister to provide any kind of arbitration [at the "round table" commissioned to deal with this problem]. Wisdom requires that the government be 'left out of it' altogether" (*L'Express*, January 30, 1958). Its abstention thus appears as the reaction "that will divide us least." The same may hold true for a party or a group attempting to prevent its own "explosion," and even, by means of a unanimous abstention, to preserve an appearance of "discipline."

The only exception to all this, it was held in political circles under the Fourth Republic, was when a government was still very young, when it had been in existence such a short time that it did not yet seem proper to end it. "A government can scarcely do very much during the first months of its existence," wrote one journalist (Jacques Fauvet in *Le Monde*, March 29, 1955). Since governments "can survive by immobilism"—and even, it was then thought, by no means other than immobilism—one observer (Pierre Uri) felt able to add the opinion that "a change of government has often proved the only means of recovering a possible margin of action for two or three months" (*Le Monde*, February 7, 1958).

29. When things are left as they are, the cause for this is very likely to be attributed to the wise apprehensions of those tempted to do otherwise. "This conference," writes an observer (Georges Rotvand) of the M.R.P. party conference in 1955, "has been marked first and foremost by a desire not to 'stir things up.' This explains why even the question of the party chairmanship has not been raised and M. Teitgen not reelected to that office, since it was generally known that the selection of a successor might bring a certain number of leaders into conflict" (*Bulletin du Centre d'études politiques*, May 24, 1955).

30. Though it may appear advantageous to abandon a routine in order to avoid a diminution of the pleasures it affords (see chap. 2, sec. 15), it may also seem wise, on the other hand, to stay with it in order to reap full advantage from it. "I don't like changes," Paul Léautaud admits, speaking of love. "I need the greatest possible physical freedom and intimacy. . . . Habit is one of the conditions of my pleasure" (Léautaud, *Propos d'un jour*, p. 16).

31. To be parted from one's habits is in itself extremely unpleasant. Habit, Marcel Proust observes, is "a fearful divinity, so welded into us, its bland face so incrusted in our heart, that if it detaches itself, if it turns away from us, this deity that we are scarcely able to distinguish from ourselves inflicts sufferings upon us more terrible than any other" (Proust, *La fugitive*, p. 420).

At the time of his accession to the premiership, during the Third Republic, a party leader (Emile Combes) was received by the president (Emile Loubet), who said to him: "Now you'll be setting about forming your cabinet. I have one request, only one, to put to you. I follow foreign affairs very closely, and I've got used to Delcassé. So let me keep him. I would appreciate that." (Combes, *Mon ministère*, p. 22). At the height of the economic expansion of the fifties, the "technocrats" urging the highest possible rates of modernization were much given to complaining of the Frenchman's "stay-at-home" nature. Apparently workers who had lost their jobs in one department of the old "static France" were refusing to accept offers of employment coming from the new "dynamic France": the people in the east aren't like us. . . . If it only meant going somewhere else in these parts. . . . You see, we buy all our meat from a cousin ten miles away . . . and besides I'm president of the local whist club . . . and there are our plots in the cemetery. . . . If I wait, I may find something else here.

32. Aside from this, to pull oneself out of a rut is an extremely arduous business. Habit may be stultifying, but there is no doubt that it is restful. "I keep going along a furrow that cost me a great deal of trouble to dig," declares a sort of everyman imagined by a contemporary writer, "getting out of it would require a super-human effort" (Jean Dutourd, Doucin, p. 197).

33. In order to introduce anything new into a life that is already a whole, something already in it, something to which one is attached must be sacrificed. Montherlant speaks of "those moments when there are too many people in our lives. There is a placard saying 'House Full.' Such moments mean that a newcomer, however sympathetic, will be kept out, simply because of that 'house full' board. Montherlant, *Carnets,* 1930–1944, p. 312). But are we not likely to have rather a lot of such moments, whether it is a matter of the people or of the objects that are filling our lives?

34. The creation of a new rut is seen as an arduous affair; all "running in" is. "I cannot conceive," Montesquieu declares, "given the extreme brevity of life, what purpose it would serve for men to leave . . . the habitual way of life they have acquired" (*Mes pensées,* p. 1153). Here is Mitsou explaining why she does not want to change to a new friend: "I'm not the sort of customer that changes tradesmen for a yes or a no. And besides, the idea of upsetting things, of complications. . . . The very thought makes me determined to stay put" (Colette, *Mitsou,* pp. 44–45).

35. And even apart from the discomfort of the change itself, what is the likelihood that the final state will prove preferable to the orginal one? Is it not sensible to bank on the contrary?

"I do not change easily for fear of losing in the change" Montaigne says (*Essais,* bk. 2, chap. 12). André Gide presents us with a whole series of remarks that seem to him to be "specifically French," such as, "All man's unhappiness comes from one thing, which is being unable to remain quietly in one room," "From now on I stay right where I am, and I shall be a hundred times better off," "What the devil was he doing on the ship?" "He shouldn't have gone in the first place" (Gide, *Journal 1988–1939,* p. 675).

36. And how often the expected advantages of an innovation are canceled out by unexpected disasters! Having determined

to win Gilberte back with gifts, Marcel makes up his mind to sell a Chinese vase, for which he obtains a much higher price than he had expected. Having left the antique shop, he has to pass through the Champs-Elysées, where he sees Gilberte with a man: "I went home, despairingly clutching the unlooked-for ten thousand francs that should have enabled me to offer so many little pleasures to Gilberte—whom I had now decided never to see again. Certainly my stopping at the antique dealer's had brought me delight . . . but if I had not made that stop, if the carriage had not taken the avenue des Champs-Elysées, then I should not have encountered Gilberte and that young man. So can the selfsame act bear opposing branches, and the misfortune it engenders annul the good fortune that caused it" (Proust, *A l'ombre des jeunes filles en fleurs*, p. 624).

37. The expectation of deriving benefit from a given change is often felt to be mere blindness; perspicacity reveals the opposite. The man who is "chained to the city" sees the country as "all freshness, all goodness," Paul Valéry points out. Whereas in fact, "there are some parts of the country that are merciless." This is because "the imagination of desire never sees more than . . . a fragment . . . of things." But "the man who sees everything desires nothing and trembles at the idea of change" (Valéry, *Tel quel*, 2: 20). He knows in advance that "changing governments isn't worth the trouble." A character in Jean Bernard-Luc's light comedy *Carlos et Marguerite*, explaining his ex-wife's inability to choose among three men, claims that normal people marry without knowing why, whereas those who suffer from loss of will need to know why; so lack of will is honesty, in a way.

38. The presence of contrary desires within the same soul is likely to render the advantage of any change very doubtful. Paul Valéry, describing a state of equilibrium, writes: "While the acrobat is at the mercy of the most unstable equilibrium imaginable, we make a wish. And that wish is strangely double, and *null*. We wish him to fall and we wish him to stay up" (*Tel quel*, 2: 189).

39. This being so, it is easy to justify a rejection of change by applying, with varying degrees of sincerity, the following formula: I am, needless to say, in favor of a certain kind of change, but not of the particular variant that is being suggested to me at this moment. The passage of time will show—or would show according to an opponent—that the bride is never beautiful enough. "The debate on tax reform has shown, as expected," notes a journalist (Jacques Fauvet), "that those very members who are demanding it are never actually satisfied with the one proposed." This "unwritten law" also applied, it appears, to con-

stitutional reform (*Le Monde*, March 25, 1954). "They want a Europe of course, but not this one," observed a "European" (Robert Lecourt) of those less enthusiastic than himself, "just as they want tax reform, but never the one actually proposed, or administrative reform, but never the one actually suggested" (A.N., November 27, 1953; *J.O.*, p. 5634). Several years later, a man of the same persuasion (Maurice Faure) was still referring to "those who claim to be in favor of a European community, but not this particular one" (A.N., July 5, 1957; *J.O.* p. 3302).

40. Opposing the inclination toward immobility we find the desire for mobility. "The mobility of the French mind" Paul Robert gives as an illustration of the noun in question; to say of an object that it is *mouvant*—meaning a thing that "ceaselessly changes its position, its form, its aspect" according to the same dictionary—is usually meant as a favorable comment. Whereas "the motionless water of a pond"—one of the most often employed political images under the Third Republic—conjures up the epithets "sleeping, idle, stagnant."

In the language of love, words conveying movement play a large role. Though the woman who wiggles about too much—a type thought of as not uncommon—is said to irritate men, men claim, on the other hand, that they are often attracted by women who, having learned from their mothers' mistakes, take care not to be "lifeless" and "lumpish," and, being of a lively temperment, are not afraid of "moving about a bit." "The loving of the stupid (the *empotés* or "lumpish") . . . is not loving," says Paul Léautaud (quoted by Paul Robert under *empoté*). "A man feels in love with life," says one of Audiberti's characters, "when it moves about in front of him" (Audiberti, *La fête noire,* act 2). According to Molière (quoted by Paul Robert as an illustration of *agile*) love "can lend . . . the heaviest soul agility."

Whereas, on the one hand, a peasant talking to Jules Renard is in agreement with Montaigne when he says of his wife: "a good woman . . . she doesn't shift about. It isn't till the end that she moves" (Renard, *Journal,* p. 105), La Fontaine, on the other, voices a powerful aversion for "motionless attractions" (La Fontaine, *La fiancée du roi de Garbe*). The "plank" is, for example, some foreign woman who is likely, simply for that reason it is generally thought, to be frigid, or some girl who is just a beginner at making love ("Nineteen, a white skin, hair that smells of vanilla; and then in bed, eyes closed and arms flopping at her sides," says one of Colette's characters in *Chéri,* p. 118); agitation is a sign of pleasure. When his desire flags beside a motionless Solange, Costals conjures up the vision of Rhadidja: "Suddenly he thought . . . of that little Moroccan girl . . . whom he had called *terremoto* because, with her way of clutching, of squeezing, of shaking her man . . . she was like an earthquake trying to tear him up by the roots. . . . At this recollection, life reawakened in him, rose up . . ." (Montherlant, *Le démon du bien*, pp. 140–41).

The decline of life means the transition from agile youth through to rigid corpse, from vivacity, through torpidity, to eventual immobility.

41. Suppleness ("rippling" if need be) is seen as a quality that is, if not always admirable, certainly most useful; whereas inflexibility creates a certain uneasiness and augurs badly—even worse perhaps than a want of "firmness"—for the person to whom it is attributed: "An inflexible character that cannot be softened" (Paul Robert)—how disturbing that sounds! Moreover, Pascal includes "flexibility of thought" in his description of "acuteness of mind"; for the Cardinal de Retz "flexibility" is "of all qualities . . . the most necessary for the managing of great affairs" (Retz, *Mémoires*, p. 104). After developing at length his ideas on physiological matters, Montesquieu concludes: "It will be seen how necessary it is that the fibers of the brain should be flexible" (*Essai sur les causes qui peuvent affecter les esprits et les caractères*). One of the major types of great politicians is essentially "a monster of flexibility" (Maurice Barrès, speaking of Briand, Chamber of Deputies, January 17, 1911; Georges Bonnefous, *Histoire parlementaire de la Troisième République*, 1: 215); according to a generally held opinion in political circles, one of the groups comprised by them (the radicals) enjoys an appreciable advantage in the "game" by virtue of its "legendary flexibility."

When one is apprehensive of having to pay the dues of nobility on account of this precious quality, one can always resort to praises of that combination—as dazzling in matters of love as in matters of business—evoked by Paul Valéry when he writes of a dancer: "She was deliciously hard and inexpressibly supple" (*L'âme et la danse*, p. 138).

42. The desire to maintain the established state of things is opposed by a feeling of hostility toward "ruts," "beaten paths," and "well worn tracks"; conflicting with the cherished "featherbed comfort" of habit there is often a lively aversion to that very temptation (see chap. 2, secs. 40–46).

"Beware, beware of habits!" Montherlant cries (*Le solstice de juin*, p. 140). "Thumbing one's nose at habit" tends to be experienced as a moment of joy, in imagination at least, whereas the spectacle of something being renewed, merely continued, can easily produce a certain feeling of displeasure. André Gide speaks of "the dreariness of habit" (La tentative amoureuse, p. 31), and the heroine of *Bonjour tristesse* says of her father: "He wasn't

really suffering from or being eaten away by anything but habit
. . . as I myself was" (Françoise Sagan, *Bonjour tristesse*, p. 164).

43. To persevere in an established state of things is, it is often
felt, to suffer a fall from grace.

"Habit . . . weakens but stabilizes, it leads to disintegration, but
it makes it last indefinitely," declares Proust (*A l'ombre des
jeunes filles en fleurs*, p. 644), while a political leader (Pierre
Mendès-France), seeing the country gripped by "immobilism"—
a conventional attitude under the Fourth Republic—referred to
"this interminable trudging round and round a rut in which an
entire nation is becoming embedded" (A.N., June 9, 1954; *J.O.*,
p. 2855).

Those who were known, under the Third Republic, as "the
professors of energy" clamored for the abandonment of all ruts
(defended at that period by "master enchanters") since to persevere in them was to condemn oneself to becoming "soft and
sleepy" (Montaigne, *Essais*, bk. 1, chap. 26), to pass from
drowsiness into numbness, in other words into weakness and
paralysis.

44. These dangers spur one on to the great effort by which
one "tears oneself up" out of the rut.

But how difficult it is to make the decision! And even more so
to translate such a decision into action! In *La fugitive*, the narrator, refusing to leave with his mother, resolves to remain in
Venice. But at the very last moment, he joins her all the same—
"thanks to the unforeseeable defensive power of inveterate habit,
thanks to the hidden reserves . . . that it hurls into the mêlée at
the last moment" (Proust, *La fugitive*, p. 655). "I am utterly
amazed," Gide notes, "at my having managed to travel occasionally. Far from giving way to a temptation, I had to make an effort
to set out every time" (*Journal 1889–1939*, p. 512).

This being so, a "shock" coming from outside may be seen
as extremely valuable, even indispensable. If it is a long time
coming, then we may try to administer a "jolt" of our own in order
to achieve the same end. "Writing of the politician who was prime
minister in the spring of 1940, another politician (Anatole de
Monzie) writes that "Paul Reynaud's mind, whether during his
time as minister of finance or while he was premier, was entirely
absorbed by his search for the psychological shock" (Monzie,
Ci-devant, p. 231). One of the Free French military leaders
(Georges Catroux) referring to the Vichy forces in Syria, wrote:
"A grave moral shock is essential to shake this profound apathy"
(letter to Charles de Gaulle, November 3, 1940; de Gaulle,
L'appel, pp. 366–67)—a routine remark that is applied to a great
many situations.

45. But when one has succeeded in tearing oneself out of the

rut, one often becomes very quickly aware that the "adventure" one has entered upon is developing into another routine; what was intended to lighten my life eventually becomes a burden to it. One of the great themes of French light comedy, for example, is the lover who before long begins to look like a second husband, the mistress who is transformed into a second wife. Here is a "very Parisian" character in a novel talking to his friend about that friend's wife: " 'I envy you, I wish I were in your shoes!' 'Aren't you ashamed, you with all your women?' 'But that's just it, it's always the other fellow's I want, the one I haven't got. . . . My life is horribly channeled, governed by timetables, there's no place for the unexpected, for adventure; all those dates at exact times, it's so wearing" (Jean-Louis Curtis, *Les justes causes*, pp. 255–56).

46. To gain a better understanding of the conflict between the desire for movement and that of immobility, one ought first to look more closely at certain experiences of the child. Here are a few speculations on this matter.

"Keep still," is an order addressed to the child by parents and teachers with both vigor and tenacity, and in a great variety of situations. The good child is often the child that does not fidget; the French metaphor for goodness in the child is the immobile statue in church. "Wherever I put him, there he is still when I get back," one of the mothers interviewed by Charlotte Roland exclaimed with delight. "He's a good boy, he loves his mother." A child psychologist, talking to a mother about her son's homework, asks: "In what way do you make sure he does it properly? Do you make sure he keeps his nose in the book, do you stop him shifting his legs about?" (*L'école des parents*, May 1952, p. 35). Another child psychologist (André Berge) feels it his duty to remind parents that "it is necessary for children to move about, to play, to yell sometimes, and not to feel restricted in any of their impulses" (Berge, *Education familiale*, p. 86). "Never a day goes by," states another pediatrician, "without my having a child brought to me for 'instability.' . . . But this is in fact a normal state for the child" (C. Koupernik, *L'école des parents*, March 1956, p. 27).

Nevertheless, grown-ups are often acutely irritated, secretly terrified, by the brimming excitability of the children around them, "I was the one who abandoned Marc," said a father who had just left his three-year-old son in a *métro* station corridor. "He was more than we could cope with; he was always hungry and he got on our nerves because he fidgeted about so" (Combat, October 4 and 5, 1958).

Grown-ups (as I have already noted) are very prone to take

the child's inability to "keep still," either at home or at school, for a pathological symptom; an inability that suggests to specialists the broad symptom of "motor instability," otherwise known as "the fidgets." Corresponding to the insistence upon immobility there is the terrible image of the unstable child with its "anarchic wobbling, its agitation, its stamping, its fiddling with any available object on meal table or desk, its insuppressible grimaces, chewings, giggles, gurgles, and chatter" (Gilbert Robin, *Les difficultés scolaires chez l'enfant*, p. 100). In school, there is a dread of children that "constantly fidget with their arms and legs, move their chairs about, push their desks, drop their erasers . . ." (Maurice Debesse, *L'élève difficile*, p. 7). How reassuring it is that the blast of a whistle can instantly cut short the unleashed chaos of a play period!

The disorder produced by the child's mobility is painful to contemplate and tiresome to repair. Here is another of Charlotte Roland's mothers explaining the measures she imposes upon her children when putting them to bed: "I've always fastened the bedclothes with a diaper grip, but now I use an extra grip to fasten the nightdress at the same time. In that way I've got the children into the habit of not wiggling, of not moving about in their beds. I've made them understand that beds aren't places for doing gymnastics. I don't like them to move the pillows or pull the bedclothes about, and all the other things children do as long as they haven't been got into the habit of keeping still."

The child's movements also constitute a threat to grown-ups' cherished possessions. Here is a little girl in a contemporary novel:

"What bothered Flore was that she could scarcely move about at all inside the apartment . . . it was too full of things . . . dreading her acts of vandalism, she [the mother] pursued Flore with her cries. 'Don't sit on the runner!' Or else: 'That's it, now she's going to smash my shell for me!' . . .

"Flore, on the other hand, was always in the process of banging herself against everything, of knocking something over. 'My things, my lovely things!' her mother would cry. . . .

"Flore preferred to stay in her room. . . . But even in her room she still could not move much. Her mother had put piles of things in there too" (Jean-François Revel, *Histoire de Flore*, pp. 9–10).

"There's a punishment I give her sometimes," explains another of Charlotte Roland's interviewees, "of sitting her down on a chair and not letting her move for a while." The child may also find itself put in a corner or out on the landing, shut up in the box room, sent to its room and made to go to bed, deprived of an outing: all forms of immobility that are supposed to be both unpleasant and calming.

On the other hand, grown-ups are as horrified by laziness in a child as they are terrified by the fidgets; and when important occasions require movements, these are forthwith insisted upon instead of being forbidden. Here is a small Paris park in a working-class area as observed by Montherlant: "Around the seats, the urchins . . . were being chivvied by the charged-up batteries they were unfortunate enough to have as mothers.— 'Don't touch!'—'Why not?'—'You mustn't touch things.' The kid would try something else.—'Will you stop running!'—'Why?'— 'Because.' The kid went on to something else.—'Play, for heaven's sake, can't you. I didn't bring you here to stand around looking dopey!' " (Montherlant, *Les célibataires*, pp. 182–83). And here is a play period in another novel: "Flore . . . refused to run about during play periods, despite the orders conveyed to her by the assistant teacher, who saw this immobility as a first step toward vice" (Revel, *Histoire de Flore*, p. 33).

47. It is this conflict between the tendency toward immobility and the desire for movement that seems to produce the interest shown in various kinds of small-scale mobility, whether amorous, furious, simply pleasant, or indeterminate in their emotional shading. Into this category come the beings or things that are seen or imagined as quivering, shuddering, wriggling, teeming, swarming, trembling, bubbling, vibrating, sparkling, shaking, or fluttering.

48. The object in the grip of such movements nevertheless remains in the same place. "Quivering immobility of an animal or dancer," Paul Robert gives as an illustration of the participle in question. "I feel my statue shivering," says the *Jeune parque*, while the roof of the *Cimetière marin*, which "flutters among the tombs," is also "still." To Montherlant, as a soldier in the Great War, a burst of artillery fire appears "quivering and immobile like the vibration of light" (Montherlant, *La relève du matin*, p. 61); looking at the Mediterranean, he perceives "the motionless . . . vibration . . . of the sea" (Montherlant, *L'histoire d'amour de la Rose de Sable*, p. 81). The world of politics sees itself as "splashing about," "fermenting" "under glass." Though André Gide may say "Nothing irritates me except things that turn round and round without getting anywhere" (*Paludes*, p. 107), it is, on the other hand, rather serious to be thought of as the sort who "prevents things from going round," who "puts a spoke in the wheel."

49. In general, there is evidently great attraction in a situation that is, in certain respects, in motion, while at the same time

being, in a way, motionless. In *Le cimetière marin,* Valéry speaks of "so much marble . . . trembling on so many waves," and in *La jeune parque,* of "the mobile and supple mummy." Though a man who likes things kept down to earth may rebel at this point: "Barrès . . . does he know what he's trying to say? . . . We must stay at home near our dead, fine. We should expand our energies far and wide, fine. We must combine the two, oh! forget it!" (Renard, *Journal,* p. 834).

50. *Plus ça change.* . . . What could be more normal than the combination of a moving surface and immoveable depths, after the model of the sea, which is only agitated on the surface? Under the Fourth Republic, for instance, there were constant reminders that "in this country, so much criticized for the instability of its governments, the same men have been governing and applying the same policy for many years" (Pierre Mendès-France, A.N., June 9, 1954; *J.O.,* p. 2855). "The fall of a government," declared another leader (Edgar Faure), "ought to signify the condemnation of a policy. One changes governments in order to change policies. Yet no ministerial crisis has had such a signification for a long time now" (*Le Monde,* March 27, 1953). "Today," another politician (Edmond Barrachin) confirmed, two months before the collapse of the regime, "the fall of a government does not signify a change of policy but simply a change of prime minister" (A.N., March 11, 1958; *J.O.,* p. 1532).

And what is more, it is precisely the change of facade that may enable the depths to remain undisturbed. Thus we find Charles de Gaulle writing of the governmental crisis during the "phony war": "Without anyone actually advocating some other military policy for which the means were not available, everyone was nevertheless venting his uneasiness and bitterness against the one in force. In conformity with its usual habits, the regime, incapable of adopting the measures that would have assured success, but searching for a way of providing both themselves and public opinion with a red herring, forced a ministerial crisis" (de Gaulle, *L'appel,* pp. 24–25).

51. Akin to this there is the great constellation within which one is allowed to "renew the lease" in fact, on condition that one innovates in intention or in sketch form: an extremely common attitude of the imaginary rebel with an explorer's soul and a stay-at-home nature. "They all say things have got to change and they get ready to vote for the same people again." Imagination—the madwoman in the attic—thus guarantees that the management of the house remains always in the same hands.

52. In accordance with a reaction akin to the one just noted, one only changes when compelled to by force. As in the case—

according to a widespread belief in political circles—of those who governed during the Fourth Republic; just as their predecessors under the Third Republic, according to a high-ranking official who was also a great writer, "persisted in always confronting the French nation with the event, never with the age" (Jean Giraudoux, *Sans pouvoirs*, p. 54).

53. "Solely governed by their present apprehension of good and bad," like the Beotians, "the dullest witted of all the Greeks" referred to by Montesquieu (*Considérations sur les causes de la grandeur des Romains et de leur décadence*, chap. 5), the leaders of the country are thus thought of as resembling a certain politician under the Third Republic (Ferdinand Sarrien), described by a colleague as follows: "Action was repugnant to his nature . . . which dreaded . . . displeasing anyone. . . . Sarrien's dream was to have none but friends in every camp" (Emile Combes, *Mon ministère*, p. 229). And indeed, if I am aspiring to accumulate the greatest possible number of "accessions to power" before "going down for the last time," it is essential that I should not imprudently risk "displeasing" any given group or individual; though it is a risk necessarily entailed by action. "Insofar as a calculated . . . policy entails choices," a former premier (Pierre Mendès-France) reminds us, "it is bound in the first place to displease a section of the country." So that "by attempting to go against no one's wishes one condemns oneself to immobilism" (*Le Monde*, April 10, 1953). But in a time of governmental instability, "the race for portfolios" requires that the would-be minister should "attempt to go against no one's wishes," and for at least two reasons. He will be in danger of having to leave such and such an office before a particular policy that is initially displeasing has time to become a "paying proposition"; and at the next ministerial crisis—which prudence will oblige him to suppose imminent—he might very well already be in need of those he has been clumsy enough to displease. All this being so, "Above all no fuss!" is a maxim it will involve grave risks to his career to disregard. He will therefore be inclined to act only in order to ward off difficulties already apparent, difficulties in the face of which "keeping things as they are" would cause even more displeasure, and which will make his action appear to be determined by *force majeure*.

54. "To go out and meet problems halfway" may thus appear rather unusual. No one openly rejects the notion that one should look ahead, of course. But it does tend to take on the status of a counsel of perfection, one inapplicable to the difficult circumstances with which one is actually struggling, in the midst of which all that one can attempt is to "face up," "day to day" and "in accordance with the needs of the day," to events "as they occur,"

and "under the pressure" of those events. "It is true that I am young," said one deputy of the extreme right (Jean-Marie Le Pen), "but ever since I have been a citizen of this country, the leitmotiv I have constantly heard, the one characteristic of French politics, has been: too late, too late, always too late! The salutary maxim 'Prevention is better than cure' seems to have been relegated exclusively to edifying books for small children" (A.N., November 12, 1957; J.O., p. 4725). Anyone who takes such maxims seriously is in danger of being considered a jackass.

To announce—as one prime minister (Pierre Mendès-France) did when introducing a number of questions (all to do with North Africa)—a resolve to deal with problems before they arise: "It is another thing to resolve them in cold blood, as we intend to do" (A.N., December 10, 1954; J.O., p. 6042) seems to be a boast rarely followed by the action to justify it. One day, the chairman of the Assembly's Finance Committee (Charles Barangé) emphasized that "the finance debate . . . we are now embarking upon presents itself under very different conditions from those that have marked so many of the other debates in which we have taken part since the Liberation." Generally, this experienced politician continued, the government has been "under the pressure of difficulties" that "required immediate action"; but this time, "the prime minister is asking us . . . to assume . . . responsibilities in cold blood that we have been accustomed . . . to assume only in the heat of events" (A.N., August 5, 1954; J.O., p. 3860).

On another occasion, a prime minister (Edgar Faure) told the house that: "There has been something satisfying in these meetings of the French and Tunisian delegations, leading as they have to subsequent agreements. Those agreements were reached as the result of a clearsighted act, without waiting for events to outstrip it or for necessity to appear threatening."

But a few moments later, the premier "let the cat out of the bag." Addressing an opponent of the agreements, assuring him that he, the premier, had "followed" him when he "spoke of the Tunisians nearest to us," he added: "But it is perhaps on behalf of those very people that we ought to have made an effort earlier, an effort to bring them the elements of development they were demanding of us, without waiting for them to be left behind by the current with which we find ourselves faced today" (C.R., August 3, 1955; J.O., pp. 2189–90).

55. "In the industrial field, our country holds a world record," a finance minister announced in the autumn of 1957; "in the years since 1952, it is in France that the fastest rate of increased productivity has been recorded: 10 per cent per annum" (Pierre

Pflimlin, A.N., November 14, 1957; *J.O.*, p. 4783). Since the state plays such a considerable role in the French economy, this manifestation of the new "dynamic France" could scarcely have occurred without its active collaboration. Yet as the world of politics conceives it, the state appears to be principally a department of the old "static France."

For according to the majority belief noted above, government, parliament, and civil service departments all act only when they have "their backs to the wall," "when their hands are forced," "because they cannot do otherwise," when "they are unable to avoid" a decision other than that of "maintaining the *status quo,*" when it is no longer possible "to put off settling the accounts."

After a vote in the Assembly in favor of his successor (Edgar Faure), a former prime minister (Pierre Mendès-France) observed that: "The prime minister, furnished as he is with a vote of confidence, has now been granted liberty of action." M. Mendès-France then went on to demand that M. Faure "should use [that liberty of action] and not wait until events impose a choice upon him that ought to spring from his own resolve (*L'Express.* October 20, 1955).

But since such a thing appears highly improbable, such an exhortation assumes the aspect of an attack. Almost a half-century ago, an observer (Robert de Jouvenel) expressed a suspicion that members of the government "were getting into the habit of never acting any more except when forced to by events" (Jouvenel, *La république des camarades,* p. 141), a notion that rings a little odd today, but which is easy enough to change, with modification of the verb, into the most worn-out of clichés: they are in the habit . . . .

56. So politicians claiming to be innovators may be reduced to basing their calculations on the anticipation of a *force majeure* exerted in the right direction.

When a newly appointed prime minister (Félix Gaillard) was anxious to refute the prediction that the cohabitation of opposing forces within his government would render it incapable of action, he announced that "governmental immobilism is not to be feared immediately; since events will impose action upon us in several fields" (*Combat,* November 4, 1957).

Given these conditions, there are a few who conceive the plan of throwing the whole country into the water so as to make it learn to swim. One of the favorite arguments of the "Europeans" in favor of the C.E.D. and the common market was that France would never consent to "renovation" unless subjected to the "electric shock treatment" of entering a united Europe in which, if it remained in its ruts, it would know that it was condemned to "sink without a trace."

So we find one of the leaders of this persuasion (Pierre-Henri Teitgen) daring to say in the Assembly itself, on the subject of the common market: "And from the general point of view of our economy, what do we all of us say . . . when we study our general situation objectively . . . ? We say quite plainly that our methods, our habits, our ways of doing things must all undergo a profound transformation. . . . But shall we bring it about, dear fellow members, shall we undertake it, this gigantic effort, with grace and good will, if there is no external force obliging us to do so? When we discussed the ratification of the Schuman Plan, we listened to the lament of a great many of our steel producers, who explained to us that they were in no fit state to cope with German competition. . . . We went ahead nevertheless . . .and under the pressure of that common market, our industrialists, the state, and successive governments have been forced to make the necessary effort. The effort that led us to build in Lorraine, for example, an industrial complex that is one of the finest and most productive in all Europe. Without the pressures created by the common coal and steel market, I believe we would not have made that effort. . . . If we abandon this treaty [the Common Market treaty] . . . we shall also be dispensing with a compelling force that is certainly indispensable to our recovery" (A.N., July 6, 1957; *J.O.,* pp. 3363–64).

57. The most acceptable innovation is still that which can be presented as merely a ratification of something that is in any case in the process of taking place, or has already been achieved. This was an important argument in persuading the Assembly to agree to the rearmament of West Germany; it is also a method that has no lack of applications in "pure politics." According to an observer describing the parliamentary situation toward the end of a long term (that of the secretary general of the Socialist Party): "M. Guy Mollet does not seem to be in the position of having to look for a fresh majority. He seems to want to leave things to trickle out within the Palais-Bourbon itself. It is solely in the event of the Communists' taking up a stand against the government and of the latter's being supported on the other hand, in a more or less constant fashion, by the center and certain representatives of the Socialist-Republicans, that M. Guy Mollet would consider that a new majority had manifested itself and think of reshuffling his government in consequence. . . . But to the prime minister's way of thinking, the situation is not yet ripe. He is not concerned with anticipating a possible new majority by reshuffling cabinet but, on the contrary, solely with consolidating it at such time when circumstances demand it. These tactics have the advantage of avoiding discrepancies within the Socialist Party itself, to a certain extent . . . since the prime

minister is making it clear that his course of action is being imposed upon him by the facts of parliamentary life themselves" (Georges Rotvand, *Bulletin du Centre d'études politiques*, May 2, 1956).

58. Parents sometimes attempt to "calm down" their children with the strap; under the French Republic, a great many acts on the part of the authorities are supposed to be attempts at "appeasing" certain groups with loud voices and an ability to make dark threats. Politics then becomes, in the words of one journalist (N. Jacquefont) an activity "that consists in stopping up, day by day, the hole from which the loudest voice is coming" (*Le Monde*, December 25, 1953). A political leader (Pierre Pflimlin) confirms that, normally, "the government tries to stop up the holes as they appear beneath its feet" (quoted by *France-Observateur*, May 23, 1957), though this can always be justified by adding that "governing people is not the same as pleasing them" (René Pléven, U.D.S.R. Congress, October 21, 1951; *L'Année politique*, 1951, p. 377).

"Very often," one deputy recalls, "the Palais-Bourbon is said to be a house without windows. . . . Nothing could be more untrue. There is much more justification for criticism on the score of its being far too open to the thousand and one variations and sudden surges of opinion, too accessible to any and every claim from outside. . . ." (Jacques Isorni, *Le silence est d'or*, p. 14). But in order for politicians to become "accessible" to such a "claim," it must often have assumed the form of a *force majeure*—the only kind of "claim" to which it is normal to yield; preventive action is forbidden.

Here is how a president of the Assembly's pensions committee (Lucien Begoin) referred to the economy measures taken by Félix Gaillard's government with regard to ex-servicemen, and the revoking of those measures by the same government: "The way in which ex-servicemen reacted to this violation of the law and of the commitments made them is no secret. Their riposte was so powerful that it has not been without its influence . . . on the tabling of the justificatory letter we have before us today" (A.N., March 26, 1958; *J.O.*, p. 1986). Toward the end of the Fourth Republic's last winter, a great many policemen besieged the Palais-Bourbon demanding an increase in their salaries. A leading politician (François Mitterand) recounts the sequel: "In the end, the demonstrators obtained the satisfactions they had hitherto demanded in vain, and their leaders were in a position to claim that the march on the Palais-Bourbon had paid off." He also refers to the events leading up to the march: "And yet, for several weeks beforehand, the prefect of police had kept the minister for the interior informed of the growing discontent among his subordinates, the minister for the interior had discussed the matter with the minister of finance, the dispute had been gone into by interministerial committees, and that very morning the National Assembly had voted a discreet increase" (*La Nef*, April 1958, p. 11).

A deputy (Jean de Lipkowski), insisting upon the distressing situation of the country's war widows, was thus able to ask: "Is it because this particular social category does not manifest its displeasure in a noisy and disruptive manner that it is so obstinately refused what is owed to it?" (A.N., March 26, 1958; *J.O.*, p. 1995).

If one invariably "deals with whatever is most pressing," the "management" will lack continuity. Its progress will look like that attributed by a satirical newspaper (*Le canard enchaîné*) to an aging politician (Henri Queuille), whose infirmity was often taken as a symbol of the entire regime: "moving along like a dead leaf fluttering in the wind" (*Le canard enchaîné*, December 16, 1953). Under the variety of pressures thus produced, movements in quite opposite directions will ensue. A deputy (Pierre de Chevigné) describes as "habitual meandering," "this jerky and vacillating policy in which weakness succeeds toughness at the whim of the latest squall or of parliamentary arithmetic" (A.N., July 28, 1955; *J.O.*, p. 4438).

59. Or else one is faced with an acute crisis which must be reduced—with a remedy certainly directed at no more than the symptoms—to a convenient state of latency sufficient for one to ignore it again until the next outbreak: "It is not the symptoms of crisis, it is the crisis in full spate . . . that imposes . . . whatever action is strictly necessary . . . upon governments" (Charles Morazé, *Les Français et la République*, p. 133)—the converse of which is the frequently proclaimed desire for a total and freely granted reorganization of some given field.

In the sphere of agricultural policy, a journalist (Pierre Drouin) has extrapolated a particular rut from his observations of various departments: "The policy of simply stopping up gaps will continue. All these various organizations will teem with feverish activity whenever the market is affected by some disturbance, then subside into lethargy again during between-crisis periods" (*Le Monde*, October 16, 1953). Discussing the economic decisions made under the Fourth Republic, the same journalist wrote, after the regime had ended: "France has become accustomed, during recent years . . . to 'choices' determined solely by the concern to resolve some particular burning problem (the remedy applied immediately creating difficulties in another area)" (*Le Monde,* December 28 and 29, 1958). In the words of a deputy whom many, under the Fourth Republic, considered a major representative of the nation's large-scale employers (André Boutemy), speaking on behalf of a committee set up to control the use of military financial allocations: "The impression that remains is that in the realm of military policy we are . . . simply in the tow of events, as we continue to be in that general policy. In both cases . . . one ought rather to talk of absence of policy. There are no solid foundations to our activities as a nation, no rules governing our actions, no firm objective. We react to everything as it comes. . . . We merely try to resolve the difficulties deliberately created for us from outside with as little trouble as possible" (C.R., March 12, 1958; *J.O.*, p. 481). The obscure power that imposes so deadly a law—André Boutemy speaks of "a lack of will or imagination"—creates the danger that routine exhortations will seem entirely devoid of force, as with this one, made by a former minister with military powers (Jean Crouzier): "Our military policy ought not to be a day-to-day policy, devoid of all ambition except that of satisfying whatever is most pressing in the vague hope that better days will come in some indeterminate future" (A.N., February 27, 1958; *J.O.*, p. 1098). And here is a deputy (Valéry Giscard d'Estaing) wondering why the attempt at constitutional reform begun during the regime's last winter "arouses no interest, and even less enthusiasm." Among other reasons, he puts forward the following: "We did not set out from any general political idea. We . . . worked like garage mechanics setting out to find the cause of a breakdown" (A.N., March 18, 1958; *J.O.*, p. 1630).

During the autumn of 1953, the "spectacular" demands for independence staged by Vietnamese nationalists forced the Assembly to debate the Indochinese question, a thing it had avoided doing throughout three years of war. One member of parliament (Raymond Dronne) observed at that time: "The debate on Indochina that we have been demanding for so long is at last being undertaken in our Assembly. It is likely that . . . it would have been evaded even longer had not a new development alerted public opinion. It is the fate of our Assembly never to come to grips with problems until they are posed in some dramatic manner, to be perpetually towed behind events instead of anticipating them. It took the August strikes, for example, to make it involve itself in the social problem at home, and the demonstrations of our farmers' anger to make it take an interest in agricultural problems. The tradition continues. The present debate on Indochina is a direct consequence of the emotion aroused by the recent statement by the National Vietnamese Congress in Saigon on relations between the state of Vietnam and France" (A.N., October 23, 1953; *J.O.*, p. 4545). Alluding to events in Indochina, another deputy (Vincent Badie) spoke on the same occasion of "questions that every Frenchman is asking himself and that we can no longer allow ourselves to evade" (A.N., October, 1953; *J.O.*, p. 4595). What an extremity!

60. "Monsieur," the Cardinal de Retz tells us, "never acted unless under pressure. . . . Of all the means one could use to exert such pressure, the most efficacious was that of fear. . . . [He] felt . . . a natural inclination in himself to refrain from action when he was not frightened" (Cardinal de Retz, *Mémoires*, pt. 2, p. 589): a portrait that, where the world of politics is concerned, seems very modern. "An Italian nobleman" once said to Montaigne, referring to the French, "that we needed to see danger with our own eyes and touch it with our own hands before we could be frightened by it" (Montaigne, *Essais*, bk. 2, chap. 11); that too seems topical enough.

There can be no serious question of taking action, then, unless one is placed under threat of imminent disaster. The action that does impose itself without any possibility of evasion is that of "filling in the holes as they occur." One deputy (Valéry Giscard d'Estaing), commenting on the French economy's unpreparedness for the common market, remarked that "it is as though there were a tendency to wait for some external compulsion before taking action. It seems as though there is a desire to wait for the difficulties that the common market will produce before undertaking the necessary reforms. This would be a sort of method of government by catastrophe" (A.N., January 17, 1957; *J.O.*, p. 94).

According to one widespread current of opinion in political circles, the country will not emerge from the "ruts" in which it is said to be "embedded" except under the demographic pressure exerted by those born after 1940; only such a massive factor will ever succeed in "shattering" the "fossilized structures" with which the country is believed to be encumbered, but to which it remains extremely attached, while waiting for the *force majeure* that will compel it to cast them off. Similarly, according to Charles de Gaulle while he was still waiting for his moment under the Fourth Republic, only "a serious crisis" could "revive" "the current of desire for the public good" in the country (press conference, December 4, 1954)—or "drive it ignominiously into greatness of soul," as Tristan Bernard put it.

61. This means that one acts, not in order to achieve a better state of things, but in order to prevent the worst. There is a great readiness to admit that the recommended "solution" has many

disadvantages; but does it not, after all, avoid the catastrophe that would ensue in its absence?

Under the Fourth Republic, the concessions made by certain groups, clans, or individuals in order to permit the "solution" of various governmental crises were often justified by those who decided upon them, not so much because of the advantages that the new combination would afford them as because of the grave dangers that would result from a continuation of the interregnum. The arguments put forward by the Center-Left and the Left in order to explain why they accepted the consequences of May 13 are often of the same kind. For instance, at a conference of the M.R.P. on August 26, 1958, at which the already imminent referendum was discussed, this "reasoning" was "taken up" by several of those attending: "When the referendum campaign begins, it will no longer be a question of deciding whether such or such an article is satisfactory or not, but simply of voting 'for or against de Gaulle.' . . . And it is not possible, in fact, to be against de Gaulle without risking chaos" (*Le Monde*, August 28, 1958). If it is a question of ratifying a treaty or not, this is the argument that is likely to become dominant at the decisive moment: Of course, dear fellow, I know this innovation has a great many disadvantages; but just think of the really catastrophic consequences of a refusal to ratify it! Such was the principal argument that almost overcame the "reservations" about the C.E.D., for example, and actually succeeded in overcoming those about the U.E.O. In both cases, as the time of decision approached, the arguments putting forward the advantages of either "framework" paled into insignificance beside the apocalyptic image of what would happen if they were rejected: "resumption" by the "Anglo-Saxons" of a "peripheral strategy," "unilateral" rearmament of West Germany under their auspices. . . . In order for the decision to be "extracted," it had to be, to a large extent, a "gesture of resignation," and also a gesture of ratification in a double sense: free consent to a treaty negotiated by the government, but also the compulsory codification of an imminent reality that it was thought impossible to prevent. One of the incentives used by the former C.E.D. supporters to make sure that the "alternative solution" (the U.E.O.) was rejected was to make their principal argument in favor of the C.E.D. a reality, to wit, that its rejection was likely to "lead to chaos." On the other hand, after the Assembly's first rejection of the U.E.O., on December 24, 1954, at the time when this decision was being "reversed" by the sudden veering of opinion manifested by a score or two of members (on December 30), "it was assuredly with great relief that several parts of the house greeted the prime minister's unambiguous declaration that 'our allies would not agree to fresh negotiations' " (Raymond Barrillon in *Le Monde,* December 29, 1954).

Six months later, an opponent (Edmond Barrachin) of the Franco-Tunisian agreements was able to point out that "we are told: if you don't vote for these agreements . . . it means chaos" (A.N., July 7, 1955; *J.O.,* p. 3678). And another (Raymond Pinchard) addressed the prime minister in the following terms: "You will certainly not fail to tell us that the ratification of the Franco-Tunisian agreements . . . is . . . inevitable and that not to ratify those agreements would be an even greater cause for apprehension than their ratification. The Assemblies have already heard this argument from resignation with reference to both the European Defence Community and the Paris Agreements" (C.R., August 3, 1955; *J.O.,* p. 2176).

Fifteen years beforehand, the Assemblies had heard (at Vichy, on July 10, 1940) the argument of a leading politician of the Third Republic (Pierre-Etienne Flandin) in favor of the projected delegation of powers to Marshal Pétain: "If the project were rejected, what would happen in France? What would be said abroad? Terrible damage would be caused to the country. I therefore consider its adoption necessary" (quoted by Jacques Benoist-Méchin, *Soixante jours qui ébranlèrent l'Occident,* 3:226). Another argument (by Pierre Laval) heard at the same time was: "I have mounted this platform in order to emphasize an argument put forward by M. Flandin: 'If you did not vote for this project, what would happen?' " (ibid., pp. 229–30).

Fifteen years later, the Assembly was perfectly willing to "vote for" another "project" already in course of execution (the Suez expedition): "The argument that won the support of the great majority of members was finally this: 'The government is conscious of the gravity of the decisions it has just taken; it is conscious also, and even more so, of the gravity of the consequences that a failure to make decisions would have entailed' " (Jacques Fauvet, *Le Monde,* November 1, 1956).

62. In such a context, the havoc that would ensue from any course of action other than that envisaged frequently appears to its supporters as of a much higher order than the disadvantages it will bring; which understandably makes them to feel an absence of choice. Noting the contrast between one leader (Edgar Faure), inclined to say that facts decide the issue, and another (Pierre Mendès-France), who is an advocate of reasoned choice, an observer (Michel Martin du Bois) had the following comment to make on "P.M.F.'s" term in office: "An analysis of M. Mendès-France's weekly speeches suggests . . . that the man who believes

in choice has justified his policy with arguments fundamentally very closely related to those used . . . by Edgar Faure. In Indochina, there was nothing to do but sign the armistice; in Tunisia the only solution was to negotiate with Destour; in Europe it was impossible not to rearm West Germany. We are not concerned here with evaluating the appropriateness of the measures decided upon by this politic leader. What we are concerned with is to demonstrate the recurrence of a certain type of argument, a veritable platitude of parliamentary rhetoric. Yet, if the word 'choice' has any meaning at all, it signifies that, in the face of a given situation, there are several possible solutions. . . . Whereas, in fact, M. Mendès-France has never presented the acts of his government in this form, but, quite to the contrary, has put them forward as the only solutions open to him in the various circumstances in which he found himself placed" (*Esprit*, September 1958, pp. 220–21).

4

DISTINCTIONS AND MIXTURES

1. The course of things carries them toward a state of mixture, the nature of things maintains them in that state.

"Everything is mixed in men," declares Vauvenargues (quoted by Paul Robert under *mélange* (mixture). According to Chamfort: "In things, everything is *mixed dealings;* in men, everything is *interlocking pieces.* In the moral as well as the physical world, everything is a mixture: nothing is one, nothing is pure" (Chamfort, *Maximes et anecdotes*, p. 36). To the degree to which one happens to examine an object closely—whether it is a man, a group, or a set of laws and decrees—one perceives, behind a facade of proper compartmentalization, the most amazing mixtures. "Everything in France is mixed together," affirms one observer (Emmanuel Berl). "In Proust, Jupien's niece, a little dressmaker, is a neighbor of the duc de Guermantes: moreover, she ends up being adopted by the baron de Charlus. I wonder whether any English novelist of the Victorian period could have depicted a family in which the alcoholic laundrymaid is a cousin of the great banker, in which the rebel miner of *Germinal*, the mechanic in *La bête humaine*, and Nana, the theatrical aspirant turned whore, are all related to the prime minister? . . . This inextricable web of kinships and sexual encounters . . . produces a network of secret solidarities between the militant communist and the blacksmith, between the high-up in the civil service and the village artisan" (Emmanuel Berl, *La France irréelle*, pp. 65–67).

2. Mixture is a various thing: some mixtures are "delicious," others are "frightful" or "monstrous." Though a general survey indicates that aversion is probably predominant.

"Beware of mixtures," Paul Robert gives under that noun.

"Nothing good comes from mixtures," André Gide tells us (*Journal des faux-monnayeurs*, p. 62), and: "Mixing is not a source of beauty" (ibid., p. 94). Having affirmed that "it is politics that have spoiled everything in France," the mouthpiece of a movement (Pierre Poujade's) directed against the established government adds: "Their sort of politics is the art of mixing and confusing everything" (*Fraternité française*, May 5, 1956).

3. Love is a mixture.

"Lovers who mingle their gazes and their sighs. A kiss that would mingle their two beings" Paul Robert gives as an illustration of the verb in question. The presence of male and female garments thrown down pell-mell in a room plays an important role in many divorce cases; and one of Armand Salacrou's characters is able to exclaim: "Look at his cigarette ends and hers with lipstick on them . . . all mixed together, mingled, just as their bodies have been for six whole months in a bed" (Salacrou, *Dieu le savait*, act 3). "To make an idyll out of the love of two metals," Jules Renard proposes to himself. "First of all we see them inert and cold between the fingers of the mediating professor, then, as the fire begins to act, mingling themselves, impregnating themselves with one another and identifying themselves in an absolute fusion such as even the wildest of loves will never attain" (Renard, *Journal*, p. 49). Human beings must, in effect, content themselves with an inferior degree of union, albeit one in which "the lips tear themselves away from the skin with as much difficulty as postage stamps from old envelopes" (ibid., p. 111). Is it not possible—frightful and delicious idea—that those who have mingled in love may nevermore "unstick" themselves from one another? Lovers, Paul Valéry says, "have knotted the day that is ending to the day being born, with the knots of their limbs" (*Mélanges*, p. 319). "Why," Montherlant asks, "do not two beings who love one another ask to be buried, not in the same tomb, but in the same coffin? So that their bodies, as they decompose, will penetrate the one into the other and mingle indeed, surpassing those epidermal minglings in the bed. That, it seems to me, is love" (*Le fichier parisien*, p. 167). The same writer speaks of "the eternal astonishment that our mingling with the aqueous consort is not a 'sin,' so good is it" (*Les lépreuses*, p. 252).

Like making love, causing death also conjures up the idea of the *mêlée*, of a "confusion of combatants fighting hand to hand" (Paul Robert).

4. The two beings who mingle in love are thought of as separating themselves in many respects from the rest of the world. The desire for mixing or mingling may then manifest itself in the breaking down of such partitions: a fairly frequent theme, in literature at least.

If one's partner is not the person one desires most, why not bring the reality nearer to the desire by thinking of the other while actually kissing the one who is present? In this way, it is claimed, unfaithful husbands and wives can sometimes lighten the task of keeping their marriages going.

It is also possible for a person, quite deliberately, to introduce into an intimate relationship nuances or objects that evoke another. A lover in a novel recounts, for example: "I got into my car. Hanging from the ignition key was the fob with my initials on it given to me by Irene. Doubtless her husband also had a fob of the same kind on his ignition key. And who knows, perhaps both he and I were wearing the same gay, diagonally-striped shirts that Irene bought for us in half-dozens during sales in the big department stores. As for the toilet water, it was quite certain, openly admitted. Irene provided us both with the same so as not to be betrayed by the scent" (Jean Freustié, *Auteuil.* Paris 1954, pp. 35–36). In another story, the lover, while escorting his mistress, has a tune played that he knows to be associated for her with a previous love affair. Later on, having left that mistress, he plays their favorite tune at the time of their affair when she comes to visit him and his wife (Françoise Sagan, *Un certain sourire,* pp. 109–11, 138–39).

Not only does the idea of infidelity play its usual well-known role in life and literature, but there is also a slight emphasis put on the possibility that someone—usually a man—feels a desire, whether deep down or overt, to be deceived; that he may, without realizing it, work hard to ensuring that he is.

There are many plots that establish close contacts between several characters of the same sex who are all sharing the favors of another character of the opposite sex.

We are easily inclined to imagine that relationships, say friendships, are strengthened by the appearance of bonds provided by love. For example, the husband's friend becomes the wife's lover, the husband himself, without knowing it, being a factor in creating this relationship. Or two couples who are friends decide to "swap partners."

A person may wish to enter into contact with another who,

like him or herself, is intimately bound to a third. Seeing Lélie, whom he believes to be his wife's lover, Sganarelle exclaims: "There's my man, or rather my wife's" (Molière, *Le cocu imaginaire*, sc. 9). A mistress in a play may wish to know the wife; the wife likes to make friends with the mistress. Two men talk about the woman of whom they both are lovers, and compare their troubles.

A person may take part in acts by means of which another, to whom he or she is very close, keeps up his or her equally close relationship with a third. The lover in *Le diable au corps* helps the wife write to her husband. "A possible scene," writes Jules Renard. "The child is dead. The mother and father are in tears. But the lover takes the wife's hand, claps his hand on the husband's shoulder, and says: "Now, now, pull yourselves together! We'll make another" (Renard, *Journal*, p. 65).

Jealousy can swing round into desire. "The idea that a woman might have had relations with Albertine," Proust's narrator notes, "no longer aroused anything in me but a desire to have relations with that woman myself" (Proust, *La fugitive*, p. 599).

Over against the idea of separate attachments—in turn-of-the-century terms, home on the one hand and the love-nest on the other—we have that of the *ménage à trois* and wife-swapping. These extremes in the breaking down of partitions may be experienced as a second form of purity to set beside that depicted in *La princesse de Clèves* and *Le bal du comte d'Orgel*, in contrast with the prudent compartmentalization in time and space of the Paris of 1900.

5. Certain combinations are bad because the substances they bring into contact do not go together. There are "monstrous couplings"—certain words "shriek with terror at seeing themselves coupled with others," says J. B. Rousseau (quoted by Paul Robert under *accouplé*, coupled)—and others that are "disparate," "motley," "chequered." Aragon describes a dag that is "an appalling mixture of Saint Bernard and spaniel" (quoted by the same dictionary under *mélange*, mixture). "A contrast is agreeable, an incongruity is . . . shocking," observes Madame de Genlis (ibid., under *disparate*, incongruity or mismatch), going on to explain that "one may term incongruity . . . any opposition that is too glaring, and contrast, one that is delicate."

On the other hand there are the happy mixtures, produced in general by an adequate knowledge of how to match things. "To match (*assortir*)," Paul Robert explains, "is to put together two or more things that are suited. . ., to put together people that are suited to one another." "To choose," Monsieur Teste observes, "is the power to make, with a moment and with oneself, a pleasing whole" (Valéry, *Monsieur Teste*, p. 106). And a character in a Montherlant comedy says: "You know, I can recognize all the red wines from our country by taste, and then tell you, to complete the picture, exactly which cheese it ought to be served with at the end of the meal; there, Monsieur, that's what being French means" (Montherlant, *Brocéliande*, act 2, sc. 6).

Mixtures range, therefore, from the excellent to the appalling. On the one hand, for example, there is Paul Valéry's view of France: "Territorially, France offers a very happy proportion of mountains and plains, of river valleys and sea coasts. . . . The men that inhabit it constitute an ethnic and psychological mixture of unique complexity and quality whose elements all complement and temper one another" (Valéry, *Regards sur le monde actuel*, p. 180). On the other hand, there are the frightful results of violence: "A horrible mixture of bones and tattered flesh" says Racine (quoted by Paul Robert under *mélange*, mixture). On the morning of June 22, 1940, there was a series of sudden explosions outside the Bordeaux prefecture, where a council of ministers was in session: two tanks had, by mistake, opened fire on one another. "We were sitting there, talking together, Marshal Pétain and I," Albert Lebrun recounts, "when a tank battle broke out in front of us. . . . We said to ourselves . . . if this were the reality, what a horrible mixture of flesh and steel!" (quoted by Jacques Benoist-Méchin, *Soixante jours qui ébranlèrent l'Occident*, 2:433).

6. A mixture may threaten the integrity of the objects placed together by affecting their forms, or even completely annihilate their individual existences in order to form a new object in which they are fused.

"Well-formed" objects, whether it be a matter of stools, breasts, or words, are superior to those that are less so. Things that lose their forms fade away. In an abandoned park, "the paths can no longer be distinguished from what were once the lawns" (Paul Robert). The highest degree of destruction an object that once possessed a framework can undergo is that which involves its being crushed, smashed, and flattened until it becomes a shapeless mass. "Boredom," Paul Valéry observes, "has no form" (*Tel quel*, 1:203).

And there are some mixtures rather like certain kinds of baby food, which the mother concocts from a variety of substances that are then minced and beaten until "they are well blended": all their forms disappear in the shapeless and foul gruel that results.

"And everything mixes together until it melts into shit" (Marcel Aymé, *Le chemin des écoliers*, p. 169)—a development fre-

quently expected. "How much better to "stay beside one another
without melting together," Paul Robert gives us under *fondre* (to
melt). A less extreme variant is the confusion-mixture, creating
an object "whose elements are so mingled that it is impossible to
distinguish them" (Paul Robert defining *confus,* confused),
which casts doubt on their very existence.

7. Mixtures that are bad in normal times may nevertheless be
salutary in times of crisis, such as a daring organ transplant
when the patient is under threat of death. "Rights at the front and
duties at home, let all today . . . be mingled into one," exclaimed
Clemenceau in his ministerial address during the Great War
(November 20, 1917; quoted by Georges Bonnefous, *Histoire parlementaire de la Troisième République,* 2:346).

Given extreme conditions, certain qualities ordinarily kept
separate come together. Montherlant writes of "those extremities
of sensation in which beauty produces unease, in which pleasure
has the taste of pain, adoration that of hate, desire, or disgust"
(*La relève du matin,* p. 163).

8. Grown-ups require of the child not only that it should know
what it wants but also what that is; it is taught a system of categories that permit it to impose clearcut classifications on the
objects it encounters.

Having become a grown-up itself, the former child retains the
desire to classify things in discontinuous compartments; he often
tends not to notice the many gradations between two extremes. In
the political field, for example, the debate on German rearmament during the early fifties turned, to a certain extent, on the
question: will these measures recreate a *Wehrmacht,* or a German *General Staff?*

But, coexisting with the continuation of a certain childhood
atmosphere, there is also a certain converse tendency leading
precisely to an affirmation of the existence of numerous "half-
shades," of the possibility and the advantages of "introducing
imperceptible transitions" that will avoid a "disruption of continuity."

The most precious and useful objects and actions appear to be
"neither wholly this nor wholly that." Valéry, in a parable, says
of man:

> For the ANGEL is ANGEL and the BEAST is BEAST
> And there is nothing of the one in the other
> And nothing between them.
> But THIS ONE was neither the one nor the other
> [Valéry, *Mélange,* p. 200.]

Such and such a thing, we are inclined to say, is "this without
being this, yet being this all the same." During the first months

of the Vichy government, Marshal Pétain "confided to his intimates that 'they were a Republic without being one while being
one all the same' " (Henri du Moulin de la Barthète, *Le temps des
illusions*, p. 111). When, toward the end of the war in Indochina,
the government was considering offering Marshal Juin high office
to deal with the affair, "the result was a sort of game of hide-and-
seek, the government approaching him, without approaching,
while still approaching him, and the marshal accepting, without
accepting, while still accepting (Jacques Fauvet, *Le Monde*, June
3, 1954).

Or again, the nature of one thing in relation to two others, both
of them clearcut, can only be described as being "between the
two." Here is Paul Valéry describing a session of the French
Academy: "Joffre was attending the session. I woke him up:
'Monsieur le Maréchal, can you give us the correct definition of
the word machine gun?'—'Difficult,' said Joffre. 'It's not a field
gun, it's not a rifle. It's between the two and it goes pah, pah, pah,
pah, only very fast' " (Gaston Poulain, *Paul Valéry tel quel*, p. 26)
According to a compleat seducer's manual: "Friendship . . . is an
ambiguous sentiment, and ambiguous sentiments are the most
useful. . . . Where does love begin? Where does friendship end?
There lies between them a strip of territory . . . upon which fruitful skirmishes may well be engaged" (Dutourd, *Le petit Don
Juan*, p. 247). One of Montherlant's characters claims "to love
nothing so much as the uncertain fringe where one thing inter-
penetrates another" (Montherlant, *Pitié pour les femmes*, p.
243).

This penetration may seem so profound that one comes to see
a propinquity where the superficial glance sees a contrast. Thus
we find Paul Valéry describing Anatole France as being "lazy
when it came to reading books so enormous that they were difficult to distinguish from studies" (*Variété*, p. 726).

Yet feelings in respect of objects that manage to evade all
categories remain divided. When Léon Bloy describes Emile Zola
as "something indefinable between cow dung and rabbit drop-
pings," the mixture and its ambiguity are intended as a powerful
reinforcement to the violence of the insult.

9. When the child appears "unable to let anything alone,"
grown-ups are angry. Many a mother who manages to remain
ignorant of her child's tendency to fiddle with itself is extremely
observant when dealing with the same child's fleeting desire to
enter into unwarranted contact with objects around it. "When
they're still very small," one of Charlotte Roland's mothers tells
her, "and they try to touch something, I say 'Tch, tch' very loudly
and give them a long look. If they don't obey, I slap them." Another mother said much the same: "I've always slapped the

children, too, when they touched something; I've managed to make them stop it completely. They don't touch anything now except their own things." "Every time a small child touches anything at all," continues a third mother, "I give it a slap on its hands." Given these conditions, the child may perhaps grow up with a deeply ingrained feeling that there are a great number of things one must never touch.

10. The child is taught that such and such a mixture is a good one to make and such and such another bad. The result, in adult life, is a multiplicity of combinations between obedience and rebellion. André Gide suggests one of them in the following childhood memory: " 'You don't seem to understand, sir,' my teacher, good old Lyon, would often say, 'that certain words are made to go with certain others; there are relationships between them that there can be no question of changing.'—'But my dear M. Lyon, what can you expect; I'm afraid I believe that words should keep bad company too!' " (Gide, *Journal 1889–1939* p. 346). Proust speaks of "the . . . depravity of taste . . . that drove Sainte-Beuve to break all the alliances formed between words, to alter any even slightly customary expression" (*Sodome et Gomorrhe*, p. 1087).

But it goes without saying, in this matter as in so many others, that it is often our obedience to rules learned upon the threshold of our lives that dominates all the rest.

11. The horror of being abandoned finds its continuation in the common apprehension of a "break" between things (various sectors of the nation, for example) that ought to be closely linked; we are constantly noticing a "gap," a "weakness in the links," a "breach that has opened," a "loosening of ties," a "loss of contact" between individuals or groups that ought to "be at one." It is common, for example, to note and deplore the lack of contact between teachers and students. In the words of a report on the attitudes of a class (that of 1952) in one famous school (the *Polytechnique*), "the conversations between students and teachers could prove fruitful; contacts as they stand are insufficient" (quoted by Bertrand Poirot-Delpech, *Le Monde*, January 9 and 10, 1955).

One of the ploys that can help reduce the unease I have just alluded to is to initiate rather than to undergo, to cut oneself off of one's own accord rather than to become the abandoned victim. Though the notion of "stewing in one's own juice" is frightening, that of constructing a perfectly hermetic and self-sufficient world of one's own may be attractive.

12. The inclination to mingle, whatever the incentives—"To mingle with all others and mingle them with oneself. To stir oneself in with other beings as though in a stew," as Maurice

Sachs suggested to himself he should do (*Derrière cinq barreaux*, p. 59)—may give rise to a converse effort aimed at counteracting its excesses. One of Montherlant's characters, out walking with a new mistress, feels a desire to kiss her: "He indicated a secluded walk, though taking care that it should not be one of those in which memories already lurked for him: no superimpositions! He already had only too great a tendency to mix everything up" (Montherlant, *Les jeunes filles*, p. 253).

13. "There is an enormous amount to be gained, in many areas of life," declares another of the same author's characters, expressing an important attitude some of whose underlying motives I have remarked upon earlier, "from things' being clearly compartmentalized without any overlaps" (Montherlant, *Fils de personne*, act 2, sc. 4). "Let us not confuse the orders (of things)" says a third (Montherlant, *La ville dont le prince est un enfant*, act 2, sc. 2). "Anyone who studies dreams," Paul Valéry notes, "will observe that some awakenings are singular pieces of good fortune . . . because of the way they make a clean break at the right place or the right moment" (*Tel quel*, 1:98).

14. And yet the desire to touch, to mingle, persists. A compromise between this tendency and its opposite results in a liking for brushing, grazing, caressing, skimming over things, like the child's crouching in a park with its buttocks as close as possible to the dirty ground but not quite touching it (an observation made by Martha Wolfenstein). There is a fascination in achieving the greatest possible proximity between two things whose actual contact would provide disaster; for example, by arranging to meet various lovers or mistresses at neighboring times and places. At the same time, one should also maintain the "respect for distances" that Gide attributes to Barbey d'Aurevilly, of whom he recounts this anecdote: "The scene is the rue Royale. It is late. No one about. D'Aurevilly, having drunk a lot of white wine in the company of his friend X that evening, is relieving himself. A policeman passes: 'You could at least stand over by the wall, Monsieur,' for Barbey has not forgotten his respect for distances. At which he turns around and replies: 'Would you have me graze myself?'" (Gide, *Journal 1889–1939*, p. 948).

15. Grown-ups check the child's tendency to enter into contact with "strangers," whether children or otherwise, who are prone to be viewed as sources of various dangers. "Stay here! Come back here!" says the child's mother in the park, unless she wishes to be "a mother who does not seem to see the mischievous boldness and the indiscreet advances of her children . . . who are calling out to people she does not know" (Proust, *Du côté de chez Swann*, p. 176).

16. Once a grown-up itself, the former child still retains to

some extent a belief that "any contact with a human being is imprudent" (Montherlant, *Pitié pour les femmes*, p. 240). People who have been well brought up excuse themselves if they so much as brush against one another in the street or on a staircase. To provoke or permit a contact that I could avoid—for example by greeting some person whom it is permissible for me to pretend I have not seen— is, after all, an implicitly burdensome act—I shall have to find suitable "padding," since good-days are seldom accepted straight—as well as a potentially risky one: how am I to exclude the possibility of a gaffe on my part or an unpleasant reaction from the other person? Here is a character (Alban) in one of Montherlant's novels who is content, at a particular moment, in the absence of the woman he loves (Soledad): "Alban perceived the duke and duchess and Soledad in their motor from a distance and observed that the duke never initiated an exchange of greetings. He did not make himself known. To what purpose? Everything was fine as it was. Who knows whether the word she would speak or not speak might not disturb this state of happy equilibrium? (What a prudent young man)" (Montherlant, *Les bestiaires*, p. 152). In certain circles, a direct contact with someone whose decisions are important to me is seen as colored by the danger of losing control over what would happen; I might "let the wool be pulled over my eyes," or I should perhaps prove incapable of preventing the other from asking me to say yes or no on the spot. (Communicating with him in writing protects me from such disasters.)

17. In one of the more usual plots to be found in novels and plays, we are first shown a certain number of people—whether it be a family or a whole neighborhood—living in a state of equilibrium within a space allotted to them. Then an intruder appears who is allowed, by the kindly feelings or cunning calculations of those occupying it, to gain access to this enclosure— always supposing he does not effect his entry by force. Whereupon the activities the intruder begins before long to indulge in, and the chain reactions they provoke, begin to threaten with collapse the equilibrium that existed before his arrival. A cascade of catastrophes then ensues, or is only avoided at the last moment by his expulsion.

The real events that seem to correspond to such fears tend to take on a particular emphasis because of them. Here is a newspaper account of the "toughs" produced by one of the famous upper-middle-class Parisian *lycées*: "In order to earn the reputation of a 'tough' at Janson, one must first belong to the mysterious 'Etoile gang,' whose rackets are possibly imaginary, but which is a source of terror in the sixteenth *arrondissement*. . . . The Etoile gang specializes in 'gate-crashing' parties. Every Saturday, fourteen or fifteen or so members introduce themselves by force into the most exclusive parties being given in the neighborhood. They 'do' five or six. If anyone tries to get rid of them they smash the place up. A fortnight ago, on the boulevard Emile Augier, they removed all the staircarpet rods and rolled them away down the street, having put the elevator out of action on the way out. If they manage to get in, they insult the hostess, 'glue' themselves to the terrified young girls present and insist on dancing with them like that" (*Paris-Presse*, May 14, 1958).

18. But there is also an effort to combat these fears of what might happen if an outsider succeeded in making an entry.

In the comic mode, for example, we have descriptions of how the torpor that comes from living in a rut (see chap. 3, sec. 43) is replaced by livelier sensations and more intense pleasures when that rut is destroyed by the appearance of someone foreign to it.

In contrast to the anticipation of the catastrophe an intruder might cause there is also the argument according to which, given certain conditions, the possible damage would be minimized by admission rather than by exclusion. Here is a wife in a novel describing the somewhat unusual application of this view that has led her to accept a *ménage à trois:* "As long as I had to put up with adultery, I preferred to have it at home. . . . Experience had taught me that a mistress in the home, if, alas, mistress there be, is still the lesser of two evils" (Claire Sainte-Soline, *Le dimanche des rameaux*, p. 70). But there are other less shocking examples of this reasoning. Here, according to Charles de Gaulle, is how Marshal Pétain became vice-premier in the spring of 1940: " 'It is better,' said M. Paul Reynaud, employing the customary formula, 'to have him inside the council than outside it' " (de Gaulle, *L'appel*, p. 43). The man thus introduced having rapidly taken over the premiership itself, here is how he justified (in July), to several of his intimates, the inclusion in his cabinet of a certain precious and dangerous personage (Pierre Laval): "Laval's intrigues will be less dangerous inside the cabinet than if he were to create an opposition outside it" (Robert Aron, *Histoire de Vichy*, p. 86).

19. The fact remains that the approaches of outsiders are very often seen as attempts at encroachment one would be wise to fend off from the very outset.

"Always keep him at a certain distance from your person," writes Rousseau (quoted by Littré under *distance*).

20. Since the world tends to become intrusive, to invade my terrain, to force my door, it is a good thing to shut off that terrain

with a surrounding wall or some other such arrangement; to render myself unapproachable, inaccessible, by means of impassable barriers, gates, screens interposed between my inner world and the outside; let the paths that lead from outside inwards be barred, so that the inside shall be impermeable, impenetrable!

"To cross, break down, force open, overthrow barriers" is often seen as being less agreeable and more perilous than "raising, interposing, setting a barrier between. . . . Creating an impassable, insurmountable barrier against . . ." (Paul Robert under *barrière*).

Attempting to stress the unusual atmosphere that reigned in her parents' house, Colette recalls that "The garden around the house where I was born lost . . . the habit of keeping intruders out. I never knew it with anything more than a permissive iron fence and doors always ajar day and night. As for the carriage gate, the whole village knew how to shake one of the halves so as to dislodge the great iron bar on the other side that was supposedly there to bolt it. Any final recommendations at bedtime were always the reverse of commonsensical: 'Whatever you do don't close the door onto the porch, one of the cats isn't in! Is the heyloft door open at least? If it isn't that tom will come miaowing under my window at three in the morning to be let in!' " (Colette, *Flore et Pomone*, p. 209) For since he is often "inhospitable . . . the Frenchman treats the immediate approaches to his home with great defensive care, surrounding himself with dogrose bushes, blackthorns, and junipers; if needs be he will surround his garden with barbed wire, and his first imagined debauchery is one of enclosure. In the Midi, the vendor of little plots has invented a way of tempting the customer. He surrounds every little square of land in his development with a little wall, which he then tops, just to make sure, with a fence. Whereupon, reassured, delighted by the "homey" feeling produced by his iron fence and his lock, the new proprietor, safe behind his bars, displays a smile that shows just a little too many teeth" (ibid., pp. 208–9). Jean Anouilh's Eurydice says "very gently" to her Orpheus: "It's nice in your arms. Like a little house all shut off in the middle of the world; a little house that no one can ever come into again" (*Eurydice*, act 1). "Now that you know the way here . . ." the person who has allowed you to enter his home graciously says to you. But how much time has had to go by, how many preliminary conditions have had to be met before it could happen; and do not the homeowner's words also express—beneath that appearance of cordiality and that ploy of making the first move— a secret apprehensiveness in case his action should have started an avalanche? "It's one of God's houses" is a familiar expression applied, according to Paul Robert, to "a particularly welcoming house." But think of the price a human being may have to pay for the presumption of playing at God!

21. Places that "anyone can just walk into" arouse a contempt that masks the attraction they may exert. Under the Fourth Republic, the Palais-Bourbon, so often referred to as a house without windows, was often alleged by nightclub satirists to be in such a state of disorder and dilapidation that everyone could get into it and anyone who wanted to could stay there indefinitely ("If France could be brought wholly within these walls, that would be the ideal, that would be perfection," Gambetta had once declared of the same spot [Georges Bonnefous, *Histoire parlementaire de la Troisième République*, 1: 148]). This coexistence of opposites produces an image of parliament as another kind of brothel; which is a reminder that the situation within it is frequently, in the jargon of the lobbies, a "f——-up," which is to say a hopeless-mess.

22. To be open is to risk disaster. Permitting oneself to be open is therefore an act of madness.

"You've been robbed, but you were most imprudent; a drawer can be locked!" Paul Robert gives under *se fermer*. One of Marcel Aymé's characters in *Les quatre vérités*, the mistress of a house, asks her maid, while under the influence of a "serum" that changes the personality, to let in anyone who calls unannounced. In a novel, we are told of a woman who is sinking into madness: "She no longer closes anything. Anyone is allowed in. She watches people walking through her garden. . . . The local urchins come in and eat her plums, the chickens are eating the lettuces. . . . The other day . . . a pig . . . was eating holes in her asparagus. . . . So her grandmother said: 'Well, so you're happy with your open doors, eh? Next time it'll be a cow' " (Marcel Arland, *La consolation du voyageur*, pp. 47–48).

23. I believe I have built a "hermetically sealed" obstacle—but what if it turns out to be nothing but a "sieve"? We believe some obstacle, natural or artificial, interposed between us and the outside world, to be impassable—only to see it suddenly crossed by means of some shock tactic bringing disaster in its wake. Even the best protected home is not safe from anonymous letters. That "security device" or "defense line" built at great expense to "cover" a territory against the threat of enemy forces—is it really "watertight" (for example, the Lattre Line in Indochina)? Or again, are we sure it can't be "turned" because we haven't made it as long as it should be (for example, the Maginot Line)?

24. Corresponding to the danger of intrusion from the outside into my domain, there is that of venturing outside its protective walls myself (see chap. 3, secs. 16–29). "To withdraw within one's lines," "to retire into a place where one considers oneself to be in safety"—Paul Robert's definition of *se cantonner*—"to remain in one's shell," or to go back into it if one has already emerged from it—these all describe a line of action whose value, combining prudence and enjoyment as it does, is often seen as being greater than that attributed to the possibly exhilarating but oh so very dangerous game of "exploding a rigid framework" (instead of "living quietly at home").

25. If certain contacts between myself and others seem to me to be dangerous, there are relationships between the various other people with whom I am connected that are no less so.

Prudence requires that I should not bring together those who, fortunately, do not already have any connection with each other; it is natural that one should be rather upset if they should manage to get to know each other on their own (a fact exemplified in an incident in *Le bal du comte d'Orgel*, pp. 192–96).

The establishing of relations between two persons of the same world, each of whom knows who the other is without their yet being personally acquainted, may be viewed as a crucial and difficult business. Here, in the words of Paul Léautaud talking about Léo Larguier, is a glimpse of the Paris literary world in the early years of the century: "Meeting him today, Van Bever said to him: 'You know, Léautaud was asking me the other day if I'd seen you.'—'Ah, Léautaud, he'd very much like to know me!' Larguier replied" (Léautaud, *Journal littéraire*, V. 1:318).

Going even further than refusing to be a go-between, one may even attempt to create a division between those who, annoyingly, do happen to have connections, after the example of the little Blaise Pascal: "When Monsieur Pascal was a year old . . . it happened that the child fell into a decline . . . accompanied by two circumstances. . . . One was that he could not drink water without flying into a rage; and the other . . . that he could not suffer to see his father and mother near to one another; he suffered the caresses of both individually with pleasure; but as soon as they came close to one another, he cried out and struggled with an excessive violence." When he had recovered, his niece also informs us, the future author of the *Traité de l'équilibre des liqueurs* "diverted himself by pouring water from one glass into another, in his mother's arms" (Marguerite Périer, *Mémoires sur la vie de Monsieur Pascal*, p. 57).

Pushing this maneuver even further, I may attempt to "set people against one another" if I feel that their being connected is a threat to me. Quite often, indeed, we find it at least plausible that A should have engaged in a series of maneuvers tending to "poison" the relations between B and C, to "sour" their feelings for one another.

This is perhaps a way of defending ourselves against a secret temptation to play the go-between. One of Montherlant's characters, having brought his mistress and his best friend together, "left the house with that delightful feeling truly altruistic, almost maternal, that flowers in you when you act the go-between. More than one man, whose heart has never before been touched by the slightest pang of human sympathy, has suddenly discovered what an agreeable thing it is, as he closes the door of the room where two persons are coming together through his agency, to make people happy" (Montherlant, *L'histoire d'amour de la Rose du Sable*, p. 122).

26. Serious meetings, it is often felt, must be between two people only: the tête-à-tête is the most efficacious setting for exerting influence. If a meeting of several people is unavoidable, at least let it be prepared for by a series of two-person interviews! (Though the tête-à-tête is seen as a good formula for negotiations, it can also be viewed as a deadly condition of existence in general—either I am faced with an equal, which means being locked in a never-ending and exhausting struggle the outcome of which will be fatal in the absence of a third party, or else I am faced with a stronger partner who will in consequence have every opportunity to crush me: a principal tenet of belief among those who opposed the C.E.D. because Britain was not included.)

27. In a well-organized life (as both Margaret Mead and Rhoda Métraux have observed), I share certain secrets with each of the persons with whom I am connected from which the other members of my circle are supposedly excluded. There are also "the parents who allow themselves to make their children their accomplices, as with the mother who says, 'You mustn't tell your father about this'" (Guy Durandin, *L'enfant menteur*, p. 11). A pleasant and useful exchange between myself and a friend, with or without quotation marks, may possibly put in that friend's possession a great many things that would be of interest to some other friend of mine but which I should find it unpleasant for him to hear, such as wounding remarks about himself, or regrettable facts about me. It would therefore be scarcely prudent on my part to increase the chances that the two friends in question might meet "behind my back." In both private and public life it is usual to speak in varying ways to different people, whether it be a matter of information to be passed on, opinions to be expressed, or promises to be made. Here again it is fairly

unlikely that my various conversational partners will meet one another. As for those who talk "to this man in one sense, to that one in another," Montaigne asks: "and what if by chance those men should meet and share such contrary information like plunder, what becomes of that fine art?" (*Essais*, bk. 1, chap. 9). This "fine art" therefore requires, as its necessary complement, either the cleverness to prevent such an outcome, or sufficient lack of concern to remain untroubled by the possibility of it.

28. If I effect an introduction between two people of my acquaintance, I am running the risk—assuming that I have taken the trouble to introduce some measure of variety into my life (see chap. 2)—that they may loathe one another, and also that they may each loathe me because I do not share their feelings toward the other one. Apart from which, I may myself be disappointed by the divergence between their reactions and my own. Here is a character in a novel thinking about his girl friend and his best friend: "Simone would like me to bring Gérard to see her. I don't particularly want to. My friendship for her, my friendship for Gérard are the only things I really have . . . of my own. . . . If they didn't appreciate each other's value, I should love both of them less" (Roger Stéphane, *Les fausses passions*, p. 221).

29. The same character also says: "If they became friendly, I should probably be jealous of them both" (ibid.)—to which must be added the danger that in becoming friendly with one another my various friends may grow more distant from me. During the Great War, Paul Morand noted in his diary: "Marie Scheikevitch, who has quarreled with Madame Bulteau, talks about her with a gentle fury. One day, at luncheon at her house, Briand asked her: 'Who is the schoolteacher?'—'Don't you know her?' Marie Scheikevitch replied, 'that's Madame Bulteau. . . . Get someone to introduce you *mon cher Président*, she may be useful to you.' Briand did so. . . . 'After which,' Marie Scheikevitch went on, 'I received two successive express letters from Madame Bulteau that sum up everything about her. First: 'Will you come to luncheon next Saturday? Bring your friend Briand.' And then, two weeks later: 'My friend Briand is lunching here on Friday, would you like to come?' Then Marie Scheikevitch was no longer invited at all" (Morand, *Journal d'un attaché d'ambassade*, pp. 264–65).

Those on whose behalf I have acted as go-between may even go so far as to forget that it is to me they owe their connection, since one of them once dangled in front of me the idea of what a boon an introduction to the other would be; from having once been privileged and envied I have now fallen to the status of the excluded.

Or those whose relationship I have imprudently encouraged could even form a coalition directed against myself. One of Montherlant's characters who has just made himself the go-between between a friend and a mistress comes to regret what he has done: "Here they are both conspiring against me, and I myself am the cause of it all!" (*L'histoire d'amour de la Rose de Sable*, p. 129). According to the same writer, a director of conscience must never hesitate to bring together two people who do not know one another when he thinks it is for their good, even if there is in his mind "the precept that those you bring together will one day form an alliance against you" (Montherlant, *Carnets* 19–21, p. 159).

30. If one cannot resist the inclination to bring people together, one should at least do so in conditions that appear to permit some measure of control over the effects of one's imprudence: an attitude often attributed to salon hostesses who expected their guests to pay more attention to them than to one another. This is what Sainte-Beuve (quoted by Paul Robert under *assortir*, "to match or arrange together") is presumably implying when he writes of a great eighteenth-century salon: "Mlle de Lespinasse's salon, aside from a nucleus of five or six constant friends . . . was . . . made up . . . of people who did not know each other particularly well, chosen from various quarters, and whom that sprightly-minded lady intermingled with infinite art." And here is how Madame Verdurin felt about her relationship with the "little clan": "In her, the need to preserve their friendship was increasingly dominated by the need to ensure that this friendship was never impeded by any that they might feel for each other" (Proust, *La prisonnière*, p. 281).

31. There is another thing: a life may unfold on several levels (see chap. 2) if the necessary partitions have been arranged within it. In *Le blé en herbe*, Madame Dalleray muses about her young lover: "That timorous little middle-class boy gets angry with me when I ask him how his family is, he does all he can to avoid telling me about his school, and he locks himself inside a positive fortress of silence and modesty as soon as he hears the name Vinca. . . . He brings it here and takes it off and puts it back on with his clothes, this . . . this . . . [points of suspension in original]. She realized that she had hesitated before the word 'love'" (Colette, *Le blé en herbe*, p. 124). In *La ville dont le prince est un enfant*, a teacher-priest says to one of his students: "It would be better if you didn't tell your mother about everything that goes on here; home and school are two quite separate worlds, and there is no point in mixing them" (Montherlant, *La ville dont le prince est un enfant*, act 1, sc. 3). If I must pursue several

activities whose coexistence within the same life could create difficulties, then I may attempt to reduce the uneasiness thus provoked by separating them clearly in space or time. (In this way I may succeed in increasing the pleasure I derive from my diversity.) In one of Armand Salacrou's comedies (*Les invités du bon Dieu*), a young man discovers that he is sharing his mistress with his father-in-law to be. When he exclaims: "What! You mean at the same time you . . .," she replies sharply: "No, not at the same time at all. With him, only on Fridays!"

32. Man's spontaneous tendency is to tangle things together. (*Embrouiller*—"to combine things with one another to such an extent that they become difficult to distinguish"—Paul Robert.) Upon awakening, Paul Valéry notes, one becomes aware that "Sleep has confused everything, shuffled the cards, . . . our dreams have tangled everything together" (*Tel quel*, 2: 121). "There is something confused, something tangled in youth . . . a jungle" (Maurice Sachs, *Derrière cinq barreaux*, p. 46).

33. One is often afraid of being a person of whom someone else may say: That man gets everything he touches into a muddle; he gets everything mixed up, he's a blunderer! In order to avoid that agonizing awareness of error heralded by the words "you must have made a mistake!" we become very watchful of ourselves; we must be careful never to confuse one thing with another; in order to combat the fear of falling into a "monstrous confusion" (Pascal), we determine inwardly to "draw up a plan that will avoid all confusion" (given by Paul Robert as an illustration of *confusion*).

"To take one person for another, one thing for another" (Paul Robert under *autre*, "other"), what a horrid thing to happen! There are many kinds of "substitution" that create apprehension. There are those much publicized affairs of child substitution in maternity hospitals. And those that occur at the end of life. "Bergson's funeral?" Valéry is claimed to have said to a friend. "The wretched creatures! . . . The worst of it was that they mistook the grave. . . . They didn't put him in his" (Gaston Poulain, *Paul Valéry tel quel*, p. 12). "The undertaker's men confused the corpses" ran one newspaper headline; the story was an account of a court case resulting from the discovery that the two graves two widowers had been respectfully visiting each contained the other's wife (*Paris-Presse*, March 30 and 31, 1958). Another court case stemming from somber events under the Occupation (centered on the Charbonneau Clinic in Carcassonne) and an important film (André Cayatte's *Le dossier noir*) both center upon an error, or a maneuver, of the same kind. It is also possible that the objects confused may be parts of corpses impounded for legal ends. Here, in the words of one journalist (Pierre Scize) is what is alleged to have happened when a group of objects of this kind was despatched from a small town to a larger one (Marseilles) so that they could be subjected to examinations that might prove of use in the trial of a woman accused of multiple poisoning (Marie Besnard): "No one, it seems, had been capable of drawing up a proper inventory of the jars and boxes despatched to Marseilles. Not only was the number of those that arrived different from the number sent, but the contents of the glass urns was only vaguely indicated. It was not known exactly to whom any given piece of anatomy belonged. In some cases there were organs missing, in others there were duplications. An eye was found packed with a skeleton that had been buried for twenty years. There were tangles of hair from different bodies. The record office in Poitiers, unless it was the laboratory in Marseilles, had treated these . . . remains in the most cavalier fashion" (Pierre Scize, *Au grand jour des assises*, pp. 110–11). In school, the child is afraid of mixing up its various exercise books, each of which must be devoted exclusively to one subject: a confusion in this case being a possible, and justified, reason for getting a zero. And apparently most of the many letters of complaint received by the office of the *Baccalauréat* examiners refer to the possibility that there has been a "mix-up in the files" (Bertrand Girod de l'Ain, *Le Monde*, June 20, 1957).

34. Opposing this tendency to confuse things there is the effort to "disentangle"—"to separate out what has been mingled" (Paul Robert)—to "distinguish between things that have been mixed, confused." "He will disentangle this whole mixture of passion and reason, he will separate the one from the other," says Bourdaloue (quoted by Paul Robert). The "scatterbrain" is in effect a major variant of the idiot; "to have things neatly arranged in one's head like clean linen in a closet" (Gide, *Journal 1889–1939*, pp. 834–35) is a quality of the intelligent man. Those who are not particularly successful at this appreciate and admire the entertainer whose act embraces a consummate use of the stammer, thereby demonstrating once again that an appearance of total muddle may conceal extreme skill.

35. If the adult sorts out his affairs (thereby achieving success, as the French idiom *se débrouiller* implies), he is once again shaking off his past. All through childhood one is forced to undergo a long and hard apprenticeship before achieving the clearly distinguished movements, gestures, words, and intentions that characterize the fully formed human being. "You're very kind," an old and tired Paul Valéry said one evening to his guests, "You never say 'for goodness sake speak clearly' to me, the way that

irritable Degas used to" (Mondor, *Propos familiers de Paul Valéry*, p. 171). It never becomes entirely easy to maintain the
required degree of distinction that certain things in nature
achieve spontaneously, like the tree described by Proust: "All
that needed to move, a few chestnut leaves, was moving. But
their minute quivering . . . perfectly executed down to the slightest detail . . . did not run into the rest, did not blend into it,
remained circumscribed" (Proust, *Du côté de chez Swann*, pp.
32–33).

36. It is in this context that we ought to consider the emphasis
that is often placed on the postulate that things ought to be kept
separate from one another (the contrary tendency finding its
expression in the "romantic" and "impressionist" movements).

"I have . . . a repugnance for any fading of the outlines that
my whole upbringing strove to emphasize," André Gide confesses
(*Journal 1939–1949*, p. 254). "Jean S——," he also writes elsewhere, "criticizes Racine's characters because they stop living
once the curtain is down; whereas Shakespeare's . . . appear for
an instant behind the footlights, but we feel that they do not
end there and that we could meet them again elsewhere, after
the play is over." But for his own part, "this precise limitation,
this refusal to break the frame, this hardness of outline is exactly
what I like" (Gide, *Journal 1889–1939*, p. 1187). "I like the sea-
sons to be clearcut and take care not to confuse the different
genres" (Gide, *Feuillets d'automne*, p. 1087). "It is well known,"
says Montherlant in his turn, speaking of the theater, "that the
differentiation of the *genres* . . . is dear to the French heart"
(Montherlant, *Les lépreuses*, p. 62). "The edging, I tell you, the
edging!" Colette cries when discussing gardens (*Flore et Pomone*,
p. 250), thereby reminding us of the way in which peasants are
influenced in their choice of crops by the degree of clearcut separation their crops will permit from those of their neighbors.

37. Ideas may be perceived above all as objects that are distinct from one another: a precious quality, comparable to that
displayed by a "lefthand breast, a darling breast" on a beautiful
woman in being "always far from its companion."

Consciousness is a process of division:

> At the heart of the night, at the center of the night
> The spirit's awakening deeply opposed to
> the substance of the night:
> Remarkably alone, distinct, and restful.
> Divided from the night,
> Sharply dividing its powers!"
> [Valéry, *Tel quel*, 2:117]

As darkness and sleep confuse things, so light and lucidity separate them: "The operation of the consciousness is to disentangle itself, like a man ceaselessly awakening and ceaselessly freeing himself from the interlacings of his limbs and the tanglings of his previous perceptions" (Valéry, *Tel quel*, 1: 55). What man "calls his intelligence," is always, according to Paul Valéry, to a large extent his "power . . . to break down his intentions into distinct actions" (*Pièces sur l'art*, p. 111).

In an argument, it is useful to know how to employ the adjective "other" in order to "differentiate": "That is another question, another affair, another song, another story altogether" (Paul Robert): you are digressing from the argument!

38. The verbs that denote the act of separating in the mind come to acquire a supplementary—or even principal—signification: that of "isolating" the truth. Thus "to distinguish (*distinguer*) takes on the sense of "perceiving . . . without confusion" (Paul Robert) and completely ("An experienced eye that distinguishes the slightest details"). Everything, it may be felt, depends on making a clear distinction. "If this distinction is not accepted," a believer in military glories prophesies in the Assembly (Pierre Koenig), "if we refuse to admit it, then total confusion must reign in our debates. If, on the other hand, this distinction is accepted, then everything becomes clear" (A.N., June 23, 1955; J.O., p. 3252).

Although the slightly archaic meaning of *discernement* (discernment) is "the action of separating," this noun has now come to denote "a disposition of the mind to make sound judgments upon things" (Paul Robert).

Démêler, to disentangle, also means to substitute truth for falsity, as in "to disentangle the confusions in which superficial minds enmesh themselves" (Renan quoted by Robert). Indeed, this verb, having begun by signifying "to separate what is tangled," has eventually come to mean "to understand . . . to clarify, to explain": "to unravel a delicate affair, a historical point, a difficulty . . . a plot . . . someone's character."

Similarly with *débrouiller;* Marivaux (quoted by Robert) can refer, for example, to "the art of reading people's hearts and disentangling the secret feelings hidden there," and Baudelaire (again quoted by Robert) can declare: "I have a passionate liking for mystery because I always hope to unravel it."

39. To mingle or tangle, on the other hand, means to succumb to error.

The person he is talking to having sighed that "the most difficult part is seeing what is," Monsieur Teste replies: "Which means . . . not to get our words mixed up" (Valéry, *Monsieur*

Teste, p. 40). *Confondre* (to confuse)—meaning in the first place "to take . . . one thing for another"—finally comes to mean to make a mistake: "I may have got things confused." "To confuse people's minds" often means to fill them with beliefs that, however clear in themselves, the speaker considers undesirable. A similar interpretation may be in order when one hears someone assert that "a spirit of confusion reigns in the government" (Paul Robert under *confusion*); when someone speaks of "one of those minds . . . accustomed to the confusion generally agreed to abound in parliament" (ibid., quoting Jules Romains); or when we hear this kind of dialogue in the Assembly between one leading politician in power and another (a member of the same party, moreover) who is opposed to him:

"René Mayer: You are confusing everything.
Pierre Mendès-France: No, I am not confusiong everything."
[A.N., January 1, 1952; *L'Année politique*, 1952, p. 419].

40. Separation is also order.
"Imperceptibly," says Rousseau describing the beginning of the world, "this chaos disentangled itself, and everything took up its allotted place" (quoted by Paul Robert under *insensiblement,* "imperceptibly"). One of the meanings of *démêler* is "to sort out," to "put in order"; "to put one's things in order before leaving on a journey," Paul Robert gives under that verb.

41. Whereas to mingle entails a risk of disorder. In one familiar meaning of *mélanger* (to mix), the reference is to a process of "putting together [things] without attempting or managing to put them in any order. . . . He has mixed up all the files . . . It's impossible to find anything now" (Paul Robert). "To mix" can even signify "to create inextricable disorder in things."

42. All this being so, separation may assure one of mastery over things.
Writing of a leading politician in whose opinion one should consider all the problems one has to deal with as a "whole" (Pierre Mendès-France), one journalist (Pierre Drouin) also supposes that he "will doubtless divide up all economic difficulties into as many smaller areas as proves necessary in order to solve them better" (*Le Monde*, July 13, 1954).
One of the figurative senses of *démêler* (to unravel), is, according to Paul Robert, "to get oneself out of a difficulty."

43. The converse to this is that anything irremediably mixed up is likely to be "a mess." What cannot be unraveled is "inextricable"; and an inextricable situation is heavy with the threat of disaster.

44. All separations are not good, however.
To "feel good in myself" is often to be experiencing the sensa-

tion that everything inside me is well packed together, firm and sound. Whereas, on the other hand, one of the most widespread variants of mental discomfort is the feeling "that I am going to pieces." Perhaps, after all, the various parts of some apparently solid "whole" may suddenly fly apart with terrifying facility? "Creatures as fragmented as this puppet," one character in *Les faux-monnayeurs* says of another, "need every scrap of egoism they can muster to hold the separate elements of their personalities together. They only have to forget themselvs for a moment and they'd fall to pieces" (Gide, *Les faux-monnayeurs*, pp. 290–91). "When people are too nice to me," one of Colette's women characters says, "I don't know whether I'm coming or going, I could just run all over the place like soup" (*La dame du photographe*, p. 154). When we see someone else on his way to an energetic bout of love-making, we may offer him the prudent advice: "Not to come back in shreds!"; one of the French idioms for great devotion is "to divide oneself into four" for someone.

Under the Third and Fourth Republics, many a government came to an end after going through long death throes during which it was thought of as "tearing itself to pieces."

45. A thing, too, can "fall to pieces," or "crumble," when it is eaten away gradually. Under the Fourth Republic, for example, it was always expected that any projected law would be "torn to pieces" by the appropriate parliamentary committee. Or again, someone is said to be intent on "breaking down" some imposing whole "into small pieces." This is a technique often considered useful in reducing the power of a dangerous group, while insisting upon one's own right to remain one and indivisible. After the first World War, for example, Germany was supposed to be broken up into "the Germanies"; after the second World War, its armed forces, according to the C.E.D., were to be broken up into scattered units, thereby rendering it impossible for them to join together to form a new "Wehrmacht."

46. Among the images of murder, that of cutting up seems to occupy an important place; the victim's body is broken down into many small fragments, often scattered over a wide area. "Only twenty-four pieces found (including the head without ears); a quarter of the corpse" one newspaper heading ran in a case of this kind, continuing: "The remainder? One foot was found in a goods wagon standing in Pont-Sainte-Maxence station. . . . 'Other pieces,' the judge remarked, 'might equally well have been found at Castelnaudary or Quimper'" (*Combat*, February 28, 1952). When Jacques Prévert refers to "the pieces of the husband chopped up by the widow" (Prévert, *En mémoire*), he can be sure of arousing a lively reaction in his readers. And the same is true of Binet's test, when he poses a problem to those whose

"intelligence" he is testing that begins: A corpse has been found cut up into eighteen pieces; it is apparently a case of suicide. . . . When I wish to make it quite clear that the efforts another person is making to persuade me to do something are doomed to failure, I may say, idiomatically: Even if you were to cut me up into little pieces. . . .

Here, described by Marcel Aymé, is what happened to a German soldier in a Paris street one August day in 1944: "He was knocked to the ground and in a few moments completely torn to pieces. The women and children . . . were particularly determined in their ferocity. They were vying with one another to lop off a finger, an ear, a strip of flesh. When the crowd dispersed, there was nothing left of Schulz but a few smears of blood on the road" (Aymé, *Le chemin des écoliers,* p. 16).

"Madame Poujade in pieces" ran a newspaper headline once, at a time when that lady's husband seemed destined for some sort of future. Her portrait had been stolen from an "art gallery," after which "a quarter sheet of paper . . . representing the right half of a female forehead and the cheek down to the level of the lip" had arrived under plain cover addressed to the head of the research department of an evening paper (*Combat,* April 26, 1956). Having brought off his first investiture on his own birthday (November 5, 1957), the Benjamin of the Fourth Republic's prime ministers (Félix Gaillard) then went on to Lipp's in order to blow out the candles on a cake which had as its base a model of the National Assembly. "I don't mind sharing out this base," he remarked, "but I refuse to slice up the National Assembly, even if it were made of marzipan" (*Paris-Match,* November 16, 1957).

In a poem by August Barbier included in André Gide's anthology, some hounds tear a boar to pieces; "each insisted on his share," and having got it, went back to his bitch "and cried, throwing his lump of carrion down: There's my share of royalty!" (Gide, *Anthologie de la poésie française,* pp. 448–49). The cliché "some dead people must be killed anew" comes from a stanza Fernand Desnoyers claims to have pinned to the statue of Casimir Delavigne in le Havre:

> Born in le Havre, a good Havrais,
> I've come from Paris, all the way,
> To smash to bits this new statue
> Of Delavigne (called Casimir).
> Some dead people must be killed anew.
>   [Othon Guerlac, *Les citations françaises,* pp. 230–
>   31]

However, the idea of tearing or being torn to pieces is not always, in the conscious mind at least, accompanied by rage; a certain exaltation may be present instead. Montherlant, in a note on *Port-Royal,* recalls the "pious dismantling of the corpse of Saint-Cyran into tiny pieces." A member of the *Canard enchaîné* staff (*René Lefèvre*) tells how one of his colleagues (Henri Monier) claimed to have been overwhelmed, during a trip through Brittany, by the discovery that "no precise information was available on the distribution of the various items of offal (with the exception of the heart) originating from the body of the Constable of France Du Guesclin, who was stewed after his death: "It was at this point that Monier entered into an ecstatic trance and declared . . . that he too wished to be stewed after his death . . . and that the various parts of his body were to be distributed throughout the country by the Hachette freight service . . . that he wished to be chopped up very finely and that bits of him should be flung about everywhere, everywhere, everywhere!" (*Le canard enchaîné,* April 30, 1958). And here is a woman in one of Armand Salacrou's plays reminiscing about her days as a medical student: "Ah! how comfortable and relaxed I used to feel . . . with the corpses, cutting them up into tiny pieces!" (Salacrou, *L'archipel Lenoir,* pt. 1).

Since the idea of cutting up a body has such powerful emotions associated with it, a figurative sense tends to become added to the literal meaning of the verb to cut up. Any activity of the mind —since it is essentially a labor of division (see above, secs. 37–39) —may be seen as a task of cutting up. "To take to pieces" (*dépecer*), Paul Robert notes, signifies by extension "to analyze minutely"—and has the result, one might add, of destroying the object thus analyzed: "The critics picked his work to bits." And similarly, "to tear to bits" (*déchirer*) also means "to speak ill of": "to tear someone's character to pieces."

When politicians entertain the notion of voting according to the smaller division of the "arrondissement" rather than by departments (as in the autumn of 1955), this implies "cutting up" the country into small pieces. An opponent of this change (Pierre-Henri Teitgen) could then speak of "butchery" (Bulletin de Paris, November 24, 1955), and another openly declared in the Assembly: " that . . . voting by arrondissements, as it has existed up till now, is nothing more nor less than skilled butchery" (Joseph Pinvindic, A.N., November 29, 1955; J.O., p. 6041). Before a weekend during which the government had recommended all deputies to visit their constituencies (*circonscriptions*) in order to discuss the boundaries of the future voting *arrondissements* with their prefects, the *Canard enchaîné* came out with the following main headline: "After the big slice, the deputies are sent back to their circumsisions (*circoncisions*)" (*Le canard enchaîné*, November 23, 1955).

But after the slicing up there also comes the reconstitution, after the model of Saint Nicholas finding the pieces of the three children put into the salting tub by the wicked butcher. A vaudeville song tells the story of a man who has been murdered by being cut to pieces but who succeeds in collecting all the pieces and sticking them back together; when he discovers that "the most important" is still missing, he goes to the Place de la Concorde in search of the obelisk. A conjurer persuades a young woman in the audience to cut her escort's tie in two. First he ties the two pieces together again with a very clumsy and obvious knot; then, saying that he can do still better, he produces a perfectly intact tie apparently identical to the one that was cut.

47. Apart from division by cutting, we also find preoccupations with several other methods of turning an intact body into a mass of fragments.

In primary school, children are shown a picture of how Queen Brunehaut was "dismembered," "cut to ribbons," tied to the tail of a galloping horse by her feet and dragged for miles over a road covered with rough stones.

They are also shown Ravaillac being "quartered" between four horses all pulling in different directions. Later, one learns from Pascal that if "hostile passions occupy the heart" they "tear it into a thousand pieces" (Pascal, *Discours sur les passions de l'amour*), just as, under the Fourth Republic, the budget proposed by the government, seized upon and "pulled in every direction" by the Assembly's finance committee, would always be "torn to shreds."

Moreover there are so many human groups— in politics, such and such a political party, or parliamentary grouping, or government—that seem to be in constant danger of "exploding."

48. Even when a complex group or object does not fly into pieces, it may be harmed by a lack of connection between its constituent parts, by the fact that certain internal partitions have not been "breached" or "knocked down."

49. Under the Fourth Republic, members of the political world often criticized one another for not having paid sufficient attention to certain other "problems" while attempting to "resolve" one particular difficulty, which, according to their critics, they had "isolated" quite mistakenly from what was in fact its vast and true "context." On the one hand there is an inclination to believe that "one can't do everything at the same time": a gem of wisdom only too frequently imparted by grown-ups to children who may,

later on, stubbornly refuse to occupy themselves with more than one "file" at any given moment, resolving to close all the others "for the time being." "These words—which the prime minister employs continually," said a journalist (Gilles Martinet) of a leader in power (Pierre Mendès-France), "are the key to his behavior" (*France-Observateur*, November 4, 1954). "I am a man of one thing at a time," the politician himself said; "at the moment"—since the Assembly's debate on economic, financial and social affairs had recently been concluded and that on North Africa just postponed—"the menu for the day is the C.E.D." (Georges Mamy, *Le Monde*, August 12, 1954).

Can we be sure, however, that this is the right method? "To govern," a rival (Félix Gaillard) was able to reply to the aforementioned believer in the virtue of "staggering" one's actions in time, "does not mean opening one file after another" (Congress of the Radical Party, November 24, 1957; *Le Monde*, November 26, 1957). For is not everything part of a whole? Certainly Félix Gaillard could have quoted some rather famous words in favor of such a point of view, spoken by the very person he was attacking. (See Pierre Mendès-France's investiture speech, June 3, 1953, *L'Année politique*, 1953, p. 490.)

50. In contradistinction to the rut of "piecemeal" or "fragmentary" measures, there is a constant clamor for an "overall" plan in which each element is seen as a function of all the rest, an "overall policy," a "totality of measures approached as a single entity."

Discussing an "assertion by one critic with reference to the unity of *Les fleurs du mal*," Paul Valéry points out that "the term unity is so vague that one can always deny or support its existence in a work without any risk of being conclusively contradicted" (letter to Cambiaire, 1930; *Lettres à quelques-uns*, p. 186). Similarly in the political situation touched on above. Since no definition of the broad terms in question is ordinarily offered, it is easy for the government to claim that it is putting forward a "whole," and equally easy to criticize it because "the suggestions put forward do not form a whole"—"the argument most in use today" in the words of a prime minister (Guy Mollet) summing up a sitting during which his downfall had been prepared. So it is always possible to apply La Bruyère's description of quietism to any position one's opponents take up: "a monstrous conglomeration of wholly ill-assorted components" (La Bruyère, *Dialogues sur le quiétisme*, dialogue 4). And one can just as easily claim for oneself the merit of having been the first to do better. After seven years of war in Indochina, General Navarre noted: "The overall plan I have presented to the government—the first to my knowledge since the outbreak of the war . . ." (Henri Navarre, *Agonie en Indochine, 1953–1954*, p. 87). To admit when referring to a policy of which one does not wholly approve that it can scarcely be accused of the defect of form being discussed here is to display a great deal of respect toward it; as with this opinion delivered by the *Le Monde* economics expert (Pierre Drouin) with regard to the "Rueff plan" adopted by the government at the outset of the Fifth Republic: "Whatever fundamental criticisms one may be led to make of these . . . decisions . . . they do form part of an overall economic policy. . . . The government . . . is treating . . . interrelated matters as an overall entity" (*Le Monde*, December 28 and 29, 1958). It goes without saying that Charles de Gaulle was in agreement with this—"this totality in which all the parts are linked and complementary to one another . . ." (speech made on December 28, 1958; see *Le Monde*, December 30, 1958)—as were his "faithful followers": "the measures taken constitute a whole" (Jean-Paul Palewski, *Le Monde*, December 30, 1958).

An opponent, however, will be inclined to attack the coherence of the measures he is rejecting before—or even instead of—examining their content.

"I cannot accept the claim or the illusion according to which this conglomeration is supposed to be looked upon as . . . a policy" declared one deputy (Raymond Boisdé), referring to the very same measures (A.N., January 16, 1959; *J.O.*, p. 75), while another leading politician, one experienced in such matters (Edgar Faure) commented: "It is impossible to make out any coherent and interconnected policy. We are dealing with a *juxtaposition* rather than an *articulation*" (*Le Monde*, December 30, 1958). This eminent critic then went on, in an unexpected manner, to name certain measures "that are out of tune with others or even contradictory to them." In general, it seems to be sufficiently normal and scandalous that a so-called "whole" should be nothing more than a "patchwork" for anything more than a statement that this is the case to be unnecessary. The man actually in power is scarcely ever viewed as capable of taking into account Boileau's advice (in *L'art poétique*) that: "The well-matched components of a nicely-judged work of art / Should form but one whole from various parts." He is pictured much more often by others—outside the political world as well as within it—as resembling Chateaubriand's Montlosier: ". . . a motley mind made up of shreds and patches, Montlosier gives birth . . . to mismatched ideas" (quoted by Paul Robert under "motley" (*bigarré*).

For though man-made combinations may be injurious in their effects (see above, secs. 5–6), they may also do no more than

merely create a futile and unseemly, though not harmful, inco-
herence. As is the case with the *assemblage* (collection or conglomeration). "The bizarre conglomeration of so many diverse
objects / May seem to you perhaps the work of chance," says
Racine (quoted by Paul Robert under *assemblage*).

"It's a strange thing for someone to have thrown together
[caused the *assemblage* of] a person like yourself and a man like
me," declares one of Molière's characters (quoted ibid.). Lesage
claims: "My versification is by no means a collection (*assemblage*) of common sentiments and trivial expressions sustained
merely by its rhymes" (quoted ibid.). And Fénelon paints the
following portrait of a bad builder: "an architect who thinks he's
done everything there is to be done, provided he has assembled
a few grand columns and a great deal of well trimmed stone,
without any thought for the order and the proportion of his
building's ornaments. . . . His work is nothing but conglomeration
(*assemblage*)" (quoted ibid.). That is precisely how political
leaders and their works tend to be viewed.

51. Just as governmental policies pursued simultaneously are
seen as destined to failure if they are not sufficiently well linked
together, so human groups are seen as doomed to a bad end if
their component parts are too much separated from one another
—an impression only too easily given, however.

The theme of the division between the "real country" and the
"legal country" is one often expressed in a variety of terms; there
was nothing surprising, for example, in Pierre Poujade's setting
out in a letter to all deputies what he considered to be the necessary conditions for a "resumption of state-nation relations" (*Le
Monde*, March 15, 1955). When, at the beginning of the Fifth
Republic, "a group of a hundred and twenty-five militant members of union movements, both professional and in the home"
decided to create a new "power grouping" (an attempt that was
swiftly abandoned), their arguments were based upon "the divorce existing until this time between political action and all
other forms of action in the national life." According to one
journalist (Georges Mamy), they were aware of "a watertight
compartment between the 'living forces' of which they were a
part and political life" (*Le Monde*, January 20, 1959).

The same feeling may spring up with regard to any one of the
larger bodies within the nation. Writing about his life as a general
staff officer during the "phony war," a historian recalls: "I realized more clearly than before that there wasn't, in fact, a
French Army, but several private preserves within an army"
(Marc Bloch, *L'étrange défaite*, p. 121). Referring to "the compartmentalization of the administration," a future head of the

government (Michel Debré) felt able to say that "there is no longer an administration, but several administrations" (Debré, *La République et ses problèmes*, p. 42).

Those who oppose the creation of a new department (in order to bring it into line with new conditions) in some given institution are therefore very likely to invoke the danger of internal breakdowns in communications. When, in 1934 and 1935, Colonel de Gaulle put forward the idea of a "specialized body" of armored troops, General Weygand immediately baulked at it: "Accepting a priori that my concept would split the army into two sections: 'Two armies never! Not at any price!' he protested" (Charles de Gaulle, *L'appel*, p. 14).

BOOK 2

UNREASON AND WISDOM

5

THE HORROR OF COMPLETION

1. Grown-ups are opposed to what they consider a tendency in children not to follow their actions through to a conclusion.

2. When setting a child some principal daily task, the adult often insists that the child shall "stay there till it's finished," whether it is a question of a bottle, the potty, some particular dish, or homework; it must execute the undertaking assigned to it in its entirety; it must "get on with it!"

3. This insistence is indispensable, it is generally thought, because the child tends to do only as it pleases; and there is a risk that the pleasure impulse may not keep him going to the end. Children may be seen as resembling the cats observed by Montherlant at their twilight games: their swift rushes stop dead, their fury changes to disdain, their disputes are suddenly discontinued, and they are subject to abrupt fits of indifference (Montherlant, *La relève du matin*, p. 43). Against the pleasure impulse that produces a sudden onslaught and then, just as abruptly, wanes, adults raise the voice sometimes of economy—it may be necessary that the child should scrape its plate—and always of morality: "Finish your bread, greedy!" (quoted by Paul Robert under *finir* "finish"), and also that of wisdom: not to finish is to fail.

"He begins something, then he doesn't finish it," said one mother discussing her little boy's use of his spare time in time-honored terms. "My husband says to him . . . 'You see, it's just the same at home as at school; you never finish what you begin.' It's serious, because we're afraid he'll go on being like it all his life" (see chap. 3, secs. 3–9). "Several times, when I asked for advice at his school, they told me they insisted on his finishing one thing before beginning another." And, in fact, "I felt they were instructions I ought to follow" (*L'école des parents*, December 1956, pp. 30–31). "It's rare for him to follow anything through to the end," says one young boy's father, "whereas we'd like him to carry anything he starts on right through to the end" (ibid., March 1957, p. 48)—remarking upon which, a child psychologist confirms that "many parents require their children to finish anything they do," whereas "the child . . . abandons certain things very easily" (Doctor Giabicani-Teyssère, ibid.).

4. Performing a reversal already observed a number of times in these pages, the ex-child tends to perceive—and does not fail to criticize—in the authorities governing adult life this very lack of "the will to finish things" that was held against him by those who controlled him in his youth.

5. As for himself personally, the child who has become a grown-up falls heir to a situation in which he can proffer much freer and more varied answers to the question "whether it is a good thing to finish things or not."

6. Far beyond the domain in which "not going on to the end" is to reveal oneself as "frigid" (La Fontaine, *Le magnifique*) and in which not to finish does harm, there is the risk eventually that one will adopt on one's own account the same horror of things half done that was expressed by one's childhood authorities— "that which is unfinished is less far advanced than that which has not been begun," Valéry declares (*Mélange*, p. 375)—as well as the condemnation of the man who does not finish them off satisfactorily: "A failure is only ever a failure because it has been abandoned," Valéry also affirms elsewhere (*Tel quel*, 1:154).

7. But nevertheless—and this is the subject of this chapter— rebellion, whether in imagination or in deed, against the compulsion to finish things off flourishes just as strongly.

"Try to see that the child complies with good grace," Fénelon advises all grown-ups (quoted by Paul Robert under *s'exécuter*, to perform some required action), "and all you then have to do is to soften the unpleasant task it has accepted"; for once grown up, may he not always avoid that unpleasant task in future?

Having felt that he himself was abandoned, may he not now abandon some given enterprise in his turn, and by extension some person; increasing his distress, if need be, by leaving the unpleasant task at the very moment when it appears to be on the point of coming to fruition.

Having recognized his weakness when he was compelled to finish things, may he not experience a feeling of strength by exercising his freedom to drop them?

Valéry pities "the man who has never, even if only in a dream! grasped the outline of an undertaking that he has sufficiently mastered to abandon" (Valéry, *Variété*, p. 1181). He is "terribly jealous of what is worthy of me; never of the thing, but of the power of doing it— and above all of the power not to do it" (Valéry, *Tel quel*, 1:189–90). "One day, in a town of Islam," Montherlant recalls, speaking of the arrangement of his pleasures, "everything was ready for the great moment of wonder; at the price of what complicated plotting! The setting, the people: one word and everything was mine. I didn't say the word. The pleasure that I experienced was a thousand times greater than what I should have tasted by going through with it to the end. The powerful satisfaction of having refused; being able, and not to have wished it!" (Montherlant, *Aux fontaines du désir*, p. 120). Having traveled from Algiers to an outpost in southern Morocco in order to make love to a friend's mistress there, one of Montherlant's characters abandons his intentions at the last moment: "The pleasure of not taking her, having traveled more than two thousand kilometers in order to take her, was so much more delicate than the other!" (*L'histoire d'amour de la Rose de Sable*, p. 127).

8. The path from project to deed is readily suspected of being a long one; and there are many slips twixt cup and lip.

"It was a long way," says Retz, "from the whim to the will, from the will to the resolution, from the resolution to the choice of means, from the choice of means to the application of them" (Retz, *Mémoires*, p. 410). "Much is undertaken, but no one executes," one of Corneille's characters claims (quoted by Paul Robert under *entreprendre*, undertake). And Robert also refers under *distance* to the "distance there is between willing and doing." Though it is a dubious honor to belong to "the vague legion of those who sketch without finishing" (Benjamin Constant, quoted by Robert under *achever*, to finish), it is also delightful.

9. So the act of pushing something on to the end may be viewed as something remarkable.

"To perform entirely, from beginning to end, completely," Robert gives under *exécuter*, to perform; he also quotes Brunot to remind us (under the noun *achèvement*, finishing off, and the adverb *complètement*, completely) that the French language designates "the complete action, the action continued until it is finished (*poussée jusqu'à l'achèvement*)" in a very particular fashion, while using other means to denote cases in which the action "is not carried through to the end (*exécutée jusqu'au bout*"), in which "there is only semi-execution."

10. A man may boast of not being the sort who abandons things.

"I have never abandoned an affair when it was worth finishing," says Chateaubriand (quoted by Robert under *to abandon*), "there are certain things that I have pursued for fifteen years of my life, as full of ardor on the last day as on the first."

11. As for the future, it is often acceptable to say that one possesses "a firm intention to carry things through"; or "a firm resolution," according to the expression of one politician, "to perform in one rapid action the tasks I have assigned myself" (André Marie, investiture address, A.N., July 24, 1948; *L'Année politique* 1948, p. 337); or "a considered intention," in the words of another, "to fight the customary postponements and to hurl ourselves resolutely along the road of realization" (Gaborit, A.N., October 13, 1955; *J.O.*, p. 5012). "The resolution has been made, I intend to fulfill it!" exclaims a Racine character quoted by Paul Robert under *achever*, to bring to a successful conclusion.

During the early days of the Fourth Republic, when the Palais-Bourbon was the target of a minor attack, the prefect of police (Lahillonne) declared: "I intend this enquiry to be pursued to its conclusion, it must be carried out to the last detail" (*Le Monde*, February 7, 1958). Did that not go without saying?

12. But the French language itself presents the act of completing in a rather unfavorable light.

Under *achever* in the sense of "finishing something one has begun," Robert gives two uses that are neutral or moderately favorable: "to finish one's education," "to conclude an enterprise." The other two are less so: "this stroke completes the picture" and "he is completing his ruin." *Achever* applied to a person signifies at the very least that he has been "struck low, or his ruin, loss, discouragement completed": "what finished him," Alphonse Daudet writes, "was the news that . . .". Though *achèvement* (completion) is perfection, that which is *achevé*, in the sense that "it is no longer lacking anything, concluded, complete, entire, finished, meticulously finished, perfect" is, despite this list of favorable aspects, obscurely linked to the misfortune that is apparent in three out of four of the authors Robert quotes: La Fontaine speaks of "a perfect portrait . . . of an unhappy wretch"; Bossuet, of the "mysterious finish that misfortunes add to great virtue"; and Faguet, again, "of the mysterious finish conferred by misfortune." After this we find *achevé* making up phrases intended to be "taken in bad part": "completely ridiculous," "a complete fool"; a Corneille character declares that "a more complete tyrant has never been seen"; another prophesies: "But one more court case and I am finished"; and there are the *précieuses ridicules* who are "finished" in more than one sense by their infatuations.

"*Fini*," in the sense of "complete, perfect of its kind" is even "in these days solely pejorative": a perfect rogue, a perfect rotter, a perfect liar.

As for *consommer* in the sense of "bringing (something) to completion or fulfilment," two of the usages Robert gives are mildly favorable or neutral: "to conclude one's work," "to consummate the marriage." The other three are very serious: "to succeed in committing an act of wickedness, a crime, an attack," "to consummate one's sacrifice," "everything is over." Of the four quotations given, one illustrates "consummate the marriage" (Montesquieu), the others "complete his ruin" (Balzac), "complete his martyrdom" (Bloy), and "complete [his] misfortune" (Camus). But it is true that *consommé*, broadly speaking, is favorable in connotation.

Though "to execute (*exécuter*) something" is "to put it into effect, to bring it to fulfillment," the reflexive *s'exécuter* on the other hand means "to determine to do something painful, disagreeable," or, more particularly, "to resolve . . . to fulfill an engagement," which Robert, following the Académie, illustrates with a reference to someone who "executed himself [i.e. met an obligation] in order to avoid prosecution."

13. The inclination not to finish things is easily combined with the horror of being interrupted.

14. Though grown-ups attempt to counteract what they consider a tendency in children to leave things unfinished, they also often prevent them from continuing one occupation upon which they are already engaged in favor of another, which the children may well feel is an unwelcome chore.

15. Having attained adulthood, one has a greater capacity for making sure that one is not disturbed by irritating and troublesome intruders: in which case "nothing comes to interrupt me" (La Fontaine, quoted by Robert under *interrompre*, to interrupt).

16. At the same time, the desire arises to treat the authorities in one's adult life as one has oneself been treated by those that governed one's childhood; to harry them with interruptions in the execution of their plans just as one was irritated oneself, as a child, by the sudden changes of activity inflicted upon one by grown-ups.

17. As for all that ado about not finishing what one has started, one can always, to begin with, go no further than talking about it: words, words, words . . . .

La Fontaine observes that the court "teems with counselors," "when deliberations only are needed," but that "there is no one to be seen" "when execution is required": Bossuet remarks likewise that there are "men of great deliberation . . . but no execution" (Robert under *exécution*); and Rousseau speaks of men "enchanted with this project in appearance, but all taking it at bottom for a pure castle in the air, something to talk about . . . without any intention of executing it in effect" (Robert under *effet*); men who, by applying "the combined tactics of boldness in words and prudence in their actions" (de Gaulle, *L'unité*, p. 294), eventually provoke the reaction: "So he says!"

18. Or it may be a case of resolutions presented as having been firmly taken, but then hardly ever followed by the actions they appear to require.

As in daily family life, "vigor of speech" in the Assembly under the Fourth Republic "usually heralded some colorless compromise" (Georges Mamy, *Le Monde*, February 13, 1958), if not a mere continuation of things as they were. Having reminded the house during the Algerian war that "everything must be done . . . to ensure that the nation's youth shall have confidence in the government's action," a deputy went on to explain: "In order to attain this, it is true that firm and courageous *declarations* must be made, but also—you are ministers and I have been one, and I know that this is the main difficulty of authority—there must be detailed *application* of the decisions that we take" (Robert Buron, A.N., June 2, 1956; *J.O.*, p. 2272).

19. This tendency is perhaps even more pronounced in periods of danger.

"The official decision to defend Paris," said Léon Blum of the situation on June 11, 1940, "still held good in the sense that it had not been expressly rejected; but everything went on as though it had in fact been abandoned, or even as though it had never been accepted in any full sense, with a real intention of carrying it out" (Blum, *Mémoires*, p. 27). According to Sir Edward Spears, the plans formed by Paul Reynaud at the same period for a "stronghold in Brittany" or for an evacuation toward North Africa demonstrated a kinship between that politician and those described by La Fontaine "who spend all their time wishing and lose in such fancies the time they would do better to spend on their affairs." "This colloquy," Sir Edward writes, of a conversation between himself and the French premier on June 15, "left me with the impression that Reynaud was still clinging to the idea of fighting on in Africa, but as a vague idea, something to talk about, not a clear plan that must be carried out and to which everything must be subordinated" (Spears, *Assignment to catastrophe*, 2: 252–53).

But a resolution hardly needs to be somewhat vague in order to prove futile.

During the night of May 13–14, in the Palais-Bourbon, Pierre de Chevigné, having been picked as minister of defense in the Pflimlin government then being formed, is said to have declared off the record: "If we're put in power, I shall be on a plane to Algiers by three in the morning, and I beg you to believe that two hours after my arrival, everything there will have been settled" (*Le canard enchaîné*, May 16, 1958). At the same time, his colleague André Mutter, who had been allotted Algeria itself, was making the following prediction: "I shall put on my decorations, I shall take the plane, I shall step off it in Algiers, and I shall say: Here I am," to which the journalist reporting his words added: "No one asked him to go" (Jean Ferniot, *L'Express*, May 22, 1958).

20. Conscious of the cynical predictions with which announcements made to his colleagues or to the public may be greeted, a politician may attempt to suggest that his words will in fact be followed by action.

"I was present yesterday [October 28, 1947] at the sitting of the Assembly," notes an important official of the Fourth Republic in his diary. "Chaban-Delmas spoke in decisive tones intended to convey great firmness" (Jacques Dumaine, *Quai d'Orsay 1945–1951*, p. 228).

21. But the very expressions that originally served to indicate firmness have come to create a certainty of the converse, since it is generally held that "firmness is not common in France" (the Cardinal de Retz quoted by Henry de Montherlant in his "Notes à Port-Royal," *Théâtre*, p. 1055).

The same is true of those expressions that affirm its presence very emphatically while imputing the responsibility for its absence to the past and to others.

In consequence, the emphasis put upon the announcement of any resolution at all out of the ordinary may be precisely what suggests that the actual results will be puny.

When a prime minister under the Fourth Republic declared that "we shall be as hard as steel with regard to any individual who . . ." (Guy Mollet, A.N., June 2, 1956; *J.O.*, p. 2276), the extravagant character of the expressed intention automatically aroused contrary expectations.

22. An energetic leap followed by a collapse, or a phase of

efficient execution followed by one that is no longer so: these are the major images of the tendency not to follow things through.

"The Frenchman," according to Montesquieu, "always does half of anything admirably well, and the remainder sometimes very ill" (*Réflexions sur la monarchie universelle*, 17). For Rousseau, though "the French are all fire when it is a matter of undertaking something," "they are unable either to finish or maintain anything" (quoted by Robert under *feu*, fire). "Too many people," a "Gaullist" member of parliament declared during the Fourth Republic, "do not believe that France is capable of persevering in any line of action" (René Moatti, A.N., October 13, 1955; *J.O.*, p. 5088).

23. Those who are satisfied with the initial stages of their undertakings are often apprehensive lest the remaining stages should prove less so.

"Youth must not fall by the wayside," proclaimed one youth movement during the fifties. "Show Pflimlin," the Committee of Public safety demanded on May 14, 1958, recalling the glories of the previous day, "that it was no flash in the pan" (*Le Monde*, May 15, 1958). And a short while later, the ex-soldiers and Resistance members of the special defense services demanded the adoption of a certain attitude "so that the national upheaval unleashed on May 13 shall not sink into oblivion" (*Le Monde*, July 4, 1958).

24. Corresponding to this fear, there is the resolve, or the claimed intention, never to let go.

There are only too many stories told of leading politicians according to which, whether in the spring of 1940 or the spring of 1958, they expressed their resolve to die if needs be in the pursuit of a line of action which they later, and apparently without the slightest difficulty, simply abandoned. It is possible, on any occasion, to present one's conduct as "unflinching," claiming for oneself that rare firmness of character exemplified by carrying on with what one has once undertaken (de Gaulle, *Le fil de l'épée*, p. 55). "Every Frenchman," declared one prime minister under the Fourth Republic "will understand . . . the necessity for a determination not to yield" (Paul Ramadier announcing the reshuffle of his cabinet in May 1947. *L'Année politique*, 1947, p. 329). A president of the Republic once voiced a presumption that "men of inflexible character" would be chosen for the essential posts, and this was just at the time when he was offering the task of forming a government to a politician of entirely the opposite reputation (Vincent Auriol's request to André Marie to form a government, July 21, 1948; *L'Année politique*, 1948, p. 333).

25. For not falling by the wayside before completing some

undertaking, however vigorously begun, not slowing down one's onslaught after having ridden into the tourney full tilt, in Montaigne's expression, may well be viewed as something very extraordinary: magnificent—or disastrous.

Valéry reminds us of "the demon of *Obstination*, the famous *Block Head* and all his many mottoes: *perseverare diabolicum*, 'I will maintain,' 'Against and in face of all' " (Valéry, *Mauvaises pensées et autres*, p. 221).

26. It is accepted as normal that whatever stands tall at the outset will eventually get bogged down and fizzle out, even if it means giving up when the goal is in sight; it is accepted that impulses will prove capricious, ephemeral, passing whims, mere fancies. "Some men," Lammenais reminds us, "begin with ardor, and then sicken [of a task] before they reach the time of harvest" (quoted by Robert under *ardeur*, ardor).

"It is part of nature," says one of Montherlant's characters, "that what endures also tires" (*La Reine Morte*, act 2, tableau 1, sc. 1); "I have blown myself out," says another, "like the desert wind that first of all drives waves of sand before it like a great cavalry charge, and that finally spreads and exhausts itself: there is nothing left" (ibid., act 3, sc. 4).

It is expected that movements or governments aspiring at first to make profound changes should "agree to play by the same rules" as the existing order of things; it is not considered particularly astonishing that the rigor of those who have decided with much publicity upon such and such sanctions should be seen to decline in the course of their execution, or that the sanctions themselves should before long shrink in scope, be annulled, or simply allowed to become dead letters; we are all familiar with "those many . . . learned men . . . particularly in French universities . . . for whom a few brilliant works at the outset of their careers have earned a reputation that they have not been able or concerned to keep up" (André Weil, *Nouvelle revue française*, January 1955, p. 100); just as the high scholastic performance necessary to win one a place in one of the famous higher educational establishments is generally thought of as declining once entrance has been achieved.

27. Will some slightly arduous resolve I have taken prove able to maintain itself during the interval, however exiguous it may be, between the moment of its origin and the instant when I may translate it into action?

If it had been possible to vote immediately after such and such an event, it was often claimed in the Assembly under the Fourth Republic, then such and such a spectacular result would have ensued; but because it was necessary to wait—on account of constitutional or procedural provisions, or as a result of some clearsighted delaying action on someone's part—the resulting atmosphere of resignation led to things continuing just as they were before. The government survived yet again; the bold measure, so attractive at first, was not passed.

But perhaps the measure was only attractive insofar as everyone concerned was secretly aware of the coming delay, and therefore of the possibility for second thoughts.

28. Even when fatigue and the cessation of desire do not cause an enterprise to be abandoned, the resistance of things themselves may succeed.

29. Here again, perseverance is often seen as a rather rare reaction, one worthy of notice.

"He had convinced himself," says Charles de Gaulle of General Gamelin, "that at the stage he had now reached, the essential thing was to fix his mind, once and for all, upon one definite plan and not let himself be diverted from it henceforward by any possible change of fortune" (de Gaulle, *L'appel*, p. 28).

30. If I am suspected of a tendency to yield to outside pressures—and if I myself am perhaps inclined to believe so too— than I may be inclined to affirm the contrary, right up to the moment when I finally give way.

On February 6, 1956, Guy Mollet was to sacrifice Catroux to the discontent in Algiers. On January 31, presenting himself to the Assembly, he described his attitude to life: "We do not want much, but we do very much want it" (*J.O.*, p. 139). "You have before you," he declared to his colleagues assembled to invest him, "a man of good will who is quite ready . . . to attempt . . . to prove to you that he is also a man of will" (ibid., p. 150). As for his first important act, he reminded a group of Algerian deputies who visited him at the Hôtel Matignon in order to protest against the choice of Catroux: "I am the boss" (*Le Monde*, February 4, 1956). "I am the boss and the entire government stands behind the minister in office" he is said to have affirmed once more, in Paris, before finally ridding himself of that very minister in Algiers instead of riding with him there, as he is alleged earlier to have said he would: "I shall be in General Catroux's car when he arrives in Algiers" (Jean Fabiani, *Combat*, February 7, 1956).

31. As for the variants of the "dropout" caused by pressure of circumstances, in the first place there is the halt called at the precise moment when the irremediable, the dangerous can no longer be postponed. In French, this is properly referred to as *se dégonfler* (to deflate), defined by Robert as "to lose courage or energy at the moment of action"). Or it is *flancher* (to flinch), for which Robert gives: "He seemed resolute, but flinched at the last moment."

When the R.P.F. was going through a bad patch, one often heard people repeating a witticism at de Gaulle's expense said to have been originated by Malraux: "He led us to the Rubicon, but only to fish," a remark that "activists" like Léon Delbecque, disappointed by the beginnings of their mentor's second reign, were to change to: "It wasn't in order to sit fishing that we crossed the Rubicon." Victor Hugo had already conjured up a human form "sitting down to fish on the brink of infinity" (quoted by Michel Chrestien in *Esprit es-tu là?* p. 274)—a posture whose plausibility is emphatically denied by Republican rhetoric, for example, in such statements as: "The Republic has never retreated in the face of . . . ."

32. It is also possible to "let things drop" at any point during the enterprise when faced with some unexpected obstacle.

This obstacle may be a minor one. "I am going to tear up this letter," Valéry suggests as an imaginary situation, "but the paper resists, and in that moment of resistance I change my opinion; I file it.—How many people were about to kill and have not done so, disturbed, put off by a nothing . . ." (points of suspension in original) (Valéry, *Tel quel*, 1: 68–69).

33. Or again, lassitude may lead one to yield to some pressure kept up for too long.

In a light comedy, the wife may warn the husband that she will end up by yielding to the man who is importuning her if the husband does not succeed in ridding her of him in a certain fixed time. The feeling she is expressing does not appear to be too unlike that referred to by Paul Reynaud when recalling the death of the Third Republic at the birth of the Fifth: "M. Lebrun," he explained to the committee formed to consult on constitutional matters in the summer of 1958, "had it within his power to authorize the then prime minister to constitute a free government abroad. If he did not do so, that was a result of intervention by military authorities, who recommended the conclusion of an armistice"; for "one would have needed to be made of bronze or marble to resist them" (*Le Monde*, August 2, 1958).

34. The world may also block the conclusion of an enterprise not—or not only—by resisting it, but by seducing those engaged upon it into other and more attractive paths. Such defections are the despair of grown-ups who have to deal with an "unstable" child. Having begun its work, "suddenly, his attention is seized by anything at all, and off he goes" (a mother writing to *L'école des parents*, May 1954, p. 45); "as soon as any difficulty occurs, [he] immediately abandons that task for another" (Clément Launay, *L'hygiène mentale de l'écolier*, p. 33).

35. The collapse that follows the original impulse may itself be followed by a further bout of energy.

Is it not perhaps a law of humanity—which according to Georges Sand "becomes discouraged and recovers again with great facility" (quoted by Robert under *se décourager*)—that things shall proceed by leaps, sudden onsets, sallies and starts, that they shall advance by alternating retreats and resumptions?

Or at least a law in France, since, according to Charles de Gaulle, "equally precipitate impulses and moments of weakening are one of our characteristics" (de Gaulle, *Vers l'armée de métier*, p. 33). During the Great War, Abel Ferry made a disconcerting discovery: the C.Q.G. "could fight only every six months. Two months of intense activity followed by three to four months of stagnation" (Ferry, *Les carnets secrets*, p. 156. December 18, 1916).

36. Though I am often appalled by the tendency toward non-conclusion that I sense in myself, I may also reach a compromise with it; I may accept it as serving some end that I am prepared to admit, to myself at least.

37. "What is the good of executing plans," we may ask with Baudelaire, "since the plan is sufficient pleasure in itself?" (quoted by Robert under *exécuter*).

38. Such pleasure may even be reduced if we imprudently put the plan into action.

"There is nothing so fine," Valéry reminds us, "as that which does not exist. . . . There is no work, however excellent, that does not swiftly reveal to the keen eye of jealousy a sufficiency of flaws, holes, and weaknesses" (Valéry, *Mon Faust*, p. 184). Colette describes certain "grand gestures . . . so minutely premeditated, so magisterially accomplished in thought that the error of performing them drains away their savor. . . . What woman who has meditated a crime of passion has not been let down by the crime itself? 'It was so much finer when I planned it. Is it always so dark and dull, blood on a carpet? And that mysterious discontentment, that disapproving sleep in a face, is that death, is that really death? . . .' She liked her crime better when she was still carrying it inside her, stormy and alive, completed down to the last detail, and ready to burst forth into reality, like a child in the final hours of its gestation. . . . But it did not really need reality all that much. . . . Reality has made it seem old, hackneyed, boring" (Colette, *Ces plaisirs* . . . , pp. 232–33).

39. Is not finishing something a small death? There are certain meanings of *achever* and similar words that seems to suggest it: "to finish off," "to be finished," "to reach the end."

40. Constantly to finish things, is that not at least to lose one's soul, as happened to one of Valéry's characters not unlike Napo-

leon: "Never a regret, never a reproach, never a pang of remorse, never a moment's yearning . . . [points of suspension in original]. But every action is money spent!" (Valéry, *Eupalinos*, p. 105).

41. To go as far as the act itself is also to reduce the freedom I enjoy while I am still able to posit that act or not (see chap. 1, secs. 5–6).

42. How blind one must be to all the reasons urging one not to perform an action in order to dare commit it!

"Intelligence," says one of Roger Martin du Gard's characters (quoted by Robert under *agir*, to act), "leads only to inaction. It is faith that gives man the impulse he needs in order to act and the obstinacy he must have to persevere."

Is there not a danger, therefore, that the very fact of my carrying some undertaking through to the end will reveal the fact that I am by nature a pigheaded bastard?

43. Moreover there is the sheer boredom of finishing things!

Under *épuiser*, to exhaust, Robert quotes La Fontaine, who had a horror of long works and formally banned the exhausting of any subject.

44. To push on to the end means to leave moderation and plunge into excess.

When he asks himself, "what have I suffered from most?" Monsieur Teste replies: "Perhaps from my habit of developing my thoughts to their full extent—from keeping on to the very end inside my own head" (Valéry, *Monsieur Teste*, p. 74).

45. But in any case, it is not incumbent upon me to reach a conclusion; that is someone else's responsibility!

In the parliaments of the Third and Fourth Republics, for example, "it is not necessary that the discussion of a subject should end with the taking of a decision," even though the majority of debates do end in that way. The fact remains that "a debate is in no way irregular if, for example, a statement on the part of a minister is followed by two or three speeches, and then the Assembly simply passes on to the next item on the agenda" (Lidderdale, *Le parlement français*).

This being so, "no official formulation of a subject is necessary in order to begin a debate": the debate may "consist simply of the free discussion of a subject and not of a precisely expressed proposition." "Usually," of course, it will become evident that "a formulation . . . has arisen from the course of the debate itself" which then "terminates in a decision for or against" that formulation; but "not necessarily," in which case the Assembly "passes on to another subject" (ibid., p. 144). Grown-ups, privileged as they are, no longer even feel they must force themselves to know what they want. They may be content with having simply "faced up" to a difficult problem—is that not already a great deal? —with having "achieved an awareness" of it and "examined its various aspects" in a debate that would perhaps be even less "complete" if they had already—magnificently, but also tiresomely—achieved a "division." "The councils," Abel Ferry noted on July 27, 1915, referring to the cabinet meetings presided over by Poincaré since the beginning of the war, "ought to be a continuous act of will on his part; they are nothing more in reality than one long inconclusive chat" (Ferry, *Les carnets secrets*, p. 45).

46. It becomes easier for me to limit myself to the task in hand if I exaggerate its importance to the outcome of the general enterprise of which it forms a part.

Man is inclined to overestimate the consequences of his inner impulses.

"How many children there would be," Valéry remarks, "if eyes could fertilize! How many dead men if eyes could kill! The streets would be jammed with corpses and pregnant women." Since crime is "the transition from the internal to the external," "criminals are those who take nothing into account but deeds" (Valéry, *Tel quel*, 1: 71–72); for would ordinary men allow themselves to be taken in by a faint illusion of omnipotence, in the way that politicians, according to one reputable observer, tend to "believe that a problem is resolved once it has been thought of" (Jacques Fauvet, *La France déchirée*, p. 38)? "He wanted to write articles so hard-hitting," Jules Renard notes of a journalist, "that they would reduce the entire world to a heap of broken glass" (Renard, Journal, p. 122). Under the Fourth Republic, politicians were often accused of being unable to distinguish between the act of vigorous speech and that of changing the world in the way the words uttered suggest; they were also said to feel that verbal ripostes were an adequate response to very real attacks made upon them. This being so, anyone opposed to the "regime" might well find it useful to remind the country that "even the greatest plans only acquire real value by virtue of the practical measures that are taken to realize them" (de Gaulle, speech at Constantine, October 3, 1958; *Le Monde*, October 5 and 6, 1958), just as Jules Renard reminded professional and dilettante users of the word that "those who have talked best about death are dead" (Journal, p. 404).

47. Is it expeditious to go as far as a full realization of the goal assigned to any given enterprise?

Not finishing things, that childish vice, becomes an adult subtlety. In the grown-up play of grown-up persons, it may happen that not one of them has "any desire to succeed" (Saint-

Simon, *Mémoires*, 1: 227); some of them are simply trying to "distract" the others with "the shadow-play of action (La Rochefoucald, *Apologie de M. le prince de Marcillac*).

48. It may be seen as naïve to be actually aiming at the goal that one says one is pursuing, or to suppose that others do so; any real objective, it is frequently believed, must be considerably different from the one that is announced.

49. If it does happen that some particular player is believed to be without ulterior motives, that in itself may be seen as a ruse; is it perhaps because he is trying to dissociate himself from a world that is criticized for the deviousness of its calculations?

This way of seeing things was applied, during the last few years of the Fourth Republic, for example, to several politicians who presented themselves to the world as innovators. "Is M. Guy Mollet thinking (or hoping) to ensure the failure of his attempt?" asked one journalist when that leader was endeavoring to form a government at the outset of a long crisis, "thereby making it possible for himself, if the crisis continues, once more to become the man of the moment? Some may have calculated along those lines, but the former premier, who considers . . . that in the judgment of public opinion he passes for the possessor of 'authority in simplicity,' means for his part to confront the test ahead without any mental reservations" (Georges Altschuler, *Combat*, October 5 and 6, 1957).

50. When we propose an objective that is certainly admirable, though for that very reason somewhat unusual, do we not do so with the precise calculation, or a secret presentiment, that we shall not be called upon actually to achieve it? If so, then we are approaching the finessing tactics of the character in Saint-Simon who went looking for someone at his home "when he had made quite certain he would not find him there" (Saint-Simon, *Mémoires*, 1: 351).

51. To engage myself in the initial phase of a praiseworthy enterprise may seem sufficient to appease my conscience, as well as to guarantee a favorable image of me among those upon whom I depend. I can, with a serene mind and no apprehensions, follow a sweep of the hat with a clean sweep of the broom (see Jean Benedetti, *Paris-Presse*, February 27, 1958).

Having remarked that in both houses during the Third Republic "nothing less resembled the laws projected than the texts finally adopted," a celebrated observer then added: "As for knowing whether the baroque law thus arrived at will ever even begin to be put into execution, who is concerned about that?" (Jouvenel, *La république des camarades*, pp. 87–88). Under the Fourth Republic, a party could bring maximum pressure to bear on those deputies who were members of it in order to decree that none of them would continue to participate in or support a government unless it satisfied certain very stringent conditions; but the decree once made, the party could remain, imperturbably, a pillar of governments that it never embarrassed to any great extent with capricious demands for reform. The Ninth National Congress of the M.R.P., for example, when it demanded, in spring 1953, "the participation of workers in the responsibilities of management," claimed to have reached a capital political conclusion: it demanded "that the M.R.P. should participate only in a government determined to take the first step, without delay, toward orienting the efforts of the nation in that direction" (*l'Année politique*, 1953, p. 46). But things went no further than that; the M.R.P. continued to "participate" without thereafter feeling obliged to claim that the government had "taken the first step" in question. Moreover, a deputy belonging to that same party has given us a very accurate description of this widely recognized ploy on an occasion when he was asking for a debate upon an important reform of the Constitution: "Moreover, the National Assembly, having declared the urgency of a discussion on the matter, has of course lost no time in ensuring that it shall not appear on the agenda drawn up by the premier and the president at their meeting" (Edouard Moisan, A.N., March 2, 1956; *J.O.*, p. 612).

The child may already be familiar with this mechanism, since in the home, too, authority may content itself with the vehement expression of its wishes, insisting less upon their realization.

" 'After all, I couldn't just let him go and do such silly things without saying anything!': that, according to a psychiatrist, was the reaction of a mother who knew perfectly well in advance that whatever she said would be wholly useless, and might even have an effect wholly contrary to her intentions. The feeling that she 'must say something' was stronger than her desire actually to prevent the 'silly things' she claimed to dread" (André Berge, *L'école des parents*, February 1954, p. 8).

52. The act of making a claim may also suffice in itself to justify my image of myself as someone who can look after himself.

"Parisians in restaurants," Montherlant observes, "ask for attention, call the waiter, but so timidly that one feels that what is important, for them, is to have made a request, not to have obtained it. When they have given a puny tap on their glass, even if the waiter has obviously not heard them, they feel they have obtained satisfaction" (Montherlant, *Carnets*, 1930–1944, p. 294).

53. By making a gesture, even if only a verbal one, in the direction of instituting some change for the good, I am emphasizing that I cannot be held responsible for the continuance of the present bad state of things; it is others who are preventing the completion of what I have begun.

The fact that I may have counted on their doing so, or even provoked them into it, is another story altogether.

I may know that I would act as they are doing if I were in their shoes; this doesn't make the ploy less useful however, because I am not in their shoes.

This is often the case, it is said, when a deputy passes on to a civil service department some claim made to him by a constituent; or when, under the Third and Fourth Republics, the Assembly expressed particular wishes—particular peremptory resolutions—that would have required serious action on the government's part to be put into effect. (The constitution of the Fifth Republic was to contain clauses intended to make this maneuver more difficult.) Faced with such a situation, the government, in its turn, was very fond of "making a ploy that we are all familiar with" (in the words of Michel Debré), "and which consisted . . . in tabling the texts in question while hoping that they would never come under discussion" (A.N., May 26, 1959; *J.O.*, p. 557). Or while foreseeing that they would not—which may also have been the case with some great men of the Fourth Republic who managed to keep their reputations for honesty intact by proposing immediate and radical reforms knowing that the chances of their being put into effect were very slim indeed. One prime minister, for example, when on the verge—though he did not know it—of dissolving the Assembly (Edgar Faure), not content with proposing that the Constitution should immediately be revised so as to render dissolution obligatory in the case of a government's premature demise, also went on to demand that, if such a revision were not instituted, all the deputies supporting him (the radicals) should voluntarily consider their electoral mandates at an end in those same conditions (speech at Chamblay, November 1955). There were few indeed who believed that such an unlikely event as the realization of either wish would take place; but the man expressing them had thereby made it clearly understood all the same that he held not the slightest brief for the existing state of affairs, of which many were critical and in which his own career was flourishing.

Everyone may, in this way, simultaneously enjoy the evil present and clamor for a better future, relying upon others to express divergent but equally insistent preferences. Everyone can accept such and such an innovatory principle yet reject any application of it he finds undesirable by proclaiming it to be a violation of that principle if properly understood.

54. In certain spheres, and at certain periods, the "usual theme of reforms" can in this way provide "the table of contents for a book that is never written" (Edgar Faure on the subject of North Africa, A.N., June 21, 1955; *J.O.*, p. 3179) and the composition of which is, in the customary phrase, demanded with more insistence than conviction.

The subsidy system, the Assembly under the Fourth Republic was once told, has been "many times denounced in this Assembly, and always maintained, if not aggravated" (Jean-Marie Louvel, A.N., January 17, 1957; *J.O.*, p. 116). "For fifty years," another deputy recalled at the same period, "there has been talk in this Assembly of administrative reform, and numerous bills have been tabled by each and every one of the parliamentary groups. Not one of those bills has been allowed to come to anything" (Raymond Marcellin, A.N., July 26, 1956; *J.O.*, p. 3688).

55. Given such a context, one may find the same proposals being put forward again and again, indefinitely, or one may, on the contrary, find ideas, and extremely important ones, making sudden but fleeting appearances.

When the Assembly, under the Fourth Republic, was discussing electoral laws (in autumn 1955), the Anglo-American system was scarcely ever referred to. And then, quite suddenly, the most numerically powerful group in the Assembly proposed the adoption of the latter system. "The pitiful results of uninominal voting and a double ballot," announced a spokesman for the moderates, "together with the dislike of the electorate for multiple ballot papers, have led the three moderate parties . . . to propose this uninominal single ballot by *arrondissement*" (Raymond Marcellin, A.N., October 30, 1955; *J.O.*, p. 5394). The proposal seemed to be one of great import; had the entire system of electoral laws in France been turned topsy-turvy? By no means; after this polite gesture toward the need for a drastic solution, it was scarcely ever mentioned again.

56. If proposals for change are uttered with the certainty that they will never come to anything, by the same token there is a likelihood that they will be made more discreetly if their realization appears less improbable.

During the last years of the Fourth Republic, *Le canard enchaîné* commented, several months before the collapse of the regime: "This is all part of Charles the Great's classic scenario. Before the crisis breaks. But as soon as it has, then de Gaulle will only be interested in saying, 'Anything at all, except that'" (*Le canard enchaîné*, March 5, 1958). "Gentlemen," one prime minister of that period said to the Assembly, "those of you who clamor for fiscal reforms, when they see them coming step aside and cut them dead very swiftly" (Félix Gaillard, A. N., November 5, 1957; *J.O.*, p. 4652). "Those [deputies] who are hostile to voting by *arrondissement*," noted a journalist at that time "are basing . . . their hopes on certain migratory supporters of the *arrondissement* system who will quickly find a way of turning their coats as soon as the reform begins to have any real chance of actually being applied" (Jean Benedetti, *Paris-Presse*, February 26, 1958).

57. In the atmosphere just indicated, it may appear more natural and less risky to assume that any proposal of reform is made with a lucid awareness of its futility, rather than with excessively naïve sincerity. "I regret," we find a deputy saying, "that certain positions recently taken up, certain criticisms, should be looked upon as cleverly calculated attitudes" (André Bettencourt, A.N., March 26, 1957; *J.O.*, p. 1858).

58. It may even appear expeditious to make conspicuous advances in the direction of realizing some proposal, provided one is sure of being able to retrace one's steps later, relatively unobserved.

It is normal for virtuous "legislative measures" to have "their effect attenuated or even canceled out entirely by memoranda," as one journalist commented with reference to "the new legislation on home distilling" under the Fourth Republic (Jacques Fauvet, *Le Monde*, September 13 and 14, 1953). This ploy is used with particular frequency where budgets are concerned. One finance minister (Félix Gaillard) insisted (in the summer of 1957) on immediate and massive economies (600 billion francs); his purpose in doing so was said to be that of creating an image of himself as a bold statesman, thereby increasing his chances of succeeding the present prime minister (Maurice Bourgès-Manoury), which he in fact did. "In any case," the *Canard enchaîné* noted, "there will be 600 billions' worth of real economies or I resign, the stern young man announced at the time. To which end, draconian cuts were inflicted upon the military estimates. These cuts are going along very nicely. They have just come to light again in the form of overdrafts in the equalization [*sic*] statement received by deputies last week" (*Le canard enchaîné*, November 20, 1957).

59. One may also deliberately excite adverse reactions in some matter one is engaged upon, not so much because they will help to prevent completion of the undertaking (since that seems unlikely in any case) as for reasons that have nothing to do with what is apparently at stake on the surface.

In *Andromaque,* Oreste has come to Epirus as ambassador to Pyrrhus from the Greeks, who want possession of Astyanax. It so happens, however, that Oreste is in love with Hermione, who is herself in love with Pyrrhus, from whom Astyanax must be obtained. Pylade indicates to Oreste how his claim to the boy may help him in his real intent to win the woman:

> My Lord, conclude your embassy.
> Await the king. Then picture in his mind
> The Greeks all sworn to have great Hector's son.
> Far from granting them his mistress' boy
> Their hate will wake his heart to tenderness.
> If we seek to part them, we'll bind them closer yet

Therefore:

> To be granted nothing, insist on all.
> [Racine, *Andromaque,* act 1, sc. 1.]

"What was at stake?" one journalist asked when a number of Mendès-France supporters voted in the Assembly in favor of elections by *arrondissement.* Were they trying to win acceptance for this new electoral method, at that time very much favored by politicians of that particular persuasion? Not especially; the real motive, it appears, was "to bring about a union of those in favor, and even more so of those only pretending to be in favor of the *arrondissement* plan . . . with the double purpose of, on the one hand, breaking up the cabinet by forcing the departure of all the M.R.P. ministers—all savagely opposed to the proposed electoral reform—and, on the other, of preventing elections being held— thanks to the crisis thus provoked—before the end of the year" (J.R. Tournoux, *Combat,* November 1, 1955). Two weeks later, after another vote in favor of the same electoral method (its second reading on November 17, 1955), another journalist felt secure in saying that "many" of those who had voted for the bill were "in reality hostile to voting by *arrondissement;* they had only voted for it on its second reading with a view to embar- rassing . . . the government and . . . delaying the elections" (Jacques Fauvet, *Le Monde,* November 19, 1955).

Toward the end of 1959, the reputedly left-wing "Gaullist" who was at that time keeper of the seals (Edmond Michelet) intro- duced into the draft of a parliamentary bill for the reform of the commercial law code a clause concerning the obligatory presence at board meetings of employees' representatives. Did he do so in order to translate the "social justice" he so often spoke of into action? Or "in order to detonate M. Pinay," "a result that did not fail to ensue" (Jean Cau, *L'Express*, January 14, 1960)? When M. Pinay in fact left the government without giving any public explanation, he was widely credited with a lively aversion to a measure aimed at the "sovietization" of industry.

60. The reaction I am counting on from the other person may be that of paying me not to continue what I in fact began with the very intention of its coming to such a happy and advantageous halt: the method of the criminal blackmailer, to which many less scandalous precedures bear a strong resemblance. All sorts of people may call attention to the existence of such procedures should customary politeness or perquisites be forgotten; or, in less crude terms, they may treat the preliminaries of an act as a sort of small change. (More prudently still, instead of making the preliminary gestures of some unpleasant action, for the inter-ruption of which I count on being paid, I may let others make those gestures while waiting for an offer from a third party before employing my power to stop them).

In the mid-fifties, when there was question of taking steps toward the "internationalization" of the war in Indochina or toward the rearmament of West Germany, did the supporters of these movements in political circles consider them above all a stage on the way to a situation in which American soldiers would be fighting in Asia beside French soldiers, and German soldiers serving in conjunction with them in Europe? No, their concern was above all to add another "trump" to the hand of those ad-ministering France's foreign policies; not a "card" that would be "laid on the table," but one to be "kept on hand," thereby inciting the adversary to modify his line of action sufficiently to ensure that it would not be. The uncompleted action bestows power—because it contains the threat of completion—whereas carrying it to its conclusion may very well turn out to be a wasted thrust.

61. Under the Fourth Republic, "sham exits" on the part of eminent personages were thought of as being very frequent occurrences, even apart from the many so-called "virtual" resig-nations, meaning those that were openly conditional. When the radical congress in autumn 1957 was unable to agree about where the next congress should take place, the newly elected president of the party (Edouard Daladier) remarked: "You don't want Toulouse, you don't want Vichy, you don't want the committee to decide. So what do you want?" And then: "If there's nothing you want, then I'm going!" Whereupon, "suiting the action to the word," recounts one journalist, "President Daladier took up his hat and began to go." Since "the sham exit is a classic ploy among radicals," "before catching up with him" and making him stay,

in the epic series of mix-ups in Marseilles, "he was allowed to take a few steps" (*Paris-Presse*, November 26, 1957).

62. Any resignation that is at all voluntary tends to be interpreted along these lines.

Since it was found hard to accept in the political world of the Fourth Republic that anyone in possession of some fraction of power would give it up for reasons to do with his convictions, the few ministerial resignations for which the minister concerned nevertheless advanced such an explanation tended to be viewed as "sham exits" that went wrong; the imprudent minister must have misjudged his prime minister's feelings in the matter, and the latter was able to seize upon the opportunity to get rid of him.

63. At the very least, it was thought that any minister who did resign was expecting to be very swiftly recalled, and under conditions rendered satisfactory to him by the reactions that the resignation itself was intended to excite.

"Since the situation has not deteriorated," noted the only high-ranking official of the day whose diary has been made public, "de Gaulle is afraid that people will become accustomed to doing without him" (entry for September 26, 1946). In other words, the General "has made a very bad move" "thinking he was merely making a sham exit" (Jacques Dumaine, *Quai d'Orsay 1945–1951*, p. 120).

64. Even though I am not sure of not wishing to complete an undertaking, I may feel that it is impossible for me to predict just how far I may wish to go before I actually undertake it. It may be only during the actual course of the enterprise that it will become clear to me whether I intend to complete it or ensure that it miscarries.

"In cold blood" I am opaque to myself; "in the heat of the moment" I come to know myself. Before, there is no way of knowing; one can only reflect truthfully upon things as they are actually happening, or perhaps not until after they have happened. According to a maxim that is often repeated at moments when claims to Cartesian thinking are forgotten, "events make us known" not only "to others" but "even more to ourselves" (La Rochefoucauld, *Maximes*). And de Retz, referring to the La Rochepot plot, notes that "the effect its imminent possibility made on my mind" was "quite different from what mere speculation had produced" (Retz, *Mémoires*, p. xvii). Imagining his future as emperor, Titus, while his father is still alive, sees himself as married to Bérénice; once summoned to the succession, he begins to become aware of the incompatibility his love and his office, even though no new factor has appeared in the meantime. He looks back into the past:

I loved, I sighed for love in deepest peace:
Another bore the burden of the world;
Master of my fate, free to sigh for love,
My love accountable to none but me.
But scarce had my father been recalled to heaven,
Scarce had my mourning hand closed those dead eyes,
Than I beheld the error of my love:
I felt the burden now imposed upon me.
  [Racine, *Bérénice*, act 2, sc. 2]

Yet it was an entirely predictable "burden." Bérénice herself alludes to this fact as she struggles to understand the change in Titus:

The hatred of Rome, is that what he fears?
Rome's hate if he should dare to wed a queen?
Alas, if that were true . . . but no, a hundred times
Titus himself has reassured my love
Against the harshness of the Roman laws.
  [Act 2, sc. 5]

Such is the impotence of reason that Titus was incapable of foreseeing his reactions in a situation that was in itself entirely predictable and about which he thought a great deal. Reminding him that she loves him, Bérénice feels justifiied in asking him:

. . . Did you not know the law
That day when I first told you of my love?

Whereupon Titus reminds her of the necessarily erroneous nature of calculations made in advance:

Then I could live and lead myself astray.
My heart took care not to venture ahead
Searching for what might part us one day.
. . . .
I looked into nothing, I hoped for the moon.
. . . .
. . . But Fame, Madame,
Had not yet spoken in my youthful heart
As it speaks in the heart of an emperor.
  [Act 4, sc. 5]

Had he been more perspicacious, Titus would have followed the example of Valéry's artisan: "Just as the ancients submitted their plans to their sibyls, trembling with awe . . . and just as they entrusted to the fury of a female soothsayer the function of formulating replies that they were unable to obtain from either cold reasoning or learning, so the potter or the glassblower addresses the problem of his pot or vase to the fire; and the fire's answer is an oracle" (Valéry, *Pièces sur l'art*, p. 10). "My mother," Colette tells us, "never learned anything, as she put it, without burning herself" (*La naissance du jour*, p. 39). When unsure of whether she wants a child or not, a woman may refuse to use contraceptive aids with the explanation: "When it's happened I shall know whether I want to keep it or not." How can one know in advance?

"In France," at least, Léon Blum suggests, "collective movements of opinion are not constituted as in other countries by the aggregation and grouping together of individual feelings developed separately in the depths of individual consciences; it is in public discussion . . . that personal opinions are revealed" (Blum, *Mémoires*, p. 102).

It is only by being asked to form a government, or at least by being a likely candidate, that any politician under the Fourth Republic seems to have been able to make it possible for his colleagues to decide whether they wanted him as prime minister or not, whether they were for or against the particular political acts that he would be inclined to perform. Nothing less than an actual trial could prove sufficiently clearcut indications. "M. Soustelle's attempt," said a journalist of one such "trial run" that was heading toward certain failure (during the crisis brought about by Antoine Pinay's resignation) "is of great interest to the majority also," since "it makes possible a much more precise definition of the various points of agreement and disagreement" (Jacques Fauvet, *Le Monde*, December 28, 1952), and also the size of the forces drawn up in the various camps. Calculations of this kind are, in effect, prevalent at the beginning of any governmental crisis. Here is the same journalist writing six years later at the time of the final "power vacuum" of the Fourth Republic: "Have either M. Soustelle's or M. Bidault's policies a chance of attracting a majority in the Assembly? This question can only be answered by offering one or the other the opportunity to try. After that, we should need to find out whether a policy oriented more to the left, rather than to the right as in the past, would have majority support. . . . The proof of this may be incumbent on M. François Mitterand. If it is decided that such a trial cannot be afforded, then a doubt will remain" (Jacques Fauvet, *Le Monde*, April 17, 1958); the cold light of reason is incapable of predicting the reactions produced by the heat of the moment.

65. This means that in order to obtain any true information as to what my opponents and partners in a game as devious and passionate as politics "are made of" I must go beyond mere enquiries;

nothing can be as revelatory as their reactions to actual moves apparently made for the purpose of seizing some advantage, the real aim of which is in fact reconnaissance—a ploy I have dealt with elsewhere (*Du malaise politique en France,* chap. 2).

"He tried out various formulas," one politician under the Fourth Republic (François Mitterand) writes of Charles de Gaulle's line of action with regard to Algeria. These formulas were "rejected one after the other before having been put into practice." Why did de Gaulle act in this fashion? "Probably because he had very little faith in them and was merely desirous of gauging the capacity of the army and the activist opposition to resist the developments he was getting under way" (*L'Express,* December 15, 1960).

66. To provoke a dangerous situation in order to achieve a better understanding—one tells oneself—of the enemy's intentions, and therefore an increased ability to forestall him, is a ploy that may get out of hand, thus bringing about the realization of what one consciously fears and perhaps secretly desires.

This is the case with Orgon when he remains under the table allowing Tartuffe to press his advances upon Elmire to greater and greater lengths; so that when he does finally emerge, Elmire is able to address her husband ironically with the words:

> What, out so soon? You can't be serious.
> Back underneath! Things aren't yet at a head;
> What you've seen so far is inconclusive,
> You mustn't rely on mere conjectures
> [Molière, *Tartuffe,* act 4, sc. 7]

—which recalls the story of man who was shown his wife with another man in a position universally considered to be entirely unambiguous, but who still went on sighing: "Always these doubts!" While an unfaithful wife in a comedy, surprised in the same situation, immediately rounds on the husband and exclaims: "Now what are you going to get into your head just because you've found me in bed with Henry; I can see from here all the conclusions you're going to jump to!" And there is the delightful, and frightful, image of the man who, having piled the status of total cuckold on top of that of perfect idiot, gratefully accepts the pitiful pretexts that are negligently tossed his way.

67. Within the general context of attitudes described in this chapter, one is often confronted with one variant or another of the sequence that begins with a desire to emerge from the state one is actually in but finishes back in that very same state; having felt the desire to break away without any thought of returning, one finds that one has never left or has already returned. And

yet, though "the whole thing was only picked up from the floor in order to fall back on it again," we must not forget that "the falling back would never have occurred without that original impulse toward flight" (Montherlant, *Carnets,* 1930–1944, p. 240).

68. In one variant, my desire to change steadily shrinks as the moment of making the jump approaches; or it suddenly collapses at that moment (see sec. 31 above).

During the early fifties, for instance, a high percentage of candidates for rural "redeployment" "did not follow up their original requests. . . . When the moment came to 'make the jump,' they changed their minds" (Pierre Drouin, *Le Monde,* September 11, 1953). This is a frequent theme in literature, formulated, for example, by André Roussin's Nina when she explains to her lover: "Why am I married to Adolphe, who isn't the right husband for me? Why am I your mistress and why aren't we happy together? Almost all women know, just as I do, that they haven't got the husband who's right for them; and almost all those who have a lover also know that they're not happy with him. And almost all men know that they haven't quite hit the truth, either in their homes or in their love affairs. . . . You're like all men who lie in their beds at night thinking, without saying anything. And I'm like all the women who lie there pretending to be asleep. What do they think about . . . ? They think about going away to Mexico . . . and then, suddenly, they say to themselves one day: 'I'm leaving' and . . . for two days or a week or a month, they suffer, and when they've smashed everything to pieces . . . when two or three people have narrowly escaped death . . . they find themselves back where they started, with their office hours and their visits to their mistresses or their lovers and the times when they're together at home, just as they were before—each with his or her own happiness—under the same roof and in the same bed. Neither of them has actually gone to Mexico" (Roussin, *Nina,* act 3).

69. And when the lover replies: "I shall go, Nina," she admits it—"You may leave perhaps"—and explains why: "Because you're more of a child than the others." The others, because they can foresee the disadvantages of the change, which will be even worse than those of things as they are, do not leave (see chap. 3, secs. 16–19). In Colette's *La seconde,* for example, the wife, having discovered that her best friend is her husband's mistress, is tempted to throw the friend out; but having been strong-minded enough to make a fairly detailed comparison between the advantages and disadvantages of the new state of things she would thus be creating and those of the situation as it is, she decides, wisely, to leave things as they are.

70. The very imminence of the moment of decision conjures up more truthful attitudes to the states one must choose between, and provides an incitement to consider them in a more sober and detailed way (see sec. 64 above).

In both the field of light comedy (for example, Albert Husson's *Les pavés du ciel*) and that of serious drama (for example, Jean Anouilh's *L'alouette*) we find scenes in which a character works out in her imagination the consequences of some change in the state of things by which she is tempted (in the one case it is a question of murdering an excessively unfaithful husband, in the other, of renouncing an excessively tiresome vocation). In both cases, the disadvantages of the change appear so much greater than those presented by the situation as it is that it is decided to leave things as they are.

Or again, like the heroine of *Carnet de bal*, I may exorcise my regrets at not having chosen differently in the past by achieving a more sober and detailed appreciation of what would have happened if I had done so.

71. In the other variant of the image of a change that gets me nowhere, I do in fact leave; but then I come back. In the end, it is as though nothing happened at all; yet many things have in fact occurred. It was only by doing what I shouldn't have done, as one comedy character observes, that I was able to see what I ought to have done. Becque's *La Parisienne*, having been left by a lover who has proved to be an aberration, returns to her official lover and says, in fact: "What a lot of useless talking to get us back to the same place"; but she must know that her escapade has served to deepen her rut.

We are faced, then, with an image of stable equilibrium in direct contrast to the one of the unstable situation described earlier (chap. 3, secs. 16–28). An exact and truthful view of the situation should therefore permit those who wish to preserve it to put their trust in the forces that will eventually bring the one who has left back to his starting-point; according to the classic piece of advice on such matters, such a course is more likely to succeed than attempts to keep him or bring him back.

72. Having left, I discover that I have underestimated, after all, the value of what I abandoned.

73. The very fact of my departure may provoke reactions that reveal to me unsuspected qualities in what I have just abandoned; a theme expressed by the comedy plot in which the woman attempts to rid herself (preferably by death) of a man whose weakness she abhors, but whose reaction to her attempt demonstrates a strength that draws her back to him.

74. Or else I discover that I have overestimated the attractions of the new state I was intending to achieve.

Those upon whom I now have to count do not perhaps behave as I expected them to; or else their expected behavior does not really produce in me all I had wanted to feel; or else, again, I find I cannot free myself from the pull of my point of departure, which then, though not really appearing less disagreeable to me than before, takes on the aspect of something impossible to avoid: the case with the heroine of Villiers de l'Isle-Adam's *La révolte*, still in the repertory of the Comédie Française. Or again, what was intended to be so different turns out to be quite simply the same thing—as with the man who comes home after a round of the taverns, kisses his wife, and says to himself, Why all that effort, after all? According to Montesquieu, this is, in one way or another, the case with France "which, when leaving home, looks upon glory as the sovereign good, and in far-flung places, as an obstacle to her return home" (Montesquieu, *Réflexions sur la monarchie universelle*).

75. The very fact of having changed one state for another means that the first state has lost, and the second acquired, the disadvantage of being dominant; it deprives the second state of its adventurous quality and bestows it on the first.

In a much used comedy plot, the husband who has been abandoned aquires the attraction of a lover, which is therefore lost by the man whom the husband has been abandoned and who becomes a husband in his turn. There is always, therefore, a tendency to return to the initial situation.

"The habit of rebellion he had acquired," one of André Gide's characters says of an adolescent who has left home, "is driving him to rebel even against his own rebellion" (*Les faux-monnayeurs*, p. 282).

76. Since leaving (home or anything else) can be viewed as a necessary condition of my remaining henceforward in the place from which I have briefly absented myself, it may appear expeditious to block another's enterprise by causing it to miscarry rather than by preventing its actual conception. He must be allowed to go quite a long way with his undertaking—and incited to do so if needs be—so that he can be prevented, in the end, from completing it; it is by urging the other forward that one is enabled to play him the nastiest, the most profitable, the most elegant trick.

In one plot that is often used, a wicked character is sufficiently clear-sighted to perceive that there is only one possible method of separating two persons who love one another: removing the obstacles to their union.

"Instead of driving the devil out by force," Valéry counsels us, "you can ask him to sit down; ask him to tell you more about these kingdoms he says he's offering you, haggle over the bargain for a long while . . . wear him out with arguments; it is rarely indeed that promises, and even realities, can stand up to a knowledgeable and clearsighted gaze. . . . 'You say you're promising me these kingdoms. . . . Would you mind describing them? Let's go into this matter in detail. Tempt me lucidly. Win me over with clearly defined images'" (Valéry, *Tel quel*, 1: 77).

According to Montesquieu, Louis XI allowed the duc de Bourgogne "to console himself with his wars, his defeats, his victories; it is more likely that he gave him support in order to help him ruin himself" (Montesquieu, *Mes pensées*, p. 1105). When "a relative of M. de Vergennes asked him why he had allowed the Baron de Breteuil, who was regarded as his possible successor, to become minister of Paris," this, in Chamfort's version, was his reply: "Because, having always lived abroad, he is a man who is not known here; I know that he has no right to his reputation; but many people believe him to be worthy of becoming first minister: they must be disabused; the Baron de Breteuil must be seen for what he is" (Chamfort, *Caractères et anecdotes*, p. 183). After the fall of the Second Empire, certain supporters of the Orléans branch "considered bringing back Henry V simply to make it immediately apparent that it would be impossible to compel him to abdicate, thus making the way easy for the Orléans branch" (Jacques Chastenet, *L'enfance de la Troisième République*, p. 161–62). Henri Wallon, on the other hand, employed the following line of persuasion: "If the Republic is not suitable for France, the surest way of having done with it is to institute it" (ibid., p. 190). Referring to a moment in 1881 when Grévy summoned Gambetta to power, Jean-Jacques Weiss notes: "They came to say to him, Take over the country; and at the same time they let him know that he was being urged to assume power, not in order to elevate him, but in order to hurl him into it as though into an abyss" (quoted by Jean-Jacques Chevallier, *Histoire des institutions politiques de la France de 1789 à nos jours*, p. 365). I have written elsewhere of the use to which this ploy was put in the Assembly of the Fourth Republic, when it was referred to as "taking up a mortgage" (*Du malaise politique en France*, chap. 2).

The Fifth Republic has perhaps not entirely broken with this tradition.

But first, another look into the past: early in 1871, the government resigned itself to the surrender of Paris to the Germans, but "one obstacle still remained: the vehemently, if not very sincerely expressed intention of the Garde Nationale to pursue their "struggle to the bitter end" to the last man. In order to remove this obstacle, it was decided that a final sortie from the city be attempted . . . a battle demanded by the Garde Nationale and one in which they would be very much engaged. This was the battle of Buzenval, fought and lost on January 17, a battle the government had never believed would end in victory, and of which the true object was to convince those in Paris of the necessity for its surrender" (Chastenet, *L'enfance de la Troisième République*, pp. 42–43). In the same way, according to several observers, the true object of Charles de Gaulle's policy in Algeria from the spring of 1958 to that of 1961 was to convince the army and the Europeans in Algeria of the necessity of what might seem to them to be a surrender to the F.L.N.; to convince them by means of the failures that he foresaw would be the result of the various other policies he tried during those three years.

"Since it was the sole possessor of power" in Algeria, one journalist who held this view explained in the summer of 1958, "the army has found itself, during the course of July, progressively more unable to cope with the tasks incumbent upon it. It is one thing to be a general, quite another to be a prefect. And it is, in any case, very difficult when one is quite alone to be on both sides of the fence at once. Moreover, the overburdening and incompetence of the military administrators was complicated even further by the unenthusiastic attitude of the civil service officials. Deprived of their authority and blamed, by the 'system,' for all the Republic's failings, these officials were crippling their new bosses with the paralysing weight of their inertia. Only the nomination of civil deputies as laid down in the decree of June 28 could remedy this situation. M. Pelletier [minister for the interior] —who was in full possession of all the facts after his visit to Algeria in late July—refused absolutely to allow this." Why? "The minister for the interior is credited with the intention of having wished to let the military drink their cup of adversity to the lees. Having proved themselves unable to cope with civil power, they were then expected to renounce it and hand back civil authority to a new set of administrators" (*France-Observateur*, August 28, 1958). A year later, two journalists were interpreting a large-scale military operation in much the same way: "At General Massu's headquarters, it is now being said . . . that operation "Jumelles,' in its more spectacular aspect, has a quite different objective in General de Gaulle's mind than that officially announced; the intention is much less that of 'crushing the rebellion in Kabylia,' as one general affirmed in an interview published several days ago in *L'Aurore*, than of proving that even by 'throwing in our lot' there is no solution possible in Algeria by military means alone, and that the political phase must be entered as soon as possible" (Claude Estier and Edouard Roermond, *France-Observateur*, August 6, 1959). Having remarked during the following year that military prospects were considered at the Elysée (that is, by General de Gaulle) to be rather gloomy, *Le canard enchaîné* then added: "But don't go thinking that Mongénéral is disturbed by this. He is even said to have explained recently that, on the contrary, such prospects fit quite splendidly into his plans, which evidently consist in leaving the army there to convince themselves by their own efforts that a military solution is impossible" (*Le canard enchaîné*, April 6, 1960).

6

GOOD LUCK AND NEAR MISSES

1. Since a great many things are necessary for our content-ment, there is a great likelihood that they will not all be present at the same time. And since the absence of a single one is suffi-cient to make us unhappy, there is a strong probability that we shall be, as the Chevalier de Méré put it, in lamentable case.

La Rochefoucauld says of "the great and the ambitious" that "they require the accumulation of an infinity of goods to make them happy" (*Maximes*)—but is that not perhaps also true of many "average" men?

Even if we suppose with Flaubert "that to be stupid, an egotist, and healthy, those are the three conditions . . . for happiness," the fact remains that "if we lack the first, then all is lost" (quoted by Robert under *heureux*, happy).

2. It is a characteristic of the fool, or of the child, not to know how many conditions must be fulfilled in order for satisfaction to be achieved. "Two tiny urchins are wandering along the avenue du Bois," runs one of André Gide's favorite stories. "A sumptuous carriage rolls past. 'You see that woman?' says the elder; 'well, buddy, yesterday I could have had her.'—'Do you know her then?' —'No, but I had a hard on' " (Gide, *Journal 1889–1939*, p. 243).

3. Any happiness there may be is therefore fragile, threatened; a privilege "that one senses, night and day, to be at the mercy of fortune" (Henri Bosco, quoted by Robert under *fragilité*); if only it will last!

4. Apart from the element of chance, there is also the fact that "life . . . likes to laugh at us"; "she amuses herself by showing us happiness and then immediately snatching it away" (Paul Léautaud, *Journal littéraire*, 1: 57). In fact, chance itself is "a great mocker" (Robert).

5. When I experience a desire, shall I be able to satisfy it? Presented with an opportunity, shall I feel the desire?

"In small towns," Montesquieu notes, "people have no chance of enjoyment, and in large ones, no desire" (*Mes pensées*, p. 1268). "Society is composed of two broad classes," says Chamfort: "those who have more dinners than appetite, and those who have more appetite than dinners" (*Maximes et pensées*, p. 46). It is a funny thing, life always sees to it that one has what one does not really want, yet obstinately refuses to grant one's most heartfelt wishes. The princesse de Polignac, having expressed astonishment at the reason offered by her husband for his unhappy mood —"I am in love and beloved"—was then given the explanation: "It's a different person in each case." There is no one more punctual at rendezvous, it is said, than the woman one is not in love with, and Montherlant describes "the dance of cross-purposes": "How difficult it is for people to give us the very thing we want or need! The invalid who would benefit from champagne is sent flowers. The man who wanted fame is given happiness, the one who wanted decorations is given money, and the one who likes his meat gamey is offered virgins. There are men who have spent their whole lives being given *everything*—everything except the thing they wanted" (Montherlant, *Carnets* 19–21, p. 161). "Every time a long bout of reading had put me in the mood for a chat," Proust remembers, "the companion to whom I was burning to talk had just finished basking in the pleasures of conversation and was now asking nothing better than to be left quietly alone to read." And also, "If I had just been thinking about my parents with affection and making the most sensible decisions of a kind most likely to give them pleasure, they had always been engaged, during that time, in learning of some peccadillo that I had already forgotten and for which they would begin criticizing me severely the very moment when I rushed forward to embrace them" (Proust, *Du côté de chez Swann*, pp. 155–56). Later on, he was to experience the evenings "when Albertine had formed some plan for the following day that she did not wish me to know of. . . . The moment she came in . . . I had already perceived the unknown, restive, implacable, untamable desire." Moreover. "this was often on those very evenings when I had awaited her return with the tenderest of thoughts, when I had counted on throwing my arms around her neck with the utmost tenderness"

—"misunderstandings such as I had often had with my parents, whom I found cold or angry with me at the very moment that I rushed toward them brimming over with affection" (Proust, *La prisonnière*, pp. 87–88).

6. As for the passage of time, it is considered normal that one condition of a happy outcome should cease to be realized at the exact moment when another comes to fulfillment; that during the brief span when such and such a condition is present, such and such another, normally fulfilled, should vanish.

"Those things most desired do not occur," La Bruyère observes; "or if they do occur, then it is neither at the time nor in the circumstances that would have enabled them to afford extreme pleasure." "One could," it is true, "defend oneself for feeling a certain joy at seeing a wicked man perish"; "His death finally occurs, but in a situation such that our interests do not permit us to rejoice at it; he dies either too soon or too late" (La Bruyère, *Les caractères*, "Du cœur," 62 and 66); for time has a fondness for such annoying mistimings.

Perhaps it takes a de Gaulle talking about France itself for it to be affirmed that there exists a "secret harmony in accordance with which events are ordered" and which, in the summer of 1943, "caused the rebirth of French power to coincide with the weakening of her enemy's" (de Gaulle, *L'unité*, p. 131).

On the other hand we find a humorist (André Breffort) reminiscing, When I was young, the girls my age all liked forty-year-olds. Now that I'm forty they all like boys in high school.

The nature of things may well be the same when our concern is to diminish an evil rather than to attain some good.

"One always falls ill on Sunday," Montherlant notes, "when the pharmacies are closed and the doctors out gallivanting. One always needs urgent professional advice in August, when Paris is deserted" (*Le démon du bien*, p. 104).

7. Having ceased to love I shall begin to be beloved. "In love," Proust declares, "the barriers . . . cannot be broken down . . . by the man who is thrown into despair by them; and it is when he is no longer concerned with them that . . . those barriers, stormed before without success, will fall quite uselessly" (*A l'ombre des jeunes filles en fleurs*, p. 613).

Having refused a love that was offered me, I begin to fall in love when I have succeeded in killing the other's desire for me.

8. Such movements in contrary directions are not seen as being solely the work of chance; have not both been provoked in many cases by the same cause?

"It is in summer," Jules Renard muses, "that the springs would be coolest if they didn't dry up" (*Journal*, p. 673).

According to a belief that has perhaps still not entirely disappeared, making love weakens the feelings of the man but arouses the woman's. "Women," La Bruyère comments, "become bound to men by the favors they accord them," whereas "men are cured by those selfsame favors" (*Les caractères*, "Des femmes," 16). ("The woman," Montherlant observes, "begins to love when he [the man] has stopped" [*Les jeunes filles*, p. 173]). "Before they love / He desires her / After they've loved / She wants him," sings one of Audiberti's characters (Jacques Audiberti, *Les naturels du Bordelais*, act 2).

9. If youth only knew, if old age could do, the proverb has it. During the course of his life, a human being attains the plenitude of his powers at a time when he is still in the process of acquiring the skill without which he cannot enjoy those powers to the full; by the time his skill is at a peak his powers are already declining. By the time one has learned how to live, it is already too late.

10. Too late even if there has meanwhile been an increase in the resources available outside of oneslf.

"And what good will it do us to have wealth," Harpagon's son asks, "if it does not come to us until we are no longer of an age to enjoy it? (Molière, *L'avare*, act 1, sc. 2). But that is precisely the way things are, as La Bruyère points out: "When one is young, often one is poor. . . . One becomes rich and old at the same time; so rarely is it that men are able to combine all their advantages!" (*Les caractères*, "Des biens de fortune," 39): and so difficult for them, therefore, to gain any advantages from them. It is "the story . . . of the nuts and the teeth; when one has teeth one has no nuts, and when one has the nuts one no longer has the teeth" (Nicole, *Les lions sont lâchés*, p. 22). "That's life," comments one of the characters in the film *Le plaisir*, "old age and salmon, youth and sardines."

11. As desires arise in childhood and adolescence slightly before the time when one is in a position to satisfy them, so they survive after the means of sating them, a fact, the aging Léautaud assures us, that "still poisons my existence today" (Léautaud, *Entretiens avec Robert Mallet*, p. 307).

"I am old . . . and disgusting, but I am not in the least disgusted," declared Voltaire (quoted by Robert under *dégoûtant*). Thus "you can love, but you can no longer be loved" (Chateaubriand, *Mémoires d'outre-tombe*, bk. 10. chap. 3).

But on the other hand there is the image of the eternally sprightly old man who declares: "What amuses me is that I still receive orders to amuse myself from my decidedly eternal organs" (Jacques Audiberti, *La fête noire*, act 3) and whose ways of amusing himself are not, for all that, either risible or pitiable. But to what degree is this image in fact intended as an antidote to our apprehensions of age-the-decline?

12. So many near successes are such very near misses. Only one little thing is needed for everything to be all right; that one little thing is precisely what is lacking, and everything collapses.

"Do not be surprised," Pascal explains when talking about man, "that he is not reasoning clearly at the moment; there is a fly buzzing in his ears. . . . If you want him to be able to find the truth, then chase that insect away" (*Pensées*, p. 850). "Who was torturing you? What, after all, was the cause of that pain and those cries?" Valéry asks. "Who bit into you so deeply, who weighed down upon you, mingled with your flesh like the fire coincident with the coal, who made you twist in pain and twisted inside you the whole order of the world, all ideas, heaven, actions and the very least of distractions? Was it a monster, a pitiless conqueror, an omnipotent being familiar with all the resources of horror and your nervous geography? Here is is: a tiny thing, a little stone, a rotten tooth" (Valéry, *Tel quel*, 2: 96). "Happiness," remarks one of Marcel Aymé's characters, "depends sometimes upon so little." And another replies: "It's true. . . . It sometimes depends on very little indeed. One seems to be achieving it, and then, almost always, some unforseen and often very slender circumstance snatches it away from us for ever. Haven't you experienced it yet . . . that sickening disappointment as you watch some immense joy turning tail in the face of the most minute, the most ridiculous obstacle?" (Marcel Aymé, *Aller retour*, pp. 212–13).

13. Sometimes it is the most minute lack in our resources that is at fault; Valéry's angry exclamation "just one term missing and my whole work is in ruins" (quoted by Mondor, *Propos familiers de Paul Valéry*, p. 55) can be varied at will.

When losing a war, military commanders are only too ready to maintain that such and such an extremely modest addition to their resources would have meant a radical change in the course of things.

"Those four areas [the zones controlled by the A.L.N.] I told you about," the supreme commander in Algiers explained to a journalist in the fourth year of the war; "All I need is thirty thousand men, and not one more, to reduce them to order. But thirty thousand mobile, acclimatized, determined men is something I just can't get hold of." Already "in 1956, during the Suez crisis, all I needed was the mechanized division operating out there to finish the whole thing off." In fact, "it's always like that" (Robert Lacoste, reported by Jean Daniel, *L'Express*, May 2, 1958). During the same period, "there are commanding officers in various sectors . . . tearing their hair out," one deputy told the Assembly, "as they watch the fruits of several months of patient efforts at

pacification being lost for lack of a half-company" (Pierre Clostermann, A.N., May 13, 1958; *J.O.*, p. 2263).

14. Can we be sure, therefore, that some tiny economy may
not in the event prove murderous?

In his sketch of what the French tank corps should be, Charles
de Gaulle insisted in 1935 on two tendencies that "should be proscribed above all else": "the more-or-less" and "penny-pinching"
(de Gaulle, *Comment faire une armée de métier*, p. 135). According to the report drawn up by six experts at the request of the
courts after the bursting of the Malpasset dam, the collapse was
in fact "caused by an economy of nine million francs" (*France-
Soir* headline, February 21, 1961).

15. We often feel that our safety depends upon our having
finished a certain action before a certain time; for example upon
our having left here and arrived there before such and such a
moment. In which case a minute's delay leads straight to disaster, so that one can then exclaim: Just at the moment when
I was going . . . what awful luck! On other occasions, in order to
avoid the catastrophe one has to keep going exactly as before
until a certain moment; but one lets go, or is let go of, just a little
bit too soon. A device frequently resorted to in the plots of films
or plays.

16. Modeling my own behavior on the malignity of fate, I may
make it my project to cause the other fellow to fail just at the
moment when he seems to be on the verge of attaining his goal
(see chap. 5, sec. 76).

Under the Fourth Republic, for example, the idea of permitting
a candidate for the premiership to gain a number of votes just
short of what he required to succeed was often seen as attractive
and occasionally possible.

17. An insistence upon the tendency of things to wreck our
plans with trifles, to doom us to near-misses, may often be intended as an antidote to the "complacent optimism" that would
have us believe that the catastrophe will always be skirted, that
the decisive reinforcements will always arrive on time.

In Paul Robert's dictionary, the only phrases given under *de
justesse* (by a narrow margin) refer to the fact of winning. For
the figurative sense of *frôler*, on the other hand, the same dictionary gives: narrowly to escape (*frôler*) death, disgrace, ridi-
cule. To have avoided these things so narrowly may come under
the heading of *jouer de bonheur*, which Robert defines as "to
succeed against all the odds," to survive against all the odds on
our dying.

I often feel familiar with situations—whose return, in a
dangerous situation, I can foresee—in which I have cause to give
a "phew!" of relief, congratulating myself on having once more

had a narrow escape, knowing with a delicious shudder that the slightest thing might have plunged me into disaster, that it would have taken no more than a minute, an imperceptible change in the ordering of events (Charles Duits, *Le mauvais mari*, p. 254); while feeling all the same that the fortunate outcome that did materialize was in some way guaranteed. I shall always manage to get out of things, I shall always fall on my feet (after various things have fallen on my head), the moment of extreme peril is also the moment of a reversal verging on the miraculous.

18. This is in fact a privilege of the French and of France as a whole, her entire history being viewed as a long sequence of catastrophes and miraculous recoveries.

"One of the things that one is bound to observe in France," Montesquieu affirms, "is the extreme facility with which she has always recovered from her losses, her epidemics, her depopulations" (*Mes pensées*, p. 1099). Among nations, "there is not one," according to Valéry, "more capable of unexpected recoveries and reversals. Her history presents a picture of extreme situations, a chain of peaks and abysses more numerous and more closely packed in time than that of any other nation" (Valéry, *Regards sur le monde actuel*, p. 115). "It is her destiny," according to Montherlant, "to roll and pitch much more than other better constructed vessels, to be constantly at sixes and sevens, to have a perpetual leak in her hold, and yet for all that to get back to port just like the others, and sometimes ahead of them" (Montherlant, *Service inutile*, p. 78). "France," one great man who served under two Republics (Edouard Herriot) is claimed to have said, "is like a cat that's thrown out of a window and always falls on its feet" (*Carrefour*, September 10, 1952). "Elsewhere," comments one observer going into the matter in more detail, "when one branch of the economy dies off, the entire section of the population depending on it is visibly ruined. But in France . . . the small storekeeper without customers recoups his losses through the rise in the value of his premises guaranteed him by the rent laws, through the rise in his wife's or his daughter's wages" (Emmanuel Berl, *La France irréelle*, p. 67). For Charles de Gaulle, the Frenchman is "the loser at Charleroi attacking on the Marne" (*Vers l'armée de métier*, p. 21), and the French "a . . . people given to sudden and triumphant resurgences" (speech, June 18, 1942; *L'appel*, p. 675).

19. But de Gaulle is the man who also expresses in such striking terms the apprehension of France's death, a theme that will be treated elsewhere and as an antidote to which we have "the myth of France's automatic recovery after every crisis" (Charles Morazé, *Les Français et la République*, p. 23).

7

BLUNDERS AND THE HAPPY KNACK

1. To adults, children often seem to be creatures doomed to blunders, and therefore to failure, an inclination both shameful and to be fought against, watched for and punished.

"Youth, the season of failures," declares one of Montherlant's characters, himself no longer young (*Le Maître de Santiago*, act 1, sc. 5). "We lose the largest part of our youth simply through clumsiness," Céline says (Louis-Ferdinand Céline, *Voyage au bout de la nuit*, p. 79).

2. Frequently, adults refuse to accept that it is through its clumsy mistakes that the child, with time, acquires aptitudes. Any act on the part of a child that deviates from the rule may produce a violent displeasure in adults that renders the act literally intolerable.

Having remarked that "with great regularity . . . at about eleven or twelve months, the child manifests the desire to grasp its food in its hands," a child psychologist then adds that "this tendency often arouses violent reprobation on the part of the mother, who is intent at this juncture on inculcating in her offspring . . . a respect for cleanliness and good table manners." However, this specialist dares to go on, "it is desirable . . . to allow the child . . . to slop things about and dirty itself a little" (L. Kreisler, *L'école des parents*, January 1955, p. 29). "It is better," insists another of his colleagues writing along the same lines, "to let children try to find their own way for a while, rather than to require of them a degree of perfection that they are incapable of attaining" (René Diatkine, *L'école des parents*, February 1954, p. 35).

3. Here, as in other spheres, a grown-up is often more indulgent with other adults, or at least with him- or herself, emphasizing the normal and moral character of making a second attempt at some piece of workmanship that has not come off perfectly the first time; or, on occasion, discovering a virtue in the very imperfections of the first attempt that would be destroyed by "finicking" with it.

But these reactions themselves are possibly intended as an antidote to the horror of any legacy of clumsiness from one's childhood, an uneasiness at the idea of any first attempt falling too far short of the masterwork! "The fresco," Valéry declares, maintaining on behalf of grown-ups the postulate of instantaneous perfection, has "more virtue in it than any form of painting susceptible of reworking, retouching, repentance"; and "of all the arts, I know . . . of none more noble than those that invoke the aid of fire" (*Pièces sur l'art*, p. 8), whose action is immediate and irremediable.

4. Does not even the slightest error entail a risk of serious consequences? "An imperceptible trifle, and everything is out of joint" (Montherlant, *Le Maître de Santiago*, act 3, sc. 2)—a notion frequently expressed. Misfortunes can happen so quickly; "once one has made a blunder, its consequences become a chain reaction; you never see the end of it" (Jean-Louis Curtis, *Les justes causes*, p. 367).

In the arts that make use of fire, Valéry explains, "any deviation is fatal: the piece is ruined. If the fire dies down, or if the fire flares up . . . , the game is lost" (*Pièces sur l'art*, p. 9). And similarly, "a trifle can wreck the finest poem" (Letter to a friend, 1926; *Lettres à quelques-uns*, p. 161). And here is the day at the end of which a character in a novel feels assured of his good fortune: "Teeming with hidden ambushes, with dangerous bends, with deep-dug pits, when viewed retrospectively it was like a labyrinth constructed by some cunning and evil genius on the lookout for the very slightest blunder" (Charles Duits, *Le mauvais mari*, p. 254).

The slightest blunder on the part of a child—and children, after all, tend to make a great many rather clumsy ones—is likely, or so grown-ups frequently and passionately feel, to damage some precious and fragile object; whether, from lack of control over its gestures, it pokes its finger in its eye or its hands in its plate; whether it dirties this by touching something it wasn't supposed to, or whether it breaks that by dropping it or knocking it over.

The grown-up often seems to feel apprehensive when anticipating what might happen in the event of his suddenly lacking precision of movement, either literally or figuratively; in the event of his stumbling, or allowing himself to be tripped up.

"I made a slip while addressing the house," that consisted in no more than "the mistake of saying two or three unnecessary words," recalls one politician. But "it was a blunder," and "during those two minutes the speech lasted, I could sense the savage beast with the hundred mouths, the hundred hates, the hundred jealousies, ready to leap and tear me apart" (Abel Ferry, June 27, 1916; *Les carnets secrets*, pp. 143–44). "M. Tardieu," one of his colleagues recalls, "lost the confidence of the Senate forever, simply because one day, in his impatience, he allowed a '*Messieurs les Sénateurs*! . . .' to slip out in a cavalier tone that put the backs up of his whole audience. Another politician, making his maiden speech one evening, almost lost the entire advantage he had gained from a long exposé on the subject of scholastic reforms because he failed to recognize M. Bienvenu-Martin and addressed him as 'Monsieur le Sénateur' instead of 'Monsieur le Président'" (Jean Zay, *Souvenirs et solitudes*, pp. 394–95). A politician created by one novelist still experiences, at the end of a long and brilliant career, "that fear he had never shaken off of losing everything at one fell swoop through a single clumsy gesture. . . . He has the conviction that there are no small affairs in this domain [that of politics]: one passes through the greatest dangers, and it is on some tiny twig that trips one up and brings everything crashing down" (José Cabanis, *Les mariages de raison*, pp. 48–49).

In such cases it is often believed that things will crash down, or have crashed down, for good; there appears to be some difficulty, at the time, in foreseeing that great failures do not manage to attain the exalted status of the once and for all.

Under the Fourth Republic, for example, political leaders were sometimes viewed as having been forever diminished by some unfortunate incident or other (Georges Bidault or René Pleven in the summer of 1954), even though they were destined to make a brilliant comeback several years later. There is a feeling that because they have been "ploughed" more than once when attempting to achieve a certain post (the premiership for example), politicians must be considered as permanent "dropouts" (Pierre Pflimlin according to Claude Estier in *France-Observateur*, June 6, 1957). Then, shortly afterwards, they attain the coveted post all the same.

5. In every field, there is a certain necessary technique; there is no such thing as spontaneity that can dispense with "know-

how." "To love takes skill," Pascal says (*Discours sur les passions de l'amour*).

6. Where there is success there must have been aptitude; failure is produced by clumsiness.

"She accused him of clumsiness in his dealings with her daughter," Radiguet writes of a mother-in-law. "She attributed the sudden change in her daughter's character to this clumsiness on Jacques' part" (quoted by Robert under *maladresse*, clumsiness). The impotent man (or the man who gets a woman with child unintentionally) is clumsy; no one has the right to be so clumsy.

7. The child, the adolescent, and even the young adult is in danger of absorbing its elders' conviction that he is condemned, merely by his age, to clumsiness and failure.

"It kills me," says one of Colette's adolescent boys to a girl friend his own age, "do you hear, it kills me to think I'm only sixteen! Those years ahead . . . those years of groping my way, those years of stammering and uncertainty, being perpetually obliged to begin things one's messed up all over again, to go chewing all over again the things which, because one hasn't digested them properly, result in failure" (Colette, *Le blé en herbe*, pp. 25–26). Apologizing for what was then a shocking suggestion (the partition of Algeria), one young deputy under the Fourth Republic said: "One can be clumsy . . . at my age" (A.N., March 20, 1957; *J.O.*, p. 1731).

8. But corresponding to this apparent willingness to adopt so unfavorable an image of oneself, there is also a tendency to rebel against it by claiming that one does in fact possess great skill, "the desire to appear skillful" even reaching such proportions in some cases, as La Rochefoucauld notes, that it can prevent one becoming so or dispense one from the need to be.

9. According to many adults, there is only one sure method of avoiding the mistakes and failures that the child's own actions would lead to: to substitute oneself for the child, or at least to keep very close watch over it.

So we find a child psychologist claiming that "families in which the child is looked upon as a person . . . able 'to look after itself' are very rare" (Dr. Sautier, *L'école des parents*, July-August, 1960, p. 36). Certainly if one is in a hurry—and is that not often the case?—it may seem indispensable to act for the child. "Since time is important," writes a child psychologist describing a mother's relationship with her son, "she gets him up, washes him, dresses him" (Clément Launay, *L'hygiène mental de l'écolier*, p. 101).

10. This being so, the former child may find "managing for itself" not only "much more attractive" (Georges Duhamel quoted

by Robert under *se débrouiller*, to manage or cope), but even necessary in order to avoid—an acute fear—slipping back into childhood.

11. The child when he has grown up may often feel that anything is excusable in this world except clumsiness.

12. He will put the emphasis in a great many activities, not so much on their purpose as on the skill being exercised.

"Sometimes I used to think," says a character in a novel of his mistress, " 'how cautious she is' or 'how clever she is,' but I succumbed to the pleasure of such skilled navigation. Laurence knew our waters, our straits, our reefs by heart. I wasn't sure that she loved me. But I was sure she loved her ease as a traveler" (Nourissier, *Les orphelins d'Auteuil*, p. 139).

13. Since skill excites suspicions of artifice, the pleasure taken in it may be covered over with a layer—usually a thin one—of pious condemnation, reinforced by a concern for style (see above). "There is great skill," La Rochefoucauld notes, "in knowing how to hide one's skill" (*Maximes*).

14. Skill requires self-control.

15. The transition from childhood to maturity appears to be marked by the acquisition of this capacity.

"Sometimes one of them tripped up her neighbor," Proust recalls as he looks at a photograph of his young girls in bloom taken while they were still children, "and then . . . they shook with uncontrollable laughter. In later days . . . they still allowed themselves to laugh . . . but the laughter was no longer that . . . almost automatic laughter of childhood, a spasmodic release of tension. . . . Their physiognomies had now become mistresses of themselves, their eyes were fixed on the quarry they were pursuing" (Proust, *A l'ombre des jeunes filles en fleurs*, pp. 823–24).

16. To decline into old age is to become powerless once more with regard to what goes on inside me.

"I wanted to get up last night," Jules Renard noted in his diary, shortly before his death. "Heaviness. A leg hanging down. Then a trickle running all along it. It reached the heel before I could make up my mind. It will dry on the sheet as it did when I was Poil de Carotte" (Renard, *Journal*, p. 861).

17. In the years between childhood and old age we often retain a fear of what Montaigne considered "the worst state of man," "when he loses awareness and control of himself" (*Essais*, bk. 2, chap. 2): a state not only horrible but also terrifying. It means one no longer knows oneself; one does not know where one is, or what one is doing, or what one ought to do.

"An appalling game," says Baudelaire of the act of love, expressing a feeling that is ordinarily obscured by the taste for its pleasures, "in which one of the players must lose all self-control" (Baudelaire, *Fusées*).

To lose self-control is to lose one's head, if not one's resources, instead of keeping it solidly on one's shoulders.

"The perturbation of the passions," Robert says, "makes us lose our heads." "*S'affoler*, to run wild, means also to lose one's head, whether "from love"—"he has lost his head over that woman"—or "from terror": "stay calm, don't lose your heads!"

In losing my head I lose my grip; everything slips from my grasp, I let things slip.

Robert gives many examples of *échapper*, to escape from, conveying this feeling: "He let slip an unfortunate phrase. . . . My secret slipped from me. . . . To allow an irascible remark or gesture to slip out. He let slip an endearment in public." There is also "the object that slips from someone's hands. . . . Hair that slips from under a hat. . . . An odor or perfume that escapes. . . ." And more serious still: "His sensibility was slipping from him," Albert Camus writes of someone; ". . . it was leaving him a prey to emotions over which he no longer had control" (quoted by Robert under *maîtrise*, control). A woman having confessed to Colette that she merely feigns pleasure when making love, and having thereby provoked the question, "What you don't have . . . is it really beyond your reach?" replies: "Possibly not. . . . Abandoning myself like an idiot, not even knowing any more what you're letting slip in the way of words or gestures . . . just the very idea . . . oh, I just can't bear the thought of it" (Colette, *Ces plaisirs. . .*, p. 36).

18. A rebuff or a shock may provoke panic, cripple us, make us like "a ship . . . that has suffered damage such as to prevent it maneuvering," like France as seen by Victor Hugo:

> We are a disabled nation floating
> Without compass, pilot, masts, or anchor,
> Unguided, unpowered, at the will of the wind . . .
> [Quoted by Robert under *désemparé*, disabled or crippled]

19. Moreover the human being is also in danger of being carried away (*emporté*) by the urgency of his own passions.

"A mysterious something," Robert gives under *emporter*, "that carries us away. . . . A passion that hurled his heart into the abyss. His imagination runs away with him. To allow oneself to be carried away by anger, hate, generosity, eloquence, pride. . . . To allow oneself to be drawn into vengeance, into pleasures." If we let ourselves go, we shall find ourselves in over our heads. "Special foam control: no running over," runs the advertising for a detergent obviously aimed at those alarmed by such notions.

20. Corresponding to the horror of losing control, there is the pleasure, the relief, and the pride afforded by one's firmness of bearing even in the presence of the most shattering pressures.

A close friend of Degas, who was given to "dicordant and coarse-grained rages," says of him that "he would have liked to develop . . . a noble kind of anger, beautifully handled, skillfully controlled" (Madame Ernest Drouart, quoted by Valéry, *Degas, danse, dessin,* p. 50), in the same way as a beautiful act of love or noble grief. Montherlant describes "that amazing impression of remaining master of one's emotions. Of saying to oneself: "I am going to *have an idea* of what distress of mind and suffering are through this being. I know that I can stop whenever I feel like it,' as though one were holding the reins of some vehicle, utterly aware that one will never allow the horses to bolt" (Montherlant, *Carnets,* 1930–1944, p. 163).

21. Not only is it always possible to restrain oneself—one has only to . . .—there are also a great many things external to oneself, apparently unmanageable at first sight, that one is capable of bringing under control.

"The deepest things," Valéry affirms, "are tractable" (*Tel quel,* 2: 209).

As in literature, for example. "Profundity in literature is the fruit of a special process. It is an effect like any other, achieved by a process like any other" (ibid., p. 84). So "I can say a *profound* sentence just as I say a *musical* sentence. It is a matter of fabrication. *It can always be achieved.*" In fact, "if we make one, we can make a thousand, all following on one from another without apparently being alike. It is the instrument that has been created" (ibid., p. 66). And that's not all: "More good lines of verse are made coldly than are made in the heat of emotion; and more bad ones made in heat. It seems that the intelligence is more capable of making up the deficiencies of emotional heat than that heat is of making up for the deficiencies of the intelligence" (ibid., p. 156).

Though in tragedy the passions may escape from the control of the being experiencing them, comedy teaches us that "one can learn to love anybody" (Marcel Achard, *Patate,* act 3).

22. To lose self-control is to do what one did not wish to do.

23. Since "it is no good saying afterwards 'that's not what I intended' because that is precisely what one ought to have foreseen" (Gide, quoted by Robert under *aventure*), I like to believe that I have accomplished what I intended, and that I was aiming at what I have succeeded in performing. Like Richelieu reported by Mignet, I would like to have intended all the things I have

done. According to Valéry, "a great man" is quite simply "a particularly exact relation between ideas and an execution" (*Mauvaises pensées et autres*, p. 195).

24. "Of course you did it on purpose!" is one of the stock adult accusations directed at the child when it defends itself (and not always without just cause) with: "I didn't do it on purpose!"

25. This denial of intent having proved in general rather unconvincing, the ex-child is tempted to claim a defiant responsibility for the acts it is charged with.

"I've pee-peed on the carpet! And I did it on purpose too!" (Colette, quoted by Robert under *exprès*, on purpose).

26. If I appear to have failed in something, it is often advantageous to let it be known that what seems to be a setback is no more than one element in a whole sequence of entirely premeditated events. "You do . . . something idiotic. . . . You're treated as an idiot. . . . You let them go on. . . . And then . . . you announce that you did the idiotic thing knowingly, that it was intended. So now who's laughing?" (*Le canard enchaîné*, April 10, 1957). The bigger the setback suffered, the more subtle the cunning it just fails to conceal.

Similarly with character defects.

"Paul thought of himself as having succeeded in creating an image of himself," Radiguet writes of one of his characters; "in reality, he had done no more than succumb to his defects. This weed had gradually succeeded in choking his character entirely, and he found it more convenient to let people think he was acting by design when in fact it was mere weakness" (Radiguet, *Le bal du comte d'Orgel*, p. 191).

27. At the same time, I may make use of grown-up privileges in order to make things more difficult for others by accusing them of "doing it on purpose," just as my life was burdened similarly in the past—one of the impulses behind the fact that "men's minds will never accept as natural anything that can be produced by art" (Retz, *Mémoires*, p. 535).

Can we be sure, for example, that such and such an invalid isn't shamming? May it not be convenient to remark of some case of apparent madness: He's not as mad as all that, there are no flies on him!

In politics there is always an element of plausibility in asking: Is all this simply a result of chance? By presupposing a "deliberate plan," with a "ringleader" who has foreseen and determined a long series of apparently diverse and spontaneous incidents, we at least avoid the extreme of simplemindedness. "As we know," one journalist writes, "the ball does not spin impartially. It will fall into the hole it has long been intended to fill" (André Stibio, *Carrefour*, May 2, 1956).

Thus one person's failure may be seen as a put-up job by another.

"At the moment," a journalist wrote several weeks after the second uprising in Algiers, "people in Algiers are convinced that Ortiz and Lagaillarde have been manipulated as though they were children by certain officers, working under orders from the Elysée, who quite deliberately provoked the recent incidents in order to permit *Mongénéral* to smash the ultras in Algeria and his extreme right opposition in France!" (*Le canard enchaîné*, February 17, 1960).

28. Children, of course, can be manipulated: I may come down on someone else, not for having attempted something he ought not to have aspired to, but for having been fool enough not to succeed in what he intended. Though I may on occasion admit with Baudelaire that "I have never yet known the pleasure of a plan come to fruition" (Baudelaire, *Mon cœur mis à nu*) or ask myself with Valéry "is it possible to do anything without believing that one is doing something else?" (Valéry, *Variété*, p. 1157), such treatment is a thing I usually spare myself and keep for others. "On two or three occasions in *Malatesta*," Montherlant remarks, "I attempted to show a man (or a woman) performing an action that turned back against himself. But once the work had been published, letters I received made it apparent to me that what I had done *consciously* those two or three times I had repeated *unconsciously* many more times. So much so that I realized finally . . . that the subject of *Malatesta* . . . was simply this: man's blindness. . . . And observe that all these people [the characters of *Malatesta*] are presented as superb politicians, 'as cunning as foxes,' etc. You see the result" (Montherlant, *Malatesta*, pp. 547–48).

Under the Fourth Republic, when a governmental crisis was particularly long and complex, or came to a surprising conclusion, there were two recurring interpretations of the role played by the ringmaster, the president of the Republic. According to one side, he had succeeded in imposing a subtle plan upon events; according to the other, he had been outwitted by politicians cleverer than himself, or by some tiny unforeseen incident, such as the gesture of politeness made by a few deputies toward a "candidate" for the premiership whose case was generally thought hopeless, thus providing him with a few additional votes that launched him into a brilliant tenure of office (Antoine Pinay in the winter of 1952).

29. If a plan is realized, is the fact really due to the actions of

the man who has pursued it? "Although men congratulate themselves on their great actions," La Rochefoucauld observes, "those
actions are rarely the effects of a great design"; they are rather
"the effects of chance" (*Maximes*) or, at the very most, "the effects of humor and passions" (ibid.)—a theme often to be found
in the plots of films and plays.

30. "I am still clumsy," Gide remarks of himself; then adds:
"I ought to be able to be so only when I wish it" (*Journal 1889–
1939*, p. 17). "I measured out the doses of clumsiness I employed
with caution," Madame Merteuil writes of her life (Laclos, *Les
liaisons dangereuses*, letter 71). Supreme mastery also includes
that of its own absence, after the model of the comedian with his
skilled stammer, or even that of the academician's eloquence,
which includes "to a certain extent," "a slighter stammer, though
not of course too pronounced" (Georges Lecomte, quoted by
Robert under *bafouillage*, stammering).

31. When we encounter "the most agreeable facility," should
we not therefore suspect it of being an "appearance," behind
which, according to all Chamfort's observations "in society," "all
is art, skill, calculation"? "I have seen men," that author recalls,
"in whom what appeared to be the grace of a spontaneous movement was a contrivance, exceedingly swift in truth, but very
subtle, very skillful. I have seen those who combined the most
considered calculations with the apparent simplemindedness of
the most harebrained abandon. It was the cunning nonchalance
of a coquette in whom art has eliminated everything that seems
like art" (Chamfort, *Maximes et pensées*, p. 47).

When a politician seems to commit a slip of the tongue, there
are those who will hear of neither chance nor an irruption of the
unconscious as explanations and are much more inclined to
"perceive what advantages it is possible for a statesman to draw
from deliberate slips that are indistinguishable from spontaneous
slips. . . . It is seen as a subtle means of revealing, while at the
same time disclaiming, some deep thought" (Pierre Audiat, *Le
Monde*, May 10, 1956).

While reporting to the Assembly on his efforts to obtain a
greater flexibility in the terms of the C.E.D. treaty from France's
cosignatories (*partenaires*), Pierre Mendès-France was obliged
more than once to correct himself after having referred to them as
adversaries (*adversaires*). *Le Monde* referred at the time to "a
slip of the tongue that some have suspected of not being entirely
involuntary" (August 31, 1954), and a deputy, at a later date,
described the effect of this "apparently deliberate slip" when it
first occurred during a committee meeting as follows: "He [Men-
dès-France, the prime minister] corrected himself certainly, but

the word . . . had created prolonged 'varied reactions.' I said that the slip appeared to be deliberate, intended to express his secret thoughts. . . . Pierre Mendès-France was not unaware of the impression his 'slip' had caused, and several days after that, while repeating his report . . . to the Assembly . . ., having reached exactly the same point in his exposé, he made exactly the same slip, producing exactly the same effect" (Jacques Isorni, *Le silence est d'or*, pp. 145, 148).

32. Cleverness requires reflection.

According to the rules of Monsieur Teste's "personal game," the game has been won if one decides that one is worthy of one's own approbation; but it is "when the game has been won with subtlety" that "the greatest possible win has been achieved" (Valéry, *Monsieur Teste*, p. 72).

33. To lack the power of reflection is deplorable; perhaps delightful even though despicable as well; but in any case dangerous. If "he is too spontaneous to calculate his actions beforehand" (Robert under *calculer*), then he will scarcely get very far.

To act frivolously, lightly, with little consideration, is likely to entail heavy consequences. *S'étourdir* means to become stunned, dazed, light-headed: "to lose a clear awareness of oneself, of one's state, of one's acts, of reality," Robert gives. And as an example: "to throw oneself irresponsibly (*étourdiment*) into an affair" is to find oneself "without defenses." To act haphazardly is to invite the most serious hazards. The thoughtless person (*l'inconscient*, the "man who does not think things out clearly," according to Robert) is doomed to a failure that is easily explained: he did not think things out. A brainless act may leave me headless. Above all, if one permits oneself an escapade one should not let one's wits escape one. "To set out on an unconsidered adventure" (Gide, quoted by Robert under *inconsidérément*) is an attractive but frightening notion, since the merest "unconsidered gesture" "will cost him dear" (Robert under *inconsidéré*). "A wise man," Saint-Evremond declares "does not leave a single action to chance" (quoted by Robert under *hasard*, chance), since one risks "ruining one's life by chance" (Robert under the same noun). "Louis, the great Louis," Molière writes approvingly, "whose sovereign mind / Utters nothing by chance" (ibid.). "Everything unconsidered," Sacha Guitry proclaims, "is idiotic" (Guitry, *Mon père avait raison*, act 2).

34. All this is serious because the tendency children have toward irresponsibility—"childish irresponsibility (*étourderie*)" Robert gives quite naturally—is very widely held to extend to French adults. Robert refers to "the proverbial frivolity of the

French" (under *légèreté*, frivolity), and Montherlant has imagined a father, whose son wanting to join the Resistance, who "is so afraid of the carelessness of the French. To be killed by the Germans all right, if needs be. But to be killed by French frivolity! (Montherlant, *Demain il fera jour*, act 2, sc. 4). In fact, according to Voltaire (quoted by Robert under *légèreté*) the "particularly French brand of frivolity has produced catastrophes in every age. . . . Torrents of blood have flowed in France because it is often rather thoughtless as a nation." "A doctor of the university of Salamanca," Montesquieu recounts, jestingly but bitterly, in a "little preface to the History of France," "has discovered . . . that in the time between the death of Henri IV and the Treaty of the Pyrenees, all the leagues, the associations of the nobility, the deliberations of the parliaments, the various expeditions, the peace treaties and the alliances cost no more than 118 minutes of reflection by all the heads in France; that if we go further back to the reigns of Henri III, Charles IX, and François II, they were all in a state of general distraction and always killed one another without thinking" (Montesquieu, *Mes pensées*, p. 1052).

35. In opposition to this tendency there is "the ideal type" of act that, according to Valéry, is "constructed in the mind down to the last detail" (*Variété*, p. 550). "There was nothing in the manipulations and conditions of execution of her design," he writes of Hera, "that she did not envisage most precisely and discuss in the greatest detail . . . with herself": "she willed what she willed down to the very last detail" (Valéry, *Histoires brisées*, p. 53). "To calculate the least of one's gestures, of one's words, of one's acts," Robert gives under *calculer*, and even "to calculate his leap."

36. At the very least I must make others believe that every one of my actions coresponds to a calculation—preferably a complicated one.

"He is by nature indecisive," says the infanta of the king in *La reine morte*, "and his art lies in passing off his indecision as politic. He plays his fish with hesitation and inconsistency, but he manages to disguise it as profound calculation" (Montherlant, *La reine morte*, act 2, sc. 5). "A man knew that he was timid," Montherlant also recounts; "he became accustomed to saying: 'I who am so very timid . . .' Others would wink: 'Cunning devil!' and admire him" (*Carnets*, 1930–1944, p. 324). "*Narcisse triste* had come to Bertrand's pen," another writer writes of an imaginary author, "like a truth to the mouth of a child, a gaffe to the lips of a young woman: in all innocence." But "he did not admit this, since others had attributed intentions to him and a lack of such intentions would have been found shocking" (Nourissier, *Por-*

trait d'un indifférent, p. 16). "Man of genius," Valéry advises, "it is important that your genius should be so well concealed beneath your talent that the world will be led to attribute to your art what is in fact due to your nature" (Valéry: *Tel quel*, 1: 91).

37. One often attributes the image one is at such pains to construct for oneself to others, at times when the tendency to treat them all as damn fools is not uppermost.

"They consider themselves to have reached the peak of wit," the Persian says of the French, "when they are able to see minute subtleties in everything and find a thousand ingenious little features in the most ordinary things" (Montesquieu, *Lettres persanes*, letter 82).

38. Thus the determination to prove how stupid others are can and does coexist with the inclination, noted by Madame de Tencin, not to believe that the world is as stupid as it is. Retz tells us of an occasion when, after Monsieur had given a speech inspired by M. de Beaufort "on the spur of the moment, without planning it and with no particular intention," "everyone was convinced that he had composed it after profound deliberation" (Retz, *Mémoires*, p. 675).

39. So that the highest degree of astuteness comes back full circle to resemble naïveté, not fearing to believe, and to proclaim, what a truly intimate acquaintance with things suggests, to wit, that "many people who pass for Machiavellis are merely blunderers" (Augagneur, quoted by Abel Ferry, *Les carnets secrets*, p. 83). "I am perhaps very simpleminded, but I cannot believe in such deep laid designs" one great politician once dared to say (Raymond Poincaré, quoted in ibid., p. 82).

40. Closely allied to the "think what you're doing!" is the "look what you're doing!" which applies in childhood to the immediate consequences of an act but expands later in life to include its less direct consequences as well.

41. "There is nothing less attentive or less thoughtful than a child" affirms Bossuet (quoted by Robert under *attentif*), expressing a belief that has remained both very much alive and very widespread.

42. The adult must consequently shout at the child a great deal: "Look what you're doing! Will you look what you're doing! Always look what you're doing!"

43. The ex-child has more often than not absorbed on his or her own account the commandment expressed by Bossuet: "Be . . . attentive and thoughtful in all things" (quoted by Robert under *attentif*).

44. One must keep one's eye on everything, be ceaselessly on guard.

"He is always visibly attentive to what is happening," Bossuet says of Louis de Bourbon (quoted by Robert under *attentif*). "For eighteen years," a woman says of herself in one of Montherlant's plays, "to have maintained, yes, as though by the sheer strength of one's grip, this sort of balance . . . to have maintained it by dint of hourly vigilance, worry and cunning . . ." (Montherlant, *L'exil,* sc. 4).

45. It is even more essential to look what you are doing in moments of passion.

According to Valéry, artistic creation is "an attention pushed to the extreme" (*Variété,* p. 476). On their way in the darkness to the place where they are to make love for the first time, the two adolescents in *Le blé en herbe* "stumbled over a sort of hard hay that crackled. 'It's the buckwheat straw,' Vinca said. 'They were thrashing it today.'—'How do you know?'—'Didn't you hear the two flails while we were having our quarrel? I heard them. . . .' And the boy thinks: "She, she heard them. . . . She was beside herself, she was scratching my face, she was pouring out incoherent words at me—but she heard the two flails thrashing. . . .' Involuntarily he made a comparison between this vigilance on the part of all her feminine senses and the memory of another feminine skill" (Colette, *Le blé en herbe,* pp. 192–93). "What happens," Marie-Chantal, the stereotype middle-class child, asks, "when two porcupines are courting?—They're very careful" (Jacques Chazot, *Histoires de Marie-Chantal,* p. 82).

46. This emphasis on the commandment "thou shalt pay attention" is linked with the belief in a very strong contrary inclination: man tends to "turn away, distract, relax his attention" (Robert under *attention*). "There is an element of laboriousness in attention, so that it needs to be relaxed from time to time" (Bossuet, quoted ibid.). "It didn't matter how hard she tried," Romain Rolland says of a character, "the knot of her attention was always coming undone" (ibid.).

"The impossibility of fixing one's attention" (ibid.)—"one's attention, attracted by a thousand trifles, weakens, relaxes, fades" (ibid.)—is feared to the same degree as Napoleon is admired for "the facility with which he can turn and fix the whole power of his attention on whatever he chooses" (Ségur, quoted ibid.).

47. The fact that any lack of attention is likely to bring harmful consequences is implied by such exclamations as: "Take care what you're about to say" (Robert under *attention*), or "Ah, if I didn't think of everything!" or when one cries out to someone: "Careful!" or "Watch out!" (*Fais gaffe!*). For though

gaffer means in the vernacular, Robert tells us, to commit a blunder, *faire gaffe,* to be on sentry-duty, is the contrary: to keep watch—the very act that prevents clumsiness.

"Inattention" Robert explains, is a "cause of confusion and error." "It was through lack of attention that he committed this error" (Robert under *attention*).

"In the midst of all the concealments and artifices that reign among men," Bossuet asserts, "only attention and vigilance can preserve us from ambush" (Bossuet, quoted ibid.). On her death-bed, Madame de Coislin agreed that if one were very attentive one wouldn't die, though at the same time expressing her fear—well founded, alas—of being distracted. All "intimacy," Valéry reminds us, "requires an exquisite attention if it is to avoid harm" (*Tel quel,* 1: 45). "One moment's inattention," Bernanos says of one of his characters, "and there she was thrown out of her safe, cozy shelter again, into the horrible crowd of milling men!" (quoted by Robert under *homme*). "Keeping watch over oneself?" Montherlant asks: "Naturally we ought never to lose sight of ourselves—or only very briefly, and even then pretending that we have not. . . . As for the hazards of fortune, they are ravens, each of which, if not driven away, will swoop and tear and carry off a shred of our substance" (*Les olympiques,* pp. 147–48).

48. At any age the committing of an error provokes criticism —"couldn't you pay attention to what you were doing?"—a refusal of pity—"all you had to do was pay attention," "you should have thought about it beforehand"—and even approval of the harm suffered—"that will teach you to pay attention!"

49. Failure to pay attention may lead to an imprudence.

50. The imprudent man is risking catastrophe: that is part of the very meaning of the word imprudence. The vicomte de Valmont reminds the marquise de Merteuil that "in the career you are pursuing a single imprudence . . . becomes a disaster without remedy" (Laclos, *Les liaisons dangereuses,* letter 79) —a conviction also to be found among many persons far less exposed to risk.

51. It is all the more important to remark upon it because it can also coexist with a belief in the possibility of being more fortunate than wise, which is to say, "to succeed more by good luck than by prudence and calculation" (Robert under *heureux* in the sense of fortunate).

52. There are those who struggle to throw off the contemptible bonds of prudence. "They never forget to take their mascots, their dolls or stuffed pelicans up with them when they fly," Montherlant writes of aviatiors between the two world wars, "but they're quite likely to take off for a five hundred mile flight over

the desert forgetting to take water with them. And then boast about it. And everyone laughs with benevolent admiration: 'Oh, how French and brave to have forgotten to take their water' " (Montherlant, *Service inutile,* p. 173).

53. To add to this there is Danton's theory, expounded on September 2, 1792, about the necessary and sufficient quality for France's salvation, which had already been preceded by Voltaire's claim that "success has always been the child of daring" (quoted by Robert under *audace,* daring). Though "always" is clearly an exaggeration, there is nevertheless a widespread inclination to agree with Casimir Delavigne that "there are certain moments when daring is prudence" (ibid.), even though one is usually tempted to decide that the present moment is not one of them.

54. Even without rushing clearsightedly into the big risk, one can still commit the worst imprudence while thinking one is being extremely wise.

French history contains major examples of "idiotic optimism." For example the remark Colonel de Castries is said to have made when it was decided to dig in at Dienbienphu: "Well, they can have the balls off me if they get me out of there!"

55. It is in this way, it is often believed, that a strong tendency to imprudence is maintained.

"In the war we are waging in Algeria," one of the accused in the so-called *barricades* trial characteristically declared, "there are many more casualties caused by carelessness than by the fellaghas" (Serge Jourdes, November 21, 1960; *Le Monde,* November 23, 1960).

56. In opposition to this tendency there stands the postulate of prudence expressed by writers from Montaigne—"one must walk . . . reins in hand with prudence and precaution" (*Essais,* bk. 1, chap. 28)—to Montherlant, who speaks of "that great virtue whose name I never pronounce without a sense of respect" (*Mors et vita,* p. 169).

Very often, to achieve a full awareness of the situation I find myself in is also to discover "the principle imprudence not to be committed."

"In these matters," said a great politician under the Fourth Republic of a question being debated by the Assembly, "we must bring to our labors a prudence that can never be excessive" (Henri Queuille, speaking on a reform of the Constitution, A.N., February 13, 1958; *J.O.,* p. 732); and is that not also true of the majority of "matters" in most domains? A young deputy, of the same party as M. Queuille, when speaking on the subject of certain negotiations with other European states, declared that

"France has a conception . . . that has often seemed to our partners . . . to be excessive in its prudence." A frightful criticism indeed! "But I am bound to say that the government has considered it its duty to make this point of view its own" (Maurice Faure, on the subject of the common market treaty, A.N., January 16, 1957; *J.O.,* p. 70).

57. But one can try to run with the hare and hunt with the hounds by dressing up as healthy daring what is in reality— though a reality suitably concealed—no more than wise caution.

Staking his game on the predilection for this ploy, and therefore on the suspicion that it has been employed, a politician habitually in favor of the status quo will be only too eager to unmask a go-ahead colleague in these terms: "you were certain of having ninety percent of the trumps in your hand when you made your wager" (Frédéric Dupont, to Pierre Mendès-France on the subject of the latter's "wager on Indochina," A.N., June 17, 1954; *J.O.,* pp. 6517–18).

58. If imprudence there must be, at least let it be committed within prudent limits; if there is "risk to be run," let it be so "within strict limits" (Jean Genet: *Le balcon,* act 1). One of Françoise Sagan's male characters, when making love, adopts "the most careful, the most passionate gestures" (*Dans un mois dans un an,* pp. 143–44).

59. Hence the idea of combining the maximum degrees of prudence and imprudence.

"When I used to go down into the meadows, in those past days in Spain, to tease the young bulls," Montherlant recounts, "it was rarely that I did not take with me in my little football bag a packet of bandages, some iodine, dressings, safety pins, an incredible collection of things! In this way I was combining the extreme folly of confronting these beasts, without either the knowledge or the skill necessary to do so on equal terms, with extreme precautions that no one, I think, daring what I dared, would ever have taken. Anyone sensible enough to take such precautions would have begun by leaving the bulls strictly alone. But it was exactly such a combination of attitudes that I was given to summing up with the words: 'One must do crazy things, but they must be done with the maximum of caution' " (Montherlant, *Service inutile,* p. 182).

60. To avoid imprudence by paying close attention to everything is to recognize that the undertaking in hand is—as is often the case—one of "those things . . . that require care and application" (Mme de Sévigné, quoted by Robert under *application*), "an affair that does not tolerate the slightest negligence" (Robert under *négligence*), whether in its conception or in its execution.

61. But this is precisely what the child, with its tendency to laziness, inclines either not to perceive or not to take into account: an inclination strongly resisted by adults.

62. Having grown up, the ex-child is still thought of as not being quite proof against the temptation to hurry through a task rather than to finish it off properly. Even a person "full of ardor in great struggles" may, like the army after 1870 according to Charles de Gaulle, be "negligent of details" (*La France et son armée*, p. 123).

63. In opposition to this tendency we find an insistence upon not lacking care in anything, upon permitting oneself to produce nothing but work that is carefully completed, finished, meticulous, polished, in conception as well as in execution, so that one can say of oneself, with Poussin or Ingres: "There was nothing I ever neglected: there has never been any more-or-less."

64. By a total avoidance of negligence one avoids all disorder: another aspect of action—also invariably threatening—that is seen as a great wreaker of havoc, even though disorder may be viewed as agreeable and too much orderliness in a mind as rendering it rigidly systematic, a thing more often than not looked upon with horror in the land of Descartes.

65. It is only in moments of passion—and even then . . .—that a certain degree of disorder is admissible, that it is seen as normal for a young man's eyes to shine "with an animal, almost chaotic life" (Colette, *La seconde*, p. 26); but only *almost!* Giving orders on how the scene must be set in order to convince a woman when she wakes up that she has made love unknowingly, a character in a play specifies: "You will lay her on clean sheets that you will then soil as you think fit. You will open her bodice, you will undo her stockings, you will take out her combs. You will give her that splendor that she can never have approached with her . . . husband . . . the splendor of chaos" (Jean Giraudoux, *Pour Lucrèce*, act 1, sc. 10).

66. As with self-control (see sec. 30 above), genuinely beautiful examples of disorder are the results of art.

"The disorder in the gardens under my sway," Colette remembers, "was always simulated"; for "there is a certain wildness that can be obtained only with the collaboration of the pruning shears (*Flore et Pomone*, pp. 210–11).

67. Having appropriated to his own ends the disapprobation expressed at his own youthful disorder by adults, the ex-child tends to notice—or suppose—the presence of disorganization in others, and particularly in those who occupy posts of authority. It often appears plausible that some high place has been infected with *gabegie*, an already obsolescent word of which the "modern

meaning" is "the disorder reigning in a state, an administration, a business" (Robert), perhaps under the influence of such and such an eminent personage who "manages to introduce clutter everywhere" (Robert under *pagaïe,* clutter), who is capable (to use the vernacular of the country's rulers) of turning any god-damned place into a brothel.

"Malraux is really on the way to doing something amazing," Emmanuel Berl is said to have commented early on in the Fifth Republic, "he's creating chaos in a ministry that doesn't exist" (*Le canard enchaîné,* November 11, 1959).

8

WASTE AND WILES

1. Since there is a risk that his acts may prove so much wasted energy, a man must first of all overcome this danger before being able to make use of stratagems and wiles.

2. To scatter oneself over too wide an area, for instance, is to condemn oneself to impotence.

That is implied when Robert, under the verb in question (*éparpiller*, to scatter), evokes "scattered ideas; scattered efforts, attempts. A work scattered over a number of smaller works. Attention scattered over too many objects. Life scattered on frivolous occupations." And *s'éparpiller*, to scatter oneself—implying "to flit from one idea or one occupation to another; . . . he scatters himself in a thousand plans"—is to waste one's life; for "to scatter one's forces, one's efforts, one's attention" means "to disperse them without efficacy." The verb *émietter* has the same implication: "to scatter one's activities, one's time, one's existence," Robert gives. The result in every case is to reduce one's life and efforts to chaos, hence to zero.

A procedure as culpable as it is disastrous.

Such dissipation can affect more than the mind and the attention, however. To live in *dissipation*, Robert informs us, means to give oneself up to debauch; to dissipate oneself is "to deviate . . . from one's duty."

Which leads directly to failure, rendering impossible the high rate of productivity that concentration alone is able to ensure.

"With so good a mind he could have succeeded in anything," Rousseau remarks of someone, "but the impossibility of applying himself and his taste for dissipation prevented him from acquiring any but half-skills in any field" (quoted by Robert under *dissipation*). "We have no doubt," Victor Hugo announced, "that if Voltaire, instead of dispersing the colossal forces of his mind in twenty different directions, had yoked them all to pursue a single goal, the writing of tragedy, then he would have surpassed Racine and perhaps equalled Corneille" (quoted by Robert under disperser).

3. That such dispersion should be so disastrous in its results is a serious matter, because children as well as grown-ups have a tendency toward it, being very fond of doing everything at once and jumping from one occupation to another (see chap. 2, chap. 5, and chap. 7, sec. 46).

So that we are now faced with the fact that the inclination to live on several levels and to be variable, the whole attraction toward diversity, in fact, is apparently packed with perils as well as delights: a double point of view of which one is rarely conscious, since one forgets each of the two aspects when in the grip of the other.

4. This being so, the emphasis is often placed on the ban against self-dispersal.

"To dissipate," Robert explains, is "to disperse over several objects what should be concentrated on one." "Do not disperse yourself too much," is the advice he quotes under that verb. "One must apply oneself thoroughly to one thing and not scatter oneself over several," he also quotes (from Littré), adding: "An artist should not scatter himself." "I must, with every means at my disposal," Gide writes in his diary, "struggle against . . . the scattering of my thoughts" (quoted by Robert under *éparpillement*).

5. Having encountered resistance from adults in his childhood against what they considered to be his tendency to dissipate himself in this way, the grown-up will be only too ready to discover this vice in others, and particularly in those in authority.

So that it is always plausible to suppose, and easy to convince oneself, that there is a "fragmentation of power" going on (quoted by Robert under *émiettement*), that one is in the presence of "that dissipation of energies, that splitting up of the nation's power into individual weaknesses" (Romain Rolland, quoted ibid.) from which a "savior" alone can preserve us.

6. This belief in dissipation in high places is made all the stronger by the fact that the child has been subjected not only to the teaching that one cannot do everything at the same time

but also to a sometimes quite contrary practice on the part of adults—the imposition of excessive tasks on the child, thereby necessarily entailing some dispersion.

Just as parents are said to interrupt the homework they clamor for the child to concentrate upon with other chores, so teachers, it is often said, "forget that the student's stock of time is limited." So that the result, in effect, according to a professor of hygiene and preventive medicine at the University of Paris, "is as though someone has had the effrontery to pack someone else's bags for a trip without any consideration for necessary limitations of volume and weight." This specialist therefore feels it a good thing to remind those looking after children of a truth that they too teach: "You can't put everything in, you know" (Professor Joannon, at a meeting of the national union of French students, January 13, 1960; *Le Monde*, January 15, 1960).

7. Another danger is waste, in opposition to which we find the desire for exact calculations (sometimes resulting in fatal economies: see chap. 6, sec. 14).

Adults insist that the child, while performing some action, shall refrain from giving way to its inclination to agitate its whole body; that it shall confine itself rather to exactly the amount of movement necessary and sufficient to achieve its goal: you mustn't nod your head as well when you say "yes." "The distinguishing notion in skill," the Lafaye dictionary notes (quoted by Robert under *adresse,* skill), "is to employ only the quantity of force and movement that is necessary."

"That makes one vote more than necessary," claimed a prime minister under the Fourth Republic one day when, during that régime's long death throes, he had just survived by two votes; a witticism that one journalist qualified as "very classic" (Joseph Laniel, May 13, 1954. Georges Mamy, in *Le Monde* 15, 1954). Similarly, a deputy of that period was able to describe his principle of action as follows: "to make the maximum of efforts to give the government the minimum of votes necessary for its temporary survival" (Georges Rotvand, *Bulletin du Centre d'études politiques,* January 6, 1954); in less studied language: to keep the government's head just above water.

8. As with dissipation and dispersal, waste becomes a characteristic of others, above all of the authority whose precursors in childhood have resisted it so strongly.

As an illustration of *gaspillage* (waste), Robert selects "waste of public money." Under wasteful (*dissipateur*)—used of "a person who dissipates the goods put in his charge"—he refers to a "wasteful government, a wasteful management."

9. To waste can also often mean not to make use of what are

in fact precious resources; as with the 1940 campaign in France, partly lost according to some by the various stores of powerful equipment left unused in stockpiles. To waste in such a case is therefore to spoil (*gâcher*): "to lose or lack something for want of knowing how, or being able, to take advantage of it" (Robert under *gâcher*).

"A great many former students of the *Polytechnique*," a highly placed and renowned public official once pointed out during the Fourth Republic, "are now occupying posts in general administration that require no particular scientific competence, at a time when we have a college of administration and the country is short of technicians" (Louis Armand, Bertrand Poirot-Delpech, *Le Monde*, January 7, 1955): an observation revealing one manifestation of a taste for absurdity that is often thought to be detectable almost everywhere.

10. Opposing the inclination to waste our most precious resources, there is the commandment that tells us never to neglect any opportunity, to make use of even the humblest things, to leave no stone unturned.

11. For there is nothing that cannot be used.

"The fool," Valéry points out, "is the person who does not know how to use . . . what he has" (*Tel quel*, 2: 190), whereas "intelligence means making use of everything" (*Mauvaises pensées et autres*, p. 204)

12. Even the most suspect leftovers, if one knows what to do with them, can contribute in the most practical way to one's interests, after the manner of the hair from female legs that one satirist advised home-loving ladies to make into little muffs for the evening, or, if they preferred, into rings for their lovers (*Le canard enchaîné*, January 17, 1951).

In cooking, what the ill-educated are inclined to throw away is often, like the juice at the bottom of the pan, the best. If you keep all the little bits, you can make a whole lunch out of leftovers; and what's more, there's nothing better!

Tending as he did to "approach things from below," Pierre Laval, as seen through the eyes of Charles de Gaulle, "held . . . that there is no event that may not turn. . . . It was his opinion that it was possible to make use even of the worst" (de Gaulle, *L'unité* p. 229).

13. Having already utilized something, what if it proved possible to salvage it and use it again? Triumph, delight!

"When our grandfathers had taken this pill and it was taking effect," recounts a character in a novel talking about a certain laxative in the form of a small ball of antimony, "they watched for it to emerge in order to recover it. It was still more or less intact, and they took great care to wash it, then to keep it in a bottle for the next occasion. . . . There was nothing to prevent the same pill serving for every member of an entire family . . ., all that was necessary . . . was that it should not be lost in transit. . . . And . . . it wore away extremely slowly" (René Masson, *Des hommes qu'on livre aux enfants,* p. 40).

14. This being so, what glory must attach to the object that one abstains from using altogether, to the room that is never used!

15. It is not enough to avoid wastage: one must also find the appropriate gimmick (*truc*).

16. Especially since only the appearance of the gimmick can drive out the apprehension of waste and muddle expressed, for example, by Montherlant: "One only has to see the word 'French' on a box of matches to know that they won't strike" (*Le démon du bien,* p. 139). Although "there are bars and jazz bands on our beaches in the summer . . . there is no life-saving equipment or lifeguards. Or, if there is equipment it doesn't work, and if there are lifeguards then they're in the bistro" (Montherlant, *Service inutile,* pp. 172–73). The same author, writing of a magazine created for the purpose of informing Parisians about the opportunities available to them for using their leisure time, remarks: "when one sees that it is laid out in a really *practical* fashion, when one sees that one can really *find* in it what one is *looking for,* one is filled with wonder that it is in fact produced by Frenchmen" (*Les lépreuses,* pp. 57–58).

17. The aspiration toward acquiring the knack or finding the gimmick—the means that is perfectly suited to its end—is powered by the fear of a gaping hiatus between instruments and objectives.

In politics, for example, it is always permissible for an observer setting himself up as a critic to point out that there is a total noncoincidence in this respect among those governing the country and to urge them either to "provide the means of carrying out their policies" or to "form their policies according to their means": one of the constant themes of the political world under the Fourth Republic.

It is when the usual method of employing the resources at my disposal is not, quite obviously, going to achieve my aims that I become more and more eager to find an idea—one of those "hard, dense little things . . . sometimes quivering and sometimes still as ice, little lives . . . without limits" (Léautaud, *Journal littéraire,* 1: 20)—that will bridge the gap.

18. Such an outcome does not appear impossible, since very tiny things often, after all, have explosive effects: a grain of

sand, a queen's nose. To be intelligent means to know how to distinguish those tiny things from the multitude of others, perhaps conspicuous and noisily evident, that are of no consequence. Pooh! that's not as important as you think; in six months (six days) everyone will have forgotten it; life is made of rubber, the wily Briand was fond of reminding his colleagues and collaborators (See Joseph Caillaux, *Mes mémoires*, 3: 19).

"While we are seeking out . . . strong and weighty causes," Montaigne reminds us, "we miss the true ones: they evade our eyes with their smallness" (*Essais*, bk. 3, chap. 11). It is "with the slightest of movements" that "human affairs . . . are transformed from one state into another, quite different" (ibid., bk. 1, chap. 19). 'It is not only fevers, strong drink and great accidents that topple our judgment; the least things in the world set it spinning" (ibid., bk. 2, chap. 12). In fact, "our greatest agitations have . . . ridiculous causes" (ibid., bk. 3, chap. 10). "The calm or the agitation of our humor," La Rochefoucauld points out, 'depends not so much upon the most evident events in our lives as upon a combination . . . of little things" (*Maximes*). "Often," Saint-Simon notes, it is "apparent trifles that have set events in motion" (*Mémoires*, 1: 13). "All distinctions between men appear slight indeed," Vauvenargues comments. "What is it that creates beauty or ugliness, health or infirmity, wit or stupidity? A slight difference of the organs" (quoted by Robert under *distinguer*, to distinguish). Musset expresses astonishment at "the way the tiniest things decide events in this world, the fact that what are apparently the least important things and circumstances bring about such great changes in our fortunes" (quoted by Robert under *petit*, small). "Oh Phaedrus," says Paul Valéry's Socrates, "you must surely have observed in important moments of human discourse, whether concerned with politics or the private interests of citizens, or even in the delicate words suitable when speaking to a lover, when circumstances have reached a decisive point—you must certainly have remarked what weight and what importance are assumed by the least of little words and the tiniest of pauses that occur in them" (Valéry, *Eupalinos*, p. 26) And there is also Valéry's little "song":

> There is no pain so great
> A trifle will not lift its weight
> Some trifling length of time.
> [*Tel quel* 2: 96]

19. Might it not be possible to provoke consciously what can occur blindly, to find a means to that end as powerful as it is small. Though many may feel as Montherlant does that "I have never

been curious to know how one achieves little things with great efforts" (Montherlant, *Carnets*, 1930–1944, p. 139), the converse is a subject of universal and lively interest. The fact of succeeding with small effort may be as attractive as the fact of succeeding in itself; the fact that Napoleon was a small general who wore a big hat considerably increases the fascination of his performance, that of the little dog with a big tail. What makes for brilliance in a show of wit is, as Paul Valéry points out, "low mass and high velocity" (*Tel quel*, 2: 85).

20. The small thing we are here concerned with is therefore small in the first place both in extent and in weight.

"Rather than life-size decorations ('regulation size')," one observer has noted, "the French prefer 'under-sized decorations,' and particularly the simple 'miniatures' that proclaim a truly modest hero" (Eugène Mannoni, *Le Monde*, March 26, 1955), which increase to a maximum that delightful divergence between the impression produced and the dimensions of that which produces it.

"At a time when Germany was equipping itself with powerful heavy artillery," Charles de Gaulle writes of the early years of the century, "the majority of specialists were unanimous in categorically rejecting any innovation of such a kind. 'You mention heavy artillery,' the representative of the army's chief of staff replied to the Assembly's finance commission in 1909. 'We have none, thank God! The strength of the French army lies in the lightness of its guns' " (de Gaulle, *La France et son armée*, p. 133); and that was not the last expression of a fondness for so-called light artillery. Although we may accuse someone of not pulling his weight, weightiness is above all seen as disadvantageous and despicable.

21. The small, as we have already seen, is also what is light to the point of being immaterial—intelligence.

Whereas memory is seen as the intelligence of fools, and the plodder is never expected to come out top, those who aspire to higher levels of education often apply themselves to the quest for a key idea, the idea that makes its mark, the controlling idea, the central idea that, all subtleties to one side, is bound to ensure success. "Our music," Paul Valéry writes, seems "to have been attempting, by taking the path of intelligence, to outflank the formidably well-organized positions of a very great symphonic power that until recently controlled the musical world" (*Regards sur le monde actuel*, p. 193). Recommending the kind of art "that reconstitutes the maximum of our impressions or intentions with the minimum of perceptual processes," Valéry reminds us that 'nature can do nothing with a little bottle of ink. It needs an infinity . . . of raw materials. We, on the other hand, need very little in the way of things and a great deal, if possible, in the way of intelligence" (*Pièces sur l'art*, p. 113).

When the last campaign in France took a very bad turn, *L'Action française* headed its main article: "The Germans have power. The French have power and intelligence. Intelligence will win" (Lucien Rebatet, *Les décombres*, p. 361). "During the first months of the occupation," Robert Aron recounts, "there were a great many clever people ready to remind us of all the historical examples of conquered peoples who had succeeded in overcoming their conquerors by means of their subtlety" (Aron, *Histoire de Vichy*, p. 194). A little later, "Darlan confided the following certainty to several of his colleagues . . . that in a Europe organized by the führer, France would eventually occupy first place: 'The French are so much more intelligent and able than the Germans: in the end, however much their defeat in 1940 may have weakened them, they are bound to become the continent's predominant nation' " (ibid., pp. 424–25).

22. My search for the appropriate gimmick is an attempt to refute the distressing and persistent belief that nothing is ever got for nothing, that everything must be paid for, that everything has its price, that it takes what it takes, that one is in fact paying for fortune's gifts.

"You know the saying, You never get anything for nothing?" a character in a novel asks. Well, he goes on, "you do sometimes get something—and something valuable, what's more!—for almost nothing!" (Duits, *Le mauvais mari*, p. 198).

23. That there should be no pleasure without pain is a state of affairs that I can easily accept—or even help to maintain— where others are concerned, despising and criticizing their desire to run with the hare and hunt with the hounds.

"All she had to do was not do it!" Proust's Françoise says firmly when referring to the difficult birth a child-mother has just been through. "She enjoyed herself! She's no right to start making a fuss now!" (Proust, *Du côté de chez Swann*, p. 123). "You've had your pleasure, now you can pay for it!" is, according to several observers, the attitude of hospital doctors who make no attempt to spare women undergoing curettage the slightest pain.

24. As for myself, though I have no qualms about wanting to find the trick that makes things easy, I may have difficulty in believing in it.

Everything good has to be bought with some pain, La Bruyère notes, and facility inspires distrust.

25. However, there is nothing so very untoward in the idea

that "every Frenchman, faithful to his legend, preserves in the depths of his heart the tenacious hope of discovering, one day, that little tavern where for next to nothing one can eat twice as well as in the posh restaurant" (Gilles Lambert, *France-Observateur*, July 10, 1958).

Many people are thought of as being perpetually on the track of bargains and money-saving tricks, hoping—for the pleasure of it as much as for the saving—that someone is going to say to them: "I've got a bargain for you," or that they themselves will be able to ask: "Don't you know the way to get in without paying?" (Robert under *combine*, meaning trick or scheme). When Gide described his counterfeiters' "doctrine of least effort" he is giving us an account of what is possibly a very widespread activity: "Each of these children . . . made it a point of honor or vanity to obtain everything with the least possible expenditure of money and energy; whether it was some object that one of them boasted of having been able to obtain more cheaply; whether it was some problem that another had found how to solve without wearisome calculations; or a method of locomotion that enabled him to leave for school five minutes later—the principle was still the same. '*No useless effort*' was their . . . motto" (Gide, *Journal des faux-monnayeurs*, pp. 86–87). The "desire to obtain the advantages without the disadvantages," Valéry considers, "is what governs the law of movement of many things": "not wanting to pay" (*Tel quel*, 2: 311), what a burning incentive!

26. And when I can persuade myself that I've managed it, what pleasure I feel! A vaudeville comedian, having succeeded in "working" his audience so well that they had responded with great alacrity and in great profusion to his few titillating questions, took his leave of them as follows: I must thank you all very much, no really, because I've got through this part of my program *without doing a damned thing*!

27. Instead of being the result of my own cleverness, getting something for nothing may appear as a gift presented to me by a world suddenly transfigured.

Though it may appear unlikely that one is going to get even so much as a free shave tomorrow, the fact remains that love is sometimes free already.

"When we perceive," Montherlant writes, "how much money it costs to try to please people who couldn't care less, to go to law, to travel, to be robbed, to be arrested, to be sick and to die, we realize that it is the people with whom we sleep, which is to say those who give us most pleasure in the world, who, proportionately speaking, involve us in the least expense" (*Textes sous une occupation*, p. 277).

Though, in this case, "it is again what is most delicious that costs least" (Montherlant, *Carnets, 1930–1944,* p. 335), it is not essential for our stake to be so large in order for the pleasure of paying less or nothing to be profound.

"All these marvels [of nature] can be had gratis by simply traveling on a train," Alain points out. "Yes, gratis, since you are paying to be transported, not to see valleys, rivers and mountains" (quoted by Robert under *gratis*). Of one character in a novel we learn that "any idea of gratuitousness threw him into a state of wild agitation" (Jean-François Revel, *Histoire de Flore,* p. 43). Montherlant gives us a description of M. d'Auligny's joy when a tradesman makes a mistake of ten francs in his favor. And in another book he writes: "The 'great Catholic novelist,' having been invited to Morocco, confesses to you that he has no desire whatsoever to go there, but that he is going all the same 'because he likes free trips.' To do something one doesn't want to do because one can do it for nothing, to make use of something one doesn't like because one got it for nothing, and moreover when one is comfortably off . . ." (Montherlant, *Les lépreuses,* pp. 10–11). "The fact that they are not paying," the same author has also written, about a party of men on their way to a conference with whom he traveled between Marseilles and Algiers, "is like an obsession with them; it is the principal attraction, indeed, the real reason for their journey. It was not just once or twice, it was at least twenty times that I heard those words: . . . Since we're not paying" (Montherlant, *Carnets, 1930–1944,* p. 224). While held as a prisoner of war during the summer of 1940, Jean Dutourd heard other prisoners talking about the right of any soldier in legal standing to a free return ticket. "This phrase," he writes, doubtless with some exaggeration, "fell upon my ears thirty times a day during the entire time I was a prisoner. As the weeks rolled by, England not invaded, the peace still not signed, the discipline becoming steadily more tyrannical, nothing could deprive it of its virtue. It was because of it . . . that five hundred thousand men refused to escape. What did this wondrous return ticket cost in 1940? Fifty francs for some, a hundred for the others. That was the price . . . at which a third of the French army fixed its freedom" (Jean Dutourd: *Les taxis de la Marne,* p. 138). "The prophecies of the optimists" in the prison camps, this satirical eyewitness claims, "always came down to the same thing: that free return ticket. After all, it was so unfair to be expected to fork out fifty or a hundred francs to get home when one hadn't come here for one's own pleasure. Those fifty or a hundred francs were tearing the prisoners' hearts out" (ibid., p. 158).

28. Getting things for nothing does not exhaust the charms

of the successful knack or gimmick. In seeking it I am also often aspiring to a state in which I shall prove able to manage with the means at hand, thus proving to myself that I am no longer a child (see chap. 7, secs. 9–10), conforming to the law of the grown-up world which says that "everyone must manage with what he has" (Robert under *débrouiller*, to manage), showing how clever I am in Voltaire's sense: "The clever man . . . is the man who makes great use of whatever he knows" (quoted by Robert under *habile*, able). The clever woman is one who can turn a few "scraps of material" into a smart outfit.

29. If poverty of means does not exist in the first place, I may think of myself as likely to go out looking for it in order to meet the challenge, it being a necessary and sufficient condition of my skill: "I only ever make anything with small means," Valéry assures us; "if I started with larger quantities I should produce nothing" (*Tel quel*, 2: 232).

Fortunately, I have only four fingers and a thumb on each hand: this being so, "it is up to me to win back some measure of liberty by the way I use that number of digits, and the most skillful actions . . . I achieve with them will be due solely . . . to the efforts I have made to supplement with art and practice the small number of *given* means" (Valéry, *Pièces sur l'art*, p. 254).

So the art preferred by this particular writer is that in which there has been, on the creator's part, "a consent . . . to exquisite tortures of constriction" (Valéry, *Variété*, p. 476), in which the creator is therefore "reduced to creating grace when tied to the rack" (ibid., p. 456), in which he must "dance while loaded with chains" (ibid., p. 455). And that is not all; it is a good thing that the "requirements" to which the creator submits himself should be 'half senseless"—like that of a "strict" prosody—in order that the "artifice" "by exciting rebellion" (ibid., p. 480), shall give rise to the soaring skill which makes light of difficulties and which he needs in order to play well upon his instrument. And is not the French language itself "inimical to the formation of composite words . . . contenting itself gladly with a restricted vocabulary" (Valéry, *Regards sur le monde actuel*, p. 183)?

30. Instead of seeking out difficulties lucidly, I may blunder into them blindly (see chap. 7), thereby again creating the conditions for salvation, or at least those of a lively quest for the stratagem that is to rescue me from a situation only inextricable on the surface.

31. For there must always be a stratagem sufficient to the needs of the moment; it is merely a matter of finding it: all I have to do is to discover whatever I must do and do it.

32. This is a belief that must start by overcoming its opposite.

"No possible escape-route; no way of getting oneself out of it,"
Gide writes (quoted by Robert under *échappatoire*, escape-route,
which he defines as "an indirect means whereby one attempts to
escape from difficulties"). "God made everything from nothing.
But the nothing can still show through," Valéry notes (*Mauvaises
pensées et autres*, p. 220). Though "a single word, a single gesture, a single glance may suffice to destroy an entire system of
relations, a life or two lives, a play, a belief . . . it happens much
more rarely that so little is needed to create the same things"
(Valéry, *Mélanges*, p. 326).

33. Yet we still manage quite often to let our minds be dominated by the kind of confidence expressed by one mother (interviewed by Charlotte Roland) with regard to her son: "It's just a
matter of having found out once and for all the way to approach
him, and then one has no more trouble with him."

"There is a knack in everything," Montesquieu's Persian reminds us (*Lettres persanes*, letter 58).

"Here is Laval," writes an observer in Vichy, July 10, 1940,
"walking out of the Grand Casino, cigarette in mouth, immediately aclaimed by the people who have been waiting in the
park for hours for the National Assembly to finish its sitting,
and who are already seeing the State restored, the occupying
forces on their way home, and peace concluded" (Maurice Martin du Gard, *La chronique de Vichy*, p. 58). Laval was one of
those, as Charles de Gaulle has pointed out, who "held . . . that a
certain degree of guile will always control a situation" (*L'unité*,
p. 299). As for the general, at the end of a "conversation on
social problems" with a member of the R.P.F. "left wing," he is
claimed to have remarked: "there must be a simple way round
it (*un truc*); all we have to do is find it" (Manuel Bridier, *France-
Observateur*, May 29, 1958).

34. In order to find the simple way round, the trick, the gimmick, it is sufficient simply not to be a stupid ass, which is
already asking rather a lot, at least in the case of others. Since
"powerful minds," acording to Valéry, are "those that make something of nothing" (*Tel quel*, 1: 52), it is normal for less powerful
intelligences to drown in a glass of water.

35. There are many incentives (apart from those already
noted) that doubtless combine to create this desire for, this
pleasure in the trick, the stratagem, the simple answer.

The child has to work too hard, but real men, Léo Ferré's song
tells us, don't do more than they have to.

36. By learning the trick of doing things the easy way, the ex-
child shakes off the suspicion of having remained a clumsy
blunderer (see chap. 7, sec. 1).

37. The man, though not the little boy, possesses the capacity to make what is little become big; this precious capacity should be displayed everywhere.

38. And it should be laid claim to even when not in fact possessed; a ridiculous tendency in others that provides a central theme for humor (among comedians, for example): a character will treat the simplest of actions as though it were a breathtakingly difficult feat.

39. No one should perceive such efforts; therefore they must be hidden; but it is also a good thing to conceal the efforts required to conceal them.

Though he prefers "poems . . . that appear to produce . . . their beauties as though they are the delicious fruits of a natural unfolding," Valéry goes on to observe that "this surface miracle . . . requires the austerest of labors to produce, efforts made all the more exhausting by the fact that they must, in order to attain completion, eliminate all traces of themselves" (*Pièces sur l'art*, p. 116). It is essential, therefore, "to maintain one's effort until one's labor has removed all traces of that labor" Valéry, *Degas, danse, dessin*, p. 34). "One becomes aware," Valéry writes elsewhere with reference to a passage of translation "that though nothing could appear easier than this sequence, more seductive to the ear, more pleasurable in prospect to return to and appreciate more fully, nothing could have been so difficult to obtain. It is the peak of art . . . that what has just proved so natural should be revealed as a matter of such skill" (Valéry, *Variété*, p. 456). In La Fontaine, for example, "the nonchalance . . . is a product of skill; the relaxation, studied; the facility, the peak of art" (ibid., p. 475). "What could be easier or less constrained on the surface," writes Gide in his turn, "than one of La Fontaine's fables? In reality, what could be more skillfully constructed, more industriously assembled to the point where all trace of effort has been reabsorbed" (Gide, preface to *L'Anthologie de la poésie française*, p. xxi). "She appears . . . filled with ease," Montherlant writes of a woman running in a stadium, "and she is ravaged within by her effort (*Les olympiques*, p. 183). Madeleine Renaud, acting in *La reine morte* at the *Théâtre français*, seemed to him the embodiment of "concealed patience and effort: art masked by art" (Montherlant, *Théâtre*, p. 250). "No other orator appears to have such as ease as he," Jacques Isorni writes of Pierre Cot, "yet never perhaps has so much ease of manner concealed such diligence" (Isorni, *Le silence est d'or*, p. 88) "He goes to great pains to make one think he is lazy," one journalist has said of Félix Gaillard. "He arrives at meetings without papers, without collaborators. He has worked like a Trojan and he knows more about the subject than all the others. Whereupon they all say what he wanted them to say: "He's damned gifted, that man' " (Jean Farran, *Paris-Match*, November 9, 1957).

40. By these means I am able to provide assurance for myself that I have emerged from childhood, a time when what matters above all is to convince adults that, far from being lazy, I have put forth the entire amount of effort they required of me and that it is now high time I was allowed to go out and play. From now on, the most important thing is to prove to others and myself that I am well provided with powerful instruments that enable me to work wonders with very little.

41. Should the trick, the gimmick, the easy way around be simple or complicated? Or both at once? Here one is torn by several contrary reactions (see chap. 2, secs. 19–26).

42. On the one hand we have the Lafaye dictionary (quoted by Robert) apparently using an antiphrasis when it describes *adroit* as meaning "that which goes straight (*droit*) to the goal . . . ; which . . . does not deviate."

Because, in the first place, the extremely adroit action does not content itself with a single goal: it's image is rather that of the "bowl that strikes two others with a single blow" (Robert under *coup*, blow). "The reverberation of this wildly impulsive act was so universal," the Cardinal Retz writes, "that it must, in my opinion, have been performed for more than one end" (Retz, *Mémoires*, p. 439). The "multiple utilization of what she did . . . was characteristic in Albertine," Proust recounts (*La prisonnière*, p. 391), but not in her alone; we encounter it "in an enormous number of people," this "principle of the multiple utilization of a single action," this "system of multiple aims"; for example, the tendency "not to be able to content themselves where a single action is concerned, to give pleasure, by its means, to a single person only" (Proust, *A l'ombre des jeunes filles en fleurs*, pp. 938–39).

43. But above all, the adroit action is likely to be a multiple cannon shot, an action aimed at the attainment, via direct consequences, of some more distant objective.

Oreste demanding possession of Astyanax so that Pyrrhus shall take offense; so that he will thereby be led to choose Andromaque; so that Hermione will break with him; so that she will be more inclined to welcome the love that Oreste feels for her.

In politics, the really subtle operators are often thought of as approaching problems at a tangent, as deliberately provoking a series of subtle caroms; it is oafish and futile to approach things straightforwardly.

Opposing West German rearmament in the form that was to be finally accepted, a political leader under the Fourth Republic (Paul-Henry Teitgen) put forward the argument that the military force as then projected would be a "formidable pawn . . . [that] might possibly be manipulated . . . by Soviet Russia." By means of a new Russo-German alliance? Not quite. "Who can say that Soviet Russia will not use this pawn . . . in order to charge the Atlantic pact with an aggressive potential that may eventually discredit it . . .?" (A.N., October 8, 1954; J.O., pp. 4635–36): Moscow might stir up a desire for revenge in Bonn in order to aggravate conflicts within N.A.T.O. itself.

During one long governmental crisis under the Fourth Republic (in the spring of 1953), a number of M.R.P. deputies helped to shatter the hopes of the radical candidates for the premiership, while the one M.R.P. candidate was in part defeated by radicals. According to a "widely held opinion in the Assembly lobbies," these "unfortunate nominations" had been "very cleverly worked out" by the president of the Republic, who was anxious to be reelected himself in several months time: "his aim . . . was to create a veritable feud between the M.R.P. and the Radical-Socialists, so that the president of the Republic elected in December could then be neither a Radical nor a member of the M.R.P. Since M. Pinay was also, for other reasons, out of the question, the only course left open to the bewildered congress would be to beg the departing president to carry on for another seven years" (*Carrefour*, July 1, 1953).

Toward the end of the Fourth Republic, when Antoine Pinay used his power to guarantee a majority vote in the Assembly against elections by *arrondissement*, it was claimed "that in voting in favor of proportional representation M. Pinay had his sights set a long way beyond electoral reforms. It is said that he had laid a skillfully worked out plan that would eventually bring the government down by sort of chain reaction; those in favor of *arrondissement* voting would take their revenge by blocking the required constitutional reforms . . . and thereby force the prime minister either to reverse his policy or kill himself off" (*Carrefour*, March 5, 1958).

44. On the other hand, there is the horror of complications, the aversion for the man who is determined to "complicate a situation quite needlessly" (Robert under *compliquer*), at whom one shouts, in exasperation: "You just like complications!" (ibid.).

45. For the supreme guile is perhaps in perceiving that the required solution is essentially simple (even though, all the same, someone had to think of it). "It's very simple!" is an ex-

clamation quite as cutting in intent and effect as "It's not quite
so simple!"

"Why shouldn't the warships that don't draw much water sail
up the Seine and help defend Paris?" one person suggested when
the capital suddenly appeared to be threatened on May 16, 1940
(Pertinax, quoted by Jacques Benoist-Méchin, *Soixante jours
qui ébranlèrent l'Occident,* 1: 174). "This is what we must do,"
Edouard Corniglion-Molinier, the minister of state, is said to
have announced at the cabinet meeting that followed the fall of
Dienbienphu: "We must must parachute weapons down to the
French prisoners being taken to the north. Our men will pick
them up, kill their guards, and return to the struggle" (*Le canard enchaîné,* May 19, 1954).

46. To perform a truly astute or wily action is to succeed in
replacing the need for blood and sweat by less costly means,
after the model of the procedure explained to Charles de Gaulle
by Pierre Brisson during the phony war: "Don't you see that we
have already, at this moment, reached the white Marne?" (de
Gaulle, *L'appel,* pp. 22–23). Words, procedures, intermediaries,
interpersonal contacts in negotiations can thus be resorted to in
order to prevent very tangible losses; especially when one feels
one lacks more massive means. "Subtlety," Montesquieu remarks, "is the resource of the weak" (*Mes pensées,* p. 1168).

As for those who believe, in Paul Reynaud's phrase, that "we
shall contrive to make our adversaries change their position during the negotiations simply by 'chatting with them' " (A.N., June
1, 1956; *J.O.,* p. 2212), they aparently included Pierre Laval—
"constantly dominated . . . by a single idea" throughout the occupation: "to get an interview with the führer and 'chat' with him"
(Robert Aron, *Histoire de Vichy,* p. 626)—as well as Edgar
Faure, who once declared, at a time when he was prime minister:
"It is our opinion . . . and I believe it to be the theory of the nation
as a whole, that we must negotiate, always negotiate" (C.R.,*
March 26, 1955; *J.O.,* p. 1106).

47. Guile also means to use the relations existing between
others in such a way as to increase my own power far above the
level guaranteed by my own unaided resources: for example,
the extremely strong showing put up by certain small parliamentary groups under the Third and Fourth Republics (notably
the radical Left and the U.D.S.R.) whose role as pendulum between Left and Right (something of a simplification) managed
to provide their members with exceptional opportunities of becoming ministers on more than one occasion.

* C.R. denotes the Council of the Republic under the Fourth Republic.

This same balance of power is also held by the arbiter, the official referee, whose strength may come from the fact that others, more powerful but also more committed than he, are canceling one another out. And indeed, to achieve the position of arbiter is always a cherished aim on the part of the politician, since it is the distinguishing mark of the highest ranks to be attained in his world (see Leites, *Du malaise politique en France,* chap. 4). Possibly it was the attraction of such a position that to some extent reinforced Pierre Laval's hopes, during the occupation, that "between the two of them [the Germans and the Anglo-American bloc], France would be able to fulfill a role as arbiter . . . that would restore her to her rank as a great power" (Robert Aron, *Histoire de Vichy,* p. 627); while Charles de Gaulle, at the end of the war, set himself the task of "persuading . . . the states bordering upon the Rhine, the Alps, and the Pyrenees to group themselves together; of making this organization into one of three world powers and, should the necessity one day arise, into the arbiter between the two Soviet and Anglo-Saxon camps" (de Gaulle, *Le salut,* pp. 179–80).

48. The supreme stratagem may even be envisaged as an exportation industry called upon to redress a deficit in the balance of power.

"The only card he can play," a widely respected journalist (André Fontaine) wrote of the government leader (Joseph Laniel) taking part in a conference of the "great" Western powers (the Bermuda conference in the spring of 1953) "is that of ingenuity. Since it is a question of reconciling the two Anglo-Saxon sisters, we may perhaps be able to furnish formulas" (*Le Monde,* June 3, 1953).

9

EXCESS AND MODERATION

1. There is often an apparent fear of being drawn into excess, since according to Condillac "all passions exaggerate," and indeed, according to Chamfort, "are passions only because they exaggerate" (Robert under *exagérer*). Am I unfortunate enough perhaps to be excessive, which is to say someone "who is incapable . . . of moderation" and of whom it is said: "he is excessive in everything" (Robert under *excessif*), or "his excessive nature can envisage no middle course" (Jean Cocteau, quoted ibid.)? Ought I to confess with Mademoiselle de Maupin that "it is impossible for me to be moderate in anything" (quoted by Robert under *modéré*)?

2. Given this fear, the virtues of the much advocated middle course receive an extremely negative definition.

The middle, Robert explains, is "that which is removed from extremes, from excesses." To be moderate is "to avoid all excess," and moderation is therefore "the virtue of a person who avoids all excess."

3. By denying the temptation exerted by excess, it is more often than not possible to experience moderation as a completely spontaneous tendency. "Our flight that neither high nor low attempts / With a middle course would always be content" Clément Marot writes (quoted by Robert under *entre-deux*, the in-between, the middle course).

"Moderation," Vauvenargues explains, "arises from a kind of mediocrity in the desires" (quoted by Robert under *modération*). "Men almost always find it easier to adapt to middle courses than to extremes," Montesquieu says (quoted by Robert under *milieu, middle*).

"The French," Joubert declared, "are born . . . moderate" (quoted by Robert under *modéré*).

4. There is a "Parisian madness," Colette admits, "but there is also a Parisian wisdom." In fact, "the golden mean is only to be found in Paris" (quoted by Robert under *mesure*, the mean). Speaking of France, one head of a government under the Fourth Republic (Félix Gouin) drew attention to "that miraculous sense of balance which is hers alone and which is made up of moderation, reason, and . . . common sense" (speech of investiture, A.N., January 29, 1946; *L'Année politique*, 1946, p. 551). "France is a country that's not too hot," recited a little boy interviewed by a weekly newspaper, "not too hot, not too cold, temperate, and . . . well, temperate" (*L'Express*, December 24, 1958).

5. It is others that lack moderation. "How excessive you all are in Provence! Everything is so extreme!" Madame de Sévigné exclaimed (quoted by Robert under *extrême*). Many other distant parts have since been viewed in the same way.

6. Good and bad are imperfect and mingled in man: a truth very little tarnished by use.

"Perfect valor and complete cowardice," La Rochefoucauld observes, "are two extremes that are rarely reached" (quoted by Robert under *extrémité*, extreme). When Balzac remarks upon the existence of "a class that is half virtuous, half vicious, half learned, half ignorant" (quoted by Robert under *demi*, half), one may well wonder whether he is not quite simply referring to all men. "I am a man who is smart and not smart" Jules Renard claims (*Journal*, p. 98). "Though he didn't live the life of a saint, he wasn't a bad man either," Camus has someone say of a character in one of his novels. "He steered a middle course, that's all" (quoted by Robert under *milieu*, middle).

7. Manichaeanism is therefore erroneous: it is a naïve belief that is rendered dangerous by the lack of moderation that inspires it; certain foreigners are notoriously inclined to it.

8. For one thing, there is hardly such a thing as purity (which is, moreover, a good thing).

"When I confess religiously to myself," Montaigne admits, "I find that the best of goodness there is in me has a taint of vice about it." So that "man is everywhere and in everything merely patchwork and motley" (Montaigne, *Essais*, bk. 2, chap. 21.) "There is no mind, however straight," asserts Boileau in more comfortable tones, "that is not given to imposture and falsity in some point."

9. But total badness is equally difficult to achieve.

Having commented of a character in a novel that "the self-seeking love he professed to feel for his uncle included some part of genuine affection," Montherlant also adds: "One has understood nothing about life until one has understood that everything in it is confusion" (*Les célibataires*, p. 277).

10. What at first sight appears to entail a disruption of continuity can often reveal itself as capable of possibly imperceptible gradations.

The evidence shows that we are neither happy nor unhappy: we are between the two, that's all. One of Sacha Guitry's characters, asked by a friend if he is faithful to his wife replies: "So often!" (Guitry, *La prise de Berg-op-Zoom*, act 1).

Recalling Pascal's statement "that one does not prove one's greatness by standing at one extreme, but . . . by touching both at the same time, and by filling . . . the space between them," Sainte-Beuve applies this law to a particular case. "It is this gap between, so visibly conjured up in Pascal's phrase," he announces, "that I hope to demonstrate *to some degree* in Saint François de Sales" (quoted by Robert under *entre-deux*. Italics added). "It is *much more* a question of a revolution than an evolution," General Lavaud is quoted as having said with reference to nuclear weapons (quoted in A.N., October 18, 1960; J.O., p. 2555. Italics added). Simply a matter of phraseology? Perhaps; but that scarcely weakens the theory.

11. The grown-up is fond of perceiving gradations, whereas clearcut oppositions were the rule when he was a child.

"Many parents," a child psychologist notes, "see their young child as an already developed human being; many others look upon it simply as a small mechanism" (André Beley, *L'école des parents*, December 1859, p. 34); or again, the same parents may adopt either one or the other of these attitudes at different times and in relation to different kinds of behavior. "The variations that occur in a child's appetite seem to be misunderstood," observes another specialist writing on the subject of the parents he has encountered in a mental hygiene clinic. "The child either bolts its food or refuses to eat; outside of these two rigid concepts in which he has been imprisoned, everything in the way of day-to-day variations, including the child's very physical development, the mothers remain wholly unaware of" (Jean Dublineau, *L'école des parents*, November 1956, p. 20).

12. If he adopts the simple utterances with which he has been fed by adults, and uses them himself, the child may be

promptly given very short change in the way of remarks like "you take what I say too literally," a rebuff frequently administered to the naïve by the knowing. The literal, the absolute, is better tempered with a measure of moderation.

13. Though this need not hold true there is a strong impulse to the contrary, as in the case of backbiting.

"In France," Théophile Gautier observes, "admiration and contempt are always excessive." "Every writer," for example, "is either a god or an ass; there is no in-between" (quoted by Robert under *excessif*).

14. If the world tends toward the average, avoiding not only the zero but also the all, this is because all is far too much; it goes beyond all bounds. Neither too little nor too much can be the mean.

15. In fact, too much is also too little.

One is often reminded that "everything that is exaggerated ceases to signify."

16. The immoderate is doomed to disaster.

"Immoderate pride," "excessive ambition," "immoderate pretentions" (all evoked by Robert under *démesuré*) all herald catastrophe, as does "an empire that goes beyond the bounds": "the empire of Charles-Quint was vast beyond bounds" (Jacques Bainville, quoted ibid.). To illustrate "colossus" in the sense of "a very powerful empire," Robert gives: "To overthrow, to topple, a colossus. The fall of a colossus. A colossus with feet of clay."

17. Anything immoderate is also likely to be disagreeable in itself.

An "enormity," as Robert explains, is not only "a thing that is enormous," but also an extremely bad thing, because in French one can speak, write, and generally commit *énormités,* in the sense of outrageous and shocking things.

18. It is true, of course, that great men are venerated and accepted as rulers; but at the same time, there is the inclination to ask, with Stendhal, "what great action is not an extreme at the moment it is undertaken?" (quoted by Robert under *extrême*). One can also agree with Flaubert that "one should never have any fear of exaggeration. It is a quality possessed by all great men. . . . It is quite simply genius in its . . . true center, which is the enormous" (quoted by Robert under *énorme*).

But even then, one is usually merely throwing down a challenge—an important one it is true—to a cult of moderation and the mean that scarcely believes it possible to kill off, either in one's own heart of hearts or in that of others.

19. Excess becomes in no way less deplorable when applied to morality.

"One should beware of excess, even in good" is a maxim chosen by the Académie to illustrate *immodération,* excess, and quoted under that noun by Robert. "People who carry goodness to extremes" Robert gives under *outrance* (excess or extravagance), following it up with: "extravagantly pious," "carrying belief too far," and "those who carry virtue beyond the bounds." "Wisdom has its excesses and is in no less need of moderation than madness is," Montaigne suggests (*Essais,* bk. 3, chap. 5); Molière has his reasonable Philinte claim that "too much goodness may just incur blame" and that it is more proper to be "soberly wise."

20. In short, trying to make an angel of yourself will just make you into a beast.

21. And the beast is going to be an ass.

Having decided during the Algerian war to ask to be relieved of his post—because so-called "special methods" had become more or less the rule—a general officer anticipated what the reaction of his superiors would be: "There are two possibilities: either they are going to greet me with their great-leaders-of-men faces and talk about the splendors and miseries of military life . . . ; or else, and this is more likely, when I've told them that I don't agree with them they will pat me affectionately on the shoulder and say: 'That damned Bollardière, still the same as ever. What an impossible fellow you are!' That's exactly what happened one day when I went to see you know who to tell him, in the presence of two witnesses I'd taken with me, that he was a liar. Do you think anything happened? Not a thing. The person in question just decided to laugh it off: 'That damned Bollardière again. Still as bad as ever, eh?' " (Pâris de Bollardière, reported by Roger Barberot, *Malaventure en Algérie,* p. 207).

Somewhat touching and somewhat ridiculous, this spectacle of someone trying to speak his mind: "You silly duffer, be off with you now!"

22. Such a man is in the first place a danger to himself: he is certainly going to fall flat on his face. The wages of purity is failure—if not total ruin.

"I am seeking vainly through this whole affair," says a lawyer created by Courteline, referring to an accused man's case, "an affair that is throughout as limpid as crystal, for that unknown something, that tiny eddy of muddied water from which the wiles of a good lawyer can always manage to fish up an argument for the defense. . . . You can't declare a man innocent when he hasn't done anything! . . . Or at least it's very difficult to!" (George Courteline, *Les balances*).

"One has not given oneself to God," Madame de Sévigné

observes, "because . . . one does not want to destroy oneself" (*Lettre à sa fille*, June 10, 1671). "There is no opinion, . . . no attitude," Valéry notes, "that if pushed to its extreme or acted upon totally will not lead to man's destruction." For instance, "if the early Christians had been so with every ounce of strength they possessed, then there wouldn't have been any Christians—and if the whole world had followed their example, there would have been no one left on earth." In fact, "the two symmetrical doctrines, that which speaks of an eternal life and that which annihilates once and for all, are in agreement on one consequence: both deny any importance to human inventions and contructions. . . . If all had been true Christians or if all had been true pagans, they would all be dead, and they would have been dead without ever having done anything" (Valéry, *Tel quel*, 2: 89–90).

23. But he is equally a threat to the others who may be affected by his mania.

"Total supporter of a doctrine," Robert gives as an illustration of *complet*, complete. "See: fanatic, frenzied, inveterate." Then he goes on to list such phrases as "up to the neck," "to the tip of his fingers," "from head to foot," "to the bottommost depths": the general impression is by no means a reassuring one.

24. A door, adults insist when dealing with children, must be either open or shut.

"It's either the one or the other, no half-measures," cry the heirs of this doctrine in the grown-up world. "We must take either this path or that" (Robert under *milieu*); we must avoid the rough-and-ready compromise.

Toward the end of the Fourth Republic, when a prime minister (Félix Gaillard) asked a deputy (Joannès-Dupraz) who was a member of a party already represented in the cabinet (the M.R.P.) to join that cabinet, his party refused the deputy its permission to accept. Whereupon the prime minister is reported as having delivered the usual sermon in such situations: "Either one is a part of the government or one is not. If my politics are disagreeble to them, why do the M.R.P. not recall their ministers? If they agree with my politics, why should they refuse me further help?" (*Carrefour*, March 12, 1958).

25. But this is precisely the point: once they are no longer children, human beings at last achieve the privileged position of being able to take part while not taking part, of not taking part while at the same time taking part. They shoved it down our throats enough when we were little, that door and those two positions it had to be in; now we're going to leave it ajar! If needs be, we will even use a doorstop (*entrebailleur*) which

will enable us "to keep a door ajar without its being possible to open it competely": this being "a security device" (Robert under *entrebailleur*).

The best place to be is in between; six of one and a half dozen of the other. A mean is also the best means (*moyen*). "To depart from the mean is to depart from humanity," Pascal says (quoted by Robert under *milieu*); "mediocrity alone is good" (at that time mediocrity had no pejorative meaning). "One should keep to a middle course (mediocrity) in all things" Fénélon confirms (quoted by Robert under *médiocrité*). And according to Montesquieu it is not only a "political good" but also a "moral good" "to remain always between two limits" (quoted by Robert under *modération*).

26. To begin with, considerations of pleasure favor moderation.

27. When in a state of desire, one underestimates the rapidity with which satiety will be reached (see chap. 2, sec. 15). It is unfortunately true, however, that "pleasure all the time is no pleasure" (Voltaire, *Zadig*, chap. 6); it is more likely to prove the opposite, as the child learns from its tendency to choke itself: "He swallows pieces too large for him and chokes himself," Robert gives under *engouer,* to choke, and also adds: "To choke oneself by eating greedily. A baby that chokes itself by sucking too fast."

28. The man with foresight—the intelligent man—therefore knows that "mediocrity" in the old and respectable French meaning of the word is what "makes a person happy" (Ronsard, quoted by Robert under *médiocrité*), that the "rule of happiness" is "to keep to the golden mean in everything" (Diderot, quoted by Robert under *milieu*). "Moderation is like sobriety," La Rochefoucauld explains: "one would like to eat more, but one is afraid of making oneself unwell" (*Maximes*). One should maintain oneself in a state such that one can never be either sated or insatiable," Joubert advises (quoted by Robert under *insatiable*). "One should live in the country," Jules Renard rmarks, "yet abuse it no more than if one were in Paris. That way it will 'keep itself up' " (*Journal*, p. 363). "This magic spell"—under which pleasure is enjoyed to the full—"cannot be appreciated except through alternation," Montherlant discovered. "It is a sad fact," he observes, "that the best when it has lost its savor becomes something that has overstayed its welcome." Therefore, "in order to preserve its savor, one must *break* the magic spell" (Montherlant, *Aux fontaines du désir*, p. 16). So that "after our will has labored to accumulate a store of pleasures in our life, there comes a moment when it must go into reverse, when it must work at

thinning out, at restricting those pleasures in order to preserve their savors" (ibid., p. 104).

29. Just as good sense requires that one should moderate those acts that tend toward pleasure, so there is a current of moral sensibility that demands no more than moderation in the matter of sin: one is safe if "one does not go beyond the bounds with vice" (Molière, quoted by Robert under *mesure*). To "come to an arrangement with heaven" means to permit oneself a "satisfaction" that it "forbids": but only within certain bounds! (Unless, of course, one prefers to adapt the laws to fit one's desires. In which case one arrives at what is termed a morality of convenience, a compromise virtue.)

Montaigne recalls "the story of Aristippus telling the young man who blushed to see him enter the house of a courtesan that 'the vice is in not coming out, not in going in'" (Essais, bk. 3, chap. 5). Similarly, a generous wife in a comedy who announces to her husband: "From now on I give you permission to deceive me," receives the reply: "Oh I'd never do that, except on Saturday afternoons perhaps"; just one little infidelity a week is really not serious! Although Madame de Sévigné claimed to be very upset at belonging neither to God nor to the Devil, this "state" was nevertheless one that "between ouselves, I . . . find the most natural in the world" (*Lettre à sa fille*, June 10, 1671). "All honor to him!" Marcel Aymé exclaims of one of his characters, "this well-intentioned man who has contrived to pay his dues to the devil at such very moderate cost" (Marcel Aymé: *Le bœuf clandestin*, p. 202).

One is not required to attempt to eliminate the bad altogther; but it is seemly to avoid any excess of badness.

"Chitterling sausage," Laval is reported as having announced at Vichy, looking down at the one on his plate, "is like a government: there must be shit in it, but not too much!" (Martin du Gard, *La chronique de Vichy*, p. 100). During an important debate under the Fourth Republic (over the C.E.D.), when a deputy (Jean-Paul Palewski) was failing to "hold" the house, the speaker (André Le Troquer) reminded it that "nothing is more distressing for an orator than to have to speak through the noise of private conversations. I therefore urgently request you to stop, or at the least to moderate (smiles) these conversations" (A.N., August 28, 1954; *J.O.*, p. 4404).

30. The existence of a fundamental recommendation to sin within certain bounds also implies the idea that it is advisable not to overdo morality: it is a dangerous drug (see sec. 19 above).

31. Whether the mean is desirable or not, is it attainable?

Or might it be true that "middle courses are too difficult to keep to" (Fontenelle, quoted by Robert under *milieu*)?

32. *Tertium semper datur*, appears to be the reply of one huge current of opinion.

"Some say that Cardinal Mazarin is dead, others that he is alive," a contemporary is said to have remarked. And he added: "I don't believe either side" (quoted by Michael Chrestien, *Esprit es-tu là*, p. 197); rather like the railroad-workers at Sfax-Gafsa, who as a protest against Guy Mollet's visit "declared an unlimited forty-eight-hour strike" (*L'écho d' Oran*, quoted by A. Aycard and J. Franck, *La réalité dépasse la fiction*, Bis, p. 88).

Seekers after compromise solutions have been provided by the French language with the prefix *entre-* (between-), which, when added to a verb, "indicates that an action is only half performed": "*entrebailler, entr'apercevoir, entreclore, entrefermer, entreluire, entr'ouïr, entrouvrir, entrevoir . . .*" (to open slightly, to half glimpse, to half shut, to half close, to glimmer, to half hear, to half open, to half see . . .) (Robert). Added to these there are the numerous composite words formed with *demi* (half). So that after mourning there comes half morning (*demi-deuil*), which is all in halftones (*demi-teintes*), both physically and morally.

When Admiral Darlan decided to negotiate with the Allies, on November 8, 1942, he rejected an armistice and refused to go any further than signing a surrender of the town. "In that way, the general thought," a historian tells us, "the Germans will not be able to complain to the marshal that he is in league with their enemies and will have no excuse for invading the unoccupied zone. While on the other hand the Americans would not be able to blame Darlan for playing the Germans' game" (Robert Aron, *Histoire de Vichy*, p. 551). "I decided to take a middle course," Pierre Lagaillarde announced when on trial for his activities on January 24, 1960, "by taking up my position in the university, by performing an act of insurrection if you like, but a static one" (*L'Express*, November 17, 1960).

33. Frequently, the mean that has been sought for and found proves deceptive: a false mean. The measured step turns out to be a half measure.

It is then assumed to deprive one of all the advantages of the clearcut decisions it is avoiding while at the same time landing one with all their disadvantages.

Having described the three paths a certain personage might reasonably have chosen, Retz says of the fourth, which he did in fact take: "Having something in it of all the others, it had almost all the disadvantages of them all while offering, properly speaking, none of the disadvantages of any them" (*Mémoires,* p. 620).

More particularly, it is possible to combine the strong line and the gentle line in such a way that the mixed or alternating procedures that result prove to be too harsh in view of the pleasant element in them and too conciliatory in view of the element of severity.

34. One becomes conscious of this trap and swears never to fall into it again.

"He has a horror of half measures, he is forceful in making decisions, coming to the point" Robert gives under *énergie.* "It's everything or nothing! He has a horror of half measures" (Robert under *demi-mesures.* "I have a fondness for neither half revenges nor halfhearted villains," Voltaire declares (quoted by Robert under *demi,* half). "Those who make revolutions by halves are merely digging their own graves" observed Saint-Just (ibid.).

35. Such formulas often bear witness to the strength of the opposite current, of the "irresistible tendency to will . . . and not to will, to do and not to do" (Charles Benoist, Chamber of Deputies, March 26, 1908; quoted by George Bonnefous, *Histoire parlementaire de la Troisième République,* 1: 126–27). One may even confess quite lucidly that "the present situation is obliging us to take half measures that are wholly inefficacious" (Robert under *demi-mesure*). "Seeing as we then did, after the mistake we had made," Retz recounts, "that there was no course we could take that would be free from terrible disadvantages, we fell, as always happens in such situations, into the most danger-ous of all, which is to take no decisive course at all but to take a little from every possible one" (Retz, *Mémoires,* p. 588).

36. It is normal to claim that the other has made a mistaken compromise.

According to Retz, the Parlement of Paris "at one and the same sitting gave the troops marching orders and forbade them, at the same time, to provide for their subsistence; . . . [it] armed the people against the military who had their commissions and theirs orders duly signed by the court and . . . [it] fulminated, at the very same time, against those who were suggesting that those same military should be licensed" (Retz, *Mémoires,* p. 605).

According to Jacques Benoist-Méchin, General Gamelin had acquired "in the political world, where he had spent several formative years, . . . a lively taste . . . for middle-of-the-road solutions and piecemeal measures. So when the War Office department given the task of organizing our tank battalions was hesitating between the advantages of the three-tank section and the five-tank section, it applied to him for help in its decision. His inevitable reply came back: 'Look into the possibilities of a four-tank section!'" Similarly, "when it was a question of organizing the antiaircraft defenses," the responsibility for which was being claimed by both artillery and infantry, "in order to avoid giving offense to anyone, he cut the apple in two and entrusted the antiaircraft protection of the army itself to the artillery while making the infantry responsible for national antiaircraft defense. Was the army to be motorized? Very well, two divisions of light cavalry must be created, large hybrid entities composed of one motorized brigade and one brigade of horse. The result: the entire formation was compelled to march at the speed of its slowest elements or run the risk of being split up. A plan to be worked out for an advance into Belgium? Gamelin found himself confronted with several 'hypotheses.' The Belgian chief of staff wanted protection as far as possible for the entire country, which meant advancing as far as the Meuse and the Albert Canal. General Georges retorted that this would be folly, and that they mustn't risk going any further than Antwerp and the Escaut. Called upon to decide between these extremes, Gamelin decided on an intermediate position. The Anglo-French forces would advance as far as Dyle, which is more or less halfway between the Meuse and the Escaut. . . . The commander in chief was unable to see that instead of combining the advantages of the various 'hypotheses,' he was simply synthesizing all their disadvantages" (Benoist-Méchin, *Soixante jours qui ébranlèrent l'Occident*, pp. 486–99).

Toward the end of 1949, when the Chinese communists had reached the Indochinese frontier, "For France," according to General Navarre, "the hour of decision had come: either to win the war by throwing in all the forces necessary to do so before Chinese aid increased to massive proportions, or else to end it by means of a political compromise. There was no middle course. Yet it was an intermediate solution that was chosen. General Revers, the chief of general staff, . . . carried through the decision to abandon the Chinese frontier and concentrate our forces in the delta" (Henri Navarre, *Agonie en Indochine, 1953–1954*, pp. 18–19). Four years later, in much the same way, "France had to choose between two policies: either she was going to accept being no more than a partner in an anticommunist front under American command—in which case she might well be forced out by the U.S.A.—or else she intended to preserve . . . her dominant role in Indochina—in which case she must face up to making all the necessary efforts and sacrifices herself." And yet, "incapable of choosing between these two policies, the government attempted to follow a middle course that would enable us to preserve 'something'—it didn't know quite what— while at the same time making the U.S.A. take over a daily larger share of the burdens" (ibid., p. 96). From another point of view, "from beginning to end, our rulers . . . never had the courage to make an open decision between a colonial regime that they declared to be no longer in existence—but whose material advantages they were still trying to preserve under another name— and an association of free peoples that they said they wanted but the genuine realization of which they were constantly delaying" (ibid., p. 320). Thus, "through having been unable to attempt anything more than a bastard solution between the maintenance of colonial government and the granting of complete independence, we had lost the advantages of the first without benefiting from those of the second" (ibid., p. 99).

"There is no doubt that it is possible to choose between two policies," a member of the extreme Right declared in the Assembly during the Algerian war. "One half of this Assembly is advocating a policy of negotiation. The other half, a policy of war. The most terrible thing . . . is not to make a choice between two policies that may both have their advantages and disadvantages." And the speaker continued, "Every day we meet mayors of rural communities who say to us: We've had enough of having to inform families that their sons have been killed in Algeria while we are thinking that perhaps these sacrifices will be just as useless as those we put up with not so long ago in Indochina, and more recently in Tunisia and Morocco. So make up your minds: either fight the war and win it or evacuate Algeria!" (Jean-Louis Tixier-Vignancour, A.N., June 12, 1957; J.O., pp. 2686–87).

37. Fearing to be carried away by Alceste's intransigent tendencies, I may insist upon the value and demand the presence of the virtuous Philinte's tractability.

38. Given the human condition, complete fulfillment of one's desires is beyond reach: one can't expect that much from this lousy life.

39. Intransigence is likely to lead to chaos, to nothing.

To be intractable—"refusing all compromise" (Robert under *intraitable*)—difficult, or demanding, to turn up my nose at my food or on any other occasion, what good will it do me? None; it's simply cutting off my nose to spite my face!

"You are far too intransigent in that matter," (Robert gives under *intransigent*). "One must not be too difficult," he adds (under *difficile*). "Let us not be so difficult," La Fontaine advises, since "the most accommodating are also the ablest men" (quoted by Robert under *accommodant*).

40. The intractable man is a danger to others as well as to himself: he is inevitably the sort who will put a spoke in one's wheel, thereby causing a catastrophe. Naturally, since he is a close relative of Mr. Pure.

41. Far from insisting on the impossible everything, I must even know how to comply gracefully when a superior power deprives me of a further portion of my already far from complete possessions. One must not hang on without hope.

Boileau and the comic stage are agreed in mocking the wife who "twenty years after her marriage still tries / To require of a husband the attentions of a lover" (quoted by Robert under *exiger,* to demand).

42. In a more general way, it is stupid and dangerous to rebel —whether inwardly or actively—against a state of things that is certainly rather unsatisfactory but also scarcely modifiable; the only intelligent and sensible thing to do is to accept it. What do you expect? You know how it is . . . ! (He shrugs his shoulders).

Although one can use the adjective *facile* in an old-fashioned way that makes it pejorative—"he's an easy fellow to manage" —the advantages of the man who is easy in the sense that "he makes no fuss about doing what is expected of him, he puts up with things easily," are much appreciated; he is the "easy man" that Robert refers to under *facile,* the man who is a practical asset, just like the dress that is "easy to put on." Although one hears contemptuous remarks like "he is so accommodating he'll put up with anything," being accommodating is nevertheless also seen as an essential if life is to be livable: it means "to accept, to concede . . . to adapt oneself to . . . to take things as they come . . . to make up one's mind to something" (Robert under *accommoder*), to know how to make the best of things. What torment and what folly not to be able to accept things, in the sense of "submitting oneself to what one cannot prevent" (Robert under *accepter*)! "Let us seek to accommodate ourselves to this life," says Montesquieu, echoing Descartes; "for it is not up to this life to accommodate itself to us" (quoted by Robert under *accommoder*). The man who has not grasped this is still a child, foolish and maladroit. "On pain of finding life intolerable," Chamfort affirms, "there are two things to which one must accustom oneself" (quoted by Robert to illustrate *se faire,* to adapt oneself), though the list is a rather short one perhaps. "I term reasonable," Anatole France tells us, the man who tends "never to be too surprised at what happens and to accommodate himself to it as well as he can" (quoted by Robert under *s'accom-*

moder). In one of Colette's novels, when a woman friend exclaims to a wife whose husband is often unfaithful, "you amaze me . . . you're really extraordinary . . . you can accept without a sign of anger, without hurt that . . .," the wife replies: "Needs must! . . . If I didn't accept it, what would happen then? Exactly the same thing!" (Colette, *La seconde*, p. 15).

43. Fortunately, however, man's capacity to accept things is proportionate to his need to do so.

"I can't get used to it!"—"You will; one gets used to everything" (Robert illustrating *se faire*, to break or adapt oneself).

44. Since one must needs content oneself with what one does have when one doesn't have what one wants—has one ever?—one eventually comes to realize that it's really not so bad; the main thing is that at least one's got that. "A moment's peace, that's always something worth having," according to Jean Giraudoux; "a few good years, or even months, is always something gained," one of Anouilh's characters observes.

45. What one has is already infinitely more than nothing; it is better than nothing at all.

"Every morning, when we get up," Jules Renard observes, "we should say: 'Terrific! I'm not dead yet!'" (*Journal*, p. 589). When a friend "who only found the weather more or less to his liking one day out of every ten" remarked to Gide, yet again, "what awful weather!" Gide replied by quoting "the Belgian saying: 'after all, it's better than no weather at all!'" (Gide, *Journal 1889–1939*, p. 1274).

46. Even in areas where one would not suspect it, there are therefore extremely important differences of degree (see 10 above).

"She's afraid of being buried too deep," Jules Renard notes, "and has promised me a big wardrobe if I will agree to see that she's not lowered in too far" (*Journal*, p. 724).

47. Alceste is wrong to refuse Célimène's offer, one that Philinte for his part would have accepted eagerly. The "gloomy pleasure of a melancholy heart" (La Fontaine) that "would prefer not to be loved at all than to be so moderately" (Rousseau, quoted by Robert under *modérément*, moderately) is pleasure against all reason, and therefore inimical to true pleasure; for "the origin . . . of the notion of reason," Valéry suggests, "is perhaps transaction" (in the philosophical sense). But the verb *transiger* in French, though morphologically the verb of transaction, has come to mean "to compromise." So that the French language has made rational intransigence a logical impossibility: transaction already implies compromise. "We are bound to compromise (*transiger*)," Valéry therefore continues,

"sometimes with 'logic'; sometimes with our impulses or intuition; sometimes with the facts" (*Mauvaises pensées et autres,* p. 7).

There is only one good reason for not taking advantage of an opportunity: the certainty of another that will be better—provided the two are really mutually exclusive, a conclusion one should never jump to hastily.

48. Since the best result I can achieve is likely to be a modest one, it is sensible to be "modest in one's claims, one's demands" (Robert under *exiger*). One must be content with what one has, which is to say "not to ask for anything more or better" (Robert under *contenter,* to content).

49. To put up with something, Robert explains under *s'arranger,* is also "to content oneself, to be satisfied": "I can put up with anything. Don't worry, I'll manage." *S'arranger* means "to turn to one's own ends . . . , to make use of a thing as it stands." It is not impossible to "fashion what is bad to our own use, and even to our own convenience" (Colette, quoted by Robert under *commodité,* convenience).

10

HASTE AND PATIENCE

1. What is more important to any undertaking than its timing?

"If any should ask me what is the first thing in love," Montaigne tells us, "I should reply that it is knowing how to choose one's time; the second most important thing the same; and the third as well; it is a point that can achieve everything" (*Essais*, bk. 3, chap. 5). "It is a secret to no one," declared a member of the opposition under the Fifth Republic (speaking on the prerogatives abrogated to itself by the executive under that regime with regard to the limiting of parliamentary sessions), "that the particular moment, the date, the particular delay are all of capital importance to the opposition." "By refusing the Assembly as a whole the right to choose its moment," he hurled at the prime minister, "you have deprived the opposition of a large part of its arsenal" (André Chandernagor, A.N., May 15, 1960; J.O., p. 662).

2. "The moment is ill chosen": always a plausible assessment, and a verdict often feared by those who are anxious that something should succeed.

3. Any moment is in danger of being ill chosen, since there is a widespread feeling that there can only ever be one that is suitable for any undertaking: the moment when all the requisite conditions for its success are in conjunction (see chap. 6, secs. 1–11), the moment when "its hour has come." And "the hour

has come" does not mean you have a whole hour to play about with; it means you have to act during the second that the minute hand is pointing to twelve o'clock!

"There is nothing in the world," Retz affirms, "that does not have its decisive moment"; consequently, "the mark of the master in human activity is to recognize and seize that moment" (*Mémoires*, p. 119). "There is only one moment for everything," Michelet says in his account of the Revolution. "In this case it was June 10, not one day earlier nor one day later" (quoted by Robert under *moment*). "There is a certain moment," Gide observes, "a certain point of maturity in a thought on one side or other of which the sentence clothing it is either overstretched or falls into wrinkles. It is important to catch it at the right moment" (*Journal 1889–1939*, p. 861). Valéry refers to "those wines . . . that must be drunk at a certain age, just as for every type of woman there is an age that one must wait for, or not let pass, in order to love her": they are wines "as old as they must be and as old as they need be" (Valéry, *Tel quel*, 2: 37). Many a thing seems to Montherlant "to be poised for a few hours between the too little and the too much" (*Les olympiques*, p. 53).

"We must not set out either too early or too late": a hackneyed but always striking truth reportedly uttered by Guy Mollet in May of 1958 (J. R. Tournoux, *Secrets d'Etat*, p. 331). "The all-important and delicate point was this," René Coty has explained, recalling how he had to address a message to the Assembly at that same period in an attempt to overcome the hesitations of that body with regard to Charles de Gaulle: "It was a matter of communicating that message neither too soon nor too late. A few hours sooner would have been too early. A few hours later would have been too late" (ibid., p. 386).

4. But if I do not manage to take, to grasp the opportunity, the right moment, if I do not succeed in taking advantage of it, even though I watched and waited for it—is it really so serious? Frequently it is claimed that one can be sure "a missed opportunity will return" (Robert under *occasion*, opportunity), that "before the right moment is still the right time, just as after the right moment is still the right time" (*Le canard enchaîné*, February 2, 1955); but such claims are often attempts to drown out the voice that is crying: "Now or never!" "He had his hour, he did not know how to make use of it. His hour is past," Robert gives under *heure*, then quotes Victor Hugo: ". . . Is our hour gone past then? Will all our cries not bring it back again?" "Opportunity, like hair, never returns," Saint-Simon observes (*Mémoires*, 1: 251), and Proust thinks back to all those "persons with whom I allowed the moment for loving them to slip past, so that for

ever afterwards, however much I might have felt the desire, I was unable to retrieve it" (*A la recherche du temps perdu,* 2: 830).

5. It is therefore terrifying but true that "it often happens . . . that one has not been able to take advantage of certain favorable and decisive moments" (La Rochefoucauld, *Mémoires,* pt. 3).

6. "Let us not allow the moment to slip by"—a plea addressed to the French Senate by a prime minister under the Fourth Republic (Edgar Faure) very deeply concerned with the "thaw" between East and West—is an exhortation whose lack of originality does not, in such conditions, really impair its force.

We must discover the perhaps hidden essence of the present so that we shall recognize the moment clearly when it comes. "We must pay attention," the same speaker continued, "to such indications as the variations in [Russia's] military budget, which, after having shown a slight decrease recently, has . . . now been augmented again. We must now ask ourselves whether we have in fact taken sufficient account of certain indications" (Edgar Faure, C. R., March 26, 1955; *J.O.,* p. 1105).

7. But we must also ask ourselves the question, "Is this really the moment to . . . ?" and frequently reply: "It is not the moment" (Robert under *moment*). In which case it does not behove us to act, but rather "to wait for the auspicious moment." "She had just come to understand," says a novelist of one of his female characters, "that men must be left to sort things out among themselves, . . . that her moment would come, that all she had to do was wait" (Georges Duhamel, quoted by Robert under *heure*).

8. Liberty of choice between action and waiting is a privilege one acquires as one emerges from childhood.

"In certain families," observes a child psychiatrist, "each child has to do what he is told to do exactly within a given time if life is to be livable. For example, as soon as the child is told to go and fetch the bread, it is supposed to stop playing right away, to go down the five flights of stairs, to go out and bring back the bread without stopping to talk to its friends, without dawdling, without losing any of the change. . . . Children are supposed to go to bed the first time they are told, because there are still five or six pieces of sewing to be done so that they can be delivered to the boss tomorow morning, and it's not possible to work while the children are still up" (Doctor René Diatkine, *L'école des parents,* February 1954, p. 31).

9. But the ex-child becomes indignant with anyone who dares to point out to him that "he can't postpone things any longer," that "he must act" (Robert under *atermoyer,* to postpone). "It is always dangerous to compel people to make a decision," re-

marks Abel Ferry with reference to the political world during the Great War (*Les carnets secrets*, p. 95).

10. Postponing the moment of action is nevertheless, in many situations, a vice much practiced and vigorously denied. "If I am called upon, by your vote, to form a government," said a candidate for the premiership under the Fourth Republic, "I hereby commit myself to laying this project before you with the briefest possible delay" (Jules Moch, A.N., October 13, 1949; *L'Année politique*, 1949, p. 340)—a remark that was understood in more than one way.

11. But the capacity to wait is often promoted to the rank of virtue.

"It is a great and rare virtue . . . that of knowing how to wait." Who do you think said that? Joseph Prudhomme? No, André Gide (quoted by Robert under *patience*). "How well you must know how to wait, Madame Charlotte," says Colette with admiration to a mistress-wife (Colette, *Ces plaisirs* . . . , p. 32). "His deepest impulse was always to pause a little," Montherlant remarks of a character he really rather approves of (*L'histoire d'amour de la Rose de Sable*, p. 124).

12. The man who lacks the capacity to wait is powerless and buffeted by events; he is behaving like a child.

"Too prompt a vengeance is not vengeance at all," remarks one of Montherant's characters; "it is merely a riposte" (*Malatesta*, act 1, sc. 8). To defer is to demonstrate one's power" (Alfred Sauvy, *L'Express*, December 18, 1954): over oneself and over others.

13. To wait frequently means deferring something unpleasant; for example the very act of taking a decision, or the unpleasant reactions it is likely to provoke.

During a sensational trial under the Fourth Republic (that of the politician Jacques Chevallier's wife and murderess), when the judge pointed out to the victim's mistress that she must have known she would have to choose one day between her legitimate position and the one that was less so, the young woman replied: Of course, but I was putting off that moment, I was playing for time.

"Henri Queuille," a journalist has written of one of the great figures of the Fourth Republic at a time when he had not yet been transformed from a reality into a myth, "especially when a decision appeared to him a tricky one, used to evade the issue by means of an adjournment. When caught, for example, between three candidacies for the government of Algeria, those of M. Haag, M. Léonard, and M. Berthoin, each of whom had his supporters and opponents, the president contented himself with keeping Marcel Naegelen in office. Not, by any means, in order to please the latter, but in order to spare himself the unpleasantness of an immediate decision" (André Stibio, *Carrefour,* March 27, 1951). "The trickiest part of the Algerian outline-law project," a deputy announced toward the end of the same regime, "is the electoral problem. How will the constituencies be arrived at. . . ? By decree? The wisest course would perhaps be to postpone this thorny problem until some future date" (Fernand Bouxom, quoted in *Combat,* November 26, 1957).

14. The time a postponement lasts is always that much gained. "When the day comes, we shall be laughing on the other side of our faces, agreed," one may say, thinking of the settling of accounts ahead, "but it's still something gained all the same, isn't it?" (*Le canard enchaîné,* December 4, 1957).

For isn't it precisely a characteristic of the human condition that all we can do is to hold back a little—so very little, and at the expense of such stratagems—the inevitable advance toward a fatal outcome?

"One more instant of happiness," Montherlant remarks bitterly of France between the wars, "in the times we are living in, each day gained is a victory. A day will come when people will say that those who did not live in France between 1930 and 1935 have never known how sweet life can be" (*Service inutile,* p. 45). "This assembly," wrote a journalist under the Fourth Republic, referring to the first legislature then coming to an end, "contains too many dead men enjoying temporary reprieves for the ways of delaying a final settling of accounts not to have all been exhausted" (André Stibio, *Carrefour,* March 13, 1951); this is very human, in the strong sense of the word. "The policy that consists in putting the brakes on every moving part . . . has a meaning," noted a young deputy who was opposed to that policy. "It is attempting to delay the inevitable change ahead for a few more months" (Alain Savary, A.N., June 1, 1956; *J.O.,* p. 2219). " 'Just one more moment, executioner': do you want to make Madame du Barry's last words into a motto for all France?" another politican of similar persuasions asked the opponents of the common market (Maurice Faure, A.N., January, 16, 1957; *J.O.,* p. 78).

15. And what if, when tomorrow comes, we should have to pay more dearly still for having delayed? But the future is less with us than the present; and is there not a chance that the time that must pass between now and the future will settle it all for us?

16. One may also wish to wait when it is a matter of consummating a pleasure rather than suffering some unpleasant-

ness. "Let's delay, let's delay that moment," sang Lucienne Boyer between the wars.

Resisting the "impulse of excitement that hastens to fulfillment" (Valéry: *Degas, danse, dessin,* p. 106), "an artist, that deep species, . . . defers . . . that fulfillment" and thus "creates difficulties" (ibid., p. 10) from which the work will then spring (see chap. 8, sec. 29). "I must check them," Eupalinos says of his ideas, "I must interrupt the very birth of ideas. . . . I must. I prevent them from satisfying me. I postpone the . . . happiness" (Valéry, *Eupalinos,* p. 42).

17. Such postponement is necessary in the first place because "everything that is of value in life is . . . brief" (Valéry, *L'idée fixe,* p. 40), since any acute pleasure lasts only an instant.

18. But also, "it is already a pleasure to postpone pleasure, to sharpen it with skillful deferments" (Duits, *Le mauvais mari,* p, 22).

19. The man one is forced to remind that "too soon is worse than not at all" (*avant l'heure ce n'est pas l'heure:* headline of *Canard enchaîné,* May 22, 1957), at whom one is forced to shout, "Too soon, too soon! And what a time to choose!" (Colette, *La chatte,* p. 129), is probably a jackass.

While "it is never wise, during conflicts in which one is wholly on the defensive, to do anything that is not urgent," "the uneasiness of those in command under one" that Retz expects to encounter in such situations, "is the most inconvenient thing in the world": "they think that you are lost as soon as you do not act. I lectured them every day on how necessary it was to hover; on how sorties were dangerous; on how I had observed, on several occasions, that patience produces much greater effects than agitation. No one understood this truth." Once more, "the devil got into our officers' heads: they thought that we should lose this opportunity if we did not seize upon it" (Retz, *Mémoires,* pp. 307–9).

20. In some cases, stupidity is allied to weakness.

"Impatience," Fénelon observes (quoted by Robert under *impatience*), "though it appear a strength and vigor in the soul, is a weakness only": a childhood vice. "An intense desire is not a desire that makes a great show," observes one writer for the benefit of would-be seducers; "it will not jump a second too soon" (Jean Dutourd, *Le petit Don Juan,* p. 131).

21. To jump too soon—whether it is a woman or the Hôtel Matignon under the Fourth Republic that is in question—is to doom oneself to failure. What folly to "precipitate" an affair, or in other words to "hasten the progress of things," as for example "to precipitate the solution of a crisis" (Robert under *brusquer,*

to precipitate). "He was too prudent to precipitate matters," George Sand writes of one of her characters (quoted by Robert, ibid.). To precipitate things is to risk dropping and smashing them. "The impatient man," Fénélon observes (quoted by Robert under *impatient*) "is drawn . . . into an abyss of misfortunes . . . he waits for nothing . . . he precipitates everything in order to attain satisfaction . . . he breaks down doors rather than wait for them to be opened for him." "Precipitancy in sieges does not hasten the taking of emplacements," Vauban teaches us, "but often delays it, and invariably makes the scene a bloody one" (*De l'attaque et de la défense des places*).

22. It is better to follow Valéry's example and "to work with infinite patience for the most precious moments" (Valéry, *Tel quel*, 2: 99).

23. To wait is much less dangerous than it appears to fools. The clearsighted man, the experienced man knows that there is every advantage in waiting: we have plenty of time, I shall still have time for . . . It is an attitude opposed in childhood by adults urging their charges to perform on the spot and be quick about it. It is therefore a reaction that may be given full rein later; often with unfortunate results, as when General Gamelin, early in the spring of 1940, "thought he still had years ahead of him," according to Jacques Benoist-Méchin (*Soixante jours qui ébranlèrent l'Occident*, 3: 473).

"Hopes then," wrote one journalist reporting the trial of a woman suspected of numerous poisonings (Marie Besnard), "but long term ones. And why hurry? These were things as certain as a life insurance" (Pierre Scize, *Au grand jour des Assises*, p. 310). "I know that you have to face grave and difficult problems," Charles de Gaulle is reported as saying in a cabinet meeting to his harassed ministers faced with the so-called educational question. "But," he advised them "let us not rush things"; for "time will allow us to wait." When Louis Jacquinot agreed, with the words "that's what I've been saying," he evidently received the reply: "Really, you've noticed that too, have you?" (Carmen Tessier, *France-Soir*, December 6 and 7, 1959). "Time is often the great master of all things," Michel Debré was reported as having reminded Jacques Soustelle in a request not to provoke his exclusion from the U.N.R.: "What have you to lose by remaining silent for six months? What have you to lose by waiting quietly for events to develop?" (News letter, *L'Express*, May 12, 1960).

24. In fact, the child did wait: and here he is promoted to the rank of grown-up! Any faith he may have put in time will therefore have proved justified.

A child psychiatrist writing about the French (François Dolto) has said that the whole of childhood is spent in waiting for the end of adolescence. "During the whole of our childhood," said a young mother interviewed by Charlotte Roland, "and during our adolescence, all we were doing was waiting to be adults."

25. This waiting may not always be done calmly.

When the sixteen-year-old boy in *Le blé en herbe* exclaims at one point to his fifteen-year-old girl friend, "God! You're hair's a mess!" the girl replies: "I shall go on having messy hair as long as it's still too short. This hairdo is just for the meantime. . . . Mama says . . . I must be patient." Whereupon, "Phil jumped up. . . . A hated word had appeared to poison his happy high-school student's vacation siesta. . . . He raised his fists and swelled out his chest . . . challenging the horizon: Be patient! That's all you ever say, the lot of you! Whether it's my father, my teachers . . . Oh! God almighty . . ." (Colette, *Le blé en herbe*, pp. 22–24). "So many years yet," he says a little later on, "during which I shall be no more than almost a man, almost free, almost in love" (ibid., pp. 26–27).

26. Waiting is a matter of pressing necessity, since it is so extremely expeditious: that is a profound and widespread belief. Let time do its work; everything comes to him who waits: a theme often much stronger than the rejection of "this habit, so many, many years old, of perpetual procrastination" (Proust quoted by Robert under *ajournement*, procrastination).

"By snatching a little time there's nothing you can't remedy," Molière's Dorine observes. "The future, Monsieur Chavarax, belongs to those who can wait," one of Courteline's characters says (quoted by Robert under *patience*). According to Valéry, "waiting is of great price" ("Dialogue de l'arbre," p. 183); for "everything can be given birth here by infinite patience" (Valéry, *La jeune parque*).

"It is right that we should both give *tempo al tempo*" Retz once pointed out to an associate (*Mémoires*, p. 848). Although he had been opposed to the "waiting school" both in Vichy and elsewhere, and although he was soon afterward to condemn the "immobilism" of the Fourth Republic, Charles de Gaulle declared during the war that "time . . . is always a courteous fellow to those who know how to make use of him" (speech, February 5, 1945; *Discours et messages 1940–1946*, p. 562). "I believe that the best attitude to maintain in Indochina at present," he announced later on—the war had been going on for almost two years—"is not to rush anything." "One must know how to take one's time," he added. And finally, "why should we be the ones in a hurry?" "One day or another," the appropriate solution "must present itself" (Press conference, November 17, 1948; *Le Rassemblement*, November 20, 1948). Antoine Pinay likewise advocated a waiting game to those of his friends who were hostile to Charles de Gaulle after the latter's return to power. "Don't jump the gun," he is reported to have requested of them with regard to the referendum of January 8, 1961: "this is a race that's going to be won with stamina" (*Aux écoutes*, December 2, 1960).

27. We should wait in order to reduce the probability of failure, in order to allow time for all the chances of success that may occur. But we should also wait so that an opening may perhaps present itself in a situation that is at present blocked.

When Richelieu "could see his way as little to retreating from his enterprise with any honor as to concluding it without help," he decided, according to La Rochefoucauld, that "he would have to draw these negotiations out . . . in order to try whether time would give rise to some means for either the one or the other" (La Rochefoucauld, *Apologie de M. le prince de Marcillac*). It is in fact a wise formula for conduct that bases hope on waiting.

28. Often, indeed, it is considered right "to wait until the last moment before . . ." (Robert under *moment*). The eleventh hour is not only the moment one must hang on until, it is also the moment for acting at last.

29. There are, of course, unfavorable reactions to this procedure.

If I keep on waiting and waiting, perhaps I shall never perform the act in the end.

"By dint of . . . postponements," the aging André Gide perceived, "and with this mania for always keeping the best in reserve for worthier days, it seems to me that all is still to be said" (quoted by Robert under *atermoiement*, postponement).

The last minute action is likely to be performed badly, however, as one of Sacha Guitry's characters implies when he says: "It was all decided in a quarter of an hour and at the last minute . . . as is the rule in our . . . country" (Guitry, *Le nouveau testament*, act 4). And when there was a long governmental crisis under the Fourth Republic, for example, one punctuated with investiture sessions that came to nothing but were dragged on and on by endless statements, questions, and answers—in the end, when the crisis simply had to finish, weren't they going to do anything at all, anyhow, and above all as quickly as possible, in order to get it over with? If one party (the M.R.P.) was opposed at that time to the procedure for revising the Constitution being assimilated into that for the election of presidents of the Republic, it was because "an unfortunate precedent [the election of the last president] had caused it to fear that if all 940 deputies and senators were to meet all together at Versailles, such a vast congress would merely succeed in doing nothing . . . or in doing anything at all in order to get it over with" (Jacques Fauvet, *Le Monde*, May 20, 1955). "Let us not wait," the first prime minister of a still young legislature (Guy Mollet) exclaimed on the subject of electoral reform, "let us not wait until the last few months of our mandate to discuss . . . such projects in haste" (A.N., January 31, 1956; *J.O.*, p. 135). Yet eighteen months later, we find his successor (Maurice Bourgès-Manoury) being forced to repeat that "we must not wait until the end of our term so that the Assembly is forced to deliberate in a last minute rush" over the method of voting the country is to use (A.N., June 12, 1957; *J.O.*, p. 2684).

30. Such apprehensions often carry little weight, however, when it comes to combating the attractions of last minute action.

"The last to get the best," Robert gives under *dernier*, last, and goes on to explain that "those who serve themselves after the others get the best meat." "The latest would be best," one of Jean Cocteau's characters says (Cocteau, *La machine à écrire*, act 1, sc. 2). It is the judge, the arbiter, who speaks last, having heard all those above whom he sits.

"Matters are being weighed, observed, and waited upon, but no clearcut decision will be arrived at until the last moment," wrote a journalist during a crisis under the Fourth Republic (Georges Mamy, *Le Monde*, February 9, 1955): a formula capable of very extensive application. In political circles, one hears stories of deputies who—when voting was the old traditional affair—went up to the speaker's platform with an entire fistful of voting slips and didn't actually choose one till the very last moment; or who, during a debate—when reading was still the form —went up to speak holding two written speeches drawing different conclusions. During his trial, Joseph Darnand told the court, referring to the ends to which he had intended to put the militia: "I had . . . the feeling that . . . we could . . . with police forces at our disposal, if Germany lost the war, give a helping hand that would make such a situation definitive, and if she won it, be represented with regard to her in such a way as to give France a voice in discussions and the chance of a place in Europe's future."

31. Last minute action is stylish; like the Parthian shot.

"The eternal question," Montherlant writes of one of his characters, "at what instant to make one's effort? There had always lurked within her a . . . desire not to make it until the very last possible moment, the elegant darling of the hare in its race with the tortoise" (Montherlant, *Le songe*, p. 50).

32. But is it even a question of daring?

Writing of France between the wars, Montherlant discerned a "belief . . . that she can go on doing just as she likes to the very last moment, that she can always pull herself back from the brink of the abyss" (*L'équinoxe de septembre*, pp. 129–29).

Even the child, hoping that adults will forget or give up making a demand in the face of discreet inaction, can be sure of his secondary line of action: in the unlikely event of things becoming serious, he will still have the time to change over to what one might term last minute obedience (which also has the advantage of emphasizing his independence of spirit).

33. So the emphasis laid on the havoc wrought by the too-late (see sec. 4 above) is perceptibly less than that laid on the frightful consequences of the too-soon.

"I know perfectly well, whatever people may say," Valmont affirms, "that the lost opportunity can be regained, whereas one can never go back on a precipitate action" (Laclos, *Les liaisons dangereuses*, letter 33).

34. It is best to wait and thus give oneself time—elbow-room —for reflection, observation, trials (see chapters 7 and 8).

35. But there is also the time I must not allow to others. Having acted, I shall be out in the open; the less time such exposure lasts the greater will be my chance of success, the more I shall minimize my proneness to attack, to raids, and to any weakening on my own part.

36. If we wait instead of giving way to the itch for action, it is possible that everything will settle down again on its own. Our wise abstention will then have achieved a delightful saving in energy.

37. Experience teaches the child that it is a good thing to play possum during the storms to which grown-ups are inclined; the mere passage of time will calm such angers provided that one is careful to abstain from reacting against them. And when it is a question of precise requests being made by grown-ups, it is again time that may lead to eventual forgetfulness or abandonment of them, again provided one does nothing to mitigate its action.

Several mothers interviewed by Charlotte Roland have made comments that reveal the truth of this. Describing what usually happens after she has given her children an order, one of them said: "I don't watch to see that they do it; I tend to let it drop if the child doesn't do it right away, then I forget." "When you had told them to do something," another mother said, "and you could see they weren't obeying, but there wasn't time to wait any longer, well, you just let the whole thing drop." "He is very patient about listening to what you tell him, and then not doing it all the same," said a third about her son. "He probably thinks you'll forget eventually." One must therefore resist such calculations on the child's part: "If the children dawdle and try to play for time," another mother said, "you have to show them that they're not going to gain anything by waiting, because whatever happens they've got to do what you tell them, so it's better to do it right away": a statement that seems, in itself, to indicate how great a strain must have been put upon the theory behind it.

38. Having grown up, the ex-child may retain the conviction that everything will always settle down pleasantly enough again provided one only waits, instead of rushing into the action that the momentary situation appears to require.

"It is rarely that a question one has repressed does not devour itself within the instant," Valéry notes (*Eupalinos*, p. 12). And Montherlant writes of one of his characters: "It was . . . a principle with him always to postpone difficult decisions until later . . . because he wanted to give every possible chance to the theory that, as circumstances changed, he would no longer be called upon to make it at all" (*Le démon du bien*, p. 65). And again, of a mother aware that her daughter is having a love affair, Montherlant writes: "She knew perfectly well that she would be obliged to insist one day that this situation end, but she put the moment off, secretly hoping that either he or she would tire of each other and part without there having been any need for her to interfere" (*Les lépreuses*, p. 224). "I have observed," the king in *La reine morte* says, "that one almost always kills people too soon. Another few days, and the victim would no longer have been quite so guilty" (Montherlant, *La reine morte*, act 3, sc. 5, p. 152). "Everything should always be put off until the next day," says another of the same author's characters, "since three-quarters of all affairs settle themselves" (*Le cardinal d'Espagne* act 2, sc. 2.). And of himself, Montherlant says, "I have always put off unpleasant things till the next day and have always benefited from doing so, the necessity for doing those particular things in fifty percent of the cases vanished in the meantime" (*Carnets*, 1930–1944, p. 305). And similarly, "I persistently observe that we are always in too much of a hurry to render a service asked of us by some third party. By the time one has rendered the service he has ceased to need it. So that both our time and our trouble have been lost" (ibid., p. 315). If we wait, the other person will have stopped importuning us, or he may even think he has had his way: "Solicited by a charitable organization to send it a signed copy of a book, I put off doing so day after day, out of laziness, until suddenly I received a letter of thanks from the organization without having sent anything" (ibid., p.

323). When "one's fountain pen leaks . . . one does nothing about it and then, after a day or two, it stops leaking. I imagine that illnesses must sometimes cure themselves in the same way, and difficult affairs in the same way resolve themselves" (ibid., p. 283).

"I called to mind then," a politician under the Third Republic recounts, "one of the three rules that we rookies offered as matter for meditation by our comrades already on active service when we met in the mess: I don't remember the first very well; the third is unprintable; but the second went as follows: 'when you receive an order, wait for the counterorder before you obey it'" (J. Paul-Boncour, *Sur les chemins de la défaite, 1935–1940*, p. 241). "He prefers to settle things quietly," a journalist explained several weeks after Charles de Gaulle had returned to power. "In Council, he has compared the situation in Algeria to that in Paris in 1944. Were the Liberation Committees ever dissolved? Who dissolved the Home Guard? Thorez. Why dissolve the Committees of Public Safety?" (Jean Farran, *Paris-Match*, June 28, 1958).

39. If it should prove indispensible nevertheless, in the end, actually to act, at least I shall then be able to make my decision with a greater knowledge of what is at stake; the situation will have become clearer and I shall have received additional information to help me assess it; I shall no longer be groping in the dark, I shall no langer be completely at sea. Whereas an immediate decision, whatever the fools and the ignorant may think, would be clearly premature, a choice made after an additional waiting period has the possibility, in the end, of being a rational one. What is more, it may be easier. Even though the passage of time may have rendered all the practical solutions less advantageous, one of them, if one is lucky, may still appear clearly preferable to the others.

"It's not that I approve of all they do," Cardinal Suhard is reported as having said to a colleague, shortly before his death, with reference to the worker priest question, "but we must take our time. It is like afforestation, at first it's all just undergrowth. It's too early to do any cutting. You can't tell yet which are the good branches" (Adrien Dansette, *Le destin du catholicisme français*, p. 218).

40. Sometimes, the vistas only open up little by little; but "there are certain obscure futures that become clear . . . quite suddenly" (Mme de Sévigné, quoted by Robert under *s'éclaircir*, to become clear), at an instant that one ought to have waited for.

41. No affair can ever drag on so long that one can no longer expect time to bring additional information to bear on it.

"The discussion of the constitutional and electoral reforms"—
a great figure of the Fourth Republic announced with reference
to the two eternally recurring subjects of debate during the last
years of that regime—"is not yet far enough advanced for it
to be possible to express an opinion" (Henri Queuille, *Combat*,
February 1 and 2, 1958).

42. The clarification one has waited for is never too small to
be thought of as earthshaking.

After Charles de Gaulle had expressed himself briefly on May
15, 1958 on the events of May 13, and then announced a press
conference for the nineteenth, on the eve of that event "General
de Gaulle's most resolute supporters" as well as "his most determined opponents . . . seem to have declared a sort of truce while
awaiting his press conference." To tell the truth, "neither side
thinks that the general will appreciably modify the attitude he
has adopted." But, "attentive to the tone rather than the terms,
weighing the slightest shades of meaning, each listener is at
liberty to seek in his remarks . . ." (Pierre Viansson-Ponté, *Le
Monde*, March 20, 1958).

43. To wait is also to allow others to act, to perform what
will ultimately prove to be benefit to me, thus sparing me the
necessity of a stupid expenditure of my own energies. Instead of
moving into an unfurnished house—the fate of the man who
acts immediately—I shall steal the ball from under their feet
later on, I shall reap the fruit of their labors, I shall cut the grass
from under their feet. But in order to do so, I must first "give
the grass a chance" (Louis Joxe, May 27, 1961, press conference
at Evian; *Le Monde*, May 28 and 29, 1961).

"A virgin's love," Jules Renard remarks, "is as tedious as a new
apartment. You have all the work to do yourself" (*Journal*, p. 9).
"In the course of parties where other men were seizing their advantages," one of Montherlant's characters "was continually
pushing women into the arms of third parties, always leaving
at the crucial emotional moment, astonishing everyone by his
lack of push and his continual self-effacements. . . . Then, one
fine morning, the woman most desired by the group fell into
[his] arms, burning to break down his reserve, and Guiscart took
what was offered, at one fell swoop, the blunders having been
made by the others and sometimes the risks all run as well"
(*L'historie d'amour de la Rose de Sable*, p. 124).

44. To wait until the pear is ripe" (Robert under *attendre*, to
wait), until it falls, until I need make no more than a single
movement to pick it up (that's the trick of it; see chap. 8).

"When the priest asked him in catechism class: What were
Adam and Eve doing in the Garden of Eden? Jean-Louis (the

archetypal little middle-class boy) replied, according to Carmen Tessier: "Well, they were waiting for the apple to get ripe" (Tessier, *Histoires de Marie-Chantal,* p. 184). According to Chamfort: "There is in all things a ripeness that we must wait for. Happy the man who arrives at the moment of that ripeness!" (*Maximes et pensées,* p. 103). Before that moment one should say to oneself, with Valéry:

> Patience, patience
> Patience in the blue!
> Each atom of silence
> Is the chance of a ripe fruit.

Such patience is wasted time only for the man who is incapable of penetrating beyond appearances:

> These days that to you seem void
> And lost to the world
> Have greedy roots
> Searching the deserts.
> [Valéry, *Palme*]

"When one is faced with a difficult problem," Edgar Faure advises us, "one hangs it up by the neck like game. When it is properly 'high' it will fall. It is then ripe for solution" (Claude Bourdet, *France-Observateur,* November 10, 1960).

45. Before that moment has come, it is as well to maintain that "the question doubtless still needs a little time to ripen" (René Pleven, on the subject of the integration of overseas territories into the common market, A.N., January 17, 1957; *J.O.,* p. 102).

For "it is not a sound idea," Gide reminds us, "to seek to 'force' plants"; as far as fruits are concerned, "by seeking to advance their natural time of ripening, one affects the fullness of their taste" (Gide, *Journal des faux-monnayeurs,* p. 77).

Should one have the misfortune to encounter "a bitter fruit that still refuses to ripen"—as with Syria, where the Free French were concerned, toward the end of 1940 (letter from General Catroux to Charles de Gaulle, December 8, 1940; de Gaulle, *L'appel,* p. 369), do not deviate from the correct procedure: it will take as long as it takes.

46. "You're not mature enough, you say," Jules Renard is asked by his partner in an imaginary conversation. "Are you going to wait till you're rotten then?" (*Journal,* p. 30). It is Victor Hugo (quoted by Robert under *mûrir,* to ripen or mature) who provides the answer: "The good ripen; the bad rot." Although I know that the worm is there in my fruit too, I try to

think less about that than about the favorable consequences to be expected from the rotting of the other fellow's: it is when his affairs go to the bad that my undertaking ripens. Hence one of the great phrases employed by politicians: The situation is not yet ripe, we must let it hang a little. Or: We must let the matter hang awhile, then it will fall into our hands all ready for the table.

47. Time is on my side, and against the other fellow—"everyone is relying above all on the help of one and the same ally, time, to impose the solution of his choice" (François Mitterand, on the subject of Algeria, *L'Express*, February 25, 1960)—since the other fellow is certain to find himself in difficult straits: that's when I spring my attack. "To wait for someone at . . ." (*attendre quelqu'un à . . .*) Robert explains, is "to wait until he becomes involved in some difficulty. I'll wait for him as he's turning the corner." During the Restoration in France, Chateaubriand tells us, Louis-Philippe "waited for the outcome like a spider waiting for a fly to be caught in its web" (quoted by Robert under *attendre*).

48. Furthermore, the other fellow will not be able to stand up to the waiting as well as I; he will weaken, he will be worn out when I am still holding firm; then, after tiring him out, I shall have him licked.

This is a ploy that is already used between children and adults. The mother leaves the child on the potty: Stay there till you've finished, until you've had enough of not finishing. (Whether it takes a little longer or not quite as long, one always gets there in the end!) It is a procedure that the child, later on, may turn against the adult. "I was trying to explain a problem the other day to Françoise, because she hasn't been doing too well at her work recently," a mother told Charlotte Roland. "Then suddenly I realized that she simply wasn't listening to me; it was exactly as though she were saying: 'Keep talking if you like, it doesn't bother me, sooner or later the time will come when you'll do my problem for me.' When I saw that's how things were I was so furious that I began by giving her a shake, after that I threw her down on the floor and I even gave her a kick. . . . After that, I did her problem for her."

Just as the judge in Rabelais defers his judgments until the parties are worn out with pleading and paying, so Louis XVI, according to Jaurès, "still hoped to tire the Revolution so that he could tame it in the end" (quoted by Robert under *lasser*, to tire). Under the Third and Fourth Republics, all-night sittings of the Assembly were also used to force decisions out of sheer lassitude—in the same way as the drawing out of ministerial crises.

Predicting in the autumn of 1948 that Israel would keep the Negev and Galilee, Charles de Gaulle added: "The remainder . . . will probably find a solution in the general lassitude" (November 17, 1948, press conference; *Le Rassemblement,* November 20, 1948). That the same politician did not advance the date of his speech announced for January 29, 1960 after the revolt that broke out on the twenty-fourth is probably also to be explained by the same line of thought: one must give those who have worked themselves into a state of open or budding revolt enough time to wear themselves out, to weaken.

49. The passage of time may do even better still: the other fellow may disappear altogether. He may leave the post that he is using as a means to block me.

"What one government refuses them," one leading politician under the Fourth Republic remarked of "vested interests," "they count on obtaining from the government that will succeed it in a few months' time. They see to it that the problem hangs fire. They are content to play for time, and finally, in this little game, they are usually the ones who come out on top." Similarly with the highest ranks of the civil service: "A new minister is appointed who wishes to direct the policy of his department along a new channel. He works out a whole series of measures and reforms spaced out over two, three, or even four years. The civil servants concerned are asked to put these ministerial orders into execution. What is their automatic reaction? . . . Many of them say to themselves: this minister is probably right, but he is there for no more than six months, and if we commit ourselves to this policy, in six months' time there will be another minister who has different plans . . . and who will ask us to undo all that we have begun to put into effect along these lines. Better to let the matter hang fire, to wait, to keep quiet and move as slowly as we can, for fear of having to undo later what will have cost us quite some trouble to build up in the early stages" (Paul-Henri Teitgen, A.N., March 14, 1957; *J.O.,* p. 1596). "If a minister attempts to enforce his wishes," another leader under the same regime confirmed, "the civil service equivocates; they are waiting for the next crisis and his successor" (Félix Gaillard, spech at Confolens, January 12, 1958; *Le Monde,* January 14, 1958).

Or the other fellow may eventually die.

"I was young," La Rochefoucauld recalls; "the king and the cardinal were both weakening in health, and I had everything to expect from a change" (*Mémoires,* pt. 1). "When he was twenty," Roger Vailland recounts, "the Abbé de Bernis solicited the conferment of a benefice from the Cardinal de Fleury, then eighty-eight years old. . . . They had already crossed swords on several occasions. 'Monsieur, Fleury replied, as long as I live you shall have no benefice.' Bernis bowed. 'Very well, Monseigneur, I'll wait' " (Roger Vailland, *Eloge du Cardinal de Bernis*, p. 7), a remark attributed more recently to Paul Reynaud when canvassing a seat in the Académie, at the age of about eighty, and encountering an obstacle in the form of Maxime Weygand, his elder by ten years. A great politician of the Third Republic (André Tardieu), who withdrew from it before it collapsed—a politic action, he announced; a defeat by illness according to others— recalls similar expectations in the past: "I heard one of my colleagues, a doctor and radical, say of me in 1930: 'Illness will get him out of the way for us.' And another, in 1934, announcing the following diagnosis on M. Doumergue: 'The old fellow's going yellow, there's no need to bother!' " (André Tardieu, *La profession parlementaire*, p. 124).

50. Waiting is also a procedure that is useful if one is on the lookout for some compelling *force majeure* (see Leites, *Du malaise politique en France*, chap. 5).

"We always wait for the moment when we are forced by circumstances before we act," Mirabeau observed (quoted by Robert under *attendre*, to wait). "What is he waiting for?" Montherlant asks, referring to one of his characters, a shy man who is contemplating accosting a woman. "Well, the truth is, he's waiting until it's too late" (*Les célibataires*, p. 222).

51. Frequently, it is a good thing to disguise the fact that I am forcing others to wait, by amusing them.

Amuser, Robert explains, also means "to occupy while causing to lose time," and then quotes Corneille: "Keep him amused, at least, by arguing with you./Make him waste time." "He is merely trying to buy time," Robert gives under *atermoyer* (to delay), "by keeping the company amused"; and *atermoyer* is defined as "trying to gain time by means of distractions."

52. To choose to wait is one thing; to be constrained to do so is another.

"The torture of waiting is the lover's hell," Robert quotes under *attendre*—and that of many others as well, perhaps. "If God decided to give me heaven but would not give it to me there and then, I should prefer to hurl myself into hell than to be forced to await His pleasure," declares the infanta in *La reine morte* (Montherlant, *La reine morte*, act 1, sc. 1). "I am a person, not who forgives, but who forgets," says another of the same writer's characters of himself; "one who truly forgets even the most offensive actions. But I am not a person who allows himself to be made a fool of, even when it's done from stupidity" (Montherlant, *Les lépreuses*, p. 285).

53. Grown-ups, when they have felt like it, have made the child wait a great deal; they have made him waste his time. But since resistence was far too difficult and risky, he learned to commute his rage into resignation.

The ex-child continues to perform this process; but let some situation arise—at the wheel of a car, for example—in which rage and impatience do not seem quite so heavy with dire consequences, and then look out!

54. How delightful to avenge oneself by reducing the other fellow to fury, by making him wait! What a pleasant proof that childhood is at an end, that it is no longer I who am being given the medicine!

This reaction is often apparent in the staffs of all the various institutions that the majority of mankind are forced to depend on. "God alone waits for no one," Roger Vailland notes, "and only the agricultural worker has no one to keep waiting." Thus, "at the two extremes of the hierarchy, we find: God and the agricultural worker" (*Paris-Match*, December 14, 1957). As for the stages in between, here is an episode in a hospital that one well-known psychologist has dared to present as being something by no means out of the usual: "I have seen patients waiting two whole mornings to no avail in the surgical wing, having been told to expect an operation. One of them was told: 'You'll be sent for again in two days'; he was in an extremely agitated state . . . and quite ready to make a scene, especially since every time an operation was said to be imminent he had been given an enema" (Georges Mauco, *L'Express*, October 5, 1956).

55. But making the other fellow wait does not only mean malignantly depriving someone who is at my mercy, it can also mean using delaying tactics on someone who, it seems to me, could treat me a great deal worse than he is doing already: the procedure that Philippe Pétain put his trust in during the Occupation. "That's what one must always think of" he said to Maurice Martin du Gard toward the end (June 17, 1944): "Gaining time" (Martin du Gard, *La chronique de Vichy*, p. 495).

11

SWIFT MOVEMENTS AND
SLOW PROGRESS

1. Though the child may be threatened with the label "restless" (see chap. 3, sec. 46), adults are also very prone to see it as hampered by an excessive slowness.

As far as the "general behavior" of their children is concerned, "it is above all slowness in their movements that strikes and worries" the mothers observed in a Parisian mental hygiene clinic: "slowness in rising, in dressing, in washing, slowness in eating" (Jean Dublineau, *L'école des parents,* November 1956, p. 21).

2. "It is seen above all as a form of laziness" (ibid.,), something not calculated to mitigate the adults' reactions.

3. But it is also often seen as being proof of some base quality in the human being; *traîner,* to drag or hang about or dawdle, has come to denote all sorts of distressing behavior in French. Above all, anyone who is slow lacks intelligence; there is nothing to be done with him.

An inspector of primary schools, affirming the opposite, has urged parents not to confuse level and rhythm, insisting on the fact that slowness in a mind need not exclude power.

4. Many adults engage in an endless and wholly inglorious struggle against their child's slowness, a struggle of which the great battle cries are "Haven't you finished?" and "Hurry up!" (if you don't want to go without dessert, for example).

"My daughter gets up as late as she possibly can," one mother informs us, "and leaves for school at a quarter to eight. That's the moment when I'm struggling with my little boy, who's very slow" (*L'école des parents*, May, 1956, p. 45) "Quickness is a quality I would like to inculcate in my children," said one of Charlotte Roland's mothers; "but since children have an innate tendency to go rather slowly I have to hustle them a bit." "Naturally," another mother confirmed, "since they like dawdling, you have to be on their backs and hustling them along the whole time, saying hurry up." Another mother, who admitted to having "a very lively temperament herself" and "a tendency to get things over with quickly," admitted that she "hustles them along [her children] generally speaking," adding: "I would like to teach my children to do things quickly." What things? "When they're on the potty and it isn't happening I tell them to hurry up; I keep on at them to hurry up in the morning, when they've got to get to school, and in the evening when they're putting their things away, and at mealtimes because they dawdle."

In school, a primary school inspector comments, "the teacher becomes impatient at the student's slowness in performing a task, at his slowness in understanding, his slowness in obeying." "One sign of this . . . impatience," the same observer adds, "is the use of the phrase 'hurry up'" (André Ferré, *L'école des parents*, July-August, 1957, p. 33). And here is a child's point of view, given by a little girl being made to work hard because she is due to move up into the class above: "The teacher says all the time: 'Now children, you haven't any time to lose; we've got very little time left to get through the whole syllabus.' She reads out the dictations much too fast because we have less time. She says we must get used to copying out our math problems much quicker, she rubs them off the board because there's no time; and I can't go as fast as that, mommy, you see. And it's the same for my homework in the evening. The teacher says: 'That should take you a quarter of an hour, twenty minutes at most: if it takes you any longer it means you've dawdled over it.'"

5. The struggle into which grown-ups hurl themselves in this way is not an easy one to win.

"What she hates most," another of Charlotte Roland's mothers says, speaking of her little daughter, "is when I say: Hurry up and put your toys away. She immediately does the opposite, or goes more slowly." In the "frequent" case of "children . . . accused of slowness and taken to a doctor on account of it," one child psychologist observes, "one often finds this slow and passive child is active and quick when it is a matter of games or indeed of any activity undertaken on its own initiative. . . . The passivity and slowness only occur when it is a question of activities imposed on it by adults: at home, washing, dressing, doing its homework; in school, following the lessons. It seems as though every time an adult intervenes, a reflex is triggered off in the child that renders it suddenly distant, absent" (Claude Launay, *L'école des parents*, September-October, 1956, p. 32). ("This wretched little girl," says a Balzac character quoted by Robert under *lenteur*, slowness, "always obeys me with the slowness of a tortoise, and becomes as lively as a lizard whenever Justin asks her to do the slightest thing"). Our child psychologists are all saying that it is nagging, nervous, insistent parents that produce this reaction of slowness. "Exaggerated slowness in a child," one specialist concludes, "is . . . almost always a reaction against the feverish impatience of the adults in charge of it" (André Berge, *Les défauts de l'enfant*, p. 31).

6. The adult is driven to attempt to modify the child's slowness in the first place by the unpleasant effects it produces in him or her: slowness irritates, gets on the nerves.

"I can't watch them dawdling at anything, it's more than I can bear," one of Charlotte Roland's interviewees exclaimed.

7. But there is also, whether real or suspected, a wish to be rid of a burden: the slow child takes up all the adult's time, the quick child allows the adult to bother less about it.

8. Adults are often thought of as favoring methods that enable them to save time and produce quick results in the child. They are likely to choose "the quickest expedient" (Robert under *expédient*), in their determination to "despatch" the children (*expédier* in French) in the sense in which Robert—who illustrates *expédier quelqu'un* with "despatch the affairs concerning him" and in particular, "to get rid of someone, to finish with him as quickly as possible"—refers not only to the judge who "despatches cases promptly," but also the "doctor who disposes quickly of his patients, does not examine them carefully," and, furthermore, "the teacher who disposes quickly of his lecture, his lesson, his program."

"Appealing to their feelings," in order to achieve obedience in their future children, "seems to us a bad method," declared one young couple. However, "we think that we shall often . . . employ it because . . . it works quicker" (*L'école des parents*, January 1960, p. 16). "We scold them," a father says, "because that's what works quickest" (*L'école des parents*, February 1954, p. 39). "The psychological method of bringing up children is all well and good when the mothers have nothing else to do," one mother explains; "but when you've got to do everything yourself at home, then sometimes you haven't got the patience, and the psychological method goes out of the window." For "they somtimes obey much quicker with a good slap" (*L'école des parents*, August-September, 1953, p. 48). "When you've told a child not to do something several times and then it starts again, it gets a slap and you get the result you want immediately" (*L'école des parents*, October 1953, p. 51). "I'll quicken you up all right if I take a stick to you," one of Scarron's characters says (quoted by Robert under *hâter*, to hasten transitively).

9. Being anxious to move quickly, grown-ups do not always allow for transitions. Sometimes they require even more than they do of each other when forcing sudden changes on a child to which it must adapt from one day to the next. This may be the case with certain separations, which can so easily be construed by the child as desertion.

10. Having partly taken over and applied on his own account the lesson thus frequently taught him in so harsh a fashion, the child will often become an adult with rapid movements and a lively physical and mental rhythm.

11. Whereas the French, according to French belief, are temperamentally lively, many foreigners are less so. Certain nations adjacent to France, employing a vocabulary that is more or less comprehensible to French ears, make French into another language with their habitual slow-motion method of pronouncing it.

"They run, they fly," the Persian remarks of the people he is observing. "The slow carriages of Asia, the steady pace of our camels would send them into a trance" (Montesquieu, *Lettres persanes*, letter 24). "I remarked to a German officer," the same author writes in his travel notebook, "you cannot withstand our vivacity, nor we your slowness" (Montesquieu, *Voyages*, p. 807). "The action of things on their minds," he says elsewhere of the Bavarians, "is not instantaneous. It takes a great deal of time for the message to reach their souls. Whatever order you may give, you see them musing a long while in order to get it well into their heads, as though you were giving them some problem in geometry. Finally they understand you. But if you give an order and it is at last understood, do not give a second one: for it will take an even greater length of time for the second to be understood, since they return continually to the first. I have often seen quite literally happen in Germany the story of that German at Madame de Lambert's: 'In faith, I am laughing at what Madame said just now.' It does take them a little while" (ibid., p. 818).

But among the favorable consequences bestowed upon "the Latin nations" by the fact that they are "consumers of wine" we find, according to a deputy representing the Gironde under the

Fourth Republic, their "rapidity of mind" (Gabriel Seynat, A.N., November 9, 1955; *J.O.*, p. 5585).

12. Which is just as well, since "a country in which everything is slow, in which everything moves in slow motion" (Robert under *lent,* slow)—what a nightmare! One of the major aspects of the decline constituted by old age is that, as Montaigne reminds us, "liveliness and alacrity . . . fade and slowly languish" (*Essais,* bk. 1, chap. 57).

It is therefore not solely in their relations with children that grown-ups find themselves being powerfully irritated by slowness.

"His slowness makes me impatient to the highest degree," Robert gives (under *impatienter*), while under *lenteur,* slowness, he lists "as slow as a snail," 'exasperating slowness," and even "his slowness drives me to despair." "My cravat, Thérèse," Anatole France has one of his characters say (quoted by Robert in the same place), "do you hear? my cravat! Or, if you drive me any nearer to despair with your slowness, it is not a cravat I shall need but a rope to hang myself with." "These longueurs, or rather these meanderings . . . are intolerable to me," Gide declares (quoted by Robert under *longueur*).

13. So "cure yourself of your slowness!" (Robert under *lenteur*); if possible, I shall become a speed merchant. "We have direct administrative methods in our bones," Lyautey declares, since "we are not patient" (quoted by Gilbert Grandval, *Ma mission au Maroc,* p. 127).

14. "He's speed personified": what a heartwarming image! And what a useful gift; for, Monsieur Teste observes, "I am either swift or nothing" (Valéry, *Monsieur Teste,* p. 62); it is speed that gets me past such and such an obstacle, that helps me beat an opponent in "a game in which speed was the essential" (Valéry, *L'idée fixe,* p. 10); life always has one more trick up its sleeve. Gaining time does not only mean "obtaining the advantage of having a greater length of time at one's disposal," but also to "economize on time" (Robert). (That delaying tactics and acceleration of a maneuver should both be denoted by the same image is a very apt expression of the coexistence of exactly opposite attitude with regard to time, a coexistence that forms the principle subject of this chapter.)

15. Just as slowness is confused with stupidity (and clumsiness), so rapidity is the same as intelligence (and skill).

Having noted that *conception* denotes by extension "any act of the intelligence," Robert immediately gives: "lively, easy, slow, conception."

"Rapidity in intellectual processes is essential . . . to their realization," one child psychiatrist affirms. Which is to say that "there are intellectual acts that cannot be successfully accomplished unless they take place at sufficient speed," a phenomenon that "becomes more pronounced as the intellectual act becomes more abstract." "In short," this specialist concludes, "one cannot make good use of one's intelligence, particularly during one's school years, unless it functions fairly quickly . . . unless it goes leaping on from one stage to the next. Everything would be all right if, with time, the intellectual act could build itself up slowly, but it loses en route the elements that link it together and permit its completion" (Gilbert Robin, *Les difficultés scolaires chez l'enfant,* pp. 94–95).

A rapid style is that of a man with wit (in the broader, somewhat obsolete sense of the English term). "What is called wit (*esprit*) among the French," Montesquieu notes, consists of "a dialogue . . . in which everything is treated in a fragmented, swift, and lively manner" (*Mes pensées,* p. 1417). "Wit," Rivarol explains, "is that faculty which sees quickly, shimmers, and strikes. I say quickly because vivacity is its very essence. A dart and a lightning flash are its emblems." In "society . . . wit . . . asks neither delay nor a fixed moment to utter a felicity; it vibrates more quickly than simple good sense; it is . . . swift and glittering in feeling" (Antoine Rivarol, *Maximes et pensées*).

16. And yet, even when the movement is swift, the enterprise may still drag on slowly. Freed from the demands that once weighed upon him, the ex-child can at last take his time.

17. In which case he will express his ill will toward those who apparently wish to keep him in a state of tutelage, or force him back into it; though he may still submit to them occasionally in a manner strikingly at variance with such attempts at rebellion.

"He is slow and does not like to be hurried" (Robert gives under *bousculer,* to hustle or hurry).

18. Given this state of mind, an action on someone else's part may easily take on the appearance of an attempt to encroach on my precious privilege of slowness.

When a movie director (Georges-Henri Clouzot) refused to allow audiences into the theater except at the beginning of his thriller *Les diaboliques, Le canard enchaîné* was concerned about the possible extensions of this action: "Your fellow men will one day invent toilets with automatically ejectable seats. Thereby destroying the last refuge of liberty . . . that of taking as long as one likes" (*Le canard enchaîné,* February, 16, 1955).

19. How delightful to be able to display a deliberate slowness which will infuriate the other, but which he is henceforth powerless to attack!

20. What I find pleasurable myself may easily be seen as a vice when the other employs it at my expense. So that those subject to any authority, although themselves tempted to take their time, are very prone to attribute to it that same vice that its predecessors in childhood hunted down with such determination: at once a vengeance and a way of escaping from one's bonds.

"Slow justice" Robert gives under *lent,* slow, and also (under *longueur*), "the delays of justice. . . . We are worn away, we are sapped by delays." Though it is the duty of judges to give justice, La Bruyère points out, their trade is to delay it. And there are some who know their duty and ply their trade.

"He applied to the prefecture of the Aube in 1948," said a deputy telling the story of a father who had been searching for his little daughter after his divorced wife had been given custody of the child. "The child was seven years old at that time. The enquiries instituted by the prefecture lasted two years. It was only after two years that it was eventually discovered that the child was in the care of the Public Assistance" (André Mutter, A.N., January 29, 1958; *J.O.,* p. 348). It is normal, but also bewildering, that "delays of considerable duration in some cases . . . occur between the statement of a principle and its application" (Pierre Viansson-Ponté, *Le Monde,* April 28, 1960): a great theme, under both the Fourth and Fifth Republics, of the some-times spectacular protest movements from "sectors" that felt they were "forgotten," as for example certain groups of civil servants, or certain groups of farmers. "The law of August 4, 1956, provides, in article 11, for decrees made by the Council of State to fix the conditions under which the government will guarantee French agents, whether still active or retired, their retirement pension," a former councillor of state, now a deputy (Pascal Arrighi) re-minded the Assembly toward the end of the Fourth Republic, referring to the provisions to be made for French civil servants in Morocco and Tunisia who had returned to France. Yet, "more than seventeen months after the promulgation of this law, those decrees have still not been published. Since it concerns retired men whose means of subsistence are limited, this delay is deplor-able" (A.N., January 21, 1958; *J.O.,* pp. 169–70). The Fourth Republic having come to an end, and "decolonization" being now in full swing, another deputy and ex-councillor of state, this time a member of the Left (André Chandernagor), concerned for the civil servants that France might be able to put at the disposal of the new African states, reminded the house that "they are asking you for guarantees, since it is certain that the fact of serving in these young countries does entail administrative risks." The de-mand was one that apparently presented no difficulties, since "a

ruling made last October"—which was already a year before—
"promised them those guarantees." In fact, "all that is lacking in
order for this ruling to be applied is a certain number of public
administration regulations." But this final step, and this was the
crux of the matter, was tending to be deferred: "These public administration regulations should have been published before April
last.... The reply to my oral question [on this matter] was given by
the minister of state, M. Robert Lecourt. . . . That reply . . . was as
follows: 'A note has been presented to me that justifies the, alas,
very real delay'—this was on June 26—'in the publication of
these regulations on account of the very particular complexity
of this problem. I am authorized to assure you that the Prime
minister is himself following this question personally, that he
has given all the necessary instructions to ensure that the settling
of this affair will suffer no further delay' " But, the speaker concluded, "we are now in the middle of October; the regulations
have still not been published."

21. Might not the slowness that adults judge excessive in a
child perhaps be rather wise in a grown-up?

22. There is the matter of pleasure, of pleasures.

"The dark purple wings beat and beat, infinite in their slowness," Montherlant writes, watching with admiration as two
butterflies couple. "The slowness of his pleasure surpassed the
slowness of anything in this world" (*Encore un instant de bonheur*, p. 111).

23. Since it is likely that a pleasure will be brief, it seems sensible to do everything one can to make it last, to save it from
oblivion; for, Valéry reminds us, "a sudden thing of brief durat-
tion, unforeseen and without consequence or traces, does not
exist" (*Mauvaises pensées et autres*, p. 133).

"Someone there was, in the old days, who wished for a throat
drawn out as long as a crane's," Montaigne recalls, "in order to
taste what he was swallowing more lengthily." At all events,
such a "wish" is very much "to the purpose" in love, "that swift
and precipitous pleasure." In that sphere one may well fear
rather to be "defective in suddenness"; it is therefore particularly
important "to arrest its flight and draw it out in preambles"
(Montaigne, *Essais*, bk. 3, chap. 5).

24. By making a pleasure last I not only increase its sum, I
also allow it to unfold all its nuances; I can savor it.

"So much longer the path is in love, so much more does a
delicate mind feel the pleasure" (Pascal quoted by Robert under
délicat). When a woman claimed that it would take five minutes
to make love, "I protested," Léautaud recounts, "five minutes! It
takes me two hours, I take so much pleasure in the approaches"

(Léautaud: *Propos d'un jour,* p. 22). And Valéry does not hesitate to speak of the "slow acts of a skilled courtesan" (*Tel quel,* 2: 98).

25. One must take a long time because the various nuances of a pleasure are spaced out at intervals in a temporal order that one is hardly in a position to reverse.

"The more steps and stages there are," Montaigne says of love, "the greater the height and the more the honor of the topmost place. We should take delight in being led to it, as in magnificent palaces, by diverse portals and passages, by long and pleasing galleries, and by many a winding way" (*Essais,* bk. 3, chap. 5). "Some young men at court," Chamfort recounts, "were supping with M. de Conflans. They began with a song that despite a certain freedom had no excess of indecency; whereupon M. de Fronsac immediately embarked upon a ditty so abominable that it reduced even that joyous band to consternation. M. de Conflans interrupted the universal silence by saying: "Dammit, Fronsac, there are ten bottles of champagne between that song and the first'" (Chamfort, *Charactères et anecdotes,* p. 132). Similarly, a cabaret singer, refusing a request made by some of her audience to sing her most titillating number the moment she appeared, told them: "Oh no, we've got plenty of time for *Little Pussy!*"

26. It is thus rapidity, so much enforced by grown-ups, that is the expression of naïveté, clumsiness, stupidity, weakness: all characteristics of the child.

In a story of Crébillon the younger, the first lesson a young man receives from his mistress, who is older than he, deals with the necessity for gradations. "The man who takes pleasure only in the moment of pleasure . . . is not one who should mingle in our school," Montaigne says (*Essais,* bk. 3, chap. 5), reprimanding a clumsy oaf, doubtless either very young or very retarded. Such a person's desire is likely, according to one of Audiberti's characters, to be at the same time "stammering and greedy" (*La fête noire,* act 1). "I have several times observed," Retz notes, "that when men have hesitated a long while before undertaking something because they fear that they will not succeed, the impression of that fear remains with them and is the cause, usually, of their going too quickly in the conduct of their enterprises" (*Mémoires,* p. 397).

27. What is true of pleasure also provides the rule for any other reasoned act (see chap. 7): to be "rapid" in any particular phase of its conception or execution is to disrupt the correct order and to doom oneself to failure. It is desirable, in serious matters, that the act, the gesture, should be "lengthily considered," the project "lengthily ripened" (Robert under *longuement,* lengthily).

28. A great matter is likely to need a great deal of time to be achieved: "I work in depth, at length," Valéry claims (*Tel quel,* 2: 99).

Whatever Montaigne may say about the *coup de foudre* that produced instant friendship between himself and Etienne de La Boétie, La Bruyère was expressing a much more widespread feeling when he affirmed that friendship is formed gradually and is the product of a long relationship. "But is there so much hurry where friendship is concerned?" asks one of Colette's characters. "We should have become friends . . . later. I know you very little" (*La naissance du jour,* p. 163). And though La Bruyère may claim that "love is born suddenly" (*Les caractères,* "Du cœur," 3), Paul Valéry is at liberty to add that a "long labor of the soul and desire" is necessary in order to lead "the most precious" loves to "their delicious goal" (quoted by Gide, preface to *Anthologie de la poésie française,* p. xviii).

29. That which takes a long time to do is done slowly.

In order to arrive at a great many important goals one must plod (*cheminer*), which means "to follow a long and difficult road that one moves along slowly" (Robert). "The slow labor of erudition" Robert gives under *lent,* and also "a long and patient labor." According to Bossuet, Don Luis de Haro, the Spanish ambassador, "gave himself weight by his slowness" (Bossuet, *Oraison funèbre de Marie-Thérèse d'Autriche*). Pétain, according to his principle private secretary, was deeply imbued with the notion that the greatest problems could not be dealt with wisely except on the precondition that they also be settled slowly (Henri du Moulin de la Barthète, *Le temps des illusions,* p. 195). Thus, under the Third and Fourth Republics, to "precipitate out" the majority that a new Chamber concealed "in solution" was a thing neither easily nor swiftly accomplished: this "labor of decantation" was, indeed, a long and arduous one. Distinguishing between two periods in the life of an Assembly, the first lasting for more or less eighteen months, one great politician of the Fourth Republic (Edgar Faure) observed toward the end of that regime that "during the first period, the crises are usually crises caused by the search for a majority" (*Combat,* February 3, 1958).

30. An attempt to achieve his goal right off the mark, at one fell swoop, is rarely characteristic of the strong man. "To rush one's affairs," Bossuet claims (quoted by Robert under *exécuter*), "is the characteristic of weakness." "It is a weakness to do the quickest thing," one of Montherlant's characters echoes (*La reine morte,* act 2, tableau 1, sc. 1).

31. That is not how one gets ahead.

Festina lente is not too hackneyed to bear saying again. "Does one drive everything on to its conclusion with such haste?" one of Colette's characters asks (*La naissance du jour*, p. 225), a character who even confesses a "fear of all haste" (ibid., p. 235). "Take care above all," Valéry remarks when describing his way of making cigarettes, "not to place one edge of the paper over the other too quickly. Impatience delays. One must roll, roll, roll" (Henri Mondor, *Propos familiers de Paul Valéry*, p. 60).

32. Even if one achieves one's goal with ill-advised rapidity, the fact of having achieved it in such a way greatly reduces the value of the achievement itself. "It's not my taste; I do not wish with one fell swoop/To take the town, since I prefer to clamber," La Fontaine declares (*Féronde ou le purgatoire*). A successful pick-up contains a strong element of this—perhaps ridiculous, certainly questionable.

33. It is more probable, however, that the initial eagerness will fade.

In his memoirs, Jules Roy notes the danger of bringing everything down about our ears simply because we have gone at something too quickly.

34. Gently (*doucement*) does not only mean slowly, it also means evenly.

35. The tendency toward discontinuity (see chap. 3, secs. 52–62) is seen as frequently being bad and dangerous, leading to shocks and breakages.

In order to avoid "finding oneself a prey to the agonies of discontinuity" (Valéry, *Tel quel*, 2: 192), one must make sure, in Montesquieu's phrase, "that there is no interruption in the contexture" (Montesquieu, *Essai sur les causes qui peuvent affecter les esprits et les caractères*), or, as we say today, "that there is no solution of continuity"; a phrase that Boussouf is reported as having employed in a description of Charles de Gaulle's policy when smoothing the way for the acceptance of negotiations with the F.L.N. in such a way that "the ultras would not feel anything" (*Le canard enchaîné*, October 21, 1959). It is wise, in short, to avoid all abrupt, jerky, shocking, bumpy, choppy, staccato methods, to refrain from all excess in the way of hiatuses and gaps.

36. These things are all avoided by going gently.

"He who wishes to do it well," La Fontaine advises in the matter of love, "must go more gently about the task" than some clumsy fellow (*Le berceau*). "One experiences extreme delight," Molière's Don Juan affirms, "in storming, with a hundred turns of phrase, some beautiful young woman's heart . . . in leading her gently to the point where we would have her be "(quoted by Robert under *doucement*).

37. So one advances step by step.

There are, Valéry admits, some "precious things" that "are the product of an extremely rare conjuncture of favorable circumstances: diamonds, happiness." "But others are formed by the accumulation of an infinity . . . of contributary elements that all absorb a great deal of time": "fine pearls, rich wines . . . , accomplished people" (Valéry, *Pièces sur l'art*, p. 13), for example—according to his principle private secretary, if not according to the member who received him into the Académie—Pétain, "that man of slow accumulations" (Henri du Moulin de la Barthète, *Le temps des illusions*, p. 155). Baudelaire perceived a "universal and eternal law . . . of the bit by bit, the little by little": "Nothing is ever made except little by little" (Baudelaire, *Mon cœur mis à nu*).

38. Thus one plods on by degrees, transitions, imperceptible touches, like La Fontaine's practiced lover: "And still by degrees, as you may well think/From one to the other he caused her to pass" *La matrone d'Ephèse*). "All my life," the Cardinal de Bernis admits, "I have had the talent for transitions, which, to be good, must be imperceptible" (quoted by Roger Vailland, *Eloge du Cardinal de Bernis*, p. 48)—just as, on the other hand, in Buffon's words (quoted by Robert under *graduel*), the end of life "comes only by gradations, often imperceptible."

39. The imperceptible advance remains unperceived. By adopting it, one becomes Valéry's "prudent man," careful "to move in such a way that one can continue for a long while to deny that one is moving at all" (*Tel quel*, 2: 196), for example, the future Louis-Philippe, of whom Louis XVIII declared: "He doesn't move, but I feel he's on the move."

40. Other undertakings, instead of a maximum of continuity, require a sequence of stages, of distinct periods of time, of neatly cut slices (see Leites, *Du malaise politique en France*, chap. 3).

"Anything produced . . . by man," Valéry discovered while thinking about such cases, "is achieved by means of successive actions, clearly separated" (*Variété*, pp. 895–96). Thus an advertisement for a department store will offer its customers "a recipe for elegance in four stages: look, choose, order, fit" (*Le Monde*, March 25, 1959).

41. These series of successive phases, may include detours; they may, on the other hand, approach the final goal steadily; or again, they may form a much more complicated pattern of approach, as in a certain plan for a cabinet that was submitted to Pétain by his principal private secretary early in the spring of 1942, the aim of which was to prevent the return of Pierre Laval: "The Germans had, in all likelihood, greeted this cabinet ex-

tremely unenthusiastically. . . . Mistler and Romier [members of the projected cabinet] had doubtless served, as Flandin had already done [when the Germans insisted on his dismissal in the winter of 1941], as expiatory victims. But the bull does not tire until it has disemboweled several horses. The path of slowly wearing the adversary out required these hippophagistical relays. And who knows whether, veering from combination to combination, from successive suggestion to successive retreat, the marshal's storm-tossed ship might not eventually have succeeded in fetching round its bow, some months later, to face the right channel?" (Henri du Moulin de la Barthète, *Le temps des illusions,* p. 418).

42. In any case, it is futile and dangerous to "scorch the ground under one" in an effort to get ahead. When Charles de Gaulle, smiling at the terror inspired by a military monk, Thierry d'Argenlieu, observed that "the admiral is scorching nothing but the ground under him" (J. R. Tournoux, *Secrets d'Etat,* p. 7), the witticism was an attempt to skate lightly over an obstacle that was dangerously near wrecking everything.

43. Even if one were to succeed in reaching one's goal without having approached it along the prescribed route, one would thereby have reduced the value of one's conquest (see 32 above), as Molière's *précieuses ridicules* demonstrate to the men who ask their hands in marriage so unceremoniously.

44. When slow, the child makes himself "late," whether in respect of some external, terminal event or simply in relation to the exact schedule or rhythm desired by the grown-ups around it.

45. The child often finds itself being told that it is going to be late; that it will be hopelessly late if it doesn't hurry up, this very instant; or that it has already forfeited any chance of escaping that fate: you will never finish your homework!

46. So the struggle against slowness (see sec. 4 above) very largely takes the form of a struggle against lateness.

"They haven't time to dawdle," one of Charlotte Roland's interviewees says of her children. "I only allow them a very little time for everything they've got to do; I hurry them along by going and telling them to hurry. It isn't only when they're doing their business that I speed things up. . . . In the morning, when they get up, they have just enough time to wash, to make their beds, to brush their shoes, and eat their breakfast before setting off for school." For "if they dawdled the slightest bit, they'd make themselves late."

47. Any backwardness in the child (backwardness and lateness are both conveyed by the French *retard*) is likely to produce acute uneasiness in those in charge of it.

"It sometimes happens," a child psychologist writes, "that specialists are consulted about six-year-olds because they cannot read yet, or children that have been in school for three months and still cannot write legibly" (Georges Amado, *L'école des parents*, June 1958, p. 32).

48. For people are only too prone to imagine of any situation what a deputy once affirmed about equipping the army: "We know very well that, in this sphere, time lost can never be regained" (Maurice Faure, A.N., October 24, 1960; *J.O.*, p. 2724).

49. Worse still, one may risk having to face the fact—along with an inspector-general of primary education (Lucien François) presiding over a committee meeting during a UNESCO conference—that: "we are falling steadily more and more behind!"

50. In other words, a slight degree of lateness at a moment still far distant from some important day of settlement can excite apprehensions of total failure on that future but certain date.

To succeed, if not in getting into the upper grades of a state school, at least in the entrance examinations for the better-known higher education establishments—since the time available for special preparatory classes is limited by the age restrictions placed upon the candidates—can reasonably be thought of as a wager at the mercy of the slightest weakening of the body or the will, since any such weakening tends to make one drop behind. "Through having contracted typhoid at the age of twelve," one journalist has commented, "through having a mediocre math teacher in third grade, or simply through having taken an interest in the world around him, more than one high school student will be forced to abandon his dream of becoming a naval officer or an engineer" (Bertrand Poirot-Delpech, *Le Monde*, January 9 and 10, 1955).

51. No longer being a child means being able to allow oneself delays with impunity, tasting new and ever fresh delights: "I never pay, when I do pay, until the day after the bill is due" (*Le canard enchaîné*, February 16, 1955). And the pleasure of this is possibly merely increased by the fact that in many circles one is expected to express horror at the vice of lateness and to promise never to give oneself up to it.

52. Parents and teachers, for example, while constantly struggling against tardiness in the child, are themselves subject to persons in authority who are in their turn inclined to be tardy in the settling of accounts.

Though "delays are usually very considerable in great affairs" (La Rochefoucauld, *Mémoires*, pt. 6), this is not perhaps a characteristic that sets them clearly apart. "All payments by the State," a deputy observed toward the end of the Fourth Republic, "those for reconstruction as well as those for war damage, are always and everywhere made after a delay" (Marcel Darou, A.N., March 26, 1958; *J.O.*, p. 1993). "A great many repatriated civil servants," another deputy told the Assembly at the same period, "having returned from Tunisia and Morocco, are being left, they and their families, without payment of their salaries, indemnities, or allowances" (Pascal Arrighi, A.N., January 21, 1958; *J.O.*, p. 170). "It has necessitated and still necessitates," another opposition member claimed, referring particularly to members of the police, who were his particular concern, "incessant protests in order to ensure that their salaries are regularly paid" (Jean Dides, A.N., February 25, 1958; *J.O.*, p. 1009). And a journalist, again during the same period, referring to a famous case of death from the administering of a drug, wrote: "The orphans of the Stalinon have still not received a centime of the damages that have been due to them now for four years" (Merry Bromberger, Paris-Presse, February 7, 1958). "200 science students protest against the delay in paying their grants," another paper headed one of its articles later that month (*Combat,* February 27, 1958). Minor symptom of a dying regime? In the third year of the Fifth Republic, "the National Union of those engaged in higher education called upon all the professors, technicians, and general staff of the Paris Faculties to go on strike from January 4 [1961] onward as a protest against the fact that their December salaries had not yet been paid. . . . Delays in payment have become habitual, the union claims. For example, after being nominated to his first post in higher education, a teacher will not be paid until three or six months later. Moreover, remuneration for supplementary teaching is usually paid only after a delay of from one to two years" (*Le Monde,* January 5, 1961).

53. The attraction of delay is sometimes sufficient to dispose of all the obstacles so carefully set up to counteract the tendency to it.

Seeing the regime that had just ceased to exist as the great reign of delay, the creators of the Fifth Republic thought up innumerable constitutional and statutory provisions to ensure that it would be possible, for example, not to put the budget through the Assembly in a suitably short time. "The Constitution," one journalist reminded his readers, "had taken every possibility into account: there was an article laying down the procedure for passing the budget . . . , an organic law, forty-six articles long, minutely determining the forms of the discussion and of its conclusion." And yet, when "the first test came [in autumn 1959], the government was the first to put itself in the wrong by failing to respect the period of delay allowed it. It ought to have produced its entire projected budget 'on the first Tuesday in October at the latest' (article 38 of the organic law), which is to say, this particular year, on the sixth. In fact, the last of the papers were not submitted to the Assembly until October 22, and M. Debré agreed to consider the forty-day period allowed to members before voting on the first reading as not beginning until October 15. Thus, from the very beginning, he was already in conflict with the Assembly over an infraction of one week" (Pierre Viansson-Ponté, *Le Monde*, November 24, 1959). Then we come to the evening of November 24, when the forty days in question were due, according to the prime minister, to expire: "Shortly before midnight it had been decided that the clock should be stopped. This return to customs that had been so many times denounced had drawn a slight mumur of disapproval from the benches of the 'national renewal' supporters" (Raymond Barrillon, *Le Monde*, November 26, 1959).

54. In order to put pressure on the child in an attempt to make it respect some time limit, the adult tries to explain to it how unpleasant, in the very nature of things, the consequences of delay will be. If the child does hurry, however, this may be more because it has been convinced by the threats with which the adult has accompanied his or her predictions rather than by the predictions themselves. Later on, the ex-child will reach the privileged position of being able at last to unmask the arbitrariness of what were presented to him as compelling reasons: he will find it difficult to admit that those occasionally mock—and certainly, for the adult, obsolete—threats have been succeeded by a real necessity even to acknowledge the existence of a disagreeably close and distressing time limit.

Toward the end of July 1955, when almost no one could yet foresee that Morocco would in fact be independent before the end of the year, the Resident General (Gilbert Grandval) increased even further, in his communications with the government, the emphasis he had already placed upon the seriousness of an approaching time limit: that of August 20, the anniversary of the ex-sultan's deposition in 1953. He explained why major action must be taken before that date. Yet during the cabinet meeting that took place on August 6, "my plan and the telegrams with which it was followed up were considered minatory." The feeling of the government in Paris was that "it is not possible to move so fast." Above all, "France cannot allow a time limit to be imposed upon her": that would be the capitulation of a child. In vain Grandval demonstrated that "August 20 is a fact I can do nothing about; . . . as for the time limit of August 20, it is not I who am imposing it upon the government, but it exists." These facts notwithstanding, "almost the entire cabinet esteemed it unsuitable for France to allow so tight a time limit to be imposed upon her" (Gilbert Grandval, *Ma mission au Maroc*, pp. 178–80).

55. So no more of "delay leads to disaster"! A slight delay? Come now, it's not so serious as all that!

On August 10, 1955, in a conversation with the Resident General —increasingly distressed by the approach of the twentieth—the prime minister (Edgar Faure) "accepted in its entirety the plan I had submitted to the government." In fact, "there is nothing in it that needs changing . . . except, perhaps, for a slight shifting of the dates . . . which is not, everything considered, so very serious. . . . I referred to the dangers of August 20," Grandval adds, "but I could not succeed in gaining any serious attention from the premier on this point." So "when I left him . . . I was feeling profoundly uneasy to see the imperative character of the time limits so misunderstood" (ibid., p. 186): as if adult life were distinguished from childhood by a certain impunity in this respect, a feeling on the adult's part that he is no longer compelled to pay such scrupulous respect to time limits.

56. In childhood, pleasures and comforts must so often be sacrificed to time limits; once it is over, it is right and proper to invert that relationship.

On August 7, 1955, when Grandval was in Paris, still with his eyes (very correctly) fixed on the twentieth, and attempted to put forward a pertinent cabinet meeting from the eleventh to the ninth, he was unsuccessful: "apparently it would have inconvenienced ministers whose good will was needed" (ibid., p. 181).

57. The inclination to rebel against time limits extends to those one has fixed for oneself (see chap. 1, sec. 13).

Refusing to take any account of August 20, 1955, the government set itself another date for its plan (September 12). Yet "on August 13," Grandval recalls, "I was brought a letter from M. Pierre July [the minister responsible for Morocco] that expressly . . . evisaged the situation if the time limit set by the government could not be met" (ibid., p. 201).

58. When a child is behindhand, the adult says to it: you'll never finish in time, you'll never catch up! The ex-child knows better: he'll get behindhand and still make it in time. So who's going to be left with egg on his face and who's going to be laughing then? Besides, if someone always works away steadily, avoiding delays as well as a rush at the end, is that not just because he is mediocre? Is it not the shortage of time produced by the delay

that, far from being a cause of failure, is precisely the condition required to find the trick that will save me from it and prove my superiority (see chap. 8, sec. 29)?

Thus, corresponding to the last minute choice (see chap. 10, secs. 28–30), we have the last minute rush.

"To tell the truth, everything here . . . in the French camp gives the impression of being scarcely begun," a journalist reported at the beginning of the conference that was to end the war in Indochina. "And though it is true that the French are renowned for remedying lack of preparation with improvization, they will be obliged in this sphere, if they are to catch up the years they have lost, to work miracles in the next few days" (Jean Schwoebel, *Le Monde*, May 7, 1954). "If we have succeeded in not losing this match," Jacques Soustelle told the Assembly when speaking on the subject of the French delegation sent to New York for the United Nations debate on Algeria early in 1957, "it was—and I intend this expression to be between quotation marks—'à la française,' at the last moment and by dint of . . . difficult improvization, rather in the style of the taxis of the Marne, doing in one month what ought to have been done in two years" (A.N., March 21, 1957; *J.O.*, p. 1776).

12

SHORT TERM AND LONG RUN

1. Since they believe it to be wholly absorbed by the present moment, adults give the child sermons on the need to be serious: "One must look a little further than the end of one's nose" (Robert under *peu*, little); one must—strong words these—prepare for the future, one's own future, and not compromise it. And on the strength of this argument, the child, prevented from "amusing" itself, finds itself persistently having to give things up, having to do nasty things. It learns that the long view is likely, in the beginning, to have unpleasant consequences.

2. Having made this harsh lesson his own, the ex-child will conceive, and even attempt to put into execution, long-term plans of great complexity—to do with his career, for example— the success of which presupposes an ability to predict or to control a great many distant events (see chap. 7, sec. 35; chap. 8, sec. 43; chap. 11, secs. 27–43).

3. But the child compelled to sacrifice his present may also, as Françoise Dolto has pointed out, rebel. In answer to the adult who tells him he must prepare for his future and learn about life, he may cry "I don't want any part of my future, I don't want to live, I want to play." "My future can go inside me where I think," yells the rebellious and triumphant adolescent in Marcel Aymé's *Les oiseaux de la lune*.

A child psychologist, addressing himself to the country's parents, says: "You tell them that if they don't work hard they may not pass their exams when they're older." Unfortunately, however, "for them that is something very unreal" (Cyrille Koupernik, *L'école des parents*, February 1954, p. 39). There is the story of the puzzled boy, usually destined for the national Rivers and Forestry department, who simply cannot see why so many odd efforts are required of him.

4. The result is that for the ex-child, however good and sensible he may be in his actions, "not anticipating" may appear "one of the pleasures of life" (Montherlant, *L'histoire d'amour de la Rose de Stable*, p. 84); there is a certain readiness to share Taine's feeling that it is "the Teuton" or some other foreigner who "is able to persist in undertakings that will not reach maturity for a very long time" (Robert under *échéance*, maturing date of, e.g., a bond). There is a rule—not noble, but attractive, in imagination at least—that counsels one to abandon the long hope and expansive thoughts, to fend off the need that is most pressing, to apply oneself less to creating opportunities, as La Rochefoucauld puts it, than to taking advantage of those that occur.

5. What I dare not put into practice myself I am only too ready to attribute to the everyday authority I am subject to (the authority whose reign is interrupted only by saviors), against whom I then turn the criticism with which I was myself belabored as a child (see Leites, *Du malaise politique en France*, chap. 5). Just like the unreasonable child, the politician with his ulterior motives is accused of sacrificing the future to the present. But now it is even more serious, since the future in question is that of others, that of the country. "I never think what I shall be doing in six months time," or, in another version: "Know that I concern myself with nothing that is not due for completion within six months": this remark, attributed to Benjamin Constant, is often thought of as expressing the underlying attitude of the politician, constantly tempted to act according to the requirements of the moment, refusing to entertain the long-term view. According to this image of him, he neither thinks of nor provides for the future; he has no difficulty in blinding himself to the fact that he is shirking the future or to the fact that he is encumbering it with debts by pursuing a so-called policy of convenience.

6. The future is, after all, only the future, those in high places are thought of as saying to themselves.

"The most usual source of men's failings," Retz observes (after having described an action during which considerable but still distant disadvantages were accepted in order to avoid slight but imminent inconveniences), "is that men are too much concerned with the present and not sufficiently concerned with the future" (Retz, *Mémoires*, pp. 579–80).

7. The future, the person in authority is believed to feel all too often, is not my future.

La Bruyère refers to "certain people" "who can be studied in courts" and who make it evident "from all their behavior that they are thinking neither of their grandfather nor of their grandson: the present is theirs" (La Bruyère, *Les caractères*, "De la cour," 95).

8. After all, I shall soon be dead!

The Bishop of Besançon, in *Le Rouge et le Noir*, "was more than seventy-five years old and infinitely little concerned with what would happen in ten years." "All of that will certainly last as long as we shall," one of Georges Courteline's characters predicts (Courteline, *L'article 330*). "After a certain age," one of Montherlant's characters says, "there is no longer anything to be gained by achieving things through slow intrigue: there is a danger that one will not see the end of it. So give me the swiftly executed action that one can enjoy in its entirety (*La reine morte*, act 2, tableau 1, sc. 1).

"He considered the State only for his lifetime," Retz dares to claim of Richelieu (*Mémoires*, p. 67). In a less well-known version of a thought that has become a cliché in another form, Louis XV is reported as having said: "The monarchy will last as long as I do. I certainly pity my successor" (Rivarol, *Maximes et pensées*). "Agreed, we've missed all our historic aims," Clemenceau is said to have admitted, in conversation with Maurice Barrès during the conference of Versailles, "but what of that! we've lived."—"And in fifteen years time?"—"In fifteen years? I shall be dead!" (Philippe Barrès, *La victoire au dernier tournant*, p. 26). Under the Fourth Republic, a general and deputy generally thought of as anachronistic in his views reproved what he called a "triumph of the short-view policy, as though France's destiny were to be measured merely in terms of the lifespan of those who claim to govern her" (Adolphe Auermann, A.N., August 10, 1954; *J.O.*, p. 4038).

9. So many functions of authority change office-bearers so very often; even the Fifth Republic has not succeeded in making the two highest offices in the state more stable, and "a prefect who . . . wished to remain in the same *département* in order to bring some long-term undertaking to a conclusion would be obliged," now as ever, "practically speaking, to give up the idea of promotion" (*Demain*, March 15–21, 1956). Even though I may be expecting to stay alive until such and such a date, it would be imprudent, or frankly ridiculous, to foresee myself outliving my present post. In which case . . .

Under the Fourth Republic, one heard stories in the political world of men holding some degree of power who, when beset by acute difficulties, reminded themselves with relief that they had a very good chance of "dying" shortly: "Besides . . . I shan't be in the government any more in three days time, so . . . (words attributed to a Minister of Transport, Edouard Corniglion-Molinier, when faced with a strike. *France-Observateur*, December 1, 1955). According to an anecdote widely printed in the national press in 1956, Jacques Chevallier, a former mayor of Algiers, having insisted on the notion that a solution had to be found for Algeria that would still hold good in ten years time, the minister in power (Robert Lacoste) replied: "In ten years time? Where shall we be then, you and I?"

10. In view of all this, the insistence upon enormous foresight and long-term planning may be viewed as exclusively the province of an austere morality.

"The constant consideration" of Pierre Mendès-France when in power was said to be this maxim of Richelieu's: "Those who live from day to day live happily for their own part, but others live unhappily under their guidance" (Pierre Drouin, *Le Monde*, July 6, 1954). Toward the end of the Fourth Republic, a senator who saw himself as following in the footsteps of certain great statesmen of the Third Republic (Edgar Pisani), found himself, during a discussion of the military estimates, confronting a "gaullist" whom he thought of as having succumbed to the seductions of "the system," whereupon he sharply pointed out to him that "for anyone who is aware of a permanent responsibility, one that lasts rather longer than that of any Minister for National Defense, voting for a budget of this sort poses fearful problems" (C.R., March 12, 1958. *J.O.*, p. 482). "We are not concerned with seeking popularity," Michel Debré counseled France's elected representatives under the Fifth Republic, "but with earning a favorable verdict from history" (speech to the presidents of the councils general of France, February 17, 1959; *Le Monde*, February 19, 1959). "In politics," he reiterated in the Assembly, "only one verdict counts, . . . the verdict of history." "You may be certain," he told the house encouragingly, "that if you [do all the right things] . . . history will give you its entire approval and forget those that have criticized you . . ." (A.N., May 26, 1959; *J.O.*, p. 560). He then added "unjustly"; but it would truly be excessive to insist upon the intrinsic value of the behavior in question rather than upon the likelihood of eventual relief.

11. Coexisting with the cult of the long term and planning for the future—whether genuine or feigned—there is another and contrary current.

12. Is it always possible and useful to fix the details of a

long and complex undertaking well in advance (see chap. 7, sec. 35)? Or is it not rather both inevitable and salutary in many such cases to wait and see (see chap. 10, secs. 39–42)? Should those exasperated exclamations hurled at the child—"You don't know what you do want!" or "You must make up your mind what it is you want!"—now be commuted into eulogies of the reasonable man?

Although Montaigne affirms at one point that "the surest method . . . is to prepare oneself before events" (Essais, bk. 3, chap. 10), he also says elsewhere that "I enjoy starting without any plan: the first step leads on to the second" (bk. 1, chap. 4). In a secret committee of the Chamber during the Great War, when one of the prime minister's opponents hurled an accusation at him (Briand) with the words, "You went to Salonika without any aim, and probably saying to yourself: we'll see what the English and the Italians will give us and what our objective will be then" (Chaumet, November 18, 1916; Bonnefous, *Histoire parlementaire de la Troisième République*, 2: 176), many must have found the criticism a little harsh: and how is one to act otherwise, since any forecast of the future made in cold blood is such an unreliable quantity (see chap. secs., 64–65)? Writing about Laval's position in the summer of 1940, Jacques Benoist-Méchin says: "When he declared that 'the Constitution must be revised,' he certainly felt that a recasting of the present regime had become indispensable, but he had no idea of what it should consist in. If he had been asked what exactly the new institutions were to be, he would have been hard put to it to answer. He contented himself with fending off matters that were immediately pressing, convinced that the future would take care of the rest. Similarly, when he affirmed that 'we must negotiate with Germany' he did not know either how such negotiations were to be arranged or with whom he would conduct them—or, indeed, if they would even be possible." In other words, Laval "shied away . . . from anything planned"; he was "as little inclined to follow a premeditated line of action as to work out any long-term policy. . . . A plan? Laval had never made a plan in his whole life" (Jacques Benoist-Méchin: *Soixante jours qui ébranlèrent l'Occident*, 3: 568–88). At the cabinet meeting preceding the opening of the Indochinese peace conference (April 24, 1954), "M. Bidault . . . emphasized that it was much too soon to predict the conditions that would prevail at the opening of the Geneva talks, and therefore to fix upon the attitude we should take during them" (*Le Monde*, April 25–26, 1954). When, two months later, a foreign newspaper printed what it called "the main lines" of a French plan to achieve an armistice and peace, "those nearest to the French delegation . . . manifested . . . their surprise that anyone could at this time suppose the existence of a detailed French plan. True, French experts and representatives are still studying a certain number of hypotheses and propositions with a view to meeting certain foreseeable situations. But the attitude of the French delegation is marked above all by the very greatest flexibility" (Jean Schwobel, *Le Monde*, May 16, 1954).

During ministerial crises under the Third and Fourth republics, it was accepted as normal that there should be a wish to overthrow the government in power without being able, at the outset, to be at all precise about the cabinet that was to succeed it (even though there was no lack of an opposite belief in precise and complicated calculations on the part of certain "killers" in strong positions, calculations that were thought of as extending to all the phases of the operation upon which those "killers" were about to embark). "This time," one celebrated journalist wrote when commenting on the Fourth Republic's terminal crisis, "it has broken without the members, or even their leaders, having any idea of the way in which it may be brought to a conclusion" (Jacques Fauvet, *Le Monde*, April 18, 1958). Was that really so unusual?

"You are in favor of another government," one prime minister (René Mayer) threatened with "death" said to the party (the R.P.F.) that was defaulting, as they say, from his majority; "but on the strength of what program?" But he knew very well that that was not the question at that moment (A.N., May 21, 1953). "All in good time," was the answer. "All in good time! That is the motto that should be inscribed in letters of gold in the *Salle des conférences*!" (*Le Monde*, May 23, 1953).

Another prime minister (Joseph Laniel) speaking to the Assembly on October 27, 1953, said: "I ask them [the Socialists] not to repudiate what has been . . . the attitude . . . of successive French governments, unless, in the place of our policy, they have another policy that they are ready to apply. . . . If," on the other hand, the Socialists "are not capable of setting out and executing an alternative policy," then "all Frenchmen should . . . make every effort not to weaken the sole policy that France is able to follow at this time" (*Le Monde*, October 29, 1953). The following year, speaking with reference to the Geneva conference, a leader (Christian Pineau) of the party thus exhorted, when others were preparing to overthrow the same government, said: "If you do not wish the present government to represent France [at this conference] . . . "that probably means . . . that you have drawn up the government that is to replace it. . . . It certainly means that you have come to an agreement about what the attitude of our representatives in Geneva ought to be when they have been changed" (A.N., May 6, 1954; *J.O.*, p. 2151). It was easy to refute such remarks in the political world of the Fourth Republic, however, since they were obviously attempting to ignore a particular and powerful belief: that the provocation of the crisis would in itself exercise upon the course of events an influence that it would not be feasible to predict before that all-important act had actually been performed. The right thing to do, therefore, is to wait, and to go on waiting until one is in a position to formulate a plan for what is to follow.

13. Improvisation is not a necessity only; it is also a pleasure.

14. Though it leads only too often, needless to say, to grave disappointments.

"I mistrust improvisations," Georges Duhamel writes (quoted by Robert under *improvisation*); "such an affair cannot be improvised," Jules Romains has a character say (ibid.).

"The moderates," one eminent journalist (Jacques Fauvet) wrote when a maneuver on their part (during the election of a president of the Assembly) had just failed, "will have made great progress when they cease to improvise their tactics during adjournment of the house" (*Le Monde*, January 26, 1956).

It is normal to imply that a government with which one is not connected is intending to effect "an abrupt change of course, improvised like all the rest, moreover" (François Quilici, A.N., October 18, 1955; *J.O.*, p. 5135).

15. And yet, is it not precisely this same improvisation that provides the situation in which the man capable of it can bring off some extraordinary and admirable feat?

16. It is by improvising that one shows oneself, in the most dazzling way, to be creative; hence the desire to prove that "I am devilishly fine at impromptus" (Molière quoted by Robert under *impromptu*, impromptu or improvisation). "The vivacity, the fire, the ecstasy of improvisation," Robert gives under *improvisation. Improviser* is defined by the same dictionary as "finding at the last minute"; but it then adds: "see *inventer*, to invent." "To improvise," Delacroix once said (quoted by Robert under *improviser*), "which is to say, to sketch out and to finish at the same time . . . would be . . . to speak the language of the gods."

17. "The impromptu," Molière points out (quoted by Robert under *impromptu*) "is the touchstone of wit": for in improvisation, the force of that faculty, rising up in so swift and surprising a manner, supplies the want of time, which is a commodity at the disposal of all the world and one that becomes precious only when one deliberately sets out to deprive oneself of it (see chap. 8).

18. Thus the great improviser despises the hard worker; men like Briand take particular delight in the contrast between their refusal of all solid preparations and the methods of men like Poincaré or Delcassé who, "having little talent for improvisation, prepare all their replies and even their replies to possible replies" (Abel Ferry, *Les carnets secrets*, p. 55).

19. This being so, it is sometimes a good thing to feign improvisation when one has not dared to risk it (see chap. 7, sec. 31).

"Impromptu at leisure," Robert explains, has been used since Molière to express "a piece composed at leisure and given out as an impromptu." "In the morning," Gil Blas recounts, "I wrote down witticisms in my notebook, which I produced after dinner as impromptus" (ibid.). In conversation, Valéry referred to "those sovereign intelligences which, since they had never ceased to think, . . . needed no more, when the moment came, battle or poem, than to look, combine, read what was in their minds, let the world believe in their inspiration, make people exclaim at the miracle. The 'inspiration' had been ready a whole year!" (Mondor, *Propos familiers de Paul Valéry*, p. 231). "Nothing needs to be better organized," Madame Express once reminded her lady readers "than a spur-of-the-moment picnic" (*L'Express*, May 26, 1960).

BOOK 3

VELVET GLOVE AND IRON HAND

13

BRUTAL TACTICS AND CONSIDERATION

1. Civilized man has learned how to control his inclination to brutality.

The antonyms of "civilized" are, according to Robert—"barbarous" and "uncultivated" apart—"brutalize, bestialize, stupefy, brute, brutal, coarse (*abrutir, bestialiser, brutaliser, brut, brutal, grossier*)."

To civilize is a subtle operation, since "wealth with all its power can never tame the brutish" (Guez de Balzac, quoted by Littré under *brutal*, then by Robert under *apprivoiser*, to tame).

Once tamed, man acquires inclinations of which the fundamental characteristic is that they avoid brutality.

He learns to "consider" (*ménager*) the other, which is to say "to treat him . . . in a way that will not displease him (whether out of respect or out of interest)." He learns to show consideration (*ménagement*), which is "a reserve . . . one employs in dealing with someone . . . whether out of respect or out of self-interest." He avoids treating the other without consideration, which is to say "with brutality" (Robert).

When one succeeds in "softening (*adoucir*) a brutal man," he becomes capable of gentleness or softness (*douceur*), which is also "the quality of someone who lacks roughness, violence." To treat someone with gentleness is also to treat him "with consideration (*ménagement*)" (Robert).

Man is even able to become delicate (*délicat*), which is to say, to act "with a considerate attitude." He will then "employ delicacy and consideration" (Robert).

2. But this does not mean that brutality has been eliminated.

One is often able to observe "an alternation of harshness and gentleness" (Charles de Gaulle, referring to Lattre de Tassigny, speech of January 15, 1961; *Le Monde*, January 17, 1961); an unusual moment of weakness is likely to be followed by an excess of vigor, whether real or feigned.

When the moment comes, brutality is both restrained and unleashed on those occasions when one tends to say, with Montaigne, that "these acts of savagery are unworthy of French gentleness" (Essais, bk. 2, chap. 3). "A little French boy," according to Montherlant, is "all sweetness (*douceur*) and dirty tricks" (*Mors et vita*, p. 139).

3. The sweet (or gentle) and the terrible are often seen as being mingled to form "a kindly rage" (Ronsard), or "a fury so tender" (Valéry).

"In the song of the Saint-Cyriens," Montherlant asks, "what adverb is used to characterize those symbolic cassowary plumes? Are they to float 'proudly'? Or 'nobly'? Or even, to stretch a point, 'gaily'? No! "How nicely they float/Those plumes of white!" (Montherlant, *Le solstice de juin*, p. 192). "Harshness and honey, almost together; life in the style I like to see her wear," the same author remarks (*Mors et vita*, p. 43). "Tenderness transmuted into strength": that is how Valéry sees love; "the general weakness of the body, abandon, tendernesses transformed into the irresistible strength of the arms . . ." (*Mauvaises pensées et autres*, p. 166).

4. According to many adults, the child is likely to ruin, to smash the things it touches. Whatever its feelings, its intentions, it is thought of as tending to be abrupt and even brutal; and it is as a check to this tendency that all those cries of "Gently!" are directed at the child by grown-ups, seeking to protect the precious and fragile objects menaced by the young, uncontrolled, unaware being. "You don't understand . . . you can't understand," a mother described by Colette says to her daughter; "You're just a little eight-year-old murderess. . . !" (*Sido*, pp. 43–44).

5. Grown-ups—who may still be reminded by labels in fruit markets that "the fruit is fragile" and asked "not to touch me till I'm yours"—often seem secretly to have accepted the image of innocent gestures leading to terrible consequences that they had instilled in them when young. However much one may enjoy a go on the bumper cars, which requires an ability not only to weave and evade but also to stand up to rough shocks,

one still knows that in the serious things of life it is often best to "skim delicately over matters," to "touch upon them delicately" (Robert under *délicatement*). "This affair," one is only too ready to admit, "is an extremely delicate one." If I put my feet in the plate, as the French say, not only will the food be less agreeable to the taste, but I am also likely to receive a very disagreeable kick.

6. To the dangers from uncontrolled movements of the body and soul must be added those that are to be feared when one lets fly (*s'emporte*), which is to say, when one "allows oneself to be ruled by impulses of anger" (Robert).

7. Between adults and children, explosions of ill-feeling play a conspicuous role. Though adults may shout at their offspring— "My daughter says to me: You treat me as if I'm a dog. . . . Why do you start shouting like that? Don't shout like that!" one mother admits (*L'école des parents*, November 1957, p. 37)— they are nevertheless shocked in their turn by what they take to be their children's fits of rage. Even though, according to a child psychologist, "the very small child screams above all out of hunger, out of pain, out of fear, out of anxiety, out of despair, or in order to exercise its lungs," "the grown-up will say in every case: 'it's having a fit of temper!' " (Berge, *Les défauts de l'enfant*, p. 76). "Your child will sometimes display violent, terrible temper because an object resists it," a child psychologist warns parents (Cyrille Koupernik, *L'école des parents*, May 1959, p. 36): an apparently bewildering prospect. The anger of children who have been thwarted or beaten, one primary school inspector observes, explodes in yells, stamping, and wild threats of retaliation. "He flies into awful tempers," one mother says of her child; "When everything doesn't go the way he wants it, he goes red, he gets all stiff, he clenches his teeth, and his eyes flash. In the beginning, he used to throw anything at us he could lay hands on" (*L'école des parents*, January 1959, p. 46). "She sometimes flies into unbelievably violent rages, no matter where she is," says one mother of her four-year-old daughter. "Sometimes [she] gets to the point of kicking me, breaking anything that's near to her, etc." (*L'école des parents*, March 1959, pp. 46–47). And the way in which such cases are described and published seems to indicate that they are scarcely thought of as unusual.

8. That anger should unleash itself and gain a hold over me frequently appears possible, if not imminent.

"I had been reasonable for more than four years," a character in a novel says, "and suddenly I felt that I was going to fly into a rage" (Georges Duhamel, quoted by Robert under *enragé*, enraged).

9. One may count it a matter of pride that one is capable of forgetting oneself in anger, and of thinking of those people, admittedly very rare, who never speak one word louder than another as both puny and insufferable. Anyone who cannot fly into a rage cannot be very good at making love. "Since I have a very lively temperament"—a precious quality—"I am very quickly irritated," one of the mothers interviewed by Charlotte Roland explained. "I recognize my blood in that noble wrath," one of Corneille's characters exclaims (quoted by Robert under *colère*).

10. Anger is a defense against boredom.

"Disputes," as La Fontaine pointed out, "are extremely useful," since "without them one would always be asleep" (*Le chat et le renard*). "These disputes that carry us beyond the humdrumming of everyday words," one of Salacrou's characters says (Armand Salacrou, *Un homme comme les autres*, act 1).

11. Better still, to lose one's temper can provide powerful pleasure.

"I want to be as angry as I want whenever I feel like it," declares Monsieur Jourdain (Molière, *Le bourgeois gentilhomme*, act 2, sc. 4); "She seems to savor her anger like a pleasure," Colette notes of a woman (quoted by Robert under *colère*).

12. On the other hand, anger is frightening. Even though we may have some experience of the facility with which calm is restored after "the storm," we still often appear to fear the loss of control that "makes a man a ferocious beast" (Molière, quoted by Robert under *passion*). If one begins by "smashing the windows,"—the French idiom defined by Robert as "manifesting one's discontent without consideration"—what may not happen to the rest of the house?

Am I in the process of revealing myself to be, if not a brute— "a person that abandons himself to his brutal instincts," according to Robert—then at least "the old chap who never stops being angry" (Saint-Beuve referring to Lamennais, quoted by Robert under *furibond*, furious), who creates a scene about nothing, about whom people may say: With you it has to be a drama every time?

"To be constantly in a secret fury was Ursus' internal situation, and grumbling was his external situation," says Victor Hugo of one of his characters (quoted by Robert under *mécontent*, discontented). "There was secret rage against the whole world always hatching inside him, and an incessant irritation that manifested itself at the slightest opportunity, at any moment," Maupassant writes (quoted by Robert under *irritation*). Though the word humor denotes "the disposittion . . . one is in at a given moment," it also denotes in French, taken "absolutely," "ill humor," which is to say, "anger, irritation." To irritate signifies "to put into a rage," and Robert exemples it with: "a trifle, the slightest thing is sufficient to irritate him."

13. Might good humor not arise on occasion from a firm and lucid resolve to avoid humor, period?

"Pretty women do not like to be angry," Rousseau explains (quoted by Robert under *se fâcher*, to become angry), "and so they refuse to be angered by anything; they like to laugh."

14. All this being so, it is often seen as essential to put a stop to a "brawl" before it gets completely out of control—one of the principal procedures adopted by adults when dealing with children; a procedure that often seems to be a drain on their own self-control, since being a spectator of fights between children tends to create acute distress. If one allows the children to go on fighting, may one not soon be forced to say that "they fought like wild beasts" (Robert under *enragé*).

15. The other's anger having manifested itself, wisdom may demand that one shall appease it before it has had the opportunity to produce dangerous results. "One appeases a man," Littré explains (quoted by Robert under *apaiser*, to calm or appease), "when one causes his anger to vanish." But it's not always so simple: "I'm not quieting down, oh no! as easily as that/I'm far too angry," Molière has a character say (ibid.)—an attitude that may already be found in the child in a temper toward the terrified adults attempting to "pacify" it; the "pacifier" being, according to the case, capitulation, a pacifier, the strap, or some other thing.

16. The ascendancy of anger leads to pleasure in doing wrong.

If the perverse person is one who "takes pleasure in doing wrong," perversity, according to Robert, is "the special characteristic of the person who seeks to do harm." The wrongdoer "seeks to do wrong to others, likes doing harm." Hate is an "emotion . . . that drives one to wish ill to someone, and to rejoice in the ill that befalls him." The bad man is the man "who . . . likes to do ill to another"; the wicked man "does evil deliberately, or seeks to do evil to others" (Robert) by means of a dirty trick, a spiteful trick, a swinish trick.

"Men are maleficent," Robert gives (under *malfaisant*); and under the corresponding noun: "The wickedness of men, of the world"; even "the best of men have a little store of wickedness." One may maintain that "man is a wicked animal" (Robert under *méchant*), or at any rate follow Diderot in answering the question "Is he good? Is he wicked?" with: "The one after the other— like you, like myself, like everyone" (ibid.).

17. Since my spontaneity, my anger, and my wickedness create so many risks for the other, and since I imagine him easily disposed to act—and even more so to react—similarly with regard to me, prudence demands that I should not openly threaten him, unless he is entirely devoid of the means to do me harm.

18. To do serious harm to another without actually reducing him to a state that prevents him from harming me—by crushing him only in the sense of humbling him rather than in that of "reducing him to nothing"—is madness. One does not violate "the exhausting obligation to treat people with consideration" (Montherlant, *Malatesta*, act 4, sc. 7) without taking a terrible risk, if those people are the ones with whom one is condemned to live, whether domestically or politically. So that the fact of having treated them "more cavalierly than caution would advise" may be a prelude to catastrophe. "One should never attack those one is not sure of being able to finish off," Barrès notes (quoted by Robert under *achever*).

19. One should not drive people to the limit (since one does not wish, or is not able to annihilate them); one must not push the other over that threshold beyond which his self-control is put out of action by the explosion that is unleashed in him. Although Louis XIV as a child was, according to Louis Bertrand, "of a calm and gentle disposition," when "he was driven too far he flew into furious rages, veritable explosions" (quoted by Robert under *explosion*).

"One of the greatest points of wisdom in the military art is not to drive one's enemy to despair" (Montaigne, *Essais*, bk. 1, chap. 47). That remark of Montaigne's still holds good, above all outside the field he himself was discussing. Once Tartuffe has been unmasked, to "drive him" further would be, Cléante points out to Orgon, "a great imprudence on your part": "and you should seek some gentler angle of approach" (Molière, *Tartuffe*, act 5, sc. 1). "Don't drive the coward too far, you will make him valiant," one of Montherlant's characters counsels (Montherlant, *Malatesta*, act 4, sc. 9).

20. So it is often better not to insist upon all the advantages that one is capable of procuring for oneself; an "incautious triumph would soon be followed by an everlasting regret" (Racine, quoted by Robert under *indiscret*, indiscreet, incautious). "His error," Montherlant says of an anonymous character, "was in wishing to make his point at all costs, whereas a deeper discernment would have led him to be slightly more lax with his opponent, to let himself be beaten a little" (*Carnets*, 1930–1944, p. 170). "Grace in victory," in what he advises. "When the opponent admits: 'He took me in nicely,' keep the face expressionless, do

not insist, thereby hooking your fish in such a way that no one will suspect your perfidy. There is still the future to be considered" (ibid., p. 325).

21. In this way one avoids the irreparable break, the irremediable parting of the ways with people from whom one will probably need further help in a future during which any possible coalition may perchance have its moment of usefulness. It is better, therefore, not "to attempt anything that risks breaking the tenuous bonds presently hanging together after a fashion" (Pierre Viansson-Ponté, *Le Monde*, May 27, 1958) between two beings or groups condemned to live together. "To keep the whole world's friendship is your great study": Célimène's principle concern, pointed out by Alceste (Molière, *Le misanthrope*, act 5, sc. 2) is essential if one wishes to succeed, or even merely to avoid failure.

"I am addressing myself in particular to those opponents of the European Defense Community who are perhaps already thinking of alternative solutions," a supporter of that community announced to the Assembly when the opponents of the C.E.D., were preparing to quash it by means of the "previous question," without debate. "Do not yourselves compromise the eventual voting on those possible solutions by an interruption of this debate, which would create between us an uneasy atmosphere very difficult to dissipate in the sequel" (Christian Pineau, A.N., August 30, 1954; *J.O.*, pp. 4470–71).

22. Above all, by limiting the harm I inflict on the other, I hope to moderate the desire for reprisals I shall provoke in him; even while envisaging an attack upon him, I am calculating what the balance sheet of the operation will look like after his counterattack, fearful lest the affair should, ultimately, prove to my disadvantage. For is there not a risk that I may be tempted not to give full weight to my victim's offensive reactions, to the unfavorable consequences that may follow, if I give myself up wholly to the pleasure of a full-scale onslaught, which may, for that very reason, be excessive?

Montherlant watches "a cat with a dying lizard. It strikes the victim with its paw—toc!—and immediately leaps backward, like a gun recoiling the moment after it has fired. How I like that little instant of fear! (to be precise, its fear of the riposte)" (Montherlant, *Carnets*, 1930–1944, p. 264). A character in *La reine morte* says of the king: "I often saw his face at the moment when he had just scored against an opponent; the expression on it at such moments was never one of triumph, it was one of fear: the fear of counterattack" (Montherlant, *La reine morte*, act 1, tableau 2, sc. 4). "Everywhere and on every occasion, inhibition," the same author observes at the beginning of the second World War. "And why? So as not to provoke reprisals. For no other reason" (Montherlant, *Le solstice de juin*, p. 191).

23. The other may fan my apprehensions by predicting his reprisals.

"The 23rd of September 1959, (the date upon which public funds were voted for the support of non-state schools) is a date that will go down in the history of our Republic," a leader of the defeated "lay" members (Guy Mollet) told the house on that very day. "You know only too well," he reminded the victorious majority, "that a day will come, sooner or later, but certainly, even though I do not know its date, when another majority will vote the total separation of church and state. . . . And on that day, as you must also know, for it will be the consequence of the decisions you have taken here today, all those establishments and principals who have applied in the interim for public funds will be considered ipso facto as having affirmed their intention to enter the public service, and will be dealt with accordingly." After a voice from the Right had asked "Is that a threat?" he then continued: "It is neither blackmail nor threat. . . . [it] will be the logical conclusion of the decisions taken here today" (A.N., December 23, 1959; J.O., p. 3608): thus rendering them decisions whose ultimate usefulness to those immediately profiting by them was questionable.

24. It may frequently appear dangerous to exert upon another any pressure that he may resent as excessive.

25. In many situations, of course, one acts in accordance with precisely the opposite calculation: only retaliatory action pushed to extremes, one then argues, can possibly succeed. "Like the civil servants and the employees of nationalized industries before them," a journalist noted in the late spring of 1961, "the farmers are proving that nothing but violence pays, since it has obtained more for them in a week than eighteen months of administrative bargaining was able to do" (Pierre Drouin, *Le Monde*, June 20, 1961). Bringing the very maximum of pressure to bear may appear indispensable if one wants to "vindicate" one's rights according to the law. During one farmers' demonstration at La Roche-sur-Yonne (June 19, 1961), "a placard appeared on the prefecture railings that read: 'The law has granted us equality; our strength shall win it for us'" (*Le Monde*, June 20, 1961).

In the examples above, those struggling to force the acceptance of their claims felt threatened by failure, but scarcely by possible counterattacks: this seems to be the necessary and sufficient condition that enables one to aspire to exerting a maximum of pressure.

26. But when the opponent appears to be capable of reprisals, such a procedure is very likely to be considered harmful, and all the more dangerous in that one's emotions urge one to apply it even when one's reason advises against it.

27. Adults find it quite natural to obtain the behavior they require from children by exerting pressures of which they rarely trouble to evaluate or moderate the degree. The same is true to some extent of the more unpleasant areas of adult life: police stations, hospitals, or any other place presupposing a return to an impotent childhood state.

28. This being so, many people are inclined to reject any pressure on them, however slight, when it appears possible to do so without risk.

29. Hence the conviction that the velvet glove will often gain me greater advantage than the iron hand; that I shall be able to lead the other in the direction I wish, to precisely the degree in which I can create and maintain in him an illusion of independence.

30. The other must not be allowed to believe or claim that he has been presented with a *fait accompli,* that such and such a measure has been forced upon him.

31. Nor is it expeditious that the other should exclaim: "In effect you're serving a writ on me!" (Robert under *mise en demeure*, the serving of a writ or summons), that he should feel himself or be able to present himself as the object of an ultimatum, a summons, a threatening communication, an attempt at intimidation, or an outright threat; since if he does he will almost invariably shout "blackmail!" The right thing to do in such a case is to adopt an attitude of defiance—a "refusal to bow before someone or something; a refusal to submit" (Robert)—unless one can convince oneself that one is faced with a case of *force majeure*.

32. Rigidity is therefore unlikely to be a good thing except in the field of love. Elsewhere it invariably indicates weakness, and heralds death: "that which rots first becomes hard" (Gustave Thibon, quoted in *La Nef*, May 1958, p. 6). Though "many women adore one's being abrupt with them" (*Dictionnaire du Canard enchaîné*, 1958. p. 1), their reactions when not in bed to "a man who is not accommodating" (Robert under *commode*) are very mixed. Instead of rigidity (*raideur*) there is a tendency to prefer smoothness (*rondeur*), "that ease of manners which . . . enables everyone . . . to live content with himself and others" (Montesquieu, *Mes pensées*, p. 1145). When selecting a man for a role other than that of savior, there is a temptation to pass by the one who is somewhat "sectarian" in favor of the one who is "ac-

commodating in his dealings" (Robert under *coulant,* flowing, accommodating), even "something of a whore," "a virtuoso in the matter of 'damping'" (*Le canard enchaîné,* October 26, 1960). To damp (*amortir*), Robert explains, is "to make weaker, less ardent, less lively, less violent": precisely what is needed when one feels oneself secretly threatened by explosions of brutality—not only from others but also from oneself.

33. It is dangerous (and not very proper) to insist.

Since the temptation of emphasis is a strong one, this "excessive and shocking energy of expression, tone, gesture" (Robert) is often reproved. Gide tells us that "one of the great rules in art" is "not to linger too long"; but the advice seems to hold good in many other fields. "He had stressed this last article a little too much," Hamilton says of someone (quoted by Robert under *appuyer,* to press, to stress), whereas a journalist writes of one president of the Republic (Vincent Auriol) that he "never underlines anything too heavily, too obviously" (André Stibio, *Antoine Pinay,* p. 38). "Take care not to insist," "if he refuses, don't insist," Robert gives under *insister;* and under *insistance:* "a misplaced, an indiscreet insistence." Recalling the cabinet meeting that followed the entry of the German army into the Rhineland, on March 7, 1936, during the course of which the minister for foreign affairs (Pierre-Etienne Flandin) proposed military action, a great politician of the Third Republic (Joseph Paul-Boncour) recounts: "I can still see and hear M. Flandin . . . giving his conclusion without any vote even having been taken: . . . 'I can see, Mr. Prime Minister, that I must not insist.' M. Flandin was doubtless of the opinion that such an action would have required a unanimity and an enthusiasm in the government of which it was only too clear that he had encountered no promise" (J. Paul-Boncour: *Sur les chemins de la défaite,* p. 35).

It is true that one also hears the praise: "I can scarcely insist too much upon . . ." But it is used only when there is hardly any disagreement—". . . the necessity for hygiene" (Robert)—or when the person it is addressed to can scarcely be thought of as dangerous. "I . . . choose those things he most needs to be educated in," La Bruyère says of a pupil, "and insist very strongly upon them, giving him no quarter" (quoted by Robert under *insister*); this being, of course, a situation in which one can "strike the nail home" with a quiet mind.

"Christianity does not shrink from insisting upon man's vices" (ibid.). But does not "not to shrink from insisting" imply that one *tends* to shrink from it, and with good reason, moreover? "Above all, don't say anything more, don't insist," the same dictionary gives, "otherwise you will spoil everything" (under *gâter,* to spoil). Of women, Montherlant comments that "one of . . . [their] mistakes seems to me to be their faith in the efficacity of insistence" (Montherlant, *Les jeunes filles*, p. 190), because insistence, the evidence seems to indicate, tends to make the victim's hackles rise, and leads him eventually to open revolt. "The next day, thanks to what was considered a misplaced insistence, Rieux succeeded in having a sanitary committee meeting called at the prefecture" (Camus, quoted by Robert under *insistance*"): but this is a proceeding which, if repeated, would rapidly become futile and fraught with unpleasing consequences for anyone who should persevere in such perseverance. He would soon have earned the observation: "Your insistence is really excessive" (Pierre Métayer, of André Liautey when he was still persisting in his campaign against home distillers after he had already achieved great successes. A.N., November 9, 1955; *J.O.*, p. 5592). During the first months of the Fifth Republic, when the government and the Assembly were at odds on the subject of the new procedure to be adopted for "oral questions," one journalist observed that "M. Debré was unable to conceal . . . a passion and a savageness of determination that shocked and distressed the house, though more by their expression and their form than by the matter that occasioned them" (Pierre Viansson-Ponté, *Le Monde*, May 29, 1959).

In order to act in such a way one must have unfortunately strong beliefs; or a no less unfortunate blindness without the benefit, if there is one, of passion. "Stupidity always insists," Camus remarks (quoted by Robert under *insister*). The less stupid I am the more swiftly I say to myself or to others, "I understand, there's no point in going on," or, transmuting wisdom into elegance: "well, I think we can take that as read!" (Robert under *insister*).

In fact, "Let it pass!" "To slide" (*glisser*) also signifies "to pass lightly over something." Robert of course gives: "we won't insist on that, we'll let it slide," and quotes Saint-Beuve's reference to "an irony that slides past without insisting" (under *insister*). Indeed, it seems generally a better idea to slide over most things, since the famous quatrain on the skaters is a good indication of the catastrophe awaiting those who press too hard, concluding as it does: "Slide on mortals, but do not press" (quoted by Robert under *appuyer*).

34. The fear of forcing someone into a corner may even develop into a fear of wounding some susceptible spot or other, into the "great fear of giving displeasure" that Chamfort discerned in M——, of whom he wrote that "no one could ever be less abrupt" (Chamfort, *Caractères et anecdotes*, p. 149). And there is Sten-

dhal's resolution: "To ask oneself every evening: have I been considerate enough of the vanity of those with whom I have lived today?" (quoted by Robert under *ménager*). "Every time I have checked an aggressive impulse," Chardonne observes, "I have later congratulated myself. I have never written any . . . letter that was at all biting, or offered the least criticism, without later repenting of it" (quoted by Robert under *mordant*, biting). "Clashing with his feelings head-on is the way to ruin everything," one of Molière's characters says; "You musn't clash with him head-on," a Duhamel character echoes (quoted by Robert under *front*, front, forehead).

And a head-on clash from the back, as it were, is no better: as the recent case of the two young men who killed their father by hitting him on the back of the head with a shovel shows. "Needless to say," one reporter wrote, "they added, once their fit of rage was past, 'now we regret so brutal an act' " (*France-Soir*, June 20, 1961).

Under the Third and Fourth Republics, the country's elected representatives were often thought of, in political circles, as having a violent aversion to any action that might provoke any temporary discontent whatsoever, even if it could be predicted that the undertaking in question would have become extremely profitable by the time the next election came around. In such cases, it is for the nation's statesmen to point out the nuance between present and future. "The National Assembly has two and a half years ahead of it," Paul Reynaud explained, "which is to say, thirty months' immunity from electoral fever. Let it make use of that time to act. What is an unpopular measure today may have become a popular one in two years time, if it produces good results" (speech at the banquet of *Indépendants*, April 6, 1949; *L'Année politique*, 1949, p. 323).

35. Where an attempt to seize an advantage cavalierly, at gunpoint, unceremoniously, by force, would be both vain and dangerous, I must concentrate on seduction by charm, on creating an obligation with favors: instead of the lion tamer's whip, the offer of help.

36. It is not enough to avoid causing displeasure: one must please, a verb that in its absolute sense signifies "to please . . . the people with whom one is dealing." "The great rule," Montesquieu proves, "is to try to please." For though it is "of public utility that men should have . . . ascendency over the minds" of others, this is a "thing that cannot be achieved by means of an austere and grim humor" (Montesquieu, *Mes pensées*, p. 1145). It is by "charming" the other with "gentleness," Pascal observes,

that one succeeds in establishing "a more terrible and imperious domination" over him than one could ever achieve by "subjugating" him with the use of "force" (Pascal, *Pensées*, p. 966).

37. To oblige the other means to pay in advance, trusting in future repayment on his part of my courtesy or money, hoping that he will eventually send the elevator back down to me; in the end, after this exchange of kindly actions, my account will be in credit.

"To work for the advantage of others," La Rochefoucauld tells us, "is to take the surest path to one's goal; it is lending at interest under pretext of giving; it is . . . acquiring the whole world by a subtle and delicate means" (*Maximes*, 236). "Friendship," Montesquieu observes, "is a contract whereby we engage ourselves to render small services to someone so that he shall render us great ones" (*Mes pensées*, p. 1284). And we say to that someone, with Jules Renard: "Don't worry, I shall never forget the service I have done you" (Journal, p. 71). According to one journalist, Pierre Mendès-France, when reporting to Charles de Gaulle on his journey to China during the summer of 1958, is supposed to have said: "We ought to recognize the Chinese Communist government right away. . . . It is a gesture that may perhaps one day save us; in a planetary war, China could put an army of a hundred million in the field. And the Chinese have long memories" (Roger Maugé, *Paris-Match*, August 30, 1958). In Gide's *L'école des femmes*, Geneviève says of her husband: "Even in his apparently most generous actions, the ones in which he is showing himself to be most obliging toward another, I sense the hidden intention of making that other obliged to him. . . . He let certain revealing phrases slip out: 'I have certainly been ill-rewarded for my sympathy' . . . 'So and so . . . after all I have done for him, can refuse me nothing!' That was the whole reason for the existence of that magazine Robert edited . . . Under that surface impartiality it was no more than a sort of agency for ensuring mutual aid and mutual back-slapping. Robert looked upon every article praising anyone as a letter of credit" (Gide, *L'école des femmes*, p. 61).

38. Even when it appears incautious to attack someone openly, that does not mean one has lost the chance of stabbing him in the back. When the other is not looking or is absent, one can be bolder. "Augustine . . . spat on [her mistress's] dress from behind, without anyone seeing" (Zola, quoted by Robert under *méchanceté*, wickedness or spite). In politics, the temporary absence of a great personage is thought to incite others, "friends" included, to "thumb their noses at him."

39. What could be more normal than to tear some absent person to pieces during a meal, thereby increasing one's enjoyment of the food?

Illustrating *nuire* (to harm), Robert gives, among other examples: "to do someone harm with his friends . . . in other people's minds. . . . To harm, to seek to harm someone by speaking ill of him. . . . To harm someone's reputation for the sake of a witticism."

Massillon speaks of the "duplicity . . . that praises to a man's face and tears him apart in secret" (quoted by Robert under *duplicité*), and Rivarol asks "what is one to do between evil-wishers who boldly utter the ill they are not sure of and friends who cautiously refrain from speaking the good they know?" (quoted by Robert under *malveillant*, malevolent, ill-wishing). "The pleasures of society, especially in the country," Balzac observes, "consist in speaking ill of one another" (quoted by Robert under *plaisir*).

"There is no place," Robert de Jouvenel tells us, "where you can hear more stories being bandied about than in the corridors of the Palais-Bourbon. They always concern colleagues and are for the most part quite frightful" (Jouvenel, *La république des camarades*, pp. 52–53). "English politicians," a French political leader between the two wars has noted, "observed a restraint in their dealings with one another that we did not always imitate; at no time in Geneva, even between political opponents, let alone between colleagues in the same government, did I hear such remarks as were too often being hawked around among us between members of the same delegation" (J. Paul-Boncour, *Sur les chemins de la défaite*, p. 55). "At least among them," a Camus character says of the Dutch, "spitefulness is not a national institution" (*La chute*, p. 13).

How difficult it is not to speak ill of others!

"X tells you that Y is a traitor," Montherlant comments; "You say to the first person you meet: 'Y is a traitor.' X tells you: 'Z is a terrific fellow.' You say to the first person you meet: 'They say that Z is a terrific fellow.' " (Montherlant, *Carnets* 19–21, p. 75). "To speak well of someone who is absent," Jules Renard notes, "is considered by Hervieu to be an act of virtue" (*Journal*, p. 269). "If you think well of me," the same author asks, "please say so as quickly as possible, because, you know, it will pass" (ibid., p. 142).

40. Since the tendency to speak ill of others seems so strong, the anonymous letter and the denunciation may, in their turn, be looked upon as actions playing a not negligible role in the way of the world.

"There were two million anonymous letters during the Occupation denouncing . . . French persons to the Gestapo," *Le canard enchaîné* dared to claim, adding: "After the Liberation, there were two million more . . . anonymously denouncing all those the writers hoped to see flayed as collaborators" (*Le canard enchaîné,* July 22, 1953). During the fifties, when certain circles in the French church were in difficulty with Rome, it was often claimed, in Paris as well as in the Vatican, that the role played in these matters by denunciations coming from France itself would have caused astonishment down below.

41. Beyond the harmful words lurks the filthy trick worked out in the shadows, the blow below the belt delivered in such a way as to leave the victim in doubt as to its author. The French vocabulary of surreptitious aggression makes use of dropped orange and banana peels, thrown fireworks, fired torpedoes, soaped planks, and deep undermining operations.

42. If an eminent personage gets into very hot water, is it really the result of innocent chance, or of an even greater incidence of gaffes than one might expect on his part? Might the evil genius apparently taking delight in thwarting him—"it is just as though" such a genius existed, people say at first—not in reality be embodied in certain members of his entourage, of his staff, who have made the boss their dupe and victim, pressing him to do exactly what he ought not do? In the political world, anyone who dismissed as mere fantasy the idea that there could be such sabotage behind some rather odd incident would very soon win himself a reputation for being astonishingly simpleminded, or grossly hypocritical.

In the early summer of 1953, when Joseph Laniel became prime minister after a record-breaking crisis, there was a great deal of comment in expert circles about the role said to have been played in the "solution" of the crisis by *Roscius*, the new adviser to the head of government. This somewhat obscure figure was spoken of as having had a career of the sort usually referred to as full of incident, as well as being extremely attached to *Hermodore*, a former and—it was then thought—probably also a future prime minister. Might it not have been Roscius who advised Laniel not merely to diminish, but to reduce to zero the sections of the government composed of men close to Antoine Pinay and René Mayer, and to undermine the influence of the Upper House, all with the purpose of provoking a conspiracy of powerful "murderers" at whose hands Laniel must before long fall, thus leaving his post free for *Hermodore*?

Shortly after this, the Laniel government undertook certain measures with regard to the employees of public industries which, though apparently minor in nature, detonated an explosion of strikes such as the country had not known for five years. Once again there was question whether the prime minister had been the victim of sabotage. This time the matter turned above all on his desire to employ the premiership as a "stepping-stone" to the presidency of the Republic—a post for which elections were due that autumn—and also upon the desire of the incumbent of that post, Vincent Auriol, to see his "lease renewed." "What a pity!" *Le canard enchaîné* exclaimed at the time, addressing itself to Laniel. "For the country. And also for you, since everything in this world must be paid for. What a fine career as president of the Republic you have just nipped in the bud, my dear prime minister. The sewing maids at the Elysée were already beginning to change the A's on the pillow slips to L's. And it's your fault, what's more! All you had to do was choose your staff more carefully! Next time you want to 'save Republican legality' as you put it, don't take M. July and M. Bougenot as your secretary and under-secretary of state and technical advisers. M. Vincent Auriol, *who will not present himself for reelection*—that's been said and said again, and quiet snickering is not allowed—advised them, a smile on his lips . . ." (*Le canard enchaîné*, August 26, 1953) to act in such a way that the most serious "social" trouble that had afflicted the country for a long time should suddenly break out. "Certain highly placed treasury officials," one well-known journalist (André Stibio) claimed—to each his own saboteurs— "deliberately loaded the first series of Orders-in-Council with explosive measures that were the immediate cause of the strikes." But—one group of saboteurs need not exclude another— there was also the minister of finance, Edgar Faure: "Another enigma presents itself, and one that has been much discussed: the intransigence evinced by Edgar Faure. It is a fact that Edgar Faure (though this may, after all, be proof of his firmness) advised his prime minister to give priority to the most unpopular, and also the most dangerous measures. It is also a fact that during the last ministerial crisis Edgar Faure was, on the contrary, thought of as a man of the "Left." It was claimed that Edgar Faure was attempting to bring Joseph Laniel down by pushing him 'to the Right' and overbalancing him with reactionary measures for which the moderates would be left to take responsibility. The way would then be open for a government that could bring the Socialists back to swell its majority" (*Carrefour*, August 20, 1953) and one for which Edgar Faure would be the ideal leader.

43. Despite all the restraints that it is wise to impose upon my desire to attack, it happens in some cases that a sober examina-

tion of the conditions tells me that I can go ahead; that I have nothing to fear and therefore need have no consideration, since I am confronted with people "about whom one does not bother" (Robert under *gêner*), with whom it is not worth restraining oneself.

44. To begin with, there is the action of "a man who spills out his bile in language without restraint . . . because he no longer has anything to hope for" (Saint-Simon, *Mémoires*, 1: 387).

45. There is also what Montherlant boldly refers to as "the typically Parisian courtesy that consists in attacking none but those who are weaponless" (*Carnets*, 1930–1944, p. 149).

For example, regarding persons under indictment as odious.

When the Fourteenth Chamber of Summary Jurisdiction dealt with Madame Gabrielle Gaucher, reputedly "an organizer of leisure activities" for certain highly placed circles, "the people . . . after a two hour wait, were granted a fleeting glimpse of 'la belle Gabrielle' leaving the audience chamber as quickly as possible, hiding her features beneath a white veil. She was treated to a copious, unrestrained, immoderate barrage of booing and catcalls" (*Le Monde*, February 28 and 29, 1960).

The same is true of the dead, whose fame is impaired by their deaths at the same time as their power.

"Scarcely had the great man breathed his last," Valéry observed of his predecessor in the Académie (Anatole France), "when already, like his flesh, the idea he had given of himself became subject to a somewhat abrupt disintegration. The forces of the living presence were immediately no more. . . . The reverential fears vanished. Tongues were unbound. Memories (not always the most worthy memories as you can well imagine) emerged from malicious lips; they teemed, they devoured everything they could grasp of the valor, the merits, the character of the absent man": such is "the agitation . . . that eagerly squirms for some time around fresh graves" (Valéry, *Variété*, p. 724).

"Even the lowest in the social scale," one of Camus' characters points out, "still has his spouse or his child. . . . The essential, in short, is to be able to fly into a rage without the other having any right to reply" (*La chute*, p. 54). "He treated her less well than he did the maid," Montherlant writes with some exaggeration when describing a man's behavior toward his wife, "which was logical enough, since she could not give him a week's notice" (*Le démon du bien*, p. 79). "We parents, for our part," a children's doctor writes, "should take care to guard against [the danger] of looking upon the family as a sort of boxing ring where we can find relief in the evening for all the restraint we have exercised during the day. Outside, we contain ourselves, we make sure we avoid conflicts. But at home, it is possible that we may be permitting ourselves liberties that we would refuse to take outside. How many charming people we meet are in fact saving up all their temper and their ill humor for their families! . . . In the first place," he adds, "let us beware of our own explosions!" (Jean Dublineau, *L'école des parents,* November 1957, pp. 2, 3, 14).

46. This being so, my behavior may vary abruptly according to the changes I think I perceive in the balance of forces around me. "His eyes," Montherlant says of one of his characters, "were continually changing from an expression of petty tyranny to one of fear" (*Le démon du bien,* p. 107).

One novelist has a teen-age girl from a working-class family say of her mother: "There was no longer any question of her trying to clobber me one, any more than she'd've tried it with Patrick, because he'd told her straight out: 'That's the last time, I'm warning you; the next you'll get it right back again, and you'll come off worst, I'm warning you now!' And she knew that's how it was going to be" (Christiane Rochefort, *Les petits enfants du siècle,* pp. 142–43). "Bernard is stronger than I am," one of the mothers interviewed by Charlotte Roland said, "and if it came to a set-to with him I should certainly come off second best. Then every bit of authority I have would be gone." "I'm definitely conscious of restraining myself with the eldest," another mother said, "because I know the boy would fly into a temper. But with the others I don't need to be so careful" (*L'école des parents,* September-October, 1957, p. 37).

14

OUTBURSTS AND OIL ON
THE WATERS

1. The proper and the outrageous flourish side by side.

According to Charles de Gaulle, the Frenchman is "that fervent partisan of the alexandrine, the tailcoat, and the royal garden, who . . . belts out dirty songs, dresses sloppily, and dirties the grass in the park" (*Vers l'armée de métier*, p. 21).

2. In the matter of language, there is a great fondness for alternate brushes with the extremely austere and the very coarse. "When you start acting at the Comédie Française, you'll see," one of André Roussin's young men tells his drama student sister, "you'll see how you'll talk then! You'll be saying shit every third word!" (Roussin, *L'amour fou*, act 1). "A strictly oral tradition has it," Valéry notes, "that even Lamartine himself sometimes allowed the most extreme expressions to be extruded from his golden mouth . . ." (points of suspension in original text) (Valéry, *Regards sur le monde actuel*, p. 101). Moreover, according to a no less oral tradition Valéry himself had difficulty in extruding from his mouth expressions that did not contain some reference to materials very far distant from (yet also, as we know, extremely akin to) gold. During his funeral—a state one—"the procession, having reached the terrace of the Palais de Chaillot, turned right instead of halting in the center. And indeed, the plywood cenotaph was still not finished; but the observations addressed to the workmen on this subject by an official of the Beaux-Arts drew replies couched in terms drawn from Jarry's

vocabulary rather than that of Valéry" (Gaston Poulain, *Paul Valéry tel quel*, p. 31); the words of a friend who knew only too well that the two vocabularies were the same.

René Viviani always found it difficult not to be noble when speaking in the Chamber, and not to be coarse in the lobbies: the latter being the place where the male politician proves his virility by dint of crudity, just as his firmness of character is displayed in sessions by his correctness.

There is also a further compartmentalization added to this first one in that the incessant employment of rather improper expressions is generally not revealed to the outside world by the protected sectors of an institution that must be careful of its public image. Sometimes, however, such crudity is betrayed. "M. Gaillard," reported the most "austere" of French newspapers, describing a sudden and serious threat encountered by a prime minister who had been in office only two months, "was forced to announce . . . in the lobbies, that he would rather 'have his . . . [points of suspension in original text] head cut off' than allow the sitting to begin under such conditions" (Georges Mamy, *Le Monde*, January 16, 1958). Whereupon the *Canard enchaîné* was most delighted to temper its readers' wilder imaginings by providing its own version of the "complete text": "I would rather my nutlets were hacked into cutlets, and deep-fried to boot, than that I should be forced to accept what they are seeking to force upon me" (*Le canard enchaîné*, January 22, 1958).

3. Just as compartmentalization, and the most peripheral contact between lover and husband, mistress and wife, has tended to decline in favor of some approximation to the multiple *ménage* (see chap. 4, secs. 4–5), so the separating of base and elevated speech after the style of Valéry has been followed by their combining to form a single mixture, after the style, for example, of Jean Genet.

4. When it is some loss of control that permits the irruption of crudity into a fortress of propriety, the incident becomes disturbing, even frightening, unless one is rescued, in the capacity of spectator, by a feeling of unholy joy.

"The word fell, coarse and brief, into our silence," Colette writes. "All of us there would have been capable of uttering the same word, not too loudly, into a private ear. But the eclipse obscuring Renée's features . . . even as she repeated the word again . . . revealed a profound inner chaos" (Colette, *Ces plaisirs* . . . , pp. 123, 124).

5. But if someone respectable, or someone undertaking a role that carries some prestige, decides to utter such a word or words

quite openly, with either real or feigned audacity, then what joy fills the hearts of his or her hearers!

As long as c—— and s—— remain sufficiently appalling, those who appear in, for example, Parisian nightclubs will be able, with a minimum of skill, to reinforce the feelings of their audience toward them, for a moment at least, by slipping in the naughty word that in such cases need not even be subtly introduced. The series—though of course on a less shocking level— was endless at the first night of *Ubu roi,* when "everyone was greeting everyone else in the foyers with 'shit' " (Octave Nadal, *Introduction à la correspondance entre Paul Valéry et Gustave Fourment,* p. 17).

6. Beyond the pleasurable breach of convention lies the casting off of all restrictions: the roughhouse, in many ways so like the act of love.

7. But at this point, the pleasure can already turn very easily to horror. Though if you keep your ear to the ground, approaching chaos can be used to strengthen the rule of order. Since people are attached, whatever they may say, to the rough and ready compromises of which the world is composed, they often seem to be afraid that "the deeps where life is a terrible convulsion" (Colette, *Le blé en herbe,* p. 119) may rise to the surface, producing an explosion that will send everything sky-high.

8. That the proprieties have in fact been observed is often seen as a cause for relief and occasion for praise.

In the National Assembly, it is habitual to observe with satisfaction that a debate, despite its having been centered on some distressing problem and turned on "matters of conscience" has been conducted with "perfect dignity"; as when Charles de Gaulle, in taking over the functions of the president of the Republic and of the Community, referred to René Coty as "a great citizen leaving the mandate he has exercised with perfect dignity" (January 7, 1959; Le Monde, January 9, 1959). As soon as the first incident occurs during a sitting in which the atmosphere is palpably tense, the Speaker may observe that "it would be distressing if the dignity shown in this debate since this morning were not maintained" (André Le Troquer, A.N., May 16, 1958; J.O., p. 2378). "I shall now conclude, for I do not wish to cause the feelings involved in this debate to run any higher," one deputy (Audré Mutter) once said, (A.N., January 29, 1958; J.O., p. 349) thus recalling the primacy of the concern for stability, constantly threatened as it is by the possibility of chaos. "I apologize," another deputy once said, "for having contributed to making feelings during this debate run rather high" (Pierre Métayer, A.N., February, 4, 1958; *J.O.*, p. 504). On another occasion, when dignity had already begun to suffer, the Speaker said: "Do not revive an incident that could well produce unexpected developments" (Eugène Claudius-Petit, A.N., October 27, 1959; *Le Monde*, October 29, 1959).

9. One of these unexpected, but very much expected, developments is the replacement of courtesy by open hostility.

There is a fear that what was, everything considered, only a slight attack from one side will provoke a disproportionate reaction from the other, so violent that one will immediately exclaim, distressed and rather frightened: The slightest thing, and you're up in arms! Suddenly, the use of the verb in the second person plural (the polite form) and the prefixing of the opponent's name with "Monsieur," or "Madame," or "Mademoiselle" is replaced by the intimate indication of aggression, the "tu." A slight deviation from courtesy in the opponent's language is sufficient to produce massive reprisals. "This time," Zola recounts, "the saleslady committed the error of losing her temper: . . . it was what he was waiting for; she had treated him badly, and so he replied with a flood of filth" (quoted by Robert under *ordures*, filth).

The child is forced to swallow rebuffs; when the grown-up feels able to throw off restraint himself without thereby risking reprisals, the temptation to lay about him may prove irresistible.

10. In many cases, this explosion is simply the final victory of the inclination that civility had in the first place attempted to curb.

"It is probable," Valéry says of Mallarmé, "that both men and their works had value in his eyes . . . in proportion to the degree of charity with which they expressed this truth he had discovered. Which means that he was obliged to annihilate mentally, to guillotine ideally, a great many human beings. But it was precisely this fact that obliged him to behave toward all men with truly exquisite grace, patience, and courtesy." That is why "he astonished the world with that prodigious civility . . . and that system of universal consideration" (Valéry, *Degas, danse, dessin*, pp. 46–47).

11. Even as it curbs an attack, courtesy may also reinforce it. "Courtesy," a deputy renowned for his use of it has explained, "is a dreaded political weapon, often more dreaded than violence" (Jacques Isorni: *Ainsi passent les républiques*, pp. 25–26). Only the weak man and the blunderer rush to make use of the latter.

12. The threat of such explosions increases the value of the man who knows how to recognize and parry "things that settle nothing," "the man who knows the art of smoothing out diffi-

culties," the arranger (Robert), the man who posseses the "dex-
terity . . . to end all differences" (Bossuet, *Oraison funèbre
de Henriette-Anne d'Angleterre*).

Though one of Cocteau's young women may hurl at her lover,
a man much older than herself, the words: "Don't think you can
arrange things so that it'll be all right. That's a disgusting mania
of yours" (*Les monstres sacrés*, act 2, sc. 7), the grown-up who
has got over the rebelliousness that accompanies our emergence
from childhood is likely to opt for the resignation of "arranging
things" in preference to the disaster that is the apparent alternative.

13. The arranger is a person imbued with a particular capacity, and a precious one: that of always being able to find some
trick or stratagem that will resolve the most distressing situation
in the most favorable way: We'll find a way out, don't worry! In
short, everything seems easy to the person who possesses "the
voice that soothes and the hand that smooths" (Briand, according
to Abel Ferry, *Les carnets secrets*, p. 147). "It is difficult to arrange things to suit everyone" (Robert under *arranger*). Yes, of
course, for ordinary mortals. But it is at such times that the true
arranger enters into his glory, by discovering, by inventing the
accommodation, the transactional solution, the mode of application perfectly judged to damp apparently irreconcilable, and
therefore threatening ardors.

14. And does not the very current of things aid him in this
task? (A belief perhaps contradictory to the previous one, but
in any case often coexistent with it.)

Although Alphonse Allas—"Things always get settled in the
end, but sometimes very badly"—and Jean Cocteau—"In the
end, you can come to terms with everything, except the difficulty
of being, which never comes to terms"—have reservations in
the matter, Briand, on the other hand—"Oh well, it will all come
out all right eventually" (Joseph Caillaux, *Mes mémoires*, 3: 75)
—and Canon Kir—"Everything, in this country, can be settled
somehow" (A.N., December 23, 1959; *J.O.*, p. 3626)—have no
doubts at all.

BOOK 4

LIGHT AND SHADE

15

THE FACADE AND WHAT IS BEHIND IT

1. Any facade is likely to conceal something very different from itself: "As long as what one is working on still resembles what it was before one's labor," Valéry suggests, "one has achieved nothing" (*Mauvaises pensées et autres*, p. 149). What takes place in front of the scenery bears little resemblance to what is really happening on the stage as a whole. When one is included "in the secrets of the gods," when one can see "the faces of the cards" (the headings habitually used by two French weeklies for their political columns), everything looks different. So many lives, so many games are double ones.

2. There is a fondness for pointing out cases in which the facade produces a more favorable reaction to what it conceals than could be expected. "Men mock at everything," Montesquieu notes, "because everything has an underside" (*Mes pensées*, p. 1417).

When Georges Bidault said that "in the Arab world . . . the noblest words conceal the most sordid realities" (A.N., March 20, 1957; *J.O.*, p. 1753), he was exporting an attitude frequently assumed toward things at home. "Sometimes when I am reading Balzac," Valéry writes, "I have a vision of . . . the inside of an opera house, all bosoms, lights, glitter, velvet. A dark gentleman, extremely dark, extremely alone, is looking on and reading the hearts of this pleasure-seeking crowd. All those charming groups, gilded by the light and throwing such rich shadows, those faces,

those white expanses of flesh, those jewels, those charming mur-
murs, those poised smiles are as nothing beneath his gaze, which
works upon all this splendid assembly and transforms it . . . into
a hideous collection of defects, poverties, and crimes" (*Variété*,
p. 580).

The astute man is the one of whom one can say, with Péguy,
that "he knew how to discern the evil that lurks beneath such a
semblance of good" (quoted by Robert under *discerner*).

3. May a perfectly normal outside not open up to disclose an
inside that is much less so, like the respectable cupboard that
conceals utter disorder in its dark depths, and even, perhaps, a
skeleton.

"The drawing-room has resumed such a comfortable look," a
character in a play says, ". . . it has become the very image of
respectable family life, light, open, proper, almost gay—with
blood under the furniture. Where have they hidden the corpse?
Inside the piano?" (Armand Salacrou, *L'archipel Lenoir*, pt. 2).

4. A facade of affection may, without there being any call for
surprise, conceal the most acute conflict.

Family life, La Bruyère notes, is often disturbed by mistrust,
jealousy, and antipathy, while we are deceived by appearances
of contentment, calm, and affection into attributing to it a tran-
quillity it does not possess. A twentieth-century author refers to
"the contrast between the apparent serenity . . . of this house and
the dramas . . . that one senses here" (André Maurois, quoted by
Robert under *apparent*).

5. What appears strong may not be so in fact.

"Thus, beneath the appearances of glory," a historian concludes, "bitter realities were concealed" (Jacques Bainville,
quoted by Robert under *apparence*). "Beneath that apparent
glitter nothing solid is to be found" (Robert under "*apparent*).
Is the impressive facade worm-eaten parhaps? About to collapse?

6. Of the man whose convincing facade of virtue has just been
demolished, the French say: He would have been allowed to
take communion without confession! There is nothing, however
limpid, that may not reveal itself similarly disturbed and disturbing.

"The little village of Vornay," a newspaper reports, "was ter-
rorized at the same time by the jackdaw and an incendiary. The
villagers were astonished when the police discovered that the
two raiders were one and the same person, a gentle old man of
eighty, Gilbert Lafaix, whom no one would have dreamed of
suspecting. . . . For ten years no one had suspected him. Everyone
would have given him 'communion without confession' " (*France-
Soir*, May 29 and 30, 1960).

7. That vice conceals itself beneath virtue is a fact I ought not to ignore, all concern with morality apart: "The snake is concealed beneath the flowers" (Robert under *cacher*, to hide, conceal).

8. The great divergence between facades and what they conceal implies that things of capital importance tend to be invisible, and that the things we do see are not so important.

"We see only appearances," Proust says with resignation (quoted by Robert under *apparence*); "for the underside of the tapestry evades our gaze." "Everything interesting takes place, decidedly, in the darkness" Céline believes (Louis-Ferdinand Céline, *Voyage au bout de la nuit*, p. 64).

It is left to the man who likes to brag of his astuteness to claim that such and such a concealed area in fact "stares you in the face." The Goncourt brothers admitted that "both the male and the female animal in Paris society . . . take years to get to the bottom of . . ." (Robert under *percer*, to pierce).

9. What is visible is therefore often likely to be false: rigged, intended to "conceal something beneath a deceptive exterior" (Robert under *dehors*, outside, exterior), to "dissimulate the defects of a piece of merchandise beneath a glittering appearance" (Robert under *dissimuler*), to "wrap shit in cellophane"

There are a great many places of which it is thought permissible to say what Madame de Chartres said to her daughter when instructing her about life at court: "If you judge by appearances in this place . . . you will often be deceived: appearances here are almost never the truth" (Madame de Lafayette, *La princesse de Clèves*, pt. 1). "Most of our actions," Montaigne writes, are no more than "mask and disguise" (*Essais*, bk. 1, chap. 38, p. 271), an opinion elaborated upon by a "poujadiste" deputy under the Fourth Republic when he referred to "our affirmation that nothing is what it seems" (Jean Damasio, A.N., January 22, 1957; J.O., p. 195). "A work," Valéry notes, "expresses not its author's *being* but his *will to show himself*. . . . A particular intention deals with and works upon . . . the real activity of his thought; but that thought does not wish to appear what it is" (*Variété*, p. 817). Elsewhere, he adds that "the world continues . . . because of the resistance offered to us by those things that are difficult to know. The moment all things were deciphered, everything would fade and vanish, and a world entirely disclosed to the light of day would be no more possible than a confidence trick once revealed or a conjuring trick of which one knows the secret" (Valéry, *Tel quel*, 1: 67).

10. It is the fool who is not aware of the false probability in appearances, the character in *Les faux-monnayeurs* in whom

Edouard notices "something lacking that I can't quite put my finger on" because "he takes everything and everyone for what they give themselves out to be" (and who further aggravates his case by "always giving himself out for what he is") (Gide, *Les faux-monnayeurs*, p. 122).

11. In order to guard against the danger of being, or appearing, a damn fool, it is as well to scent out falsity everywhere, after the example of the Cocteau character who loses not a second in saying: "this castle feels to me like a mock ruin" (*Les chevaliers de la table ronde*, act 2). According to La Fontaine, we ought to "unwrap" the "truth concealed beneath appearances . . . at every opportunity" (La Fontaine, quoted by Robert under *apparence*).

12. Once the presumption that a vast divergence exists between the visible and the essential has become a generally accepted notion, however, it begins to give an impression of astuteness if we admit that nothing exists other than the surface, even though it may not be very subtly woven, or even because of the very fact that it is so easy to see through: we do the world too much honor in believing it to possess depths that, however scabrous, are also claimed to be complex and difficult of access. It is only upon first analysis—the point at which fools in search of intelligence stop—that the reality seems to lurk far beneath the surface; a more penetrating gaze perceives nothing behind appearances but—nothing. There are, as the subtle man never forgets, many locked cupboards that are empty, even though, if we are to believe Retz, "anything that is empty, in times of faction and intrigue, passes for mysterious in the eyes of all those who have no acquaintance with great affairs" (Retz, *Mémoires*, p. 528). This individual attempting to act with such authority, is he not perhaps a sham policeman? No, he is a sham sham policeman, the real thing with a look of the imitation. "The greatest defect of penetration," La Rochefoucauld observes, "is not to stop before the goal is reached, but to go beyond it" (quoted by Robert under *pénétration*).

"The real Albertine that I was discovering," Proust recognizes in the end, "was very little different from the orgiastic girl . . . sensed that first day on the seawall at Balbec, who had later presented me with so many successive and differing aspects, just as a city as one approaches it modifies, turn and turn about, the disposition of its buildings until it has crushed, until it has effaced the capital monument one first saw solitary in the distance, and just as later, finally, when one knows that city well, when one can judge it exactly, the true proportions turn out to be those that the first glimpse had offered in prospect, the rest, through which one has passed, being no more than the successive series of defense works that any human being will throw up to block our vision, which we must pierce, one after the other . . . before reaching the heart" (Proust, *La fugitive*, p. 609), so that the heart we read in the face can be the real one. "We need only not to put on a mask for others to believe that we are wearing one," Montherlant notes (*Le démon du bien*, p. 258), a theme he later illustrated in his *Don Juan*:

> Don Basile: . . . Everyone has totally misunderstood him. His dream has always been to be made president of the Indies Council.
> A Lady: President of the Indies Council! But he pays no attention to anything but women, and he has never been seen to show the slightest interest in public affairs . . .
> Don Basile: That's because he didn't want to show his hand. The women were nothing but a pretext, an alibi intended to conceal his all-devouring ambition . . .
> A Lady: How deceptive appearances are!
> [Montherlant, *Don Juan*, act 1, sc. 1].

16

LUCIDITY AND BLINDNESS

1. Success requires reflection (see chap. 7) and reflection requires lucidity, the conquest and preservation of which are often experienced as acute pleasures.

2. If, according to Bossuet, "there is no man easier to lead by the nose than a man who is hopeful; he helps in the deceit" (quoted by Robert under *espérer*, to hope), according to Roussin, "a husband who 'knows' is no longer a cuckold" (André Roussin, *La petite hutte*, act 1). Lucidity forearms me against the danger of being had.

Having succeeded in finding the lighted window through which he can see the shadows of Odette and the man with whom she is deceiving him, Swann is glad. "Certainly he found it painful to see that light, in whose golden atmosphere the invisible and detested couple were moving beyond the window frame, to hear that murmur revealing the presence of the man who had come after his own departure, Odette's falseness, the happiness that she was even now experiencing with him. And yet he was glad he had come; the torment that had impelled him to leave his own house had lost some of its sharpness by becoming less vague, now that he held Odette's other life, which had come to him in that . . . sudden and impotent suspicion, lit up by the bright light from the lamp, a prisoner without knowing it in that room into which he could now walk, whenever he wished, in order to surprise and pinion her; or instead he would knock on the shutters, as he used to do so often when he arrived late; then at least Odette would be aware that he had known . . . and he who had been picturing her to himself a little while ago as joking with the others about his own illusions, now it was them he saw, confident in their error, deceived in short by the man, by himself, whom they thought so far away" (Proust, *Du côté de chez Swann*, pp. 273–74).

3. Lucidity makes my pleasures keener.

Those who enjoy the other pleasures of life, as they do sleep, "without knowing them," seem to Montaigne to be preventing themselves from "savoring" them. As for himself, in order that "even sleep should not slip by me in such stupidity, I have in the past found it a good thing to have myself disturbed so that I might catch some glimpse of it" (Montaigne, *Essais*, bk. 3, chap. 13). And similarly, "with me, Venus has far greater alacrity when escorted by sobriety" (bk. 2, chap. 33). Just as a young girl in a modern novel says with reference to love: "With me, when I drink too much I feel less" (Rochefort, *Les petits enfants du siècle*, p. 193).

4. To know the details of a misfortune is to reduce the pain of it to some degree.

"Though once I had driven myself into ecstasies when I thought I was catching some mystery in Albertine's eyes," Proust notes, "now I was happy only in those moments when I had succeeded . . . in driving every scrap of mystery from those eyes. The image I was seeking . . . was no longer the Albertine who possessed a life unknown to me, it was an Albertine as wholly known to me as possible" (*La prisonnière*, p. 75) ". . . seeing her hesitate over whether it was worth her while to spend the evening with one or another" of her women friends, "her satiety when the other woman had gone, perhaps her disappointment, I might have shed some light upon the jealousy that Albertine inspired in me, I might have reduced it to its correct proportions, since by seeing her experiencing them in that way I could have measured and discovered the limits of her pleasures" (ibid., pp. 555–56).

5. Not to see clearly into things—"to have muck (*merde*) in one's eyes" (the French expression Robert gives under *merde*)— how unpleasant and how dangerous: "To be totally in the dark," or in other words "not to understand anything at all about something, to be wholly ignorant about something," is pretty frightening. "In the dark" one flounders, becomes entangled, or runs into things that are harder than oneself; the man in darkness, Valéry observes, "advances through the dense obscurity, his hands stretched out in front of him for fear of running into things"

(quoted by Robert under *obscur*); he gropes blindly, he loses his way when he is deprived of light, whether it be "in the fog" or "in the heart of the night" (Henry Trémolet de Villers speaking on Algeria, A.N. September 30, 1957; *J.O.*, p. 4453). It is only in an emergency that one makes arrests "still at night and therefore blindly," in contrast with the lucidity of "the normal and diurnal laws" (François Valentin, C.R., May 16, 1958; *J.O.*, p. 877). But the night, the dark, also means liberty. "Constantine could employ us as he saw fit during the day, even with contempt for all the laws of intelligence," Jules Roy writes in his account of a group of aviators during the second World War; "But once night had fallen, we obeyed no longer" (Jules Roy: *Le métier des armes*, p. 70); which is perhaps not unrelated to the position taken up by the first commanding officer of the training center for subversive warfare during the Algerian war: "Colonel Bigeard emphasized ... that priority must be given to night combat" (*Le Monde*, May 11 and 12, 1958).

6. The act of dissipating anything that impedes clear perception—to clear up a confusion, a misunderstanding, an uneasy atmosphere—is to enable to *see* fully: safety and pleasure.

7. The pleasure of seeing!

In literature, and in plays or movies, one often encounters the figure of the now aging man who, though he never fires a gun, is always aiming his binoculars or a periscope at someone; moreover his counterpart is not entirely unknown in real life. In conversation with the policeman who was attempting to make him confess to certain savage murders, a "patriarch" from the Haute-Provence (Gaston Dominici) "raised his head. In the sky . . . a plane was passing. The old man said suddenly: 'They're on to a good thing, those fliers.' 'Why do you say that, grand-dad?' 'From up there, with a telescope, they can watch the couples in the woods!' " (Pierre Scize, *Au grand jour des assises*, p. 269).

In depicting love, the emphasis is often placed on the act of seeing.

There is the man for whom it is important to be able to watch the woman he is giving pleasure to, as for example in Malraux's *La condition humaine*, and also in Montherlant. "That she loved the pleasure of it," he says of his principal character's mistress, "was blindingly clear from her face. . . . Costals traveled twelve hundred miles to see her face at those moments" (Montherlant, *Les lépreuses*, p. 127).

According to Baudelaire, "what one can see in broad daylight is always less interesting than what goes on behind a window" ("Les fenêtres," *Le spleen de Paris*, 35). And, indeed, in fantasies processed for public consumption we do find an abundance of scenes in which one character looks in from the outside at another who awakens his or her desire, or perhaps at a couple. Here again, the link with reality, though often tenuous, is not entirely absent. "Yesterday, at Saint-Cloud," the young Jules Renard recounts, "there were couples with their arms around one another. Other couples would look at them, laugh, and sit themselves down a little further on. . . . One good-looking couple . . . were making love in earnest. A hundred and fifty people, spaced out in a line, were catching fire as they watched them, and some very respectable persons buttoned up their overcoats, while the young girls followed the frolicking couple with grave, serious, slightly pale faces. This spectacle tickled us to such an extent that we were eventually obliged to collapse onto the grass. . . . The young man and woman became aware of the attention they were drawing but continued undisturbed, with their game. . . . One woman took out a pair of opera glasses and used them as though she were at the theater" (Renard, Journal, p. 89). "In the zoological gardens," the same observer added, toward the end of his life, "the enormous zebu follows his female and from time to time, rearing up on his back legs, darts out a long red arrow that fails to reach its goal. A pleasurably sensuous spectacle for the gentleman with a pretty woman, who blushes slightly. One goes to see the seals, because they are so close by, but one keeps a sideways gaze on the zebu and watches, out of the corner of one eye, for the next red arrow" (ibid., p. 655).

And even if one cannot see, one can still listen: there are frequent references, in literature, in the theater, in the movies, and in life, to the noises made by love-making neighbors in apartments or hotels; they are even alluded to in the repertoire of the Comédie Française (Gérard Bauer, *Un voisin sait tout*). "Even in the most cosy, the most discreet, and the most expensive . . . beddy-bye palaces," Alexandre Breffort notes, "it is customary to refrain from soundproofing the partition walls entirely" (*Le canard enchaîné*, April 8, 1953).

8. Desiring as I do to know in detail all that goes on in hidden, and therefore important, nooks and crannies, I despise the person who has not succeeded in gaining such knowledge, the thoughtless, unaware person, a danger both to himself and others; the sort to whom one would be justified in saying, as one of Cocteau's women characters does to another. "You're not wicked, it's worse than that. You do harm without even knowing it" (*La machine à écrire*, act 3, sc. 3).

9. And yet, if I wish to avoid pain, ought I not desire unawareness?

Whatever Pascal may say, man's wretchedness may seem

great precisely because he knows that he is wretched, while the tree's happiness is guaranteed by the fact that it is incapable of knowing anything. "When one considers existence as a whole," Chateaubriand remarks, "one might be tempted to long for any accident that would bring oblivion," since "happiness is not to know oneself, and to arrive at death without having felt life" (*Mémoires d'outre-tombe*, bk. 5, chap. 6). "A cat that sleeps twenty hours out of every twenty-four," Jules Renard suggested shortly before his death, "is perhaps God's most successful creation" (*Journal*, p. 701).

10. While, for Pascal, man's "advantage" over the "universe" that is killing him is that "he knows he is dying" whereas "the universe knows nothing," Montesquieu was already pointing out that naturally "the beasts" "do not have the supreme advantages that we possess," but that also "they do not have our fears; they suffer death as we do, but without knowing it" (*De l'esprit des lois*, bk. 1, chap. 1). And Baudelaire openly envied the lot of the lowest animals "which can plunge themselves into a brutish sleep—when time's skein is slowly running out!" (*De profundis clamavi*). "Damned, we're all that of course," one of Salacrou's characters remarks, "but in different ways. And to damn oneself with one's eyes wide open is a terrible one" (*Tour à terre*, act 2); but is not opening one's eyes a tendency of the human condition? One that requires all the skill man possesses to counteract?

11. "What you don't know, just isn't there," La Fontaine proved (*La coupe enchantée*). In friendship as in love, La Rochefoucauld notes, one is often made happier by the things that are concealed from one than by the things one knows. "The only remedy," Proust discovered, having tried the opposite course (see sec. 4. above) is to "be ignorant of everything so as to avoid a desire to know more" (*La prisonnière*, p. 61).

12. Since perfect ignorance is difficult to achieve, my chances of reducing my pain often depend upon my capacity to delude myself.

"Man needs illusion," Robert gives under *illusion*, "he feeds, he lives on illusion." "Hope, deceitful though it be," La Rochefoucauld observes, "serves at least to lead us to the end of life by an agreeable path" (quoted by Robert under *espérance*, hope). According to Boileau, "the biggest fool is often the most content" (*Satire 4*). Musset says of one of his characters that "he knew how misleading illusions are and he preferred his illusions to reality" (quoted by Robert under *illusion*). "The form the illusion takes is of little importance. But illusion there must be," writes Georges Duhamel (ibid.). And here is a Camus character musing: "He was conscious of the sterility there is in a life without illusions" (ibid.).

13. The only thing is, it's not quite as simple as all that, having illusions! "Flattering illusion, sweet and glaring error," Corneille writes; "how little you are able to endure, how swiftly vanish!" (ibid.).

14. And yet I must have them, those illusions, if I am to make myself do various unpleasant and unavoidable things that lucidity would never permit me to perform. Should I foresee from the very beginning how the enterprise I am undertaking is going to turn out, then some fear of or repugnance for future reality might prevent me—unreasonably—from embarking on such a course. But in fact I shall perceive what the undertaking involves in reality only when it is quite evidently too late to turn back. I shall then accept, under the compulsion of *force majeure*, what I would obstinately have continued to reject for as long as I had not succeeded in destroying my margin of liberty; I therefore present myself with an initial phase that it is up to me to equip with soothing illusions. Such and such a degree of loosening of the bonds between metropolitan France and one of its overseas possessions would lead to a new arrangement just as stable as the old one, and France would still therefore remain a solid "presence" out there; such and such a degree of increase in Germany's international power after her defeat will be as much as she can possibly attain in the foreseeable future. In this way I will without willing it, while willing it all the same, a much more radical, much more painful development along the same lines. "He did not consciously wish for it," an observer wrote of Guy Mollet's attitude to the Fifth Republic after its first eighteen months of existence, "but he helped it to come into being and has come to terms with it. A definition of the father that very often corresponds to the reality" (Georges Suffert, *France-Observateur*, January 14, 1960). "I never manage to achieve anything without misleading and cheating myself," Gide remarks (quoted by Robert under *biaiser*, to evade, take indirect paths). "What can one wish that is not simple? And if it were not simple, then the willpower would be lacking," Valéry suggestes, then goes on to explain: "For who would will the consequences of what he wills? No one . . . could will the consequences of what he wills" (*Mélange*, pp. 326–27).

15. Since the requisite simplemindedness will not always take over of its own accord, the best thing to do is to provoke it—or make it possible to lay claim to it—by an act of lucidity at one remove.

"I do what I can to deceive myself," Bérénice claims (Racine, *Bérénice*, act 3, sc. 3). And generally speaking I can do quite a lot. "To give my lucidity, when I decide the time is right, a controlled vacation at will," says one of Montherlant's characters (*Les jeunes filles*, p. 284): I don't wish to know—which means I don't wish to admit that I know, either to myself or others. Having taken a good look, having arrived at a fairly certain prognosis of what I should see if I continued to look, I choose to close my eyes. "It is sometimes good to blind oneself deliberately" (Destouches, quoted by Robert under *s'aveugler*, to blind oneself). "I consent to my eyes being forever deceived," Thésée says when he is already beginning to have suspicions of Phèdre, and he refuses to go "searching for hateful enlightenment" (Racine, *Phèdre*, act 5, final scene). "One runs for refuge to one's ignorance. Once hides in it from what one knows," Valéry notes (Valéry, *Tel quel*, 2: 35). "Wives and husbands should not look one another too much in the eyes," Giraudoux wrote, "if they wish to avoid discoveries" (quoted by Robert under *éviter*, avoid). In the autumn of 1915, Briand succeeded Viviani as prime minister: "For months," Abel Ferry writes, "the vice-premier (Briand) had been secretly undermining the position of his leader, colleague, and friend. Viviani handed over to him with elegance and dignity. When someone asked him whether he had been aware of the underground campaign that Briand had been conducting against him, he replied, it seems: 'I am the cuckold who doesn't want to know'" (Ferry, *Les carnets secrets*, p. 118).

16. In order to succeed in closing one's eyes to good purpose, one must be strong enough to refrain from the blind impulse to acquire too much information. "The weakness of men is their curiosity to learn what they do not wish to know" Molière has one character say (Molière, *Amphitryon*, act 2, sc. 3).

17. More than this, one must also draw the teeth of the dangerous moral impulse that can drive men to seek unconditional truth—the attitude of Gide's Oedipus, who rejects "a happiness made of errors and ignorance," and has no "pity" for it (*Oedipe*, act 3), and also Prévert's acceptance of all the consequences: "If the eyes must be put out in order to see everything, then put out the eyes!" (Jacques Prévert, *Lumières d'homme*).

18. The consideration one ought really to keep uppermost in one's mind, one that by-passes such conflicts, is that brought out by Sacha Guitry in *Chez les Zoaques* when a man reproaches his friend for having slept with the former's mistress: "Why did you sleep with Kiki?" "The fact of sleeping with Kiki was for me a pleasant thing," Henri offers as his "excuse," adding a counterattack: "Is it a pleasant thing for you," he asks Gustave, "to be

aware of it?"—"Ah, not in the slightest!"—"Then don't be. There's no reason why you should" (Guitry, *Chez les Zoaques*, act 3).

19. One can even go so far as to close one's eyes to something upon which they have previously been long and assiduously fixed.

"The question no longer interests me," a former supporter of the European Defense Community announced in the Assembly three months after the Community's rejection, and at a time when he was concerned with guaranteeing a majority for an "alternative solution." "I don't even know," he added, "whether I ever was a supporter of the C.E.D. (exclamations and laughter on the extreme Left, in the Center, and from several Right-wing benches) or whether I wasn't, because I don't want to know any more (further exclamations from the same benches)" (Jean Le Bail, A.N., December 22, 1954; *J.O.*, p. 6754).

20. On the other hand, one may content oneself with restricting one's power of vision just sufficiently to prevent the emergence of a distressing certainty.

"Such relationships, had they been revealed to me by a third party," Proust's narrator observes, "would have been enough to half kill me; but since it was I myself who was imagining them, I was careful to include in them an amount of uncertainty just sufficient to deaden the pain. If they are taken in the form of suspicions, one can successfully absorb enormous daily doses of the idea that one is being deceived, even though a very slight quantity of that same idea could be mortal if injected through the needle of another's wounding words" *La prisonnière*, p. 85).

21. The prestige of deliberate blindness can sometimes be extended to disguise blindness that is in fact involuntary.

"Parents are much less perspicacious than they like to seem," says a teen-age boy in one novel. "On the whole, they are heavy sleepers and quickly forget what they were like at our age. Some cunning experts assure us in high school that they are perhaps 'pretending not to see anything.' It would be an ingenious scheme. But not at all like them in fact" (Bertrand Poirot-Delpech, *Le grand dadais*, p. 65).

22. Having decided to close my eyes to some particular aspect of the world, I wonder whether events beyond by control will permit me to go on keeping them closed. I am disturbed when such events threaten my defense against unpleasantness, relieved when the danger is removed, glad when my maneuver is seconded by the course of things themselves.

In one successful comedy, a wife is afraid that the father of her husband's mistress is going to present her with proof of the infidelity to which she is closing her eyes, thereby forcing her into the position of leaving the husband. When she is let off the hook at the last moment, she exclaims: "It's inexplicable! I feel a sort of relief!" (Marcel Achard, *Patate*, act 3).

23. It is as well not to provoke others into revelations that would endanger the blindness I wish to maintain.

When a wife flings at her husband: "You poor soul . . . if you were capable of noticing anything at all . . . !" it is folly—a very natural one, but all the more dangerous for that—on the husband's part to reply: "Well? Go on . . . Tell me something I haven't noticed" (Guitry, *Je t'aime*, act 2).

Nor is such a reaction any the less reasonable if the threatened blindness is in no way voluntary: the prudent man would sense the danger.

24. "I beg those who live with me," Montaigne admits, "to coddle me and take me in with fine appearances" (Essais, bk. 2, chap. 17); their moral obligation with regard to me is not so much that of behaving well—that would really be expecting too much—as that of being careful to conceal any actions that will distress me.

"If ever she is unfaithful to me," a husband in a comedy says of his wife, "she will be clever enough about it, I hope, to see that I don't notice, and . . . no one will be either childish enough or stupid enough, I also trust, to come and tell me about it" (Guitry, *Chez les Zoaques*, act 2).

25. The other may feel it is a virtue in him to collaborate with me in my efforts to close my eyes to something he is inflicting upon me.

"I advise you to deny it," a panic-struck wife says to her lover in a Guitry comedy: "We must deny, deny, to the bitter end. . . . That's what he wants" (Sacha Guitry: *Le nouveau testament*, act 4). "Now why should you think she's going to find out?" a father in another play asks his daughter when she discovers that he is being unfaithful to her mother; "I guard your mother's peace of mind like a jealous lover. . . . If you knew how much happiness I give up for her sake so that she can go on leading her cosy little life in blissful ignorance . . ." (Armand Salacrou, *Une femme trop honnête*, act 2, sc. 3).

26. I may be acutely displeased with the other when he fails in his duty.

A man past his prime, having been told by his mistress that she is going to spend a particular evening at a particular theater, goes himself and sees her there with another man. "Lucette had so many days, so many evenings at her disposal . . . in which she was at liberty to do whatever she saw fit, to be unfaithful to him with the world at large, if that was what she wanted. Ordinarily this did not cause him too much pain, and even this evening, if he had stayed at home . . . would have gone by like any other. What Lucette was doing during that time would not have given him a moment's concern. The moment she had told him about her evening out at the theater, about the friends who had invited her, he had felt that it was not true. To know nothing, that is still acceptable, but how can one avoid trying to delve a little further, to see things as they are, just once, even though it is bound to be painful, when some verifiable piece of information is handed to one like that?" (José Cabanis, *Les mariages de raison*, pp. 79–80).

In the early summer of 1916, André Maginot, speaking in the Chamber, quoted a text (attributed to Galliéni who had recently died) against Briand that was generally believed to be authentic but was not entirely impossible to deny—which Briand did, with his usual and always admired skill. Briand came out of the exchange on top. Whereupon Maginot "dug his heels in," Abel Ferry recounts, "and the day after next compounded his original failure by attempting to prove Briand a liar. The Chamber knew that Briand was lying, but it did not want proof of it, like a man who pays a prostitute and knows he is being deceived, but does not like having the fact pointed out to him" (Ferry, *Les carnets secrets*, p. 146). In France, Chamfort claims, it is usual to leave those who start fires in peace and persecute those who sound the alarm: so great is the addiction to anaesthesia.

27. How much pleasanter a world bathed in shadows is to live in than one flattened by total sunlight! (see chaps. 1 and 2).

"He leaves nothing in shadow": the action of someone who "savagely transforms into light things whose value is that of shade" (Valéry, *Histoires brisées*, pp. 80–81), creating "a world without shadow that can be peopled only by boredom" (Valéry, quoted by Robert under *ombre*, shadow). A girl in one of Cocteau's plays talks about a man who fascinates her to another man of whom she is very fond: "Maxime has so many layers, crannies, surprises. . . . I must have shadows, and with you, Pascal, everything goes on in broad daylight, in total sunlight. You know where you are right away. For instance, I knew . . . I knew exactly what you were going to do when you stormed out and slammed the door. With Maxime, I have to search, I have to feel my way, I'm a little frightened of him. . . . But since you love me . . . I must ask you . . . not to be always all of a piece, always hewn out of one block, not to be always this white light blinding me, this trumpet that deafens me, this marble wall I'm always barging into" (Cocteau, *La machine à écrire*, act 1, sc. 10).

In other words, light does away with the excitement of doubt; it eliminates unpredictability, one of the conditions of both freedom and attachments; it impoverishes and even destroys.

28. This being so, there are a great many shadows that one scarcely experiences as such, or with which one can live on the easiest of terms.

29. When one does make a gesture suggesting an attempt to let in new light, it may be so tentative that what it is in fact expressing above all is a desire to combine an unchanged status quo with the satisfaction of believing oneself to be part of the "opposition."

Speaking of the difficulties hampering French exports, a political leader under the Fourth Republic referred to "the complexity of the regulations preventing one from making anything out" (Pierre Pflimlin, A.N., November 14, 1957; *J.O.*, p. 4780): a phrase that recurs in a great many spheres, as when a premier under the Third Republic referred to a piece of legislature as "a . . . vast thicket in which it is impossible to make anything out" (André Tardieu, *La profession parlementaire*, p. 169). Though any assault made upon such a state of affairs is likely to be weak, intermittent, doomed to failure. Robert is still able to quote Anatole France's reference, when writing about the laws, to "the obscurity in which they are enveloped" (under *obscurité*).

30. Even when I am forced to admit that I have "benefited" in some particular business, at first very obscure, "from the casting of very considerable new light," I shall frequently add: ". . . though even this, I hope I may be allowed to say . . . has not quite expelled all the shadows from every nook and cranny" (Charles Barangé, speaking for the finance committee, A.N., August 5, 1954; *J.O.*, p. 3860).

31. "Indeed, I count myself fortunate in not having been forced to observe that the shadows are still thickening around this affair" (Robert under *obscurité*), which will therefore end by being filed away "unsolved."

In which case the obscurity is really excessive, and I shall protest. And yet, even so, let us not forget that "one must be half in shadow . . ." (points of suspension in original) (Valéry, *Mélange*, p. 331), and that it is even a good thing that what is outside me should be so as well.

17

HONESTY AND LIES

1. Many adults wage a savage battle against the inclination they perceive in children toward lying.

2. "Every time a child lies," one observer notes, "it is called a lie, because the child hasn't spoken the truth." But "when a grown-up does not speak the truth, he or she does not always think of it as a lie" (Guy Duradin, *L'école des parents*, 1955, p. 26).

3. Any affirmation on the child's part that does not correspond to reality may be felt by adults to be a lie.

"When a child says 'I saw some zebras cycling in the Bois de Vincennes,' its mother will reprove it for making things up," one children's doctor notes (Chantal Rivaille, *L'école des parents*, April 1960, p. 24). "Children are often storytellers," Robert gives under *fabulateurs*. But isn't there perhaps a purpose behind the stories?

4. " 'You musn't tell lies' is a prohibition made solely to children. Adults are never asked not to lie," one of Montherlant's characters observes (*Demain il fera jour*, act 2, sc. 1). To lie is thus one of the privileges the child acquires simply by growing out of those underprivileged early years.

5. The child feels that its lying is jeopardized both by its own insufficient control over itself and by the powers of penetration that it often attributes to adults; the latter say to it: "I warn you, if you lie to me I shall know" (Colette, *Gigi*, p. 50). The child

suffers from the fact that its lies are "often detected and easily detectable" (Guy Durandin, *L'école des parents*, 1955, p. 26). But as it grows up, so it increases its power to appear opaque.

"She had discovered a new source of pleasure—lying," we are told of an adolescent girl in a novel. "She began telling lies . . . for no other reason than to be able to look at the other person's face and say to herself: 'I've just told her that, that's what she thinks, and it isn't true. . . . She's looking into my eyes, but she can't find anything out from them'" (Jean-François Revel, *Histoire de Flore*, p. 39). So the child discovers, with Voltaire, that "of all bad actions" lying "is the easiest to conceal" (quoted by Robert under *mensonge*, lie, lying).

6. The adult employs harsh methods to uncover the child's lies; methods that are no longer acceptable between grown-ups.

When a politician says publicly to another "I must tell you that you have not convinced me, and I am not really sure, commensurate as your fine intelligence is with your great talents, that you yourself are convinced" (Raymond Pinchard to Edgar Faure, C.R., March 24, 1955; *J.O.*, p. 991), it is something most unusual. Even so very pleasant a version of the childhood "you're lying!" is rarely employed, at least when those concerned are not maintaining extreme positions or involved in an extraordinary incident.

"Is it true, that lie?"—a phrase "used to indicate that one doubts an assertion"—is "often" employed "when speaking to a child" (Robert under *mensonge*).

But among grown-ups, public enquiry into lies, like public enquiry into intentions generally, is forbidden.

The reason why one must never bring lying into any particular case is precisely, of course, that one assumes it in every case. For the French, one observer claims, "a speech is never truthful and never signifies anything other than 'intentions'" (Berl, *La France irréelle*, p. 74). "Any utterance," Valéry notes, "has several meanings, the most remarkable of which is assuredly the cause that has provoked that utterance. Thus, *quia nominor leo* does not by any means mean: For lion I am named, but rather: 'I am a grammatical example. To say: The eternal silence, etc., is to state quite clearly: I intend to appall you with my profundity and dazzle you with my style" (Valéry, *Tel quel*, 2: 191).

It is precisely this atmosphere, however, that causes a wife (on the point of being unfaithful) in a Sacha Guitry comedy to propose the following agreement to her husband (whom she supposes to have been unfaithful already): "You will never question my word, and your word will never be questioned by me . . . on condition, of course, that neither goes beyond the limits of probability" (*Faisons un rêve*, act 1). Expressed with greater precaution, this becomes, in the words of one deputy, "an attitude of mind such that, if you will not allow others to impute dishonest and devious intentions to you, you are forbidden in your turn to attribute such intentions to your opponent" (Jacques Fonlupt-Esperaber, A.N., August 26, 1954; *J.O.*, pp. 4270–71). On an occasion when there are even more backstage whispers than usual to the effect that some political leader's attitude on some important problem is the result of personal motives, the victim of such whispers can therefore invoke the fundamental law: "I do not question the good faith of any of those members who, in a short while, will take up a different position from my own on the matter now before us. I hope that no one will question the good faith by which my friends and myself are actuated" (Jacques Soustelle, A.N., September 30, 1957; *J.O.*, p. 4454). "No one doubts the intentions of the government," one of those "friends" then elaborated, "or the intentions of those who are going to vote in its favor. No one even doubts their wishes in the matter" (Jacques Isorni, ibid., p. 4439). After all, those concerned could feel secure in that noble place; they were not involved in the perilous intimacy of which Boileau was able to write:

> Accept now, poor husband, a life of reproofs;
> Seeing her daily, as judge and as jury,
> Arranging each word that you say in her fury"
> [*Satire*, 10]

7. And even supposing a grown-up should in fact be proved guilty of lying, despite all the difficulties in the way of such an event: so what? Another improvement in the conditions of life as one grows older, since such a discovery in childhood would probably have entailed painful consequences.

8. Now that one is in enjoyment of "the right to the relaxations . . . of lying" (Colette, *Le blé en herbe*, p. 170), one can savor what Jules Renard called "the sensual gratification of telling lies" (*Journal*, p. 103), which according to one of Sacha Guitry's characters is "one of the greatest gratifications in life . . . a delight that never fatigues and is limited solely by the credulity of others. . . . So you can see how much scope there is" (*Mon père avait raison*, act 1).

9. It is probable that such an insistence upon the pleasures of lying also serves to combat the distress it gives rise to.

"I have carried out several enquiries into this problem of lying, I have questioned a great many people," an observer writes, "and I have discovered that eighty percent of those questioned expressed the wish to have at least one person with whom they could be totally sincere, to whom they need never lie" (Guy Durandin, *L'école des parents,* November 1958, p. 26).

10. The uneasiness that lying produces is betrayed by the formal phrases that accompany its practice.

Between opponents—political ones for example—it is referred to as "the most frank and open explanation": "we are not here to disguise our thoughts" (Henry Trémolet de Villers, A.N., October 15, 1959; *J.O.,* p. 1806).

A "moment of truth" or "a time for honesty" may be called for or heralded in terms implying that "disguising our thoughts" is precisely what everyone had been doing up to that point. It has happened more than once that "the time has come for the opposition, as for the majority, to lay its cards on the table. Let each of us decide what he wants and say what he wants" (Robert Schuman, while prime minister, speech at Lille, July 11, 1948; *L'Année politique,* 1948, p. 116).

I am speaking the whole truth and nothing but the truth! This formal and extravagant affirmation is often expressed in set phrases: "I won't hide from you the fact . . ." "in order to conceal nothing from you," "I do not wish to disguise from you," "I don't think I have misled you about the difficulties," "I am telling you without keeping anything back and with complete frankness," "I am saying exactly what I think," "I am going to tell you the whole of my thinking." Then there are other, rather less formal ways of conveying the same idea: "These problems must be dealt with honestly," one leader under the Fourth Republic exclaimed, "and I shall not try to evade them" (Edgar Faure, A.N., October 13, 1955; *J.O.,* p. 5098). Another deputy, when broaching a question that was particularly dear to him, said: "But at that point, after a long debate, I felt I owed it to myself to say . . . quite straightforwardly, without holding anything back" (André Morice, A.N., September 30, 1957; *J.O.,* p. 4452). Another felt it was necessary and useful to announce: "[I am going] to say out loud what I am thinking and what others think to themselves though they sometimes do not dare say it" (Emile Hugues, A.N., October 30, 1955; *J.O.,* p. 5382). "A politician who has been given the great charge, the heavy mission, the noble mission of governing this country," declared one prime minister with a reputation for subtlety (Edgar Faure), "owes you, not invariably the satisfaction you may require of him, but always his complete and utter sincerity. And whatever may happen, either this evening or in the future, that I shall never stint you of" (A.N., March 18, 1955; *J.O.,* p. 1686). "I had sworn to say honestly exactly what I think," one deputy once said when concluding a speech (Edmond

Barrachin, A.N., October 30, 1955; *J.O.*, p. 5398): ah, what virtue! "I am astonished," another deputy once claimed, rejecting solemnity in favor of sarcasm, "that certain of my respected colleagues should be shocked by the fact that it is possible to say things one believes in; it is not obligatory to mount the speaker's platform . . . in order to say things other than what one thinks" (Jean-Paul David, A.N., October 18, 1960; *J.O.*, p. 2563). "It is sometimes a good thing in an Assembly," a third member claimed in more sober tones, "that every member should say quite openly what he thinks about a bill and not hide his true feelings" (André Armengand, Sénat, February 3, 1960; *J.O.*, p. 38).

11. Whatever one's opinion about lying, honesty does tend to be harmful.

If one thinks over the question, Should it be said? one is quite likely to answer no! "There are many occasions," Molière has a character remind us, "when utter honesty would be ridiculous and scarcely permissible" (*Le Misanthrope*, act 1, sc. 1). Although she admits: "I believe I could without danger be sincere," Racine's Hermione (*Andromaque*, act 2), later recognizes her error. "Should one tell everything?" Proudhon asks, and answers: "To tell everything is to set fire to everything" (quoted by Daniel Halévy, *Le marriage de Proudhon*, p. 20). A character in a Guitry comedy, having succeeded in having his will read while he is still alive, draws the moral from the results: "At this moment we are being given a glimpse of what life would be like if people suddenly found out the truth about one another. It would be a frightful Armageddon" (*Le nouveau testament*, act 4). Another Guitry character, a woman, says to her lover: "Think of how fragile such a wonderful illusion is, and of how one misplaced word from you would destroy it forever! . . . I mistrust this unruly honesty of yours" (*Faisons un rêve*, act 4). "That was a narrow escape!" the wife in a Colette books says to herself, thinking about her friend and rival. "How could Jane have let herself go like that? She was going to talk, to shout it out, to talk about the whole thing . . ." (points of suspension in original) (Colette, *La seconde*, p. 127). "We should never dare to see one another again if everything were said," Valéry wrote to a friend (*Correspondance avec Gustave Fourment*, p. 121). "Neither the State, nor Justice, nor Religion, nor Education, nor any serious business could *function*," the same author writes, "if the truth were wholly visible. Judges, priests, teachers, all must be robed" (Valéry, *Degas, danse, dessin*, p. 76). "No life is possible any longer if honesty is tolerated," Montherlant concludes (*Aux fontaines du désir*, p. 38).

12. To display the truth about myself to others is to do myself

grave harm. If I begin to do so, someone who wishes me well and desires to stay close to me will unfailingly suggest: Don't you think you'd do better to keep quiet?

"He chose the course of sincerity," Retz writes of someone," with that sort of freedom that is always as futile as it is odious whenever it is employed merely to compensate for the failure of artifice" (*Mémoires*, p. 588). "What is the use, for a woman," Courteline asks, "of undressing her behavior and showing it stark naked to the whole world?" (quoted by Robert under *déshabiller*, to undress); and indeed, what would be the use for a man either? "Man," Valéry observes, "has raised himself only by disguising himself. A shaven, pink-skinned lion or a plucked eagle is distasteful to imagine. The unfortunate reputation of the domestic pig doubtless stems from the fact that it is flesh-colored" *Tel quel*, 2: 319). "One is never sufficiently pleased with oneself to be totally honest about oneself" (ibid., p. 179).

13. Offering to tell the other the truth about himself is in the first place to do him harm and in the second place to expose myself to reprisals, so that "truth is a bomb whose effects kill both the one who throws it and the one it is thrown at" (Nicole, *Les lions sont lâchés*, p. 35). Under *franchise*, (honesty, frankness), Robert gives "so-called frankness that permits itself to make wounding comments"; and: "to express oneself with brutal frankness" (ibid.), a combination of noun and adjective whose hackneyed nature has led André Maurois to remark upon the tendency "to consider brutality the only possible form of frankness" (ibid.). "Sincerity . . . with regard to others, is more often than not . . . ill-judged" (Léautaud, *Journal littéraire*, 1: 120).

14. Frankness is no less disastrous even when it has no information value for the person being addressed, when I insist on telling him what he knows sufficiently well—if not too well (see chap. 16, secs. 24–26). To shout out an open secret may destroy a state of equilibrium that is dependent upon a general silence being maintained over a universally shared certainty.

"I'm afraid you've been rather clumsy and imprudent, one of Montherlant's male characters tells a woman who has been nagging at him; "you should have kept all that to yourself so that I could go on pretending I hadn't understood" (*Les Jeunes filles*, p. 48).

15. Being harmful to the other person, frankness may be viewed as immoral.

"To be frank," Jules Renard notes, "in other words to step on other people's toes on purpose" (*Journal*, p. 150). And of his wife, the same writer says: "When I say to her: 'Be frank with me,' she can tell from the look in my eyes just how far she can go" (ibid., p. 724). "One has to be careful . . . with people who don't lie spontaneously," one of Colette's young women says; "they're just lazy creatures who won't even take the trouble to adjust the truth a little" (*L'ingénue libertine*, p. 129).

16. And when all is said and done, how very nasty frankness is!

"Sincerity prowled around her, closing in then moving away like a temptation" (Colette, *La seconde*, p. 195). "He had despised the truth," the same writer says of a man, "ever since the day when it had exploded from his mouth like a belch to sully and harm" (*La fin de Chéri*, p. 11). "It is a genuine sickness, not being able to lie," Montherlant claims (*Le démon du bien*, p. 179).

17. Idiotic, tyrannical, murderous—frankness is a childish predilection.

"He says all sorts of things he shouldn't," adults say of the child; "Out of the mouths of babes and sucklings," and "He'll get his parents hanged" (Jean Dublineau, *L'école des parents*, November 1959, p. 3). Education also means learning how to lie. It is Voltaire's Huron who proudly proclaims: "I always say . . . what I think" (quoted by Robert under *ingénu*, ingenuous).

18. Though conscious of the dangers that my own frankness might create, I may still censoriously demand it of the other: "His attitude, his behavior has not been honest in this affair" (Robert under *franc*).

19. To find dangers of frankness denied, one must look to the world of comedy, or to so-called *avant-garde* circles, or to the sort of people who are more concerned with boasting than with protecting: "France can take the truth!" "France is great enough to be told the whole truth and nothing but the truth" (Jean-Michel Flandin, A.N., July, 1955; *J.O.*, p. 3678). Is that quite certain?

20. Once the maleficence of frankness has been established it becomes easier to hint at the happy influence exerted by lies.

21. Lying is indispensable: according to Proust, it is the most necessary and the most employed instrument of conservation. Here is Gide reporting him on the subject: "He said with sudden impulsiveness: 'But my dear fellow, lying is something absolutely sacred!'" (Gide, *Journal* 1889–1939, p. 846).

22. There are always aspects of myself that it would be disastrous not to disguise, to gloss over. To cultivate my image, to maintain, to be careful of, to save appearances is essential if I am to avoid failure.

To risk—nay, the certainty of—forfeiting an attachment, the reasonable man will prefer the slight discomfort—mingled with pleasure (see sec. 8 above)—of pleasing another as someone he

is not. "One lies," Proust recalls, "in order to protect one's pleasure or one's honor. . . . One lies . . . above all to those who love
one" (quoted by Robert under *mensonge*). "In our old nation
with its mingled peasant and military ancestry," one journalist
began a disagreeable report on Algeria, "the first reflex is always
to conceal the real situation as far as is humanly possible. There
is an extremely widespread fear that by revealing unflattering
facts one is arming others against one. . . . The man who wants
to know is looked upon with suspicion" (Philippe Minay, *Le
Monde*, November 24, 1955).

23. "On how many occasions does deceit not become an heroic
virtue!" Voltaire exclaims (quoted by Robert under *mensonge*).

Valéry has written "in praise of the hypocrite": "the hypocrite,"
he suggests, "can never be as entirely wicked . . . as the sincere
man" (*Mauvaises pensées et autres*, p. 90). "Deceit," Montherlant
observes, "often creates fewer ills than truth; contrary to the
generally held opinion, one can very well lie to those one loves
most: you have lied to me, I have lied to you, I shall lie to you
in the future" (*Service inutile*, p. 269). "When everyone is happy,"
he argues, "there can have been no crime. . . . So I say: Here's
to a deception that has made so many people happy!" (*Carnets*,
1930–1944, p. 233). Colette, who refers to the "courteous deceit"
(*Le blé en herbe*, p. 270), also describes "the melodious and
pitiful deception" lived out by Charlotte, a woman who loves only
women but pretends to achieve pleasure with a man: "She waited
. . . to resume the task incumbent upon the one who loves most:
The daily trickery . . . Deferential lies, deceits maintained with
ardor, unsuspected feats of valor expecting no reward . . ."
(Colette, *Ces plaisirs* . . . , pp. 28–29).

24. There is also the lie that is no less precious because it is
not deceiving anyone: the lie that permits the liar to save appearances, either his own or another's, in a situation where honesty
would destroy a balance quite delicate enough already (see sec.
14 above).

25. And there is the lie that should not deceive anyone.

Although "it isn't possible to tell the truth . . . one can," Jules
Renard reminds us, "tell transparent lies: it's up to you to see
through them" (Journal, p. 492).

26. The practice of protective lying (whether on one's own
behalf or another's) may be accompanied by a refusal, perhaps
an indignant refusal, to lie uselessly. "A woman is honest,"
Anatole France notes (quoted by Robert under *franc*), "when she
doesn't tell useless lies."

27. It often appears just as useful to tell the truth at one point

as to lie at another (and perhaps to leave the nature of the attitude adopted doubtful in each case).

Here is an eminent journalist writing about French policy in Algeria after three years of war there: "There is no doubt that it is often criticized or even condemned openly by many of those who approve of it officially. For French policy, for two years now, has evolved in an atmosphere of total insincerity" (Jacques Fauvet, *Le Monde*, November, 16 1957). "Officially" meaning, for example, "when speaking in the house," and "openly," "in the corridors outside." It was said at this time that *Mopse*, having long advocated a policy that his opponents termed one of withdrawal, was forced, when he wished to head a government, to employ expressions of great "firmness" in his investiture speech. "Foreign diplomats," one newspaper claimed at this time, "are employing a new expression among themselves to describe the many French politicians who, like M. Guy Mollet, are thinking to themselves the exact opposite of what they say aloud: they are calling them 'the bilinguals' " (*L'Express*, March 27, 1958).

But what folly to say out loud what it is so easy to convey in a whisper! When the Euratom treaty came before the Assembly, an opponent of that institution (Pierre André) quoted a certain general, the director of special weapons and future commander in chief in Algeria (Charles Ailleret), as being of the same opinion. This provoked an interruption from another member on the other side of the house (André Monteil): "General Ailleret is a supporter of Euratom. He made a speech to say so!" But the other replied: "I can show you ten letters in which he explains quite the opposite to me!" (A.N., July 3, 1957; J.O., p. 3190). The incident was apparently never cleared up, however; it was a matter of no consequence.

28. You cannot claim beneficence on behalf of just any old lie, however; if you want to do that, then you must make sure it has not been bungled in any way. "When you tell a lie, you must do it very carefully, believe me," says one character in a Sacha Guitry comedy (*Faisons un rêve*, act 3). As Montaigne says, "anyone who does not feel he has a really good memory ought not to meddle with lying" (quoted by Robert under *menteur*, liar); it would be dangerous not only for himself but also for the other, who has the right to expect a well-constructed lie. "I suddenly felt guilt," a character in a novel says, "at not having lied carefully enough. I certainly owed it to Cécile, such circumspection" (Nourissier, *Les orphelins d'Auteuil*, p. 136).

29. It may happen that in order to work properly a lie has to be extreme, shameless; for example, in order to allay suspicion

on the part of someone who must at all costs be deceived now that a certain situation has arisen.

30. And in any case, one may have to lie in order to be believed.

A faithful wife in a Guitry comedy is tormented by the jealousy of her husband, which she is unable to appease. But when she in her turn eventually takes a lover, her mother tells her: "Now you will be able to do what you could never have managed before . . . what I would never have advised you to do if you hadn't told me what you have just told me. Now, you're going to be able to make him believe that none of all this is true. . . . You know, we women are really not very good at telling the truth. . . . But on the other hand, we're very good at lying. If your husband needs a passionate outburst, a cry from the heart . . . you'll be able to supply it!" (Guitry, *La jalousie*, act 3).

31. The disadvantages of honesty and the advantages of lying are most strikingly apparent in the matter of confessions.

32. "Many parents insist on obtaining an admission or a confession when something naughty has been done," a doctor remarks (André Berge, *L'école des parents*, March 1960, p. 14); "They attribute an excessive importance to confessions" and "believe they have won a victory when they . . . have obtained a confession" As for the child, he may find himself forgiven if he has confessed right away. But if he denies even the evidence, if he goes on denying his guilt in the face of all probability," then he is adopting "an attitude that is particularly distressing to parents" (Guy Durandin, *L'école des parents*, February 1951, p. 20), and is in danger of greatly increasing his punishment.

33. How much less difficult the situation of the grown-up is! To deny guilt when one is caught absolutely red-handed is for him a ploy by no means devoid of efficacity.

"The second law of scandals" formulated by a great politician of the Third Republic "is that everyone denies everything, even in the face of the evidence" (André Tardieu, *La profession parlementaire*, p. 335). "Even the most flagrant of errors rarely disqualify them," an observer of the following Republic comments, "provided they resist the temptation of admitting to them" (Berl, *La France irréelle*, p. 72).

34. For grown-ups, admission no longer alleviates the pain: it makes it worse.

"When you know my crime and the fate hanging over me," Phèdre tells Oenone, "I shall die nonetheless, but I shall die still more guilty" (Racine, *Phèdre*, act 1, sc. 3). And here is Anouilh's Eurydice considering the opinion of "learned men" that "the act of confessing" makes "everything all washed and shiny again": "But if it were possible that they're wrong or that they said that in order to find things out; if they were to go on living [the shameful things one has confessed] twice as strong and twice as much alive from having been repeated; if the other began to remember them for always . . . well, I think it would be better not to say anything" (*Eurydice*, act 2).

35. Confession may provoke catastrophe.

When five deputies were indicted in connection with the so-called Panama affair, "they made every effort to prove that the s ims they had received were the result of normal financial operations or represented perfectly legitimate honorariums. Baïhaut alone made a complete confession: 'In a moment of folly . . . I sank into forgetfulness of my duty. I ask my country and the Republic for their pardon.'" All "were acquitted, with the exception of Baïhaut, who found himself condemned to five years imprisonment and a fine of 750,000 francs. Of all the deputies under suspicion, the only one to be punished was the one who had confessed. The others resumed their seats in the Palais Bourbon or the Luxembourg amid the plaudits of the Republican majority" (Jacques Chastenet, *La République des républicains*, p. 318).

36. So "never confess."

"You admit it!" one character in a comedy cries to another; but the other replies: "No, I don't admit it, that just slipped out!" (Guitry, *Florence*, act 2). In another comedy, a lover in a compromising situation says to his mistress: "I advise you to deny it. We must deny, deny to the bitter end, quite shamelessly" (Guitry, *Le nouveau testament*, act 4). "Even when you're caught *in flagrante delicto*, don't admit it!" (Salacrou, *Une femme trop honnête*, act 2, sc. 5). "Mr. Prime Minister," a leader (Gaston Defferre) once said in the Senate under the Fifth Republic, "now that the time has come to explain my group's voting, I should like to make a confession"—a phrase that occasioned "smiles" and, from the Speaker of the house, the good-natured interjection: "You're a lawyer! Never confess!" (Sénat, February 3, 1960, p. 39).

18

WORDS AND SILENCE

1. Words destroy, whether they are the vehicles of frankness (see chap. 17, secs. 11–14) or of other neighboring reactions.

"We were better off *before* . . ." a wife in a Colette novel thinks to herself after her friend and rival has spoken out. "Neither of us is going to derive any profit or happiness from what is going to happen now. . . . It would be best if Jane doesn't say any more" (*La seconde*, p. 190). "I am beginning to believe," another of the same author's female characters says, "that a man and a woman can do anything together with impunity, anything, except talk" (*Duo*, p. 168).

"There are words that should not be spoken," Delcassé said in a cabinet meeting during the Great War (Ferry, *Les carnets secrets*, p. 89). "I shall take great care," someone involved in any negotiation will always say, "not to utter any word likely to compromise the prospect of a friendly settlement, while at the same time trusting that all those concerned in this negotiation will act in like manner" (Georges Bidault, minister for foreign affairs, on the subject of the Sarre, C.R., October 29, 1953; *J.O.*, p. 1684). Toward the end of the Fourth Republic, a journalist writing about French policy in Algeria expressed the opinion that "any (ministerial) crisis would force a discussion of its results and its objectives [a prediction belied by several crises that ensued], and no one knows what the result of such discussion would be" (Jacques Fauvet, Le Monde, May 4, 1957); so let the cabinet in power stay in power! "Explanations and a restatement of the whole position were expected," another journalist wrote with reference to the announcement made by the prime minister after the Sakkiet affair. "In fact, it was no more than an account of the events, and there was nothing else it could have been. The sequel was to demonstrate in effect just how difficult . . . it was not to destroy the fragile edifice of the government's majority with a single misplaced word" (Raymond Barrillon, *Le Monde*, February 13, 1958).

2. Words are made all the more dangerous by the temptation to select precisely those that will do harm and provoke reprisals. "The Abbé Calon," Mauriac writes of one of his characters, "was one of those . . . who . . . rather than swallow an angry word would willingly be hanged" (quoted by Robert under *boutade*, witticism or flash of temper); and that is what they're asking for, to some extent, when they let fly.

When illustrating *langue* (language or tongue) in the sense of "the content of discourse," Robert seems concerned almost exclusively with its aggressive and spiteful uses (the exceptions are italicized in the following extract, from which only the references are omitted): "The language of the *just* . . . of the detractor. . . . *Flattering*, slanderous, treacherous language. . . . Venomous . . . poisoned language (tongue); tongue of an asp . . . of a serpent . . . of a viper. Viperish tongue. . . . Bad language, a wicked tongue, fine language (ironically). . . . See: calumny, slander—Wounds . . . inflicted with the tongue. Flick of the tongue: slander, cruel epigram. To murder . . . with a flick of the tongue." Piquant—a word once very much in use and still of service—describes "that which stimulates the interest and the attention sharply and agreeably: . . . a piquant assortment of colors, of objects . . . a piquant beauty." But originally it describes that "which presents one or more sharpened points capable of piercing something, of wounding someone . . . that which wounds sharply, pierces (*pique*) to the quick: . . . a wounding word, piercing words" (Robert). There are "conversations during which one succeeds in . . . letting fly with a few little darts that amuse without doing any great harm" (Georges Lecomte, quoted by Robert under *décocher*, to let fly); but there are also "tiny darts . . . that make a deep wound" (Montesquieu, quoted by Robert under *épigramme*). A clearsighted man is apprehensive of the "misjudged word that may slip out and set the whole powder keg alight" (Guitry, *Le nouveau testament*, act 3).

3. Silence preserves.

Opposed to those who hold the austere view that "one must speak. . . . It is because we are silent that evil happens" (Cocteau,

Les monstres sacrés, act 2, sc. 6) there is a long tradition exemplified by the Molinists, whose "safest course," Pascal tells
us, "has always been to keep silent. And this is the cause of a
learned theologian's saying that the cleverest among them are
those who intrigue a great deal, speak little, and write not at
all" (Pascal, *Les provinciales,* 3d letter): a description that exactly fits the myth of Henri Queuille under the Fourth Republic,
once described as "that great white silence" (*Le canard enchaîné,*
November 11, 1953). "Everything," Radiguet writes, 'will soon
sink back into the shadows, in other words into everlasting
darkness" (Raymond Radiquet, *Le bal du comte d'Orgel,* p. 118).
"On Judgment Day," one of Montherlant's characters predicts,
"there will be no sentence passed against those who have remained silent" (*La reine morte,* act 1, sc. 2). "You cannot imagine," Colette observes, "what a number of subjects and words
two women who can say anything to each other will banish
from their conversation" (*Ces plaisirs . . . ,* p. 89). "It wouldn't
be the first time," she also has a character say, "that a couple's
happiness depended on something unspoken or something un-
speakable" (quoted by Robert under *inavouable,* inadmissible).
"I shan't speak another word," another Colette character announces after a moment of crisis. "Let us leave everything as
it is. All we need do is to be rather careful and continue as before"
(*La fin de Chéri,* p. 238–39).

4. Silence may sometimes heal the wounds that words have
inflicted.

In Colette's *La seconde,* the evening after the fit of honesty
that almost wrecked their *ménage à trois,* the two women involved "no longer exchanged any but the most infrequent and
everyday words. The one pretending to read, the other sew, they
both desired only . . . to put themselves into the hands of silence,
to nourish the newborn and still sickly sense of their safe escape"
(*La seconde,* p. 225).

5. The strong man "can remain silent indefinitely" (ibid.,
p. 203); it is the weak man who is incapable of restraint.

6. Silence can be used to make others exaggerate the importance of what I am hiding.

"When someone asked him to give further details of his program," Pierre Poujade is said to have replied: "Not on your life.
While I keep quiet, people all think: The tricks he must have
up his sleeve!" (*Demain,* December 20–26, 1956).

7. For the individual, silence may be the best course to steer
between alternatives.

Having announced that neither "in prose nor in verse shall

I ever refer to . . . the famous cardinal," Corneille explains: "He did me too much good for me to speak ill of him—he did me too much ill for me to speak well of him."

8. This is even more frequently true when more than one person is concerned.

The "right of nations and the right of kings," Retz argues, "never agree so well as in silence." "To evade problems," said a prime minister under the Fourth Republic at a party conference, "is convenient . . . when it comes to facilitating the first stages of forming a majority" (Robert Schuman, national congress of the M.R.P., May 24, 1953; *Le Monde,* May 26, 1953). Several congresses later, this "movement" was to furnish a minor but striking example of such evasions. "At a late night sitting, the vote on the general policy motion gave rise to a long . . . argument on the subject of quotations from speeches by General de Gaulle. Whereas the chairman . . . and the general secretary . . . wished to make their stand upon the speech at Issoudun—'A new Algeria forever linked to France of its own accord'—. . . the Northern Federations on the one hand and that of the Seine on the other wished to take their stand on the speech at Bourges, which particularly emphasized the 'universal inclusion' of all those living in Algeria and the possibility 'for all their children to decide their own destiny and that of the lands they inhabit.' After a discussion . . . the congress finally decided . . . not to quote any statement made by the president of the Republic" (May 10, 1959; *Le Monde,* May 12, 1959).

9. Though perhaps urged with less ardor and in a more intermittent fashion, the austere cry of "the whole truth!" is still to be heard. According to François Mauriac, during the Fourth Republic "there is a corpse lying about somewhere that is tainting the whole of French political life with its stench" (*L'Express,* April 9, 1955); according to Gaston Defferre, addressing himself to a prime minister under the Fifth Republic after the second Algerian uprising, "it would be unworthy . . . of our institutions . . . if the truth were not disclosed" (Sénat, February 3, 1960, p. 33).

10. But running counter to the tradition exemplified by Voltaire and Zola, the great provokers of scandals, there is still the careful traditional wisdom according to which the art of governing consists less in settling problems than in silencing (for example, by a gesture of appeasement such as the institution of an inquiry that will never come to anything) those who are posing them—unless the latter abandon their attempts to speak of their own accord. Chateaubriand expressed this in exaggerated terms: "One

must prevent the world with nothing that is not fine and noble" (quoted by Robert under *découvrir,* discover or uncover)—a tendency that balances out the tendency to self-denigration.

There are some abscesses it is impossible to drain, or whose pus, should one try, would poison the whole body. "There are decidedly some national wounds," one eminent journalist wrote with reference to the education question, "that it would be best for us to think about constantly and never to mention" (Jacques Fauvet, *Terre humaine,* March 1951, p. 107). "Everything you have read earlier about the weaknesses that . . . were undermining the country's health," writes a historian Resistance-member after an analysis carried out during the Second World War, "about the intellectual lethargy of the governing classes and their bitterness, about the . . . propaganda . . . poisoning our workers, about our gerontocracy, about the army's uneasiness over its position within the nation, all of these, or almost all, were things we had been murmuring among close friends for a long time. How many had the nerve to speak any louder?" (Marc Bloch, *L'étrange défaite,* p. 188). Right in the middle of a new period of stability, *Le Monde,* when reporting a particular affair that was causing unpleasantness (the Saar problem), remarked upon a resolve "to draw a discreet veil over the essentials of a problem that no one dares to speak of aloud" (*Le Monde,* July 26, 1952). A deputy renowned for his military feats, addressing his colleagues on the very day when the Fourth Republic was to start its death throes, said: "And then, you will have to attack that area [in Algeria] *which is never mentioned,* that formidable redoubt 250 kilometers long by 50 wide . . . that marches on the western suburbs of Algiers, on the Cherchell side, that stretches down as far as Mostaganem on the other and blocks the whole northern approach to el Cheriff. *No one ever mentions this region.* Yet we have never succeeded in penetrating into it for more than 20 kilometers. . . . It is the *fellagahs'* principle stronghold. *It has never been mentioned.* We have not the resources to attack it and we have never succeeded in doing so. . . . *It is never talked about"* (all italics added) (Pierre Clostermann, A.N., May 13, 1958; J.O., p. 2263).

11. It is even as well to *state* that I am not going to talk about such things.

"We shall earn the reader's gratitude," Victor Hugo declares, "by passing rapidly over certain painful details" (quoted by Robert under *passer*), or distressing ones. For "the more you stir muck up, the more it smells" (Robert under *merde,* muck or shit). "It is not my wish, during this seconding speech," one deputy felt obliged to say, "to evoke any excessively somber episodes in our history" (Pierre de Chévigné, C.R., December 8, 1953; *J.O.*, p. 2118). Another member, alluding to the appalling fate suffered by a French officer (Captain Moureau) at Moroccan hands, said: "We are immediately faced with a problem; but we feel some scruples at raising it in this place, so painful is it to the heart of the French people" (André Morice. A.N., March 20, 1957; *J.O.*, p. 1747).

12. But if I must touch upon some distressing subject, I should at least refrain from going into it at all deeply!

"This is a delicate matter that must not be delved into too deeply," Robert gives under *approfondir*, to deepen. And M. Teste is still more emphatic: "One must never dig right down to the bottom of anything" (Valéry, *Monsieur Teste*, pp. 89–90).

13. Thus I may limit myself—and still be thought rather daring—to indicating that something distressing is taking place somewhere without going into details; my hearer or hearers are unlikely to protest against this refusal to sate what is apparently a not very lively curosity.

During one sensational trial (that of Gaston Dominici), "both prosecution and defense," according to an eminent journalist (Pierre Scize), "seem to be shutting their ears to important statements." In fact, "in this affair . . . the journalists reporting it would like to ask one question: "Is M. Bousquet, the judge, deaf?' Statements of the utmost gravity were made during yesterday's hearing. Statements of such a nature that they might be expected to change the entire direction of the proceedings. Everyone present received the impression that M. le Président Bousquet had not heard them" (Scize, *Au grand jour des assises*, pp. 348–49); just as M. Scize apparently had not remembered them. He did not even offer the excuse of being constrained to silence by the law. When an interview was announced as imminent between Khrushchev and de Gaulle, the West German newspapers, according to *Le Monde*, "published on . . . this subject, some of them on their front pages, a number of cartoons shedding a great deal of light on certain fixed ideas in the popular imagination that are still proof against all forms of reason" (Alain Clément, *Le Monde*, October 24, 1959); the rest was left to the reader's imagination. And apparently no one complained.

14. What most astonishes a provincial about Parisian society, according to François Mauriac, is "the way any subject is broached without shame" (quoted by Robert under *aborder*, to approach or accost). But toward the end of the Fourth Republic, when the Assembly undertook to discuss a somewhat sweeping series of changes connected with certain institutions all commonly held to be in a state of collapse, one deputy declared: "We

must congratulate the government upon having had *the courage* to bring this debate before the Assembly" (Paul Coste-Floret, A.N., February 12, 1958; *J.O.*, p. 705): words often employed whenever a "debate" is likely to become "painful." During the trial of a priest charged with murdering his mistress and unborn child, "council *took the risk of mentioning* the attitude of the young girls, his parishioners, who fell victim to Desnoyers. 'All of them were consenting partners. They have said so.'" (Bertrand Poirot-Delpech, *Le Monde,* January 26 and 27, 1958). When an Algerian Moslem was shot down by a police officer attempting to aid a foreign cameraman in search of titillating material, *Le Monde,* before passing this information— already common knowledge outside France—on to its readers, felt it necessary to describe it as a "crime committed in Algeria in circumstances so revolting that it is necessary, everything considered, and may eventually be salutary, that the French public should know of it" (*Le Monde,* December 30, 1955). "During the past few weeks," the minister for foreign affairs announced at one point during the Fifth Republic, "we have heard a great deal about a N.A.T.O. crisis, and rarely, I believe has one heard such an assortment of rumors of all sorts, of pessimistic comments, and—*why not admit it?*—of criticisms of France's position" (Couve de Murville, A.N., December 28, 1959; *J.O.*, p. 3669).

19

STARK LANGUAGE AND VEILED MEANING

1. It is often as well to express what I want to say in toned down form (see chap. 13; secs. 17–34).

"The consonants in French are remarkably soft; no harsh forms," Valéry notes. Even "the letter *r*, although extremely unabrupt in French, a language in which it is never rolled or aspirated, has on several occasions almost disappeared from the spoken language altogether and been replaced . . . by some more easily emitted sound (the word *chair* becoming *chaise*, etc.)" (Valéry, *Regards sur le monde actuel*, pp. 126–28). This is a tendency often believed to be discernible in many spheres. It is not only in painting that it is possible to perform the action of softening or, in other words, "of attenuating . . . [whatever] is too pronounced, too sharply defined" (Robert). "This letter is too brutal, the expressions in it must be softened," the same dictionary gives under *atténuer*).

2. One can achieve this by making an affirmation less categorical in form than one intends it to be in reality.

"If the government was determined to send troops to Tunis," one deputy commented with reference to an expedition under the Fourth Republic when Bourguiba had rejected that regime, *"there might perhaps have been* some other way of doing it" (Jacques Isorni, A.N., January 21, 1959; *J.O.*, p. 162). The restraint of the formal expression merely emphasizes the virulence of the matter.

Claiming that the efforts announced by Pierre Mendès-France (at the time of his accession to power) to attempt to end the war in Indochina had demoralized the Indochinese fighting beside the French, one deputy argued that "the Vietnamese soldiers *may have* been very much affected by the declaration you made." "It is evident," he added, "that the military setbacks that ensued *may to some degree* have been brought about by a lowering of morale" (Frédéric-Dupont, A.N., July 22, 1954; *J.O.*, p. 3452). Pierre Mendès-France himself, that same summer, when broaching the subject of the European Defense Community, spoke in his turn of "a certain number of French people who *may* be concerned about the future political implications of the C.E.D." (A.N., August 29, 1954; *J.O.*, p. 4425).

Many French people seem, like Montaigne, to have a fondness for softening and qualifying words as such: they say, "I think," "some." Among these formulas, "I think" in particular has had a long and notable career, becoming absorbed into a large family of which other members, for example, are: "it may be thought that . . ." and "there is no reason not to think that . . ."

3. Because the meaning is extreme does not mean that the expression has any need to be so.

"We have . . . noticed that his judgment *did not entirely correspond* with our own," Guy Mollet announced after a conversation with Pierre Mendès-France, the then prime minister. Their disagreement was total (*Le Monde,* May 11, 1957). When Michel Debré "permitted himself to say" to his prime minister under the Fourth Republic that the latter's "argument *cannot be wholly accepted* (C.R., January 17, 1958; *J.O.*, p. 132), he was suggesting that it was in fact wholly unacceptable. "I even said," a minister for the interior (François Mitterand) said of the "indignation" and the "rebellion" of one of his numerous enemies (George Bidault) with regard to him, "that they ought not be limited to making interesting and well-constructed, but *not always* well-documented speeches" (A.N., July 25, 1956; *J.O.*, p. 3604): my opponent has been unable to provide the slightest hint of proof against me! "While accepting his good faith, though I do not feel there has *always* been proof of it," one politician says of another (Jean-Marie Le Pen of Pierre Mendès-France, A.N., February 11, 1958; *J.O.*, p. 674), meaning—a good faith I am quite sure is always absent. Despite the fact that *toujours* (always) is for Robert an antonym of *parfois* (sometimes), the latter is almost a synonym of the former in various specialized languages, such as that used in parliamentary debate.

4. Sometimes, when wishing to refer to something rather extreme, rather "strong," there is a hesitation in daring to name it.

Instead of "not mincing words, of coming to the point" (Robert under *mot*), a speaker will use a *demi-mot,* which is to say "a word chosen for the purpose of attenuating an excessive brutality of expression or of dissimulating one's thoughts from some part of one's audience" (Robert).

5. One does not always feel obliged to dissimulate the fact that one is dissimulating.

"The army has always had the feeling," a "Gaullist" member of parliament observed toward the end of the war in Indochina, "that this war it has been burdened with was undertaken, I will not say with a bad conscience, perhaps, not wishing to offend anyone, but at the very least with some embarrassment" (Edmond Michelet, C.R., November 12, 1953; *J.O.,* p. 1752).

6. Hostility is too intense and too dangerous a thing (see chap. 13) always to be called by its name.

Thus a "rather mixed" reception is likely to have been a very bad reception indeed; and again, the words Robert gives as the antonyms of *nuancé* (mixed, in this phrase)—opposed, clearcut —merely reveal the harsh signification that the softening word has acquired. Similarly, *mouvements divers* (mixed reactions) denotes an unfavorable reaction to an act or gesture that is *diversement apprécié* (variously appreciated). Told that "the radicals *are concerned* over the war veterans' estimates" (Jacques Fauvet, *Le Monde,* November 4, 1953), we understand that they find some parts of them unacceptable. When we meet the words "reserve" or "reticence" we know that there has been a stiff battle. "I seized her by the throat," a rapist is reported as saying, "but in the face of her reticence, I failed in my attempt to abuse her" (*Nord-Matin,* January 12, 1956; Albert Aycard and Jacqueline Franck, *La réalité dépasse la fiction,* bis, p. 35). In 1953, when Pierre Mendès-France was canvassing for the premiership, he declared, after a conversation with one of the men who had laid down the policy pursued in Indochina: "It is notorious that M. Letourneau and I are not in agreement on this matter" (*Le Monde,* June 2, 1953); the whole change of style that was to be proposed to the country is in that refusal to attenuate the truth.

7. Beyond the *demi-mot* or hint there is the antiphrasis; it may or may not be tinged with irony, "the most dangerous weapon that men can wield" (Léon Bloy quoted by Robert under *ironie*).

"Sometimes," Proust notes, "the writing from which I was to decipher Albertine's lies . . . simply needed to be read backward; that evening for instance she had tossed to me with an air of nonchalance a message intended to pass almost unnoticed: 'It is possible that I may go to the Verdurins' tomorrow; I'm not at all sure I shall go though, I don't really want to.' A childish anagram of the following admission: 'I am going to the Verdurins' tomorrow, it is absolutely certain, since I attach an extreme importance to the visit.' This apparent hesitancy signified a determined intention. . . . Albertine always employed expressions of doubt to convey irrevocable resolves" (*La Prisonnière*, pp. 90–91).

Boileau's observation that "a man may seem to applaud you though he is mocking and deceiving you" (quoted by Robert under *applaudir*, to applaud) is still very applicable, as well as the same author's remark that "to slander with art" is "respectfully to plunge the dagger home" in "honeyed tones" (Boileau, *Satire 9*). "Even *I hate you* is spoken with tenderness" (Boileau, *Satire 3*) still applies to many a subtle tongue since Quinault's. Knowing what to say and how to say it includes the habit of presenting "all sorts of harsh things wrapped up in all the polite considerations of society" (Madame de Sévigné, quoted by Robert under *envelopper*, to envelop); we must polish away at our expressions until there is not a single acute angle, not a single grating surface left!

"How many authors must have been received in that minuscule office," an author comments of a publisher (Robert Denoël) "and showered with hyperbolic compliments into which there invariably insinuated itself an almost imperceptible hint of reservation that reduced all the rest to nothing as soon as one gave it a moment's thought!" (Robert Poulet, *Entretiens avec Céline*, p. 22).

In a national assembly, no one forgets that "there are . . . praises that slander (La Rochefoucauld, quoted by Robert under *louange*, praise), that "to praise princes for virtues they do not possess is to offer insults with impunity" (La Rochefoucauld, quoted by Robert under *louer*, to praise).

An exchange of unusual acerbity having taken place between a prime minister (Pierre Mendès-France) and various members of a group hostile to him (the M.R.P.), a deputy belonging to the latter rose to speak: "I ask the Assembly to have the goodness to agree to a suspension of this sitting. The impotance of the prime minister's speech, the concern for objectivity of which he has given proof (laughs from the Center), the elevation of his thought (further laughter from the same benches) lead me to ask the Assembly . . . to postpone any further debate until three o'clock this afternoon" (Edouard Moisan, A.N., December 20, 1954; J.O., p. 6626).

When a deputy (Jean-Jacques Juglas) was refused permission by the member already speaking (Edouard Daladier) to interrupt him, a refusal that ran counter to the demands of "courtesy," it was with these words that he concluded the incident: "I must thank you, Monsieur Daladier, for your cordiality and your politeness" (A.N., October 27, 1953; *J.O.*, p. 4579). When another deputy (Pierre Cot) had interrupted a minister (Christian Pineau) without having asked his permission, the victim of the interruption resumed his speech with the words: "Monsieur Pierre Cot, I must thank you for having anticipated the fact that I should certainly have allowed you to speak if you had asked me to" (A.N., March 27, 1957; *J.O.*, p. 1901).

8. I may claim that I am not doing something that in fact, under cover of the claim, I am in the very process of doing.

If I say "I shall take care not to" make such and such a remark, or "I shall not be cruel enough" to make such and such a comment, then the remark and the comment have obviously been made. "You preferred to defer to the wishes, *I shall not say* the demands, of your official advisers," a deputy once flung at a minister (André Monteil to René Pleven, A.N., December 29, 1953; *J.O.*, p. 6956). "For how long," a venerable leader (Edouard Daladier) asked with reference to the 1954 Geneva conference, "will these negotiations, bargainings *I dare not call them,* last?" (A.N., May 4, 1954; *J.O.*, p. 2096). When correcting a particular misrepresentation of the past made by some "Poujadistes," a left-wing member used the words: "I am forced to remind my colleagues of the French Union and Fraternity party, whom we did not have the pleasure of seeing on those benches at the time (smiles)—*I say that without irony*" (Pierre-Oliver Lapie, A.N., July 11, 1956; *J.O.*, p. 3373). Referring to the relations between Pierre Mendès-France, the target of anti-Semitic reactions, and Edgar Faure, then in power, a right-wing deputy said: "Mr. Prime Minister, sir, you are being accused of all the sins of Israel (laughter), *be it said, I assure you, without any play on words* (further laughter)" (Joseph Pinvidic, A.N., November 29, 1955; *J.O.*, p. 6041).

9. In an atmosphere saturated with antiphrasis, the really sharp operator, or even those who simply wish to avoid being too much taken in, tend to interpret everything as its opposite.

10. So a denial merely strengthens the belief it is attempting to destroy, as with a particular reaction that Proust's narrator fears to provoke in Albertine: "that 'no' in which the *n* would be too hesitant and the *o* too explosive" (*Sodome et Gomorrhe*, p. 1097).

Referring to the moment in its life when the child is made to learn the passage from La Fontaine that begins "Without a word of a lie, if your feathers . . ." Rousseau becomes indignant: "*Without a word of a lie!* . . . Where will the child be if you teach it that the fox only says *without a word of a lie* because it is lying?" (quoted by Robert under *mentir*, to lie). Where will the child be when it learns that "to deny A is to show A behind bars" (Valéry, *Mauvaises pensées et autres,* p. 14)? A little farther along the road out of childhood.

Writing about events in June 1940, Montherlant says: "Every time one heard the Marseillaise or the word 'confidence' on the radio one said to oneself 'another disaster.' Every event was heralded by an announcement that it had not happened. 'The government will move, if needs be, to our American possessions' meant: 'We're going to form a new government that's going to stay here and negotiate in France.' And 'There is no question of France asking for a separate peace' was an announcement that the decision to ask for an armistice had just been taken" (Montherlant, *Textes sous une occupation,* p. 59). Shortly after the Suez expedition, Morvan Lebesque addressed the government in these terms: "The other week, one of your spokesmen announced that the sugar shortage was simply due to an exceptional demand and transport difficulties; the explanation was clearcut, closely argued, unanswerable; it was also all it needed to make sure that, next day, all the housewives in my neighborhood rushed to buy up sugar with redoubled ardor. Several days later, you explained to us that there was no shortage of oil; in a flash, all the oil left in the stores had vanished. Then came a warning against hoarding salt, which you told us was 'absurd'; the last few kilos of salt were volatilized on the instant." In short, "in 1956, the government only has to say *white* for the whole country to understand *black*" (*Le canard enchaîné,* December 12, 1956). The following week, the same publication made this comment on a statement by the minister for economic affairs: " 'Gasoline will not go up in price before February 1, 1957; moreover, whatever happens the increase will not exceed three francs a liter.' Everyone immediately deduced from this that the increase was going to occur immediately, since in France we all know what words are worth. We didn't have long to wait. Since last Monday, the precious fuel has cost six francs more per liter" (*Le canard enchaîné,* December 19, 1956).

11. "The inverted signs by means of which we express our feelings with their contraries," Proust notes, "are so transparent in nature that one wonders how there can still be people who say, for example: 'I have so many invitations I don't know where to start,' in an attempt to conceal the fact that they have not been invited anywhere" (Proust, *Sodome et Gomorrhe,* p. 1023). Yet there is never any lack of people who could justly confess, as the same author does, to using "the invariable system of ripostes

depicting exactly the opposite of what I was feeling" (*La Prison-nière*, p. 347).

12. Speak clearly and simply!—a constant cry.

Just as La Bruyère recommends direct expressions such as 'it is raining, it is snowing,' just as Boileau insists on the fact that he calls a cat a cat and Rolet a rogue, so d'Alembert criticizes Buffon because "instead of simply naming the horse, he says: 'the noblest conquest.'" "If I have anything shocking to say," Léautaud explains, "circumlocutions just irritate me and seem ridiculous. . . . For instance, I need to express the fact that a woman has wanked herself off. Should I write: She indulged in intimate caresses . . . or: she allowed one of her fingers to wander for a while . . . [points of suspension in the original] The verb masturbate? That looks as though one's trying for an effect . . . So, just put: she w—— herself off. That seems to me best" (Léautaud, *Journal littéraire*, 1: 267–68). "I say what I think," one deputy (Léon Noël) once declared. "I have not risen to speak, a thing I do rarely, in order to resort to circumlocutions, but in order to express my opinion in direct language, as is right and proper in a debate of such seriousness, however much it may displease some people" (A.N., December 21, 1954; *J.O.*, p. 6706).

13. According to another powerful current of opinion, however, naming things directly is forbidden, despite the fact that, according to Madame de Staël, "no language conveys more clearly what one wishes to say" than French (quoted by Robert under *nettement*, clearly, distinctly).

"The trouble is," Boileau tells us, that his muse, being "somewhat light," "names everything by its name" (Boileau, *Les satires*, "Discours au roi"). "Calling things and people by their real names," a Colette character says incisively, "has never got anyone anywhere" (*Gigi*, p. 32).

A new Resident General in Morocco (Francis Lacoste) was "tempted" according to one journalist (Eugène Mannoni), toward the end of the protectorate, "to perceive beneath" the agitation in that country "the existence of a 'non-nationalist current.'" In fact "the Resident was persuaded that behind the 'extremist' nationalism a movement could already be seen looming that he was taking care not to describe in any brutally outspoken manner." Thus leaving to the journalist the audacious and vulgar action of naming names: "To be more precise than the Resident himself . . . one may say that in M. Francis Lacoste's view communism is playing an important role . . . in Morocco" (*Combat*, August 3, 1954); but it is not, to say the least, useless to be so explicit?

14. The subtle man knows how "to speak in veiled words, in

hints" (Robert under *mot*); it is very important for him that his hearers, whenever he has told them something, always feel: There again, it is clear that he has not told us everything. At the court of the Roman emperors, "nothing was ever said," according to Montesquieu, "everything was insinuated" (*Considérations sur les causes de la grandeur des Romains et de leur décadence*, chap. 17). La Fontaine warns his readers to expect "many expressions . . . that tell and yet do not tell."

15. Even though we often hear of a decline in the use of allusion—these days, *Le canard enchaîné* claims, "in order to insinuate that someone is a stupid c——, you tell him he's a stupid cunt" (*Dictionnaire du Canard*, 1960, p. 4)—it is nevertheless always as well to make some sort of apology when one speaks at all directly.

Having expressed the opinion that a degree of difficulty in selling their goods on the home market "would encourage" producers "to turn to foreign markets," a prime minister under the Fourth Republic immediately apologized for having explained the situation so "crudely" (Félix Gaillard, speech on February 20, 1958; *Le Monde*, February 22, 1958).

16. To say things clearly, what eccentricity!

"In what I am about to tell you," a comedian told his audience, "there will be no allusions, no hidden implications, no attack against any person whatsoever. I beg you to take it all in its most precise, most literal meaning: fifteen minutes' intermission."

17. Naming things for what they are may be viewed as a procedure so very bizarre that it is avoided even in respect of that procedure itself.

"Under *direct*, Robert gives "to make a direct allusion"—it is still an allusion, you see. Several months after the Suez expedition, when the British government authorized its ships to pay transit dues to Egypt—a decision that provoked references to 1938 from the opposition—*Le Monde* reported that "the Macmillan government's opponents have not failed . . . to make *open allusions* . . . to Munich" (*Le Monde*, May 15, 1957).

18. To replace open allusion by direct naming, what audacity —or, to be more accurate, what folly!

After the nationalization of the Suez Canal, when Georges Bidault wished to escalate his attack on Nasser to a hitherto unprecedented level, he reminded the Assembly "that freedom of navigation through the canal has been refused to a State that my friend, M. Maurice Schumann, has referred to, *and that I now name*: the state of Israel" (A.N., August 2, 1956. *J.O.*, p. 3843).

19. There is a widespread passion for methods that provide

prudent indications without naming names, but that indicate quite clearly all the same.

"A transparent allusion" Robert gives under *allusion*: "one that is easily understood." "This allusion indicates him clearly" (under *désigner*, to denote). "So that each one of them, without naming his name, clearly indicated himself," Florian writes (quoted by Robert under *nommer*, to name). " 'The prince of critics' . . . is . . . a periphrasis," Théophile Gautier notes (quoted by Robert under *périphrase*), "understood by all which refers to Jules Janin." "Mask nature and disguise it," Pascal notes. "No more of king, pope, or bishop, but *august monarch*, etc.; not Paris, but *the kingdom's capital*" (*Pensées*, p. 834). A politician proud of his direct manner (Pierre Mendès-France) once said of a monster of subtlety (Edgar Faure) that he had made an "allusion . . . that despite its veiled nature was very precise" (A.N., March 19, 1957; *J.O.*, p. 1707).

In 1945, the prospective prime minister, Charles de Gaulle, spoke to the country on the subject of a single issue: the Communist party was demanding to be given one of three important ministries. "I found myself faced," he declared, "with the insistance of the leaders of *one of the three principal parties*." But "much as I would have liked to associate the men put forward *by the party in question* in the economic and social tasks of the government," this was an unacceptable request (November 17, 1945; *L'Année politique*, 1944–1945, p. 458). "My government," one prospective prime minister (Maurice Bourgès-Manoury) told the house, several months after the Suez expedition, "while it is resolved to reestablish its traditional links with Islam, will certainly maintain and affirm its friendship with *a very ancient and at the same time very young people; it considers that that people has a right to live and work*" (A.N., June 12, 1957; *J.O.*, p. 2684).

20. An allusion may be made clear, not only by the inclusion of characteristics exclusive to the object to be indicated, but also by a use of contrasts after the model of: "one day in the subway the train was crowded—he let his hand run over her"—the narrator pauses—"hair."

21. If need be, one can emphasize the fact that an allusion has been made, or that it is an extremely transparent one, after the manner of the comedian who, having made his insinuation, pauses: ". . . if you see what I mean?" In a movie, the priest of a village declining in its Christianity arraigns from the pulpit all the unbelievers who gather at sermon time in a café, and adds: "I shall not say in which café, especially since there is only one."

"The boss . . . always made him sweat," Céline is reported as confiding to a friend, who then adds: "he used a more Rabelaisian verb; but sweat is already pretty forthright" (Robert Poulet, *Entretiens avec Céline*, p. 71). "There is a town," said one deputy from Lyons and an important man in that place (Pierre Montel), "a fairly sizeable town that I do not wish to name, but whose name everyone can guess . . ." (A.N., November 15, 1957; *J.O.*, p. 4847).

22. One may judge, therefore, what a gulf there is between the transparent veil and nudity! "You know that Amazon's son, that prince I myself have for so long oppressed?" Phèdre asks Oenone as a prelude to yielding up her secret; "Hippolyte! Ah, ye gods!" Oenone exclaims, to which Phèdre replies: "It was you that named him!" (Racine, *Phèdre*, act 1, sc. 4).

23. While deliberately making my allusion as clear as possible, I may refuse to go beyond that point.

"This member of the sultan's council I am thinking of and whose name is on everyone's lips," a deputy opposed to Moroccan independence (Guillain de Bénouville) said, referring to a Moroccan politician about to obtain it (Si Bekkai): "This man . . . whom I shall not name" (A.N., October 7, 1955; *J.O.*, pp. 4890, 4892).

24. In certain situations, the act of naming is seen as a serious error, whatever the nature of the statement one wishes to make.

"I can name nothing unless by its name," Boileau admits, because "I have such a coarse soul" (*Satire 1*). "He is wrong," one of his critics says, "why must he name names" (Boileau, *Satire 9*). In fact, "these gentlemen have spoken of the liberty I have allowed myself in naming names as an unprecedented and unheard of criminal assault" (Boileau, *Discours sur la satire*). "I do not wish to give any names," declared one priest-deputy (Canon Kir). "I am not accustomed in my electoral campaigns to quote the names of parties, to point the finger at individuals. I have never done so" (A.N., October 14, 1959; *J.O.*, p. 1781). During the so-called "barricades" trial, the president of the court read out to a theoretical supporter of Algerian activism, Bernard Lefèvre, certain texts that had been attributed to him; the likelihood being that they were attacks on Charles de Gaulle. "Doctor Lefèvre refused to acknowledge the texts as his: 'Mr. President, that must be by Robert Martel. I personally never mention anyone by name. That's just not my style'" (November 12, 1960; *Le Monde*, November 13 and 14, 1960).

A member of the Assembly must never speak the name of an absent colleague.

Toward the end of the Fourth Republic, when Jacques Soustelle was approving a projected "outline-law" for Algeria conceived by Robert Lacoste, while rejecting that just submitted to the Assembly by Maurice Bourgès-Manoury, he was therefore forced to say: "I am thinking . . . of a project that was drawn up by a member of the present government, as indeed of the previous government" (A.N., September 26, 1957; *J.O.*, p. 4385). Wishing to point out the absurdity of a clause in the Assembly's procedure that had the result of barring from committee service a statesman as worthy of such a responsibility as Georges Bidault, one of his colleagues expressed himself as follows: "I have mentioned the name of a person in committee—I shall not repeat it in a public session—who, though isolated, certainly has both previous and present claims to sit on such or such a committee" (Jean-Paul David, A.N., January 20, 1959; *J.O.*, p. 104).

25. But if I do decide to perform the all-important act of naming names, at least let it be preceded by the proper circumlocutions!

The government having requested certain special powers during the Algerian war, a deputy (François de Menthon) wished to elucidate the question whether these powers would permit sanctions to be made against *a journalist working as a correspondent for one of the large Paris daily papers* who had recently expressed his disagreement with current French policy in no uncertain terms. It was not until later in his speech that the deputy felt able to say: "I conclude . . . from the minister for the interior's words that though *M. Raymond Aron* has doubtless felt reassured . . ." (A.N., July 19, 1957; *J.O.*, p. 3776). Several months earlier, a newly elected president of the Assembly (André Le Troquer) had observed: "Public opinion in France has been seized by doubt, its disappointment being proportionate to France's friendship for *a great nation*." That said, it became possible for him to continue: "Our *American* friends must pardon us for saying it . . ." (A.N., October 4, 1956; *J.O.*, p. 4006).

26. Or else let the effect produced by naming the name be immediately canceled out! Under *nommer*, Robert gives: "I met a friend in amorous company; it was N——, who shall be nameless."

27. I may also name someone in a less outright manner than that achieved by the clear allusion.

After a partial election (in the Ain) under the Fourth Republic, the victorious party (the National Center of Independents and Farmers) published a communiqué in which it declared that: "the leaders of neighboring groups would do well in the future, before they start giving lessons to the Independents, to gauge the exact strength they still wield in the country"—a sentence upon which *Le Monde* commented as follows: "We have received indications from the Center that this paragraph was aimed at the speech made by M. Lecourt, president of the M.R.P. party, last Sunday at Voiron" (*Le Monde*, March 27, 1957).

28. I may even excuse the act of naming someone by relating it to the good opinion I express of that person in doing so (as if morality were any excuse for bad manners!).

"I was reading an article from the pen of a journalist whose work I appreciate—why not name him? M. Wolf—which . . ." a member of parliament may say, for example (Raymond Triboulet, A.N., July 6, 1957; *J.O.*, p. 3369).

29. As for the motives behind veiled speech, it is a most effective means of reducing the embarrassment accompanying a forbidden action. A person may laugh heartily at a song about the disasters that befall a gentleman called Ducon while being unable to take equal pleasure in the utterance of what is still a very rude word (*con*, cunt), whose presence in this case, however obvious, is also in a sense silent. Often, Molière reminds us, we "forbid ourselves the name, but not the thing" (quoted by Robert under *nom*).

In the preface to the *Contes*, La Fontaine tells the reader that everything in them will certainly be veiled, but with fine gauze only, so that the reader need miss nothing; he will be the gainer, in fact, since he will not need to blush.

30. This trick, which enables us to escape our own inner sanctions, also serves as a way of evading the punishments with which we are menaced by external authority; instead of being punished, we shall savor the pleasure of having tricked the authority, of having proved our ability to dodge it. For example, in one of the archetypal scenes in classical comedy "the disguised lover converses with his mistress in concealed terms under the very eyes of the person whose task it is to keep watch over her" (Raymond Picard, Commentaire des *Plaideurs*, in Racine, *Théâtre*, p. 115). "This expression," a journalist wrote with reference to the "closing of the faucet" advocated by Pierre Poujade in his heyday, "has until now prevented M. Poujade from becoming liable under article 1839 of the Tax Act, which specifies 'a fine of from 6,000 to 12,000 francs and imprisonment for from six months to one year for any person who shall incite the public to refuse or delay payment of tax' " (Alain Murcier, *Le Monde*, March 5, 1955).

31. Unnameable (*innommable*) is an adjective qualifying that which is "too vile, too ignoble to be designated" (Robert).

If one were to give such a thing its direct appellation one would perhaps produce extremely disagreeable sensations in oneself, whereas "delicacy," as Vauvenargues reminds us "conceals beneath the veil of words whatever in things is repulsive" (quoted by Robert under *délicatesse*).

32. To do as Victor Hugo's character did who "gaily called everything by its proper or improper name" (quoted by Robert under *grossièreté*, coarseness, impropriety) is to become improper oneself. "Everything was called by its name, with the cynicism of dogs," Chateaubriand writes (*Mémoires d'outre-tombe*, bk. 9, chap. 3).

33. To accord the name by which he personally designates himself to a person one despises, even when that name is neutral in itself, is an act of recognition generous to the point of prodigality.

Under the Fifth Republic, when Charles de Gaulle conferred duties upon Louis Joxe that are normally reserved for the minister for foreign affairs, *Le canard enchaîné* suggested the following definition in its "dictionary": "Joxe (Louis)—General de Gaulle's second minister for foreign affairs. Apparently doesn't know Couve de Murville's name, since he has christened him: 'The Other'" (*Dictionnaire du Canard*, 1960, p. 90).

34. In designating a dangerous enemy by name, do we not also, by sanctioning his reality, increase his power? "The plague, since we must call it by its name . . ." But must we?

It was perhaps under the influence of this feeling that the leader of the French Republic spoke of the "West European association in which we should be . . . submerged by *you know who*" (de Gaulle, speech at Nevers; *Le Rassemblement*, June 19, 1948), and of "that situation by virtue of which there exists within our very people itself a sort of permanent plot against it . . . Ah! you know well enough of what plot I am speaking!" (Charles de Gaulle: Speech at Nice. *Le Rassemblement*, September 18, 1948). "A terrible anxiety . . . perhaps the worst of all, was expressed in the course of that debate," the minister for foreign affairs (Georges Bidault) observed with reference to the C.E.D.: "Europe, it has been said, is in danger of dividing France, the European Defense Community is in danger of dividing the French people." And he continued: "I do not think that we have any other duty than to attempt . . . to prevent . . . ourselves reaching such a point in order to benefit those," the speaker concluded firmly, "whom I shall not name" (C.R., October 29, 1953; *J.O.*, p. 1690).

35. By referring to a disastrous eventuality, are we not encouraging it to occur?

One deputy, an enemy of all overseas "withdrawal," who suspected, quite correctly moreover, that Pierre Mendès-France was intending to pursue such a course in the case of the Indian branch banks, declared that "it is indispensable that the government should state . . . whether it intends to promote a new policy whose outline and shape one would rather not guess at" (Michel Raingeard, A.N., August 27, 1954; *J.O.*, p. 4350).

36. It is possible to discern in oneself, Valéry observes, a "mixture . . . of the fear of not being understood and the terror of being understood," and also, in consequence, this desire with regard to others: "you must understand me without letting me see reflected in your eyes the idea of a man who has explained himself" (Valéry, *Tel quel*, 1: 45). And veiled language provides a way out of this conflict.

37. Veiled language also reduces the damage that can be inflicted by a refusal, both for the one who makes the refusal and for the one who has made the unfortunate advance.

"Clotilde understood and refused what had been asked of her, a matter upon which doubt was not possible, even though nothing had been explicitly requested" (Emile Henriot, quoted by Robert under *explicitement*). "I have a repugnance for the threatening style, because it commits the speaker," a Montherlant character explains, "I prefer the smooth-tongued style. It can conceal just as much solid determination as the energetic style, and it has the advantage of making retreat much easier" (*La reine morte*, act 2, tableau 1, sc. 1): an observation that could easily be applied to the veiled style too. "He never expressed any clearly defined opinion," we are told of a young man in a novel seen through the eyes of the heroine, "but she sensed that he had them, and had thought about them deeply. . . . He never went farther than allowing one to glimpse them by means of . . . a pattern of allusions . . . of exaggerations . . . of gestures and pouts: without ever compromising himself, he expressed it all" (Revel, *Histoire de Flore*, p. 71).

38. To speak in a direct way is to be brutal.

39. In the first place, it is an attempt to impose one's opinion.

Referring to one of the rare witnesses unfavorable to those accused in the so-called "barricades trial" (Colonel Fondes), a journalist said that "he displayed consummate technique as a sketch artist, never trying to overload his brush, limiting himself to discreet indications, here and there, in a phrase spoken or an incident, of what he really thought, leaving his hearers to draw conclusions that he refused to impose on them" (Jean-Marc Théolleyre, *Le Monde*, January 30, 1961).

40. To speak directly is also to force the person listening to me to face up to things that may perhaps be terrible for him (or at any rate distressing for a third party).

"They . . . parried any remark that was too direct and about to touch the bleeding spot in their hearts" (Alfred de Vigny, quoted by Robert under *direct*). To hit the nail on the head can also mean hitting the person listening on the head.

"To call things by their real names," Robert explains (under *appeler*, to call or name) is "not to attenuate with words the harsh or shocking effect of certain truths."

A politician under the Fourth Republic (René Mayer) demanded that the government should make itself "clear" on the subject of a major issue (North Africa) "not to the point of brutality," of course, but "to the point of making itself understood" nevertheless (A.N., August 27, 1954; *J.O.*, p. 4320): a tenuous boundary that it is difficult not to cross if one has been bold enough to approach it.

In order to convey the meaning of the word *net* (clear, distinct) when used adverbially—as in *refuser tout net*, to refuse point blank—Robert suggests the synonym *crûment*, crudely.

Though *cru*, crude, is linked on the one hand with "brutal," "ungracious," "without consideration," "without attenuation," there is also, on the other hand, the meaning it has in "I am telling you things just as they are" (*tout cru*), which is merely the same as saying "I'm not mincing words" (Robert under *cru*). "To speak crudely (*avec crudité*)" is perhaps no more than to "call things by their names" (Robert under *crudité*)—but isn't that already shocking enough? "Could you not have expressed the same truths while stating them with less crudity?" Chateaubriand asks (quoted by Robert under *crudité*). "The two friends told each other their slightest thoughts quite crudely, without attempting any subtleties of expression" (Balzac, quoted by Robert under *crûment*).

41. To put one's foot into it, or into the food, as the French phrase has it, is not only unseemly—it is also very dangerous.

"I named the pig by its name; why not?" (Victor Hugo, quoted by Robert under *nom*). A silly question, to which Florian replies: "Hunted, proscribed, and from his haven driven/For having dared to call things by their names,/A poor philosopher . . ." (ibid.).

"What does it cost," La Fontaine asks, "to call things by their honorable names?" But if the animal in question prefers "queen of the ponds" to "frog," then to substitute one for the other might add up to quite an amount. "Human relationships," Valéry reminds us, "are based upon ciphers. Decipherment causes confusion." "What folly to abandon "the advantage of saying without saying" and thus of "maintaining in a suspended, reversible state the reciprocal opinion," for "decisive and definitive judgments"! (*Tel quel*, 1: 43).

42. It is therefore much better to be formal about things, to keep one's gloves on, to adopt "a language swathed in veils, bounded by limits" (Valéry, *Variété*, p. 779), "to employ periphrases when touching upon a delicate subject" (Robert under *périphrase*). "I touch delicately upon delicate matters," d'Alembert informs us (quoted by Robert under *délicatement*). It is elementary as well as essential to perceive that on many occasions "this truth requires some softening" (Robert under *adoucissement,* softening or sweetening). Though the impact is being somewhat cushioned," a deputy (René Pleven) said referring to a debate in progress (on the Euratom treaty), "two conceptions . . . I will not say are colliding, for they must not collide, but are confronting one another on the occasion of this discussion" (A.N., July 10, 1956; *J.O.,* p. 3338).

43. If one presents some given matter of a difficult nature "in a form perhaps somewhat unemphatic" (Maurice Deixonne, A.N., February 11, 1958; *J.O.,* p. 680), one has every chance of avoiding the violent reactions that the same matter would provoke if presented in an unfortunately stark manner. "Under cover of this frivolous chatter," Voltaire explains (quoted by Robert under *à l'abri de,* in the shelter of), "I speak truths." "Even the most questionable situations," in the belief of one of Marcel Aymé's peasants, "do not cause offense provided you talk about them with great care" (*La jument verte,* p. 249).

44. From a fear that too violent an attack will provoke excessively violent reprisals, we often prefer to disguise it in order to reduce it to a more cautious level.

45. Thus names may often be replaced by categories, and the latter even qualified by a questionable but reassuring claim that no one in particular is being attacked.

The author of *Les caractères* defends himself by saying that "no one is named or designated" in his book, and since he has followed the procedure of writing "without naming those who are vicious," he has also written "without wounding," "using consideration for particular persons with all the precautions that prudence can suggest" (La Bruyère, *Préface au discours à l'Académie*). Not wishing to offend anyone, we say, I shall not quote any example of . . . "I fear . . . that those who are opposed to changes in North Africa," declared one politician (René Mayer) under the Fourth Republic while defending the C.E.D., "are sometimes also those who are opposed to changes in Europe"; but within this sentence he inserted the following clause: "though I do not allude to any person in particular" (A.N., August 27, 1954; *J.O.,* p. 4318).

46. The mere fact of mentioning a name creates a certainty in many circles that a murderous attack is being unleashed.

"To hear one's name," Valéry observes, "brings a whiff of the criminal court" (letter to Léon-Paul Fargue, April 30, 1917; *Lettres à quelques-uns,* p. 119). "When I referred to a certain number of underprivileged social categories," a prospective prime minister (Christian Pineau) explained to a critic (Paul Reynaud), "I did not do so merely for electoral motives, but because, as a Socialist, human suffering affects me deeply." "Mr. Prime Minister Designate," his Moderate critic replied, "human suffering is so far from belonging to any party that you have been beaten to the post in this affair, since it was our colleague M. Frédéric-Dupont who first, and long before you, submitted the proposal to which you are alluding." A name? That means they are attacking! Magnanimously, the Socialist rushed to defend his opponent: "Do not bring M. Frédéric-Dupont into the case. I know him and I know he has a warm heart" (A.N., February 18, 1955; *J.O.,* p. 825). For though *mettre en cause,* to bring into the case, means involving someone as a suspected party, it can also mean merely to bring him in as a blameless witness.

47. If I am not intent upon wounding, then I shall avoid naming names.

"I was in my prison in Nancy," Edouard Herriot wrote, harking back to 1944, "when on the morning of August 12, I saw walking into the room the man who was then head of the government." He then explains: "I employ this abstract expression because the man in question is now no more and because, even though I was his victim, I should not like to trample on a corpse" (*France-Soir,* December 24, 1948).

48. If you don't want trouble, no names!

One deputy (Paul Reynaud) having spoken disparagingly of home distillers in Calvados, a deputy from that *département* (Jacques Le Roy-Ladurie) replied to his remarks as follows: "In a region I know well, which has been referred to, and which I shall not mention by name in order to avoid rekindling a polemic of a personal nature (smiles) . . ." (A.N., December 2, 1959; *J.O.,* p. 3157).

49. Moreover, since the fact of naming is an extremely hostile act, it is natural that I should attack the name itself. So we get the name game.

A right-wing Moderate member, Jean Legendre (*le gendre* = son-in-law), addressing himself to the prospective Socialist prime minister Christian Pineau, said: "You have written a charming story, 'Plum and the salmon,' in which you take your readers with you into fairyland. I have the impression that this ministerial statement has been drawn up with the same ink, and that, like Alice, you too wish to take us into wonderland." Whereupon one of the candidate's friends exclaimed: "He's not *le gendre*, he's the mother-in-law!" Whereupon Lean Legendre himself riposted: "My dear colleague, I don't know whether that interruption is really witty or not, but I can tell you that it's not original. And allow me to add that on the Socialist benches from which the interruption came we have someone who can complete the family in Mabrut" (Mabrut is pronounced as *ma bru*, my daughter-in-law) (A.N., February 18, 1955; *J.O.*, p. 814). "To Saint Helena with Lempereur!" the Poujadistes exclaimed in protest against an energetic Socialist member, Rachel Lempereur (*l'empereur* = the emperor) (A.N., March 7, 1956; *J.O.*, p. 727). Wishing to remind the Communists of their support, during a senatorial election, for an ex-director of a nationalized bank, Ludovic Tron, an M.R.P. member (Robert Bichet) shouted at them: "M. Tron! The bankers are with us!" Whereupon a colleague (Fernand Bouxom) added a cry of *"Le Tron populaire!"* an allusion to the *Front populaire* (Popular Front) (A.N., October 28, 1957; *J.O.*, p. 4591).

50. Though the "words disguising the thing" are, according to La Fontaine, "less strong," they are also, from another angle, more powerful.

51. Abel Ferry tells us how, when a deputy (Albert Favre) called a president of the Republic (Raymond Poincaré) into question, the prime minister (Alexandre Ribot) "covered the president; but his words, because of the tone of voice they were spoken in, and certain subtle reservations that, to be truthful, I could no longer repeat, left in the minds of his hearers a sort of smear even more potent than Albert Favre's open attacks" (Ferry, *Les carnets secrets*, p. 180). "Returning from a demonstration of military aircraft in 1910, the commanding officer of the *Ecole supérieure de guerre* exclaimed: 'All that's just sport! As far as the army's concerned, the airplane doesn't exist!' "—so runs an anecdote that was used for his own purposes, before the Second World War, by Colonel Charles de Gaulle in a work originally undertaken at the request of Marshal Pétain (*La France et son armée*, p. 134). The fact that he did not name the commanding officer—Marshal Foch—need not, he evidently felt, in any way impede the force of this, as it were, only half-delivered thrust: the knowledgeable reader would still be struck by the disparity between the already astonishing surface facts and the vast iceberg of implication lying below it: the blindness of which a marshal can be capable, and the intensity possible in a conflict between two marshals.

52. A veiled attack is also a threat of open hostility if the more guarded method does not attain its goal.

A deputy who had once been a member of the Resistance (Edmond Michelet), finding himself being bluntly opposed—"Speak for yourself!"—by a colleague (Pierre Boudet), remarked simply: "Monsieur Boudet, you were much less free with your tongue in Cahors, in 1943!" (C.R., December 8, 1953; *J.O.*, p. 2123). And no more was said.

53. If an attack is veiled, then immediately the victim's capacity for counterattack is reduced.

When a deputy is mentioned by name in a public session, the rule is that he has a right to immediate reply: a privilege of which he is deprived in the case of even the clearest of allusions.

When you are made the object of an even very lightly veiled attack, all you can do is refuse to see that it is intended for you!

Under the Fourth Republic, when a Communist deputy spoke of "stock-exchange and portfolio patriots," Antoine Pinay exclaimed: "that is inadmissible!" Whereupon the Speaker reminded him of an elementary tenet of good sense: "No one can feel that he has been touched by the phrase M. Balanger has just employed" (A.N., July 19, 1957; *J.O.*, p. 3774).

But when Racine's Esther describes Aman, the minister of Assuérus, in the former's presence as "an . . . enemy of your own fame," though without naming him, the politician in question makes an even worse blunder than Antoine Pinay: "I?" he says to the king, "Heavens! Is it possible you could believe that? I who have no other object, no other God . . ." Upon which Esther is able to thrust home with: "Our cruel enemy reveals himself to your face" (Racine, *Esther*, act 3, sc. 4). I didn't ask you to say it; but I'm glad you recognized yourself! Or again: "Heavens, no, my dear fellow, how could you possibly have thought I meant you?"

54. As for the motives that make convolutions of style in others tolerable, if not actually pleasurable, there is first of all the pleasure of being treated as a grown-up.

Adults often address the child either in very simple terms or in complicated speeches seasoned with a warning that it neither can nor should understand them.

This being so, once I am no longer a child, I may appreciate the fact that someone with a reputation for being knowledgeable and subtle should suppose, or feign to suppose, that I am able to follow him; the fact that he behaves as though we understand one another even though he may be plunging me into almost total incomprehension.

55. This accounts for the persistence of a mode of expression —for instance in the quality newspapers, in the National Assembly, or in so-called intellectual discussions—involving an abundance of obscure allusions to a great many facts and ideas with which one must be fully acquainted in order to understand what is being said.

In *Le Monde* of June 15, 1961, Alain Guichard reviewed a book that gave an account of the "trend toward a reconciliation" between the Roman Church and Freemasonry (Alec Mellor, *Nos frères séparés, les francs-maçons*). The author was formulating a hypothesis, the critic remarked, based on the concealed motive behind "the first condemnation by Pope Clement XII." He abstained from indicating the year, or even the general period, in which this act took place; that would be sinking to a somewhat elementary level no doubt, even though very few readers could have provided this essential datum for themselves. It was not until the following paragraph, after a reference to an encyclical of 1884, that the critic allowed himself to specify "the bull of 1738," not with an air of providing a piece of information the reader might need, but merely in order to apply the principle of stylistic variation when forced to designate the same object repeatedly at brief intervals. The real motive behind the 1738 act was the pope's fear of "Hanoverian influence in the lodges." The reader was presumed to be familiar with the dominant role played by English affairs either in the Freemasonry movement at that period, or else in the concerns of Rome; he was offered no explanations in this matter at all. "The Masonic movement," the critic then continued with high disregard, "was at that time divided into two currents: one favoring the Stuarts . . . the other favoring the house of Hanover." The pretender James III, after the victory of the latter tendency, apparently persuaded the pope "that the interests of English Catholicism required a condemnation." And that's all there was to it.

56. But it would be a very bold man who would dare to ask: But what about the French lodges? He might thereby be admitting his ignorance of some overwhelmingly important and well-known fact of which the mere mention by the other, with a hint of disdain and the intolerable smile of those who really know their onions, would reveal him as being not merely foolish in his methods but also foolishly ignorant. The capital rule: "Never admit" (see chap. 17, sec. 36) also refers to this particular case: never admit to not having understood! To ask for additional explanations is to sign one's own certificate of nonproficiency.

"He sometimes lets fall a tiny remark that appears to be a piece of malicious wit, but which is incomprehensible. People . . . do not like to press him, for fear of being thought fools" (Jules Romains, quoted by Robert under *incompréhensible*).

It was much the same, under the Fourth Republic, with those "sibylline" remarks regularly dropped by Georges Bidault. "If we did not perceive it earlier, it was because we have waited until today to perceive it": a remark felt in political circles at the time to be a "disturbing riddle" (*L'Express*, February 12, 1955). One journalist wrote of the same politician, toward the end of the Fourth Republic: "His witticisms, requiring as they did a solid cultural education . . . enabled him on many occasions to rescue himself from a critical situation, his listeners not wishing to gain a reputation for being uneducated by asking for an explanation" (Jean Ferniot, *La Nef,* January 1958, p. 34).

"The common market reaches a critical point: the key to agricultural policy," Pierre Drouin announced in capital letters on the front page of *Le Monde* on June 8, 1961. But he refrained from informing his readers explicitly that the central fact in his argument was that the French government had recently made certain requests to the West German government concerned with agricultural matters; and that the latter had refused to consider them before the autumn elections. Yet the correspondent's article remained incomprehensible if the reader was not already in possession of these data, or if he failed to succeed in deducing them from a text affecting to take them as read. As though he were referring to some fact no more obscure than that the prime minister's name at that time was Michel Debré and that of the president of the Republic, Charles de Gaulle, the writer nonchalantly reminded his readers of the "very precise techniques . . . proposed by the common market executive of which the key," of course, "is to be found in those *notorious* 'deductions' . . . All this is elementary, but let us nevertheless insert a brief reminder." In fact, these deductions are "sorts of import taxes on the principal agricultural products that are to be lower in the case of internal trading than when the buying is done by an outside country." Impossible to put the matter more clearly, and the respective attitudes taken up by Brussels, Bonn, and Paris, as well as the public explanations of them and the less official calculations surrounding them, all become necessarily and limpidly apparent once this essence of the matter is known!

"To sum up," one journalist wrote with reference to Charles de Gaulle's chances at the end of the Fourth Republic, "the conditions of his return to power remain exactly those enumerated in *Combat* two years ago. . . . But"—but—"*at least one* of the leaders of the principal French political parties is irrevocably opposed to General de Gaulle's return" (J. R. Tournoux, *Combat,* March 6, 1958). Here then is an all-important fact—is the reader, having been thus aroused, to learn the name? Naturally not. It is up to everyone to sniff out the solution (Guy Mollet) for himself from an analysis thus transformed, in the so-called land of Descartes, into a game of riddles.

Broaching for the first time—if I am not mistaken—the affair that was to lead a prominent personage in the recently deceased Fourth Republic into the criminal court, *Le Monde* presented its readers on January 28, 1959, with the discreetly small headline: "The affair of the 'licentious ballets.'" And in the text, one read: "Sorlut . . . has particularly involved, *as we know*, a well-known official of the Fourth Republic in the case." Needless to say, it was unthinkable that the paper should go on to insult its readers by entertaining for a moment the idea that they might be ignorant of the name in question (André Le Troquer), which had been on the lips of "everyone who mattered" in Paris for quite some time!

In a book about Saint-Just that was apparently intended for a much wider public than that composed of specialists of the revolutionary period, a historian and politician (Albert Ollivier) wrote with reference to a report drawn up by the subject of his biography: *"As everyone knows,* no copy of this report has ever been unearthed in France" (Albert Ollivier, *Saint-Just,* p. 342).

Commenting indirectly on this habit, *Le canard enchaîné,* referring to the crude oil shortage after the Suez expedition, said: "Certain *'corpsards'* (the *'corpsards,' as nobody knows,* are those who belong to the corps of mining engineers) hope . . ." (*Le canard enchaîné,* January 9, 1957).

57. However, though one may accept one's inability to understand to a certain extent, this does not mean that one will not resent the fact, or that one will not make efforts to remedy the position.

58. Adults often express themselves deliberately in such a way that the child will not understand what they are saying to each other.

One of the mothers interviewed by Charlotte Roland said: "There are certain things that we feel, my husband and I, don't concern the children, and when they come up we manage it so that we can understand one another without the children understanding."

59. Children suffer from being excluded and humiliated in this way; it is, after all, an inadequacy on their part, one the adults are only too aware of, that enables this trick to be played on them.

60. When the child succeeds in outwitting the adult in this respect, then it is triumphant.

Here is an adolescent girl in a novel who has understood what her parents tried to conceal from her: "I thought I'd understood, from hints as big as houses they let slip out here and there, because they always think we're too dim to understand" (Rochefort, *Les petits enfants du siècle,* p. 118).

61. The ex-child may feel a desire to have words addressed to him that are on the verge of being unintelligible but that he can

succeed in unraveling by his own efforts. He will then be able to celebrate his triumph by remarking nonchalantly with Valéry that "even the clearest forms of discourse are spun from obscure terms" (quoted by Robert under *comprendre,* to understand). By becoming able to "take a hint," he proves both to himself and to others that he is no longer a child justly suspected of being a fool, that others ought rather to say of him now: "He has a quick mind and can take a hint" (Robert under *demi-mot,* a hint). And here is the atmosphere of an election meeting in the Salle Wagram (December 26, 1955) being addressed by the archpolitician of the Fourth Republic (Edgar Faure): "No attacks on individual opponents; scarcely more than an allusion or two; a series of velvet-pawed blows leaving the merest scratches. The whole thing brought off . . . so lightly . . . by a speaker . . . dealing with an audience sufficiently in the know to seize certain veiled implications and catch every hint" (André Ballet, *Le Monde,* December 28, 1955). The dullard is no longer myself, it is the other: "the Germans," Rivarol notes, "when one says anything witty in their presence, make an effort to understand. They never succeed without much reflection and the passing of glances between them. They club together in order to grasp a witticism" (*Maximes ets pensées*). "It seems to me, my dear one," Mme de Sévigné was to write at last to her daughter, "that I do you a great wrong in doubting your intelligence in matters that are something veiled" (*Lettre à Madame de Grignan,* July 8, 1671).

62. But the other fellow must be careful not to say too much! LaBruyère observes of "certain lively minds," that "one must leave them to complete everything" (*Les caractères,* "Des ourages de l'esprit"). "What we call wit," Voltaire suggest, is also "the art . . . of only half expressing our thought and leaving the rest to be divined" (quoted by Robers under *deviner,* to divine or guess). "Obscurity," Romain Rolland tells us (quoted by Robert under *obscurité*), "is less harmful to a great artist than apparent clarity. When we wish to understand him we will take the trouble to search for the secrets of his thought." "Whatever we have not had to decipher, to bring to light by our own personal effort, is not ours," Proust writes (quoted by Robert under *éclaircir,* to make clear).

"In a muffled but perfectly perceptible manner," a politician famed for his finesse (René Pleven) remarked during a debate on the Euratom treaty under the Fourth Republic, "two different conceptions . . . have been brought into collision by these discussions" (A.N., July 10, 1956; *J.O.,* p. 3338). If the "manner" had been cruder, the politician in question would not have had the opportunity to exercise the subtlety that alone made "perceptible" to him those "conceptions" thus locked in ("muffled") conflict.

20

PRECISION AND AMBIGUITY

1. To those who subscribe to the widespread attitude of hostility to ambiguity, the latter is in the first place a sign of intellectual weakness. When "we are floundering about in the more-or-less" (Gide, *Journal 1889–1939*, p. 837), when "the state of the mind" is "vague and uncertain" (Robert under *incertain*), when it is "eddying and confused" (Robert under *mouvant*, moving), then there is a failure of the intelligence that will lead to further disasters.

2. Ambiguity is shady.

Though "equivocal" (*équivoque*) sometimes denotes merely what "may be interpreted in different ways," it is also a word akin to "suspicious, suspect, questionable . . . disquieting . . . dubious . . . licentious" (Robert).

3. Ambiguity is a source of fear.

"Vague uneasiness" Robert gives under *inquiétude*, uneasiness. Even when *inquiétudes* denotes "distresses that produce agitation," we are still dealing with "vague" feelings (ibid.). The same dictionary gives "indeterminate fears" under *imprécis*, unprecise, and Gide recalls "indistinct fancies . . . that terrified me because I could not make out their exact contours" (*Si le grain ne meurt*, p. 286).

4. Ambiguity is related to grief.

Though Robert refers to "the uncertain joy concealed by any indeterminate feeling" (Edmond Jaloux quoted under *indéter-*

miné), he goes on immediately to quote "boredom in search of the indeterminate" under the same adjective; and it is the second type of associations that prevails. As an example of *indéfini* meaning that which "is not defined, that cannot be defined," Robert immediately offers: "an indefinable sadness." Under *incertain* he gives "disturbing and uncertain feelings; vague yearnings." The "painful sensation" constituted by *malaise* is "usually vague," in the soul as well as in the body: "vague . . . indefinable malaise." In fact, "boredom, malaise, and uneasiness have a common characteristic: vagueness" (the Lafaye dictionary, quoted by Robert under *malaise*). Melancholy, which is "of a rather confused nature" and "is characterized by uncertainty," is a vagueness of the soul; Chateaubriand speaks of the "wandering state . . . into which melancholy plunges the feelings" (quoted by Robert under *mélancolie*).

5. Rejecting the pleasures that it is nonetheless possible to extract from such unpleasurable sensations, one may resolve to "leave nothing a prey to imprecision" (Robert under *imprécision*), and take delight in "the definite boundaries of an outline" (Robert under *défini*).

6. Vagueness: a childhood defect.

"The child," one child psychologist says, "has difficulty in knowing what it is feeling"; "it is rarely precise." Above all, "its feelings are much vaguer than those of the adult." It is only "by growing up" that the child "leaves behind . . . the confused sensations that might hold it back" (Jean Dublineau, *L'école des parents*, November 1959, pp. 3 and 12) and into which grown-ups are perhaps afraid, obscurely, of falling back again.

7. Precision: the French virtue; a conventional theme that does occasionally escape from the realm of cliché in its expression.

"The land of France makes a clearcut shape on the map," Valéry notes (*Regards sur le monde actuel*, p. 180). "I did not understand until much later," Gide confesses as he reminisces over his juvenilia, "that the particular characteristic of the French language is to tend toward precision" (*Si le grain ne meurt*, p. 245).

8. Precision is an antidote to the fear provoked by ambiguity (see sec. 3 above).

"He felt a sense of relief," Romain Rolland writes of one of his characters (quoted by Robert under *malaise*) "in the same way that someone who is ill, suffering from a . . . vague . . . malaise, is relieved to find it being narrowed down to an acute pain, localized at a particular point." "I amuse myself sometimes," Jules Renard tells us, "by staring into nothing and extracting

from it, expressing in words, everything precise that it contains"
(*Journal*, p. 789): in other words, a painful sensation is replaced
by an agreeable emotion.

9. Pleasures are seen as precise (but are therefore not described).

"It took less than three weeks," a character in a novel says,
"for this passion to take on a precise form in my daydreamings.
. . . I desired her. . . . Precise ideas came into my head. . . . We
would have dinner by candlelight. My thoughts about it were
precise . . ." (Michel Déon, *Les trompeuses espérances*, pp. 102,
103, 160). A woman with considerable past experience of love
has been "formed by the precise demands of men in a hurry"
(Sagan, *Bonjour tristesse*, p. 139). "At that moment," says a
girl in a novel, resolved to make sure of her own pleasure first and
foremost, "I was busy educating Didi, the most likely to put up
no resistance to what I was looking for, which was very precise"
(Rochefort, *Les petits enfants du siècle*, p. 141). Past pleasures
leave "very clear memories" of meals or acts of love, and cases
involving morals revolve around "very precise details."

10. Precision is power.

It is the child that is in danger of being uncontrolled in its
actions; the grown-up "eventually finishes off the confused sketch"
(La Fontaine quoted by Robert under *achever*) constituted by
the first years of life. Hence the quotation of this statement in a
newspaper for its comic effect: "Marcel Rozet in the difficult role
of the eunuch was astonishing in his precision, his performance
was without a single wasted effect" (Aycard and Franck, *La
réalité dépasse la fiction*, p. 61).

11. On the other hand, however, is precision not—precisely—
a cause of impotence?

"Anything of which we can form a clearcut idea loses some of
its prestigious power, some of its reverberation in the mind"
(Valéry, *Regards sur le monde actuel*, p. 292) a lesson formulated by Valéry that appears to have been well learned in many
instances, in politics for example.

12. Is it not precision that is shady, rather than ambiguity
(see sec. 2 above)?

The products of the blackmail presses, a speciality of the Third
Republic, were "published for excessively precise ends"; a man
who attaches himself to a "doctrine" for reasons of personal and
tangible profit is "a fellow who has a very precise idea of what
——ism is."

13. Precision destroys (see chap. 17, secs. 11-14, and chap.
19, secs. 38–49).

"There are some situations and ideas," Valéry suggests, "that cannot be made precise without our perishing or causing to perish" (*Tel quel*, 1: 69). Having given the text of a letter written by a male character in one of his novels to a woman who has offered herself to him but is being refused by him, Montherlant adds this note to the missive, which ends with the words *Bien à vous* ("Ever yours"): "The B in *Bien* was in reality an R—*Rien à vous* ("Never yours")— but scribbled in such a way that it could be misread" (*Les jeunes filles*, p. 191).

"Thought"—because it tends toward precision—"is brutal—lacks consideration" Valéry points out. "What can be more brutal than a thought?" (*Tel quel*, 2: 189).

"The most precise and piercing words . . . " Madame de Staël writes (quoted by Robert under *mordant*, biting), and Valéry talks of "an almost cruel precision" (*Eupalinos*, p. 68), a phrase akin to the formula: "I shall not be unfeeling enough to specify . . ." and Madame Teste also refers to "precise and brutal actions" (Valéry, *Monsieur Teste*, p. 44).

14. But ambiguity enables an object capable of it to expand, to flower.

"Brunettes have something a little too precise in their outlines," a character in Balzac advises a woman friend, "and marabou feathers lend their clothing the haziness that they themselves lack" (quoted by Robert under *flou*, hazy, blurred). "Whether one be a man or a book," Valéry suggests, "what greater glory than to provoke contradictions? . . . The number of different and incompatible aspects we can reasonably impute to a person is a manifest measure of the richness of his composition" (*Variété*, p. 795). "A work lasts," the same author says, "insofar as it is capable of appearing quite other than its creator made it. It lasts . . . insofar as it has been capable of a thousand transformations and interpretations" (*Tel quel*, 1: 168). Montherlant speaks of "a certain haziness that is precisely that of life itself" (Preface to *Fils de personne; Théâtre*, p. 272).

15. To renounce the effort required to maintain one's state of precision—even if only for a brief interval clearly separated from everyday life—what a relaxing and delightful pleasure! It was under pressure from adults that the child first submitted to the necessity for articulation. When a famous comedian expresses himself in gibberish instead of ordinary language, how pleasant it is to be taken back to the mooings and cooings of childhood! In love, one is entitled to the pleasure of a somewhat childish enunciation and vocabulary. And in the same way, the *C'est si bon* first pronounced quite distinctly by a popular singer is gradually transformed into a confused and voluptuous murmur from the mouth.

16. And perhaps pleasure is not precise at all (see sec. 9 above), but vague?

In pleasure, the eyes become "vague," "swimming." "I long to see you," the lieutenant writes to Mitsou. "I feel so soft, so weak, so hazy, drawn toward something so velvety, so deep, so indistinct" (Colette, *Mitsou*, p. 66).

17. The same is true of happiness.

"I am very vague," Valéry writes to a friend. "It is my day for being vague. And being vague is happiness, don't you think?" (Valéry to Gustav Fourment, *Correspondance*, p. 119). "Perhaps it is only unhappiness that drives people to express themselves without any possible misunderstanding," an André Roussin character suggests. "Happiness . . . blurs the vision and makes words confused" (*L'amour fou*, act 2).

18. The ambiguity of words often encourages our tendency to treat them as ultimate realities. They can then be used as substitutes for even more unpleasant and inaccessible facts.

After a year of war, the minister responsible for Algeria (Maurice Bourgès-Manoury) remarked that "integration" was a "word that immediately excites the most passionate arguments." Now, "this word . . . does not mean very much if examined in itself, and yet means everything. . . . Even on the mathematical level, it covers some very complicated things" (A.N., October 12, 1955; *J.O.*, p. 5044).

Nevertheless, it is often seen as indispensable to make use of such a word. Another politician on the same occasion, and referring to the same subject, took the unusual course of raising this question: "Was a formula absolutely indispensable then? Is the essence of the matter not something beyond the label and beyond the bottle, the contents themselves? . . . Don't you think it would be wiser to make reforms first? There would always be time, afterward, to fit them into some doctrinal framework. . . . Words must be put in their place. And that means in second place" (Edouard Depreux, A.N., October 13, 1955; *J.O.*, p. 5105). A year later, an eminent journalist (Jacques Fauvet) was able to describe the state of the "problem" in question in these terms: "The recognition of 'Algerian status' may now be seen as no longer adequate, while that of 'the fact of Algeria as a nation' is still premature. . . . To move beyond 'Algerian status' while keeping on this side of 'the fact of Algeria as a nation' is not easy" (*Le Monde*, November 24, 1956). The world lies beneath words, Victor Hugo says, as a field does beneath its flies.

19 Ambiguity preserves freedom (see chap. 1).

Fontenelle observed of Leibniz that his exact definitions deprived him of the agreeable liberty of abusing his terms on occasion; Proust uses the phrase "a burdensome precision and finish" (*Du côté de chez Swann*, p. 150). "An artistic or political opinion," Valéry notes, "should be a thing so vague that the same individual can always accommodate it to his changing moods and interests without any change in appearances; always justify his actions; always 'explain' his vote" (*Tel quel*, 2: 43). "Retz writes," Montherlant recalls, "that it is very necessary to restrain oneself from jesting in great affairs. But there are occasions when one must jest wittingly. For example, one may deliver an ultimatum jestingly, if one wants one's adversary to remain unaware of it and to run himself into difficulties, or if one wishes to maintain one's own freedom to disregard it oneself later on: the ultimatum has two aspects, like the ancient mask, the grave aspect and the comic aspect, so that one can present the aspect one wishes according to the occasion" (Montherlant, *Carnets*, 1930–1944, p. 371). If I adopt excessively clearcut attitudes at the outset of a negotiation, I shall force the other party's back against the wall; he will see my actions as demands, as constituting ultimatum, so that I shall be depriving myself of the advantages of flexibility.

20. Thus the other's ambiguity preserves my own freedom.

"This text is infallible," Renan pretends to admit; "All well and good. But it is capable of various interpretations, and there we meet diversity again, that simulacrum of freedom with which we content ourselves for lack of any other" (quoted by Robert under *interprétable*, capable of interpretation). But is it not more than a simulacrum? "Remember that to interpret has never meant to traduce," a high school teacher says to a colleague in a documentary novel with reference to a civil service directive; "So it's up to you to interpret directives as you wish and to respect others' freedom of interpretation at the same time" (René Masson, *Des hommes qu'on livre aux enfants*, p. 389).

21. Ambiguity: a condition of compromise.

The best ground of agreement is one without clear boundaries; stable situations are very likely to be founded on equivocations. "I don't want there to be the slightest equivocation in future between you and me!" If that resolve expressed by one of Courteline's characters (quoted by Robert under *équivoque*) were serious, then it would lead straight to disaster. "Every equivocation," Camus claims (quoted by Robert under *équivoque*), "calls death closer; clarity of language alone . . . can provide protection against that death": a theory diametrically opposed to another and much more widespread feeling.

A politician too eager to criticize others for "seeking a facile assent founded . . . upon equivocation" (Pierre Pflimlin, A.N., May 13, 1958; J.O., p. 2255) was reminded that reaching an agreement was difficult enough as it was, and that without the methods he was attacking it would probably be impossible. "As far as Algeria is concerned," a prime minister under the Fourth Republic (Christian Pineau) remarked at the outset of the Fifth, "the equivocation" going on with regard to the impending referendum (scheduled for the fall of 1958) "is total. Defferre is convinced that a 'yes' can be perfectly well reconciled with negotiations with the F.L.N., Soustelle is certain that a success for him on September 28 means the green light for integration" (National Congress of the Socialist Party, September 12, 1958; *Paris-Presse*, September 13, 1958). "The margin of possibilities in this affair . . . is extremely narrow," a member of Charles de Gaulle's "entourage" confided to a journalist after the latter had proclaimed his policy of "self-determination" for Algeria. "General de Gaulle, in his declaration, has without doubt gone as far as the present state of public opinion and the psychological state of those living in Algiers, as well as that of the army, will permit; his statement can be interpreted in many ways. . . . With this sort of thing, at the outset of such an operation . . . there are points that it is better not to go into too precisely" (*France-Observateur*, October 1, 1959). The year before that, a politician (Paul Devinat) referring to one of the recurrent problems of the previous Republic, the revision of paragraph 8 (*De l'Union Française*) in the 1946 constitution, said: "I am drawing . . . the attention of the Assembly to a double danger. By attempting to regulate matters *too precisely* in advance, we risk arousing, not only reservations in this Assembly . . . which will diminish the value of the broad assent that it would be best we should accord to the reform of paragraph 8, but also suceptibilities among our friends abroad, which will make our task more difficult" (A.N., February 18, 1958; *J.O.*, p. 846).

22. "Broad assent" may be the result of fraud: the Jesuit father invented by Pascal refers to "our doctrine of equivocation according to which it becomes permissible to employ ambiguous terms by causing others to understand them in a sense different from the sense in which one understands them oneself."

23. Or else there may be a misunderstanding.

"The world," Baudelaire asserts, "functions solely by misunderstanding. It is by misunderstanding that . . . everyone reaches agreement. . . . If, by misfortune, we were to understand one another, we could never agree" (*Mon coeur mis à nu*). "Long live misunderstanding!" Montherlant cries (" How *La reine morte* was written." *Théâtre*, p. 240).

24. But does not complicity come into it as well?

"Having all united with the design of ruining M. Arnauld,"

Pascal explains after having set out the various meanings of "proximate power" among all the Jansenists' various enemies, "they hit upon the plan of all agreeing upon this term *proximate*, which they would all pronounce together, even though their understandings of it were so various, so that they might all speak a single language and thus be able, through this apparent corroboration, to form a considerable body and make up a greater number in order the more surely to oppress him" (Pascal, *Les provinciales*, first letter): a ploy used in parliaments under both the Third and the Fourth Republics when it was a question of overthrowing a government by using a motion upon which a so-called makeshift majority could reach agreement.

25. The existence of opposite reactions with regard to precision and ambiguity arouses a desire to reconcile the two. There is "nothing more dearly prized than the suggestive song—in which vagueness and precision are combined"; nothing more amusing than the comedian whose stammer is the perfection of art. Since the child is pursued by a determination on the part of adults to combat his propensity to "a confused speech that renders (children) almost unintelligible" (Rousseau quoted by Robert under *articuler*, to articulate), the ex-child naturally glories in the skill of a language that is defective and almost unintelligible, without being so, and yet being so too; or again, and even more daring, a language that is almost intelligible while resisting comprehension.

26. In more conventional terms, the reconciliation can be effected by the combination of being ambiguous in practice while expressing a great desire for precision in one's own future and on the part of others: all ambiguity must be done away with!

27. When every detail becomes a *précision* (in French journalese they tend to be synonymous), the fact that vagueness holds full sway is thereby masked, but only in the most transparent way.

28. It is easier to construct an imaginary figure of precision than it is to perform an act of precision.

Valéry asserts of Mallarmé that he worked out an idea of language for himself "that became the center of his thought" and that was—"an all-important point"—"remarkably precise." He reflected upon the conditions of his art "with a precision . . . unprecedented in literature. . . . He had constructed for himself," his discipline repeats, "the most precise . . . theory" of poetry (Valéry, *Variété*, p. 679). In fact, "Mallarmé envisaged literature as no one before him had ever done: with . . . a rigor, a sort of instinct for generalization that creates a kinship between . . . our great poet and certain of those modern geometricians who have relaid the foundations of science" (ibid., p. 700).

In what, precisely, did this so very precise theory consist? Impossible to say, since we seem to know nothing about it apart from the fact of its precision. For Mallarmé "maintained until his dying day a secret and inward contemplation of a truth he had no wish to communicate except in the form of his own prodigious application of it"—his poems—"as proofs." (ibid., p. 707).

Perhaps, after all, not entirely. We are dealing with "a sort of doctrine of which we unfortunately know only the general bent" (ibid., p. 655): a general bent that was known, therefore, but never stated. "We can do no more than make conjectures about the inmost content of his thought" (ibid., p. 679): conjectures that were never formulated. Mallarmé "drew his"—secret— "reflections from the formulas of a singular metaphysics" (ibid.): singular but never described. "I shall not attempt here," Valéry tells us, "to give any precise idea of the development of those analyses and experiments of which his works are the successive vestiges" (ibid., p. 700); in fact, Valéry was never to attempt to give such an idea, precise or otherwise. Nevertheless, "I have retained the memory of remarks he made that bore witness . . . to the uttermost refinements. He spoke, one evening, about the differences he could perceive between the possible effects of abstract words, according to whether they ended in *-té* (like *vérité*), in *-tion* (like *transition*), or in *-ment* (like *entendement*). It did not seem to him to be unimportant to have observed these nuances" (ibid., p. 685)—nuances that Valéry does not pass on.

So the myth of precision is a disguise for nothingness and oblivion.

BIBLIOGRAPHY

Books

Achard, Marcel. *Patate.*
Anouilh, Jean. *Théâtre.*
Arland, Marcel. *La consolation du voyageur.* Paris: Gallimard, 1952.
Aron, Robert. *Histoire de Vichy.* Paris: Fayard, 1954.
Audiberti, Jacques. *Théâtre.*
Aycard, Albert, and Frank, Jacqueline. *La réalité dépasse la fiction.* Paris: Gallimard, 1955.
————. *La réalité dépasse la fiction, bis.* Paris: Gallimard, 1957.
Aymé, Marcel. *Aller retour.* Paris: Gallimard, 1927.
————. *Le bœuf clandestin.* Paris: Gallimard, 1939.
————. *Le chemin des écoliers.* Paris: Gallimard, 1946.
————. *La jument verte.* Paris: Gallimard, 1933.
————. *Théâtre.*
Barberot, Roger. *Malaventure en Algérie.* Paris: Plon, 1957.
Barrès, Philippe. *La victoire au dernier tournant.* Paris: Nouvelle librairie française, 1932.
Baudelaire, Charles. *Œuvre.*
Bauer, Gérard. *Un voisin sait tout.*
Beley, André. *L'enfant instable.* Paris: Presses Universitaires de France, 1951.
Benoist-Méchin, Jacques. *Soixante jours qui ébranlèrent l'Occident.* 3 vols. Paris: Albin Michel, 1956.
Berge, André. *Les défauts de l'enfant.* Paris: Editions Montaigne, 1953.
————. *Education familiale.* Paris, Editions Montaigne, 1936.
Berl, Emmanuel. *La France irréelle.* Paris: Grasset, 1957.
Bloch, Marc. *L'étrange défaite.* Paris: Editions Franc-Tireur, 1946.
Blum, Léon. *Mémoires, L'œuvre de Léon Blum,* vol. 2. Paris: Albin Michel, 1954.
Boileau. *Œuvre.*
Bonmariage, Sylvain. *Willy, Colette et moi.* Paris: Editions Charles Frémanger, 1954.

Bonnefous, Georges. *Histoire parlementaire de la Troisième République.* Vols. 1 and 2. Paris: Presses Universitaires de France, 1956, 1957.

Bossuet, *Œuvre.*

Cabanis, José. *Le fils,* Paris: Gallimard, 1956.

————. *Les mariages de raison.* Paris: Gallimard, 1958.

Caillaux, Joseph. *Mes mémoires.* Vol. 3. Paris: Plon, 1947.

Camus, Albert. *La chute.* Paris: Gallimard, 1956.

Céline, Louis-Ferdinand. *Voyage au bout de la nuit,* Paris: Gallimard, 1952.

Chamfort. "Caractères et anecdotes." *Maximes et anecdotes.* Monaco: Editions du Rocher, 1944.

————. *Maximes et pensées.* ibid.

Chastenet, Jacques. *L'enfance de la Troisième.* Paris. Hachette, 1952.

————. *La République des républicains.* Paris: Hachette, 1954.

Chateaubriand. *Mémoires d'outre-tombe.*

Chazot, Jacques. *Les carnets de Marie-Chantal.* Paris: Hachette, 1956.

Chevallier, Jean-Jacques. *Histoire des institutions politiques de la France de 1789 à nos jours.* Paris: Dalloz, 1952.

Chrestien, Michel. *Esprit, es-tu là?* Paris: Gallimard, 1957.

Cocteau, Jean. *Théâtre.*

Colette. *Le blé en herbe.* Paris: Flammarion, 1950.

————. *Ces plaisirs . . . ,* Paris: Ferenczi, 1933.

————. *La chatte.* Paris: Grasset, 1933.

————. *Chéri.* Paris: Fayard, 1956.

————. "La dame du photographe." *In Gigi* (see below).

————. *Duo.* Paris: Ferenczi, 1934.

————. *La fin de chéri.* Paris: Flammarion, 1953.

————. *Flore et Pomone.* Paris: Flammarion, 1939.

————. *Gigi.* Paris: Ferenczi, 1945.

————. *L'ingénue libertine.* Paris: Albin Michel, n.d.

————. *Mitsou.* Paris: Fayard, 1946.

————. *La naissance du jour.* Paris: Flammarion, 1928.

————. *La seconde.* Paris: Ferenczi, 1929.

————. *Sido.* Paris: Ferenczi, 1930.

Combes, Emile. *Mon ministère.* Paris: Plon, 1956.

Courteline, Georges. *Œuvre.*

Curtis, Jean-Louis. *Les justes causes.* Paris: Julliard, 1954.

Daniélou, Charles. *Dans l'intimité de Marianne.* Paris: Editions Musy, n.d.

Dansette, Adrien. *Le destin du catholicisme français.* Paris: Flammarion, 1957.

Debesse, Maurice. "L'élève difficile." *L'école des parents.* Paris, n.d.

Debré, Michel. *La République et ses problèmes.* Paris: Nagel, 1952.

Déon, Michel. *Les trompeuses espérances.* Paris: Plon, 1956.

Duits, Charles. *Le mauvais mari.* Paris: Editions de Minuit, 1954.

Dumaine, Jacques. *Quai d'Orsay 1945–1951.* Paris: Julliard, 1955.

Durandin, Guy. "L'enfant menteur." *L'école des parents.* Paris, n.d.

Dutourd, Jean. *Doucin.* Paris: Gallimard, 1955.

————. *Le petit Don Juan.* Paris: Laffont, 1955.

————. *Les taxis de la Marne.* Paris: Gallimard, 1956.

Fauvet, Jacques. *La France déchirée.* Paris: Fayard, 1957.

Ferry, Abel. *Les carnets secrets d'Abel Ferry.* Paris: Grasset, 1957.

Freustié, Jean. *Auteuil.* Paris: La Table Ronde, 1954.

Gaulle, Charles de. *L'appel.* Paris: Plon, 1954.

————. "Comment faire une armée de métier." *In Vers l'armée de métier* (see below).

————. *Discours et messages 1940–1946.* Paris: Berger-Levrault, 1946.

————. *Le fil de l'épée.* Paris: Berger-Levrault, 1944.

————. *La France et son armée.* Paris: Berger-Levrault, 1945.

————. *Le salut.* Paris: Plon, 1959.

————. *L'unité.* Paris: Plon, 1956.

————. *Vers l'armée de métier.* Paris: Berger-Levrault, 1944.

Genet, Jean. *Le balcon.*

Gide, André. "Ainsi soit-il" ou "Les jeux sont faits." *In Journal 1939–1949* (see below).

————. *Anthologie de la poésie française.* Paris: Gallimard, 1949.
————. *Les caves du Vatican.* Paris: Gallimard, 1922.
————. *L'école des femmes.* Paris: Gallimard, 1944.
————. *Les faux-monnayeurs.* Paris: Gallimard, 1925.
————. "Feuillets d'automne." In *Journal 1939–1949,* (see below).
————. *L'immoraliste.* Paris: Mercure de France, n.d.
————. *Journal 1889–1939.* Paris: Gallimard, 1948.
————. *Journal 1939–1949, Souvenirs.* Paris: Gallimard, 1954.
————. *Journal des faux-monnayeurs.* Paris: Gallimard, 1927.
————. *Œdipe.*
————. *Paludes.* Paris: Gallimard, 1926.
————. *Si le grain ne meurt.* Paris: Gallimard, 1928.
————. *La tentative amoureuse.* Paris: Gallimard, 1948.
————. *Un esprit non prévenu.* Paris: Editions Kra, n.d.
Giraudoux, Jean. *Pour Lucrèce.*
————. *Sans pouvoirs.* Monaco: Editions du Rocher, n.d.
Grandval, Gilbert. *Ma mission au Maroc.* Paris: Plon, 1956.
Guerlac, Othon. *Les citations françaises.* Paris: Armand Colin, 1954.
Guitry, Sacha. *Théâtre.*
Halévy, Daniel. *Le mariage de Proudhon.* Paris: Stock, 1955.
Herbart, Pierre. *L'âge d'or.* Paris: Gallimard, 1953.
Husson, Albert. *Les pavés du ciel.*
Isorni, Jacques. *Ainsi passent les républiques.* Paris: Flammarion, 1959.
————. *Le silence est d'or.* Paris: Flammarion, 1957.
Jouvenel, Robert de. *La république des camarades.* Paris: Grasset, n.d.
Koupernik, Cyril. "La colère." *L'école des parents.* Paris, n.d.
La Bruyere. *Œuvre.*
Laclos, Choderlos de. *Œuvre.*
La Fayette, Madame de. *Œuvre.*
La Fontaine. *Œuvre.*
La Rochefoucauld. *Œuvre.*
Launay, Clément. *L'hygiène mentale de l'écolier.* Paris: Presses Universitaires de France, 1959.
Léautaud, Paul. *Entretiens avec Robert Mallet.* Paris: Gallimard, 1951.
————. *Journal littéraire.* Vol. 1 Paris: Mercure de France, 1954.
————. *Propos d'un jour.* Paris: Mercure de France, 1947.
Leites, Nathan. *Du malaise politique en France.* Paris: Plon, 1958.
Lidderdale, D.W.S. *Le parlement français.* Paris: Armand Colin, 1954.
Luc, Jean-Bernard. *Carlos et Marguerite.*
Malraux, André. *La condition humaine.* Paris: Gallimard, 1933.
Martin du Gard, Maurice. *La chronique de Vichy.* Paris: Flammarion, 1947.
Masson, René. *Des hommes qu'on livre aux enfants.* Paris: Laffont, 1953.
Molière. *Théâtre.*
Mondor, Henri. *Propos familiers de Paul Valéry.* Paris: Grasset, 1957.
Montaigne. *Essais.*
Montesquieu. *Œuvre.*
————. *Mes pensées, Œuvres complètes.* Vol. 1. Paris: Gallimard, 1949.
————. *Voyages.* ibid.
Montherlant, Henry de. *Les Auligny.* Paris: Amiot-Dumont, 1956.
————. *Aux fontaines du désir.* Paris: Gallimard, 1954.
————. *Les bestiaires.* Paris: Grasset, 1926.
————. *Carnets. Années 1930 à 1944.* Paris: Gallimard, 1957.
————. *Carnets 19 à 21.* Paris: La table ronde, 1956.
————. *Les célibataires.* Paris: Grasset, 1934.
————. *Le démon du bien.* Paris: Grasset, 1937.
————. *Encore un instant de bonheur.* Paris: Grasset, 1934.
————. *L'équinoxe de septembre.* Paris: Grasset, 1938.
————. *Le fichier parisien.* Paris: La Palatine, 1952.
————. *L'Histoire d'amour de la Rose de Sable.* Paris: Plon, 1954.
————. *Les jeunes filles.* Paris: Grasset, 1936.
————. *Les lépreuses.* Paris: Grasset, 1939.
————. *Malatestiana.* In *Théâtre* (see below).
————. *Mors et vita.* Paris: Gallimard, 1954.

————. *Les olympiques.* Paris: Gallimard, 1954.

————. *Pitié pour les femmes.* Paris: Grasset, 1936.

————. *Le relève du matin.* Paris: Grasset, 1933.

————. *Service inutile.* Paris: Grasset, 1935.

————. *Le solstice de juin.* Paris: Grasset, 1941.

————. *Le songe.* Paris: Grasset, 1922.

————. *Textes sous une occupation.* Paris: Gallimard, 1953.

————. *Théâtre.* Paris: Gallimard, 1954. Published subsequently to this volume: *Brocéliande, Don Juan, Le cardinal d'Espagne.*

Monzie, Anatole de. *Ci-devant,* Paris: Flammarion, 1941.

Morand, Paul. *Journal d'un attaché d'ambassade 1916–1917.* Paris: La table ronde, n.d.

Morazé, Charles. *Les Français et la République.* Paris: Armand Colin, 1956.

Moulin de la Barthète, Henri du. *Le temps des illusions.* Geneva. Editions du Cheval ailé, 1946.

Navarre, Henri. *Agonie en Indochine 1953–1954.* Paris: Plon, 1956.

Nicole, *Les lions sont lâchés.* Paris: Julliard, 1955.

Nourissier, François. *Les orphelins d'Auteuil.* Paris: Plon, 1956.

————. *Portrait d'un indifférent.* Paris: Fasquelle, 1958.

Ollivier, Albert. *Saint-Just et la force des choses.* Paris: Gallimard, 1954.

Pascal, Blaise, *Œuvre.*

————. *Pensées, Œuvre.* Paris: Gallimard, 1950.

Paul-Boncour, J. *Sur les chemins de la défaite 1935–1940.* Paris: Plon, 1946.

Périer, Marguerite. *Mémoire sur la vie de Monsieur Pascal.* In Pascal, *Œuvre* (see above).

Poirot-Delpech, Bertrand. *Le grand dadais.* Paris: Denoël, 1958.

Poulain, Gaston. *Paul Valéry tel quel.* Montpellier: La licorne, 1955.

Poulet, Robert. *Entretiens avec Céline.* Paris: Plon, 1958.

Prévert, Jacques. *Œuvre.*

Priou, Colette. *Le miroir aux alouettes.* Paris: Corréa, 1952.

Proust, Marcel. *A la recherche du temps perdu.* 3 Vols. Paris: Gallimard, 1954. (Includes all Proust titles cited in text.)

Racine, Jean. *Théâtre.*

Radiguet, Raymond. *Œuvres complètes.* Paris: Grasset, 1952.

Rebatet, Lucien. *Les décombres.* Paris: Denoël, 1942.

Renard, Jules. *Journal.* Paris: Gallimard, 1935.

Retz. *Mémoires.* Paris: Gallimard, 1949.

Revel, Jean-François. *Histoire de Flore.* Paris: Julliard, 1957.

Rivarol, Antoine. *Maximes et pensées.*

Robert, Paul. *Dictionnaire alphabétique et analogique de la langue française.* Paris: Presses Universitaires de France, 1953.

Robin, Gilbert. *Les difficultés scolaires chez l'enfant.* Paris: Presses Universitaires de France, 1953.

Rochefort, Christiane. *Les petits enfants du siècle.* Paris: Grasset, 1961.

Roussin, André. *Théâtre.*

Roy, Jules. *Le métier des armes.* Paris: Gallimard, 1948.

Sachs, Maurice. *Derrière cinq barreaux.* Paris: Gallimard, 1952.

Sagan, Françoise. *Bonjour tristesse.* Paris: Julliard, 1954.

————. *Un certain sourire.* Paris: Julliard, 1956.

————. *Dans un mois, dans un an.* Paris: Julliard, 1957.

Saint-Simon. *Mémoires.* Vol. 1. Paris: Gallimard, 1953.

Sainte-Soline, Claire. *Le dimanche des rameaux.* Paris: Grasset, 1952.

Salacrou, Armand. *Théâtre.*

Scize, Pierre. *Au grand jour des assises.* Paris: Denoël, 1955.

Sévigné, Madame de. *Lettres.*

Spears, Sir Edward. *Assignment to catastrophe.* 2 vols. London: Heinemann, 1954.

Stendhal. *Le Rouge et le Noir.*

Stéphane, Roger. *Les fausses passions.* Paris: La table ronde, 1956.

Stibio, André. *Antoine Pinay.* Paris: Editions Journal du Parlement, n.d.

Tardieu, André. *La profession parlementaire.* Paris: Flammarion, 1936.

Tessier, Carmen. *Bibliothèque rosse.* Paris: Gallimard, 1953.

————. *Histoires de Marie-Chantal et de beaucoup d'autres.* Paris: Gallimard, 1955.

Tournoux, J. R. *Secrets d'Etat.* Paris: Plon, 1959.

Vailland, Roger. *Eloge du Cardinal de Bernis.* Paris: Fasquelle, 1956.

Valéry, Paul. *Correspondance entre Paul Valéry et Gustave Fourment.* Paris: Gallimard, 1957.

————. *Degas, danse, dessin.* Paris: Gallimard, n.d.

————. "Dialogue de l'arbre." In *Eupalinos* (see below).

————. *Eupalinos.* Paris: Gallimard, 1944.

————. *Histoires brisées.* Paris: Gallimard, 1950.

————. *L'idée fixe.* Paris: Gallimard, 1934.

————. *Lettres à quelques-uns.* Paris: Gallimard, 1952.

————. *Mauvaises pensées et autres.* Paris: Gallimard, 1942.

————. *Mélange, Œuvres.* Vol. 1. Paris: Gallimard, 1957.

————. *Mon Faust.* Paris: Gallimard, 1946.

————. *Monsieur Teste.* Paris: Gallimard, 1946.

————. *Pièces sur l'art.* Paris: Gallimard, 1934.

————. *Poésies.*

————. *Regards sur le monde actuel.* Paris: Gallimard, 1945.

————. *Tel quel.* 2 vols. Paris: Gallimard, 1941, 1943.

————. *Variété. Œuvres,* vol 1 (see above).

Vauban. *De l'attaque et de la défense des places.*

Verneuil, Henri. *Pour avoir Adrienne.*

Voltaire. *Zadig.*

Zay, Jean. *Souvenirs et solitude.* Paris: Julliard, 1946.

PERIODICALS

L'Action laïque
L'Année politique
Artaban
Arts
Aux écoutes
Bulletin de Paris
Bulletin du Centre d'études politiques
Le canard enchaîné
Carrefour
Combat
Demain
L'école des parents
Esprit
L'Express
France-Observateur
France-Soir
Journal officiel, Débats parlementaires: Assemblée Nationale, Conseil de la République, Sénat
Le Monde
La Nef
Nouvelle revue française
Paris-Match
Paris-Presse
Le Rassemblement
Revue de défense nationale
Terre humaine

ABBREVIATIONS

A.N.   Assemblee Nationale (National Assembly)
C.R.   Conseil de la Republique sous la Quatrième (Council of the Republic under the Fourth Republic)
J.O.   *Journal officiel* (Official Journal)